AGAINST THE PROTESTANT GNOSTICS

AGAINST THE PROTESTANT GNOSTICS

Philip J. Lee

OXFORD UNIVERSITY PRESS
New York Oxford

To Roberta

Oxford University Press

Oxford New York Toronto
Delhi Bombay Calcutta Madras Karachi
Kuala Lumpur Singapore Hong Kong Tokyo
Nairobi Dar es Salaam Cape Town
Melbourne Auckland Madrid

and associated companies in
Berlin Ibadan

First published in 1987 by Oxford University Press, Inc.
200 Madison Avenue, New York, New York 10016

First issued as an Oxford University Press paperback, 1993.

Library of Congress Cataloging-in-Publication Data
Lee, Philip J. Against the Protestant Gnostics.
Bibliography: p. Includes index.
1. Gnosticism. 2. Protestantism—20th century. I. Title.
BT1390.L35 1986 280′.4 85-48304
ISBN 0-19-504067-8 ISBN 0-19-508436-5 (PBK.)

1 3 5 7 9 8 6 4 2

Printed in the United States of America
on acid free paper

Foreword

At once perceptive and learned, cogently argued and critically discerning, thoughtful and thought-provoking, witty and wide-ranging in scope, these chapters invite, indeed, evoke the reader's determination to see the analysis through to the end. That so solidly researched, clearly focused and challenging an exposition and interpretation of a theological thesis—and its implications for the faith and life of the members of churches today—should have emerged from the reflections, vocational commitment and extensive experience of the preacher and pastor of a demanding congregation of Christian believers in—of all places—Saint John, New Brunswick, is rare enough. The sustained level of its competence is doubly rare! "Can any good thing come out of Nazareth? . . . Come and see" (John 1:46). A serious and engaging theological work from the midst of the complexities and claims of parish life is remarkable enough. That such a work should come to us from "north of the border" can only be welcomed as a foretaste of cultural and religious reciprocity long overdue.

As the title suggests, Philip Lee's thesis and its themes are evoked by the classical exposition and criticism of gnosticism written by Irenaeus, Bishop of Lyons in Gaul, toward the end of the second century C.E. The cardinal gnostic heresies *then* were: promise of salvation by knowledge rather than by faith; stress upon secret or hidden, as against open and available, revelation; disregard and devaluation of nature in favor of the pure, free and unencumbered spirit; and concentration upon the radical individuality of the self. Consequently, gnostic pursuit and piety were escapist, elitist and syncretistic. Lee gives contemporary vitality to these themes and their consequences for piety, values and culture and subjects them to searching criticism by way of central and vivid contrasts to orthodox Protestant convictions, for example, the good creation over against an alienated humanity; knowledge of the mighty acts of God and knowledge that saves; salvation through pilgrimage and through escape; the believing community and the knowing self; ordinary people and the spiritual elite; and particularity and selective syncretism.

The thesis is steadily adhered to and extensively documented with citations and allusions. Lee draws upon basic Protestant theological sources; upon formative theological writings of the eighteenth, nineteenth and twentieth centuries, upon nineteenth- and twentieth-century poets and novelists, and upon the ways in which the faith and life of Protestantism in America, from Puritanism to revivalism and religious syncretism, have been affected and gnostically transformed. The bearers of these transformations cover the spectrum from the great to the not-so-great: in theology, Karl Barth and Thomas Torrance; in literature, Herman Melville and Walker Percy; and in social and political theory, Max Weber and Tom Wolfe. All these, and not a few others, have been used, misused and abused by fundamentalists, evangelicals and liberals in different but ultimately consensual ways, as the creative meaning and power of Protestant orthodoxy have fallen into disarray.

This book is a penetrating and provocative assessment of the promise and denouement of Protestant orthodoxy. Lee has sounded a call for a root renewal and redirection of the parish reality and structure of the community of believers to be a regenerative leaven in the churches of North America and in North American culture and society. He does not hesitate to challenge established thinkers and widely accepted values and truisms that currently mark the interpenetration of religion and culture, economics and politics in North America. No one is spared; no volatile issue is passed over. The relentless probing of these pages leads to decisive judgments about the shape of the liturgy and the trivialization of Christian nurture, about prayer and justice, and about what ought to be done and what left undone in matters such as: ordination and church discipline; psychiatric counseling and the Human Potential movement; ecology and nuclear weapons; normative and variant sexuality; marriage, procreation and the family; greed and poverty; and society and self. The author of these pages does not shrink from the risk of being dismissed or disregarded as a purveyor of antiquated nostrums that not only have been overtaken by events but have contributed more than a little to bringing about the very events he now proposes to overtake. The integrity and radicalness with which he calls into question the wisdom of the wise and the commitments of the foolish are ventured in obedience to the Protestant vision of the place and purpose of the world of time and space and things, of the nature and destiny of people, and of the freedom, responsibility and fulfillment promised and given to "the earth and all the inhabitants thereof" (Ps. 75:3), whom God has called "out of darkness into his marvelous light" (1 Pet. 2:9). At a time when theology, preaching and participation in the life of a community of believers have become as devoid of meaning and as syncretistic "as sounding brass or a tinkling cymbal" (1 Cor 13:1), these pages are as instructive and illuminating as they are astringent. They ask for neither concurrence nor consent. They are, instead, an invitation to conversation and to thinking again "about all these things that [have] happened" (Luke 24:14), and to comradeship in pilgrimage together with the Lord and Giver of life who is Himself "the resurrection and the life" (John 11:25).

Paul Lehmann
Charles A. Briggs Professor Emeritus
of Systematic Theology,
Union Theological Seminary

Preface to the Paperback Edition

Harold Bloom, in *The American Religion* (1992), has entered the debate on gnosticism in America and has responded to *Against the Protestant Gnostics* with these words: "He [Lee] sees what I see, the American Religion, but what fascinates me moves him to dread and wrath, whether he encounters it among liberal or Fundamentalist Protestants." Bloom notes the "uncanny relation" of my book to Bellah's *Habits of the Heart:* "What Lee protests in American Protestantism is the exaltation of the elite self as against community, a protest pragmatically parallel to the feeling of Bellah and his associates. . . ." Bloom maintains, however, that the American Religion (gnosticism) "cannot be extirpated," that "urging the need for community upon American religionists is a vain enterprise. . . ."

Bloom concedes that "Lee deserves all praise for seeing clearly what is there to be seen, though concealed in the multiple masks of supposed Protestantism." I have found responses from these "multiple masks" to be consistent though somewhat surprising. While theological conservatives have often been open to my analysis of their affinities with gnosticism, theological liberals have, for the most part, found gnostic-liberal parallels to be contrived, unfair, unacademic, and overstated.

Although I have appreciated all critics—both friendly and unfriendly—who have joined my discussion of Protestant gnosticism, I cannot accept the charge that my argument has been overstated. In fact, I believe that five years ago I underestimated the gnostic threat. I did not imagine in 1987 that the over-spiritualization of American life would make such rapid gains. When I wrote of American Protestant elitism that the "gnostic misunderstanding of divine election as an immutable separation between real men and animal-like people . . . [has] opened the door for every sort of atrocity by the chosen few against the unchosen many," I did not believe that American attacks on Third World peoples would escalate so rapidly. When I surmised that "it is doubtful that America can be led out of the psychological malaise of Vietnam or enabled to avoid future Vietnams until Protestant elitism has been overcome," I did not foresee such immediate atrocities as those inflicted on Grenada, Panama, and Iraq. These and other social and political developments have gone beyond my darkest vision.

I believe that Bloom and I are closer than he would admit. According to Bloom, "the central argument of [*The American Religion*] is that we all of us are affected by the consequences of our national faith." Whereas, unlike Bloom, I have sought to "clarify the distinctions between gnosticism and the faith of the Church" and have urged my readers to oppose "a gnostic Protestantism in our generation," like Bloom, I have sought to expose the overwhelming gnostic influence on religion in America. My own hope is that there might be, in North America, a turning from radical individualism to a more corporate understanding of life, and from elite concerns to more egalitarian aims. Could it be that Lee, Bellah, *and* Bloom all share this hope? Could it be that it is not a "vain enterprise"?

I am gratified that the debate goes on and that Oxford University Press is making my argument available to a broader public through this edition. In his Foreword to *Against the Protestant Gnostics,* Paul Lehmann writes that "these pages . . . ask for neither concurrence nor consent. They are, instead, an invitation to conversation and to thinking again 'about all these things that [have] happened' (Luke 24:14), and to comradeship in pilgrimage together with the Lord and Giver of life who is Himself 'the resurrection and the life' (John 11:25)." The invitation is still open.

Preface

In December 1945, when Muhammad ʻAlī al-Sammān put his mattock through a pottery jar near Nag Hammadi, he unwittingly opened a new era in gnostic studies. The old leather books and fragments he found naturally attracted the attention of linguists and historians of the ancient Middle East. Interest in the Nag Hammadi library, however, has gone far beyond the usual scholarly circles. These ancient Coptic texts have fascinated ministers, priests, lay persons and the general reading public. Why would so many people be drawn to a Christian heresy rejected by the early Church as a destructive misunderstanding of the true faith? Perhaps the answer is that modern readers find in this literature an immediacy which claims their attention. These gnostic ideas strike a familiar chord for modern ears: we sense that we have heard them before—or something very much like them.

Several attempts have been made to discover the connection between ancient gnosticism and some modern counterparts. Eric Voegelin attacks the Hegelians and the Marxists (whom he considers the arch heretics of the Western world) by comparing them with the gnostics. Elaine Pagels, in her popular study, *The Gnostic Gospels,* approaches the gnostic tradition in a positive light and finds in it interesting modern parallels such as the Women's Liberation movement. Hans Jonas, representing a more objective approach, sees a connection between classical gnosticism and modern nihilism—Nietzsche, Heidegger and Sartre. In the literary field, Harold Bloom identifies William Butler Yeats, Wallace Stevens and other neoromantics as twentieth-century gnostics. All of these philosophers and critics make a strong case for their position, yet something is missing. Still, the familiar presence in our world that is brought to mind by the Nag Hammadi documents has not been satisfactorily isolated within these secular movements.

Is it possible that by identifying a gnostic thought pattern with those *outside* the Christian community, we have failed to locate it in its natural habitat? Walter Bauer, in his work on early Christian heresy, points out that the gnostics were, for the most part, firmly ensconced *within* the churches. According to Bauer, it took centuries for Christians to arrive at an "orthodox" position, to free themselves from an entangling alliance with gnostic thought.

This work attempts to demonstrate that the familiar presence of gnosticism is as close at hand as the reality we call Protestantism; that something like the ancient misalliance has occurred in our own time, particularly in the North American expression of Protestantism; and that within Protestantism the faith of Christ has become so interwoven with *gnosis* that it is difficult to separate one from the other. This study further indicates that modern gnosticism is a destructive heresy which is doing immeasurable harm to Christ's Church and to God's world. Finally, suggestions are offered for a liberation from false faith and the reassertion of a more authentic Protestant Christianity.

It may be that the other great Christian traditions, Roman Catholicism and Greek Orthodoxy, have their own problems with a reappearance of *gnosis,* but their problems are beyond the scope of this Protestant work. As a Protestant, I believe I have identified the elusive modern gnostics, and they are ourselves.

Saint John, New Brunswick P.J.L.
January 1986

Acknowledgments

It would be impossible to recall the many people who have, in one way or another, contributed to this project. However, to certain individuals and institutions I will attempt to express my gratitude.

I am indebted to my congregation—the Kirk Session and members of the Church of St. John and St. Stephen—for their continuing encouragement over several years. It is not usual for a parish clergyman to take a sabbatical year; therefore, their action to grant me a sabbatical during the academic year 1982–83 was both courageous and generous. The Rev. Dr. Robert Armstrong, who ably took over my parish in my absence, also has my sincere thanks. Furthermore, throughout my ministry here, this congregation has provided me with a hopeful example of what a Christian community can be and can do.

Those who offered such warm hospitality to my family and me during my sabbatical in Montreal should have some idea of how much I appreciate their friendship. After encouraging the sabbatical in advance, Principal William Klempa of Presbyterian College made housing and a study area available within the college. All the members of the college—faculty, staff and students—helped to provide a positive environment for research and writing.

Similar advance encouragement for my sabbatical was given by the Rev. Dr. Joseph McLelland, then Dean of the Faculty of Religious Studies of McGill University. Through his good offices I was awarded research status and privileges during my year on campus. Other members of the McGill faculty were extremely helpful. The Rev. Prof. Edward Furcha read and offered constructive comments on an early draft of the manuscript. Prof. Frederick Wisse allowed me to attend his stimulating seminars on the religious environment of early Christianity.

I also wish to thank certain librarians for their kindness. At Presbyterian College, Librarian Daniel Shute and Assistant Librarian Hilda Thompson were most helpful to me during my year there. At the Religious Studies Library of McGill, Assistant Librarian Tapis Majumbar showed every consideration in making books available from libraries on and beyond the McGill campus. In the early and late stages of writing, Chief Librarian Kenneth Duff and Reference Librarian William Kerr of the Ward Chipman Library at the University of New Brunswick in Saint John, offered me invaluable assistance.

Many friends have contributed ideas and criticism to the argument. The Rev. Stuart McEntyre, a fellow Canadian pastor, renewed my interest in Rauschenbusch. Professor Joseph Vining of the University of Michigan Law School has been a vital source of inspiration and confidence throughout the venture.

I hope that the readers of my manuscript have some understanding of my appreciation for their long suffering. The Rev. Dr. Paul L. Lehmann, my mentor since seminary days, was kind enough to interrupt his own research to take painstaking care with the first complete revision of the manuscript. The Rev. Dr. Alexander J. McKelway, a friend and advisor for many years, also wrestled with my first effort and tried to correct my more embarrassing sins—both logical and doctrinal. The Rev. R. Sidney Pinch, also a longtime friend and colleague, dealt with the pastoral sections of the manuscript and offered many helpful suggestions based on his learned experience.

Places have been important. Joseph and Alice Vining made Clear Hill in Vermont available at a critical time. Arthur and Peggy Howe allowed me to work at the Upsalquitch Parr and Beaver Club in New Brunswick on another occasion. The Villa Madonna Retreat House in Renforth, New Brunswick, has been another haven. The Sisters of Charity, the Holy Cross fathers Robert McInroy and William Boland, and the entire staff have sustained me in body and spirit during my labors. In every case, the generosity and friendship of my hosts made the locale the delight it was.

How can I begin to thank my typists for the skill and patience involved in preparing the manuscript? Mary Carter has contributed her time and skill from the earliest to the latest stages. Jacqueline Gallie gave her considerable talent in the preparation of the first complete draft of the manuscript. And the Rev. George Harper has performed an invaluable service in the areas of typing, correcting footnotes, and organizing the bibliography. The personal devotion that accompanied the work of each of these individuals has been a gift I will not forget.

The editorial staff of Oxford University Press has been more than helpful. Ms. Cynthia Read, by means of various creative suggestions and critiques, has helped me to tighten my argument. Mr. Henry Krawitz, associate editor, and Mr. Andrew Yockers, free-lance copy editor, offered invaluable assistance in regard to style, footnotes, and bibliography.

I also want to thank Douglas Leyden for ably assisting in the final stages of proofreading with his careful and sensitive work.

I am grateful to my children, Sadie, Philip, Susan, and Walter, for their confidence in me and their enthusiasm for my work. Furthermore, they have taken turns at checking footnotes, numbering pages and performing other tedious chores. My wife, Roberta, has been at the same time my most profound critic and my most indefatigable supporter. She has applied her writing talents to every phase of the revision process.

Finally, I am more and more appreciative of my parents, Philip and Sara, who, earlier than my memory, introduced me to the concrete realities of Word and Sacrament in the context of an *ordinary* congregation.

[Gnostic knowledge]?

Saint Paul exhorted Timothy: Guard what has been entrusted to you. Avoid the godless chatter and contradictions of what is falsely called knowledge, for by professing it some have altogether missed the mark as regards the Faith (1 Tim 6:20-21)

Contents

I

GNOSTICISM IN CONFLICT WITH THE FAITH

CHAPTER ONE

Gnosticism as a Type of Religion

FOR the gnostic Christian, ancient or modern, the simple faith (*pistis*) of the believer is not sufficient. Instead, there must be knowledge (*gnosis*).[1] Using this Greek verbal noun, the Church Fathers tagged the ancient heresiarchs with the derogatory name gnostics (*gnostikoi*), "those who know." Often there was the ironic implication, "those who *think* they know something the rest of us do not know."[2]

It is too simple, of course, to say that the gnostic *knew*, whereas the orthodox Christian *believed*. The New Testament writers and the Church Fathers also claimed to *know* something. In the New Testament and the writings of the Fathers, however, what is *known* is primarily an objective, received collection of data concerning "what God has done for man and to man and . . . what man owes to God in the way of obedience."[3] The gnostics, on the other hand, *knew* something which was quite distinctive from common knowledge. They knew secret information that had not been and could not be revealed to *hoi polloi*. For instance, in *The Apocryphon of James,* Christ is reported to have appeared to James and Peter "after five hundred and fifty days since he had risen from the dead." Having called these two aside, the Lord "bade the rest [of the disciples] occupy themselves with that which they were about" and then proceeded to fill these chosen ones with the secret interpretation of his generally known teachings.[4] We gather that without this "secret book"[5] and others like it, the ordinary books such as the Four Gospels would remain always baffling and unhelpful.

What the gnostics knew was *saving* knowledge, a saving technique concerning the self. Probably the most often quoted gnostic formula sums it up: "What liberates is the knowledge of who we were, what we became; where we were, whereinto we have been thrown; whereto we speed, wherefrom we are redeemed; what birth is, and what rebirth."[6] If the Gospels were written "that you might know the reliability of the *words* concerning which you were instructed,"[7] then perhaps it could be said that the gnostic texts were written so that the *gnostikoi* could know the truth, not concerning *words,* but concerning their own salvation. In gnosticism, there was not that extra step of going to a sacred literature which existed quite apart from the self and finding in it, as a fringe benefit, a truth that could be applied to the self. In gnosticism, the Scripture was sacred only insofar as it saved the self. Again, what was known in gnostic circles was personal. If it was not personal, it was not gnostic.

The more we learn about the first few centuries of the Christian era (and the Nag Hammadi discovery has profoundly improved our knowledge of the period), the more aware we become of the complexity of the religious scene. The idea once held (partly promoted by the polemics of the anti-gnostic Fathers) that there existed an orthodox church composed of right-thinking, proper Christians, on the one hand, and dozens of gnostic sects populated by wild-eyed, strange-acting deviants on the other, can no longer be accepted. As early as 1964, in an article by Arthur Darby Nock (published posthumously), the opinion was given that "you could not have found anyone in Corinth to direct you to a Gnostic church: the overwhelming possibility is that there was no such thing."[8] At the Yale Conference of 1978, Frederik Wisse argued convincingly that "the intended readers [of the so-called Sethian writings] would have been the esoteric group of 'like-minded' Gnostics, not in the sense of members of a sect but as individuals with a similar attitude towards this world, other-worldly vision, and ascetic lifestyle."[9] This assessment could also be applied to many other gnostic patterns of thought, and it is quite possible that apart from the Valentinians, the Marcionites and later the Manichaeans, very few gnostics were to be found outside the main body of the Church. The typical gnostic was a member, often a pillar, of the local and recognized Christian Church. Also valid is Bauer's thesis that at this point in Church history, the lines between orthodoxy and heresy had not been drawn. There was still a groping for an interpretation of the Gospel that could be, at the same time, catholic and apostolic. All parties would have claimed to be orthodox while charging their opponents with heresy.[10]

Despite the fluidity of the religious mix of the early churches, we do know that gnosticism was the overriding issue facing the Christian community during the first four centuries of our era. Opposition to gnostic thought and practice occupies a great deal of the Pauline corpus; there are anti-gnostic themes in the Johannine literature and perhaps even in the Revelation.[11] By the end of the first century, the attack on gnosticism had been escalated by Ignatius (d. ca. 110), bishop of Antioch; Justin Martyr (ca. 100–ca. 165); and especially by Irenaeus (ca. 130–ca. 200), bishop of Lyons. The polemic was sustained by Tertullian of Carthage (ca. 160–ca. 220), the Roman theologian; Hippolytus (ca. 170–ca. 236); Origen of Alexandria (ca. 185–ca. 254); and many others.[12] It would seem either that the gnostics posed a grave threat to Christianity or else that the Fathers were suffering from a pathological obsession, for this question to have absorbed so much of their considerable talents and energies.

Irenaeus, the gnostic fighter par excellence, records that "a multitude of Gnostics have sprung up, and have been manifested like mushrooms growing out of the ground."[13] The image is that of numerous fungi suddenly and rootlessly materializing on virgin soil. Irenaeus gives himself to the defense of that unprepared ground, the Church.

In the opposing camp, we know there were, among the gnostics, formidable philosophers and men of letters. People like Basilides, Valentinus and Marcion gain an infamous stature in the works of the Fathers. Before the recent discoveries of primary gnostic material, we were almost entirely dependent on the unfriendly critics of the heresiarchs for an understanding of their views. Now, however, we have a clearer idea of this extraordinary faith from the gnostic witnesses themselves.

What produced these able adversaries of the orthodox cause? Is there any explanation for the mushroom-like growth? Many theories have been introduced to explain this spiritual phenomenon. The Fathers often traced the secret *gnosis* to Simon Magus, the strange magician whose connection with the Church is noted in the Acts of the Apostles.[14] Adolf von Harnack, in his classic study of Christian thought, asserted that gnosticism was the result of the "lasting influence of Greek philosophy and the Greek spirit generally on Judaism."[15] He went on to say, in a phrase which for many years would remain the definitive statement on the subject, "The gnostic systems represent the acute secularising or hellenizing of Christianity."[16] Following Harnack's lead, A. D. Nock felt tempted to speak of the gnostic movement as "Platonism run wild."[17]

After the Nag Hammadi discovery as well as the unearthing of the Dead Sea Scrolls at approximately the same time, it became impossible to accept Harnack's simple hellenization theory any longer. The respected Roman Catholic scholar, Father Daniélou, opted for a Jewish influence:

> It will have become clear by now that gnosis in this sense [the knowledge of eschatological realities] cannot be regarded as once it was, as the result of Hellenistic influence, but must have been a characteristic of later Judaism.[18]

This position, with some modification, is the prevailing one today. It is a good working hypothesis if we understand with Hans Jonas that "the Jewish strain in gnosticism is as little the orthodox Jewish as the Babylonian is the orthodox Babylonian, the Iranian the orthodox Iranian, and so on."[19] If, that is, the *gnosis* emerged from Judaism, it was from a Judaism gone berserk.

Whatever the roots of ancient gnosticism (and as we have seen, they are quite uncertain), how can we possibly move from that confused, hidden-in-the-mists-of-time world to our own familiar world? What has ancient Egypt to do with modern North America? What has Nag Hammadi to do with the First Presbyterian Church, Mainstreet?

To trace gnosticism from ancient times through the Middle Ages down to the present would be, at best, a dubious enterprise. Because it is not essentially a historic faith—in the sense of clinging to particular historical structures—by the very nature of the phenomenon, it defies ordinary historical study.

The connection between ancient and modern gnosticism can be established, however, through the identification of a gnostic *type*. Max Weber taught us the value of using the "ideal type" or the "constructed type" to gain a more precise picture of whatever religion, movement or group is being investigated.[20] With this method, a typical pattern can be devised from whatever complex individualized data might appear. One of the most effective uses of this typological method is found in Ernst Troeltsch's masterful study of the "church type" versus "the sect type."[21]

In a similar way, a clear picture of gnosticism can be gained by attempting to construct a gnostic type. If that can be done, the ahistorical but essential relationship between gnostics of all times and climates should be easier to grasp. At the very least, if we can perceive a gnostic pattern, then perhaps the danger ancient *gnosis* posed for the early Church can, in an objective sense, alert us to the dangers now being posed by a modern *gnosis*.

Before delineating the various aspects of the gnostic type, it should be understood that the one primary ingredient for the birth of gnosticism is a particular mood. The mood is one of despair. The gnostic solution can be satisfying only to those who have no tangible or rational hope. Because a certain number of people at every stage of history are caught up in despair, gnosticism of one sort or other always has a following. Throughout Christian history, certain individuals and small groups have been drawn toward the gnostic way. That historical reality is not terribly alarming; every great religion has variations on the theme. When, however, we come to a period like that of the first four centuries of the Church, when the gnostic way almost prevailed, how can we speak of a mood? Can an entire culture be in despair? And if so, why?

R. M. Grant has attempted to locate the despair in the failure of Jewish apocalypticism. The final blow came, according to his thesis, with the destruction of the Temple at Jerusalem: the end of the inhabitation of God on earth. In that catastrophic moment, "faith was shaken in God, his covenant, his law and his promises."[22]

No doubt, gnosticism might have gathered strength after the destruction of the Temple in A.D. 70, but there is strong evidence to suggest that gnosticism already was in ascendency prior to that event.

A subtler solution has been offered by Ernst Troeltsch:

> A more universal reason [for the mood] was the decline of an overripe and static civilization, whose delight in life and vitality had been drained out of it, and which in dull dissatisfaction with itself was seeking for something new; . . . it was satiety, exhaustion, and fatigue.[23]

Just as despair within an individual usually does not come from an unfortunate circumstance but rather from the individual's perception of the circumstance, so mass despair might result from the way a culture views itself. Cultures with rising hopes, ambitious political and social expectations, tend to occupy themselves with revolutions, universal philosophies, artistic endeavors and ordinary life. On the contrary, cultures with declining hopes, sensing they have reached a *fin de siècle,* tend to slip into ennui, cynicism, inwardness and, finally, despondency.[24]

Whatever the cause of the particular despair of later antiquity, the mood was widespread and pervasive. And the mood resulted in a burst of creative legend and poetry to describe the feeling and to find an adequate escape from what gnostics perceived to be the dilemma of humankind. Although the basis of their despair may always remain a mystery, the following characteristics of the gnostic spirit emerge clearly from gnostic literature.

First, there is for the gnostic a sense of alienation, and the alienation is metaphysical alienation. The feeling is perhaps best summed up by the poet A. E. Housman:

> Be still, be still, my soul; it is but for a season:
> . . . .
> Ay, look: high heaven and earth ail from the prime foundation.[25]

The fundamental complaint for the gnostic is not against the powers that be, but against the powers that began, against the Prime Mover for having moved. The material world itself is the result of a cosmic faux pas, a temporary disorder within the *pleroma.*[26] The ancient gnostic, looking at the world through despairing eyes, saw matter in terms of decay, place in terms of limitation, time in terms of death. In light of this tragic vision, the logical conclusion seemed to be that the cosmos itself—matter, place, time, change, body, and everything seen, heard, touched or smelled—must have been a colossal error.

In the Valentinian formula, the world of our present existence is a hellish world, "whereinto we have been thrown."[27] In this unacceptable environment, "anguish and misery accompany existence as rust covers iron."[28] And who is to be blamed? From this peculiar perspective, "the fault, dear Brutus, is not in our stars" nor in ourselves, but in the Maker of both.

Gnosticism, unlike modern atheistic existentialism, does not accept this sense of alienation as the end of the human story. For the gnostic, there is a *gnosis* which can save humanity from this otherwise hopeless condition. The saving *gnosis* is a form of religious knowledge. This is why all attempts to identify as modern gnostics, Marx, Sartre, Heidegger and others who make no religious claims, would seem to be inaccurate, even unfair. The ancient *gnosis* attempted to answer the question of how to find salvation (transcendental salvation) through God when all evidence points to the fact that the Creator-God is either evil or incompetent. The solution of the gnostic type—ancient, medieval and modern—is to remove from God (or from the God beyond God) the stigma of Creation.[29]

Saving knowledge pertains to the secret trick of employing divine help against the Creation and therefore against the Creator Himself. As Quispel puts it in regard to Valentinian *gnosis,* "The Valentinian mystique opposes nature to grace, the human psyche to the transcendent soul, and the world to God. It is, in effect, a *tragic* Christianity."[30] This radical opposition denies the possibility of the present world being an acceptable environment for humanity on any terms.

It is generally accepted that gnosticism is a world-denying faith and that it inevitably leads to escapism. What is not always recognized is that before there can be a deliberate escape from the real world into an alternately designed world, there first must be a deliberate escape from the real God to an alternately designed God. This, in fact, is the gnostic trick. There is, to use the word Harold Bloom employs in regard to modern romantic poetry, a deliberate "misreading" of theology.[31] To call on God for saving knowledge, the gnostic first had to free God of the awful responsibility of having dealt this mess. The whitewash of God in regard to responsibility for the Creation involves, by one method or another, the refusal to accept the obstinate Judaic and Christian assertion that God and Creator are one and the same Being. The device of setting distance—theological distance—between the true God and an evil creation allows gnostics to escape the world with impunity, for neither gnostics nor their God have any stake in it.

One of the cleverest uses of this device is found in the Valentinian *Gospel of Truth,* in which the author asserts:

> Error became powerful; it fashioned its own matter, foolishly not having known the truth. It set about making a creature, with [all its] might preparing, in beauty, the substitute for the truth.[32]

That is, error has designed matter, and the end result is an artificial creation.

Having performed his metaphysical trick, his deliberate misreading of the Old Testament, Valentinus is then enabled to misread the New Testament, asserting of the Risen Christ, "having stripped himself of the perishable rags, he put on imperishability."[33] The aim of Resurrection faith, thus interpreted, is to escape the cruel bondsmen: matter and time, world and flesh.[34]

The gnostic escape, in the last analysis, is an attempt to escape from everything except the self. In the *Gospel of Truth,* the human tragedy is not a result of sin, as in the biblical understanding, but rather a result of ignorance of God and self. Salvation, therefore, becomes "the name of the work [the Savior] is to perform for the redemption of those who were ignorant of the Father."[35] *Gnosis,* having driven away ignorance, leaves the faithful at peace within themselves: "Rest in him who is at rest, not striving nor being involved in the search for truth. But they themselves are the truth and the Father is within them."[36] Because the Father is within, the gnostic always returns in a circular fashion to the self.

There is a wealth of evidence to suggest that gnostic speculation always led in this egocentric direction. Thus in Quispel's reading of Valentinus:

> Spirit is present in man, but it is dormant. Only the word of Christ, which awakens and reveals it, can lead to self-knowledge. . . . Valentinus provided us with a very original approach [to Christianity] which is not the Word and the Spirit, or the Word and the Sacrament, but the Word and the *Self.*[36]

The concentration on self is a natural result of the passionate need to escape the world. Because no one can actually escape the real world except by death (suicide being the ultimate self-actualized escape), the only other solution is to effect an escape by withdrawal into the self. The sense of impotence before Creator, matter, time, suffering and death can all be overcome through a denial of the Creator-God's power over the spiritual self and an assertion of total power within that limited sphere of isolated *pneuma* (spirit). "Hence comes the importance," writes Nock, "attached to self-sufficiency, *autarkeia*. He who has learnt his lesson aright is beyond the reach of circumstances."[38] And in his essay on the subject, Nock goes so far as to state that "some of the later developments [of gnosticism] convey a curious impression of auto-intoxication."[39] There is, in fact, a striking similarity between the gnostic and the beautiful boy, Narcissus. According to the Greek legend, Narcissus so offended the goddess Nemesis, that he was made to fall in love with his own reflection in a pool. There, because of the curse of self-love, the inability to break away from his own mirrored image, he must waste away and perish. The gnostic escape is, in essence, a narcissistic escape.[40]

The average person, of course, is neither able nor willing to leave everything and every person behind to pursue a relentless search for the true self. During the days of the early Church, the vast majority of Christians were tradespeople or common workers, uneducated folk who had little interest in philosophical speculation. Despite the ideal picture often painted of primitive Christianity, there is every reason to believe that in most respects the typical Corinthian Christian was very much like the typical Corinthian: "Not many of you were wise according to worldly standards, not many were powerful, not many were of noble birth."[41]

The *gnostikoi,* on the other hand, were an elite, whether within or apart from the Christian community. They were not *hoi polloi* or *christiani rudes.*[42] Plotinus, the great Neoplatonist of the third century, writing of gnostics within Judaism and the Christian Church as well as those who had infiltrated his own philosophical school, complained:

> Each of them is a "son of God," superior even to heaven, and without any personal effort, each can apprehend the intelligible world . . . they profess to despise the beauties of the world: they would do well to despise the beauty of boys and women.[43]

A kinder description of the gnostic personality would be that of the intellectual or poetic aristocrats who simply cannot bring themselves to understand life as the masses understand life. Randall sees the gnostic type in this more attractive light:

> The gnostic vision of life in the world is exciting and exhilarating. It makes evil intelligible and good pure . . . but it is exclusive and aristocratic: only the intellectual elite that can understand the *gnosis* can hope to be saved.[44]

No matter how we regard gnostic thought, whether with hostility, tolerance or favor, gnosticism is always an elitist faith.[45]

Finally, in constructing a gnostic type, it must be noted that gnosticism is syncretistic. Jonas observes:

> The gnostic systems compounded everything—oriental mythologies, astrological doctrines, Iranian theology, elements of Jewish tradition, whether biblical, rabbinical, or occult, Christian salvation-eschatology, Platonic terms and concepts. Syncretism attained in this period its greatest efficacy.[46]

What was true of the classical systems has been consistently true of the movement wherever or whenever it has manifested itself.[47] A modern writer, repelled by the strictures of what he feels to be an unimaginative orthodoxy, has called for a more syncretistic approach: "A single story . . . a rigid theology, and a confining morality are not adequate to help in understanding the nature of real meaning."[48] Gnostics, whether of the second century or the twentieth century, will not be constrained in the use of material. They will employ whatever is available, in whatever way they choose, to answer the needs of gnostic faith, which is to say, the spiritual needs of the self.

CHAPTER TWO

Gnosticism as a Heresy

THE gnostic typology sketched in chapter 1 is patently at variance with orthodox Christianity's faith and teaching. At the beginning, as in Protestantism now, gnosticism posed and poses the critical question of heresy. Is it possible, however, to speak of heresy in our time? Even to utter the word might seem to be a retreat into a darker age. Heresy evokes memories of the Spanish Inquisition, the martyrdoms of Jeanne d'Arc, John Huss and countless other victims of religious tyranny. It also brings into our consciousness ridiculous spectacles of Protestant orthodoxy such as that described in Burns's "Holy Willie's Prayer."

For almost two millennia, Christians have been assailing one another in court and out, with words or weapons, over the issue of who is correct in doctrine and praxis. Is it not self-contradictory for Christians to be judgmental toward one another about anything? Certainly, heresy talk does not seem kind or liberal-minded and is not conducive to the popular notion of what is ecumenical. In fact, within the Church, has heresy not become a heretical word?

Also, does not history show that heretics were simply those who had the least votes, that orthodoxy prevailed because a certain ecumenical council was packed or because one side had more pull with the papacy or the emperor than the other? Would not the bad guys have been the good guys had there only been more of them or had they played their cards right? These questions make us most reluctant to consider heresy as anything other than an interesting phenomenon of Church history prior to our present period of toleration.

Certainly, there is, in our reluctance to accept the notion of heresy, a legitimate caution. Yes, our divisions in the past have been destructive. Yes, the cruelties and self-contradictions of the Church of Jesus have been a scandal. Yes, our lack of tolerance toward Christians and others has been a disgrace. It is true that within Christianity there should be ample room for diversity. According to the Gospel of Mark, Jesus himself had occasion to remind the disciples, "He that is not against us is for us."[1] The Church Fathers were not for the most part an intolerant lot. Even Augustine, who could not be said to suffer error gladly, affirmed the principle *salvo jure diversa sentira,* that different opinions can be held without the loss of the rights of communion, without disloyalty to the Catholic Church.[2]

There are, however, limits to creative diversity. At some given point, a teaching, an idea or an action which claims to be Christian is so utterly different from the "faith which was once for all delivered to the saints"[3] that it becomes the opposite of Christianity. When that point is reached, the Church itself must "contend for the faith."[4] The defense of orthodoxy then becomes more necessary than any struggle against a secular, easily identified external form, because if the Church loses the truth which distinguishes her from error, she no longer has the right or the inclination to contend on any other front.

It was for a similar reason in the Old Testament that Israel's worst moments were those when the Children of God themselves worshiped the golden calf or were seduced by the false prophets. It was for a similar reason that Jesus himself speaks in so unkind a fashion to the Pharisees. The very fact that they are inside the faith of Israel makes the Pharisees the primary enemies of Jesus. They are to be feared precisely because of their religion: "Beware of the leaven of the Pharisees, which is hypocrisy."[5] They are a hidden danger for the faithful, "like graves which are not seen, and men walk over them without knowing it."[6] Because of their claims to embody the very essence of faith, Jesus addresses them as "Hypocrites! . . . you traverse sea and land to make a single proselyte, and when he becomes a proselyte, you make him twice as much a child of hell as yourselves."[7] Strong words to use against fellow Jews, fellow believers, but Jesus understands that his prophetic task requires not only teaching of truth, but also warning against falsehood. The blessings, if they are to mean anything at all, must be accompanied by the woes.[8]

When teachings or practises emerge that are wholly different from those of the community of faith, they must be opposed, even though they come from within the body of faith. Irenaeus found himself with no choice but to strike out against heresy in the second century. Irenaeus was far from narrow-minded. He tolerated the Montanists and was even attracted to them. He criticized, by letter, the bishop of Rome for his uncompromising attitude regarding the date of Easter. He wrote against gnosticism only because the gnostics threatened the apostolic faith. He was certain that were this heresy to prevail, the gospel of Christ would be transformed into an anti-gospel.[9]

Most often in Christian history, it has been gnosticism in one form or another that has forced the Church to "contend for the faith." As we have seen, nearly all the early Church Fathers enlisted for the cause.[10] Much later, in the Middle Ages, the Albigensian and Bogomil heresies, both extremely gnostic, endangered the very existence of Christianity in parts of France and the Balkans.[11]

It is not altogether surprising that gnosticism poses such a persistent danger to biblical faith. It almost would seem that there is within Jewish and Christian faith a constant temptation to gnostic thought. According to the great Jewish philosopher, Martin Buber, the perpetual enemy of faith in the true God is not atheism (the claim that there is no God), but rather gnosticism (the claim that God is *known*).[12] The latter represents for Buber not a historical movement, but a form of religion which would always be with us. At another point, he wrote:

> The two spiritual powers of gnosis and magic, masquerading under the cloak of religion, threaten more than any other powers the insight into the religious reality . . . the tribes of Jacob could only become Israel by disentangling themsleves from both gnosis and magic.[13]

Perhaps, in the typological comparisons that follow, it can be seen that the grave threat Buber felt gnosticism posed to Judaism is similarly a threat to Christianity. If we can understand why there could be no ultimate compromise with gnosticism for the New Testament writers and for the Church Fathers, maybe we would better understand why there can be no compromise today.

An Alienated Humanity Versus the Good Creation

The fundamental problem between biblical faith and gnostic faith begins with two different world views. Biblical faith insists that the Creation is well made. Christianity affirms with Judaism that "in the beginning God created the heavens and the earth . . . God saw everything that he had made, and behold, it was very good."[14] Christian faith goes on to claim that the Word, the Second Person in the Trinity, is co-creator with God the Father: "He was in the beginning with God; all things were made through him, and without him was not anything made that was made."[15]

Gnosticism simply cannot endorse that positive vision of the Creation. Whether the gnostics accept the Genesis and Johannine texts and thus have to interpret them in some ingenious fashion, or whether they reject them at the outset, is strictly a matter of style. The basic issue is clear: gnosticism must deny any *direct* link between the Creation and God. Jonas writes:

> The cardinal feature of gnostic thought is the radical dualism that governs the relation of God and world, and correspondingly that of man and world. The deity is absolutely transmundane, its nature alien to that of the universe which it neither created nor governs and to which it is the complete antithesis . . . the world is the work of lowly powers.[16]

Most Christian gnostics made some attempt to avoid an overt dualism, realizing that a complete disconnection between God and world could not be accepted by the Church. Their task, therefore, became that of making an indirect connection which would nevertheless exonerate the good God of all guilt in regard to this world. Often the connection was made through a series of archons (semidivine rulers) who reigned over the lower spheres in the absence of God. The more archons and spheres existed between the high heaven and the cosmos, the greater the distance between God and creation, the less God's guilt for having allowed this calamity to happen. Basilides, for example, counted 365 heavens between high heaven and universe. By the time one has worked oneself through those light years of spiritual space, it is difficult to imagine that the supreme Deity could have the slightest interest in, or contact with, the material world. And that, of course, is the point.[17]

Marcion and his followers, who were much closer to the Church than many other gnostics,[18] exonerated the high God in another manner: they declared that the God of Israel, a demiurge with no ties to the real God, is totally responsible for creation. Although the Marcionites did not view Israel's God as the Prince of Darkness, as did some of the more radical gnostic systems, they did regard Him as "just" as opposed to the good God who is "love." It follows, of course, that for Marcion the Scriptures that tell about the demiurge can in no sense be considered holy or sacred by the Christian.[19] The Old Testament is mere justice and legality.

Out of these ingenious dualist systems, or perhaps behind them, there is a picture of the world which is depressing to say the least. The cosmos is an abortion; humanity, in the fleshly sense, along with all materiality, is a mistake. "Earth, water, fire and air" wrote the Valentinians, "took their origin from the despair, sorrow, ignorance and fear to which *Sophia* [wisdom] was subjected."[20] Whether we have been thrown here by a succession of archons or by the loveless justice of Yahweh, our milieu is one of hopeless and entangling emotions.

It follows that acceptance of such a dark view of Creation would require not only a rejection of or rewriting of the Old Testament but ipso facto a serious adjustment of the New Testament Christology as well. "The gnostics were necessarily Docetist in their Christology," argues Runciman. If Christ is to be taken seriously as the Savior, how can he actually be part and parcel of this material cosmos? Again, the gnostics were compelled to embark upon another chore of distance-making, in this instance creating distance between Christ and the flesh. Valentinus spoke of Christ passing through the Virgin Mary as "through a canal."[21] Christ himself is credited with a body which is nonterrestrial:

> It was by his unremitting self-denial in all things that Jesus attained to Godship; he ate and drank in a peculiar manner, without any waste. The power of continence was so great in him that his food did not decay in him, for he himself was without decay.[22]

This anti-materialist Christology also required the gnostics to allegorize the Gospel stories. The true Christ, after all, would not be sullied by evil-created matter. Irenaeus reports the gnostic interpretation of Jesus' parable of separating the wheat from the chaff: "The fan they explain to be the cross (*stauros*) which consumes all materiality, as fire does chaff."[23] For the *pneumatic* (the gnostic term for a spiritual person) Christ's life and work were proving the exact opposite of the Pauline assertion, "We are not contending against flesh and blood." The gnostic contention was indeed against flesh and blood.[24]

Because nothing is quite so earthy (or quite so supportive of continuing earthiness) as sexuality, it is not hard to understand why the gnostics did everything they could to interpret Holy Writ in an antisexual way. Some of their allegorizing efforts in this regard are mind-boggling. The Jordan River, for example, symbolized sexual intercourse. Both Joshua and Jesus, they claimed, were able to interrupt its flow—Joshua temporarily when he crossed over dry-shod with the children of Israel and Jesus permanently at his baptism. Jesus' baptism in the Jordan symbolized the beginning of a type of birth which would make carnal begetting obsolete.[25] Once Christ is able to introduce a new form of birth, there is then hope for an end to this dreadful error called *cosmos.* Saturninus taught that Christ descended to earth to destroy the God of the Jews and "to destroy the works of the female, to bring marriage and reproduction to an end, to save men from women"![26]

In biblical religion, the Creation is viewed in a perspective utterly different from that of the gnostics. The Old Testament asserts that the Creation itself cannot be faulted. One is able, in facing the cosmos, only to offer a prayer of thanksgiving, "The earth is the LORD's and the fulness thereof."[27] Humankind, far from being an "abortion," is the direct product and responsibility of a loving God: "For thou didst form my inward parts, thou didst knit me together in my mother's womb."[28]

Even when the cosmos seems very dark and there is apparently no hope, as in the case of Job, no one can legitimately criticize the Creation: "I will question you, and you shall declare to me. Where were you when I laid the foundation of the earth?" The Creator-God then goes on to accept full responsibility for the whole earth, from the morning stars to the ostrich. He reminds Job, in the process, that only He, the Creator, is even yet responsible, lovingly responsible, for the maintenance of it all. There are no apologies and no regrets; the buck stops here. "Who provides for the raven its prey, when its young ones cry to God and wander about for lack of food?"[29]

Nor in the New Testament is there the slightest embarassment in regard to the Creation. Its authors, already faced with an incipient gnosticism, are ready for the challenge and answer this affront to the Old Covenant and to Christ in the strongest terms.[30] The firm tie between Christ and Creation established in the prologue to John's Gospel has already been mentioned. The same bond is affirmed by the author of Ephesians when he describes the apostolic mission, "to make all men see what is the plan of the mystery hidden for ages in God who created all things."[31] The Christ event is a further chapter in the overall plan of the Creator-God. In even closer accord with the Johannine formula is the confession in Colossians: "For in him [the Christ] all things were created, in heaven and on earth, visible and invisible, . . . all things were created through him and for him."[32]

The song of the twenty-four elders before the throne of grace may well be an early Church hymn chanted to protect the faithful against the gnostic disparagement of the cosmos:

> Worthy art Thou, our Lord and God,
> to receive glory and honour and power,
> for thou didst create all things,
> and by thy will they existed and were created.[33]

The gnostic diatribes against the female, sexuality and procreation are answered sharply in I Timothy. The author is aware that some are leaving the Church because of false doctrine put forward "through the pretentions of liars whose consciences are seared, who forbid marriage and enjoin abstinence from foods which God created to be received with thanksgiving."[34]

The challenge to gnostic despair over the Creation begun in the New Testament itself was picked up by the Church Fathers, reaching its most complete expression in the work of St. Irenaeus. The central purpose of Irenaeus's polemical theology was to understand clearly the relationship between creation and redemption so that the gnostic wedge between the God of Israel and the Savior Christ could be once and for all removed. For Irenaeus, the gnostic attack on the Creation was nothing less than a blasphemy against the Father and the Son.[35] Irenaeus's answer to the gnostic threat took him into every major area of Christian theology, just as the anti-Creation doctrine of his opponents had led them into a virtual denial of everything the Church confessed.

Knowledge That Saves Versus Knowledge of Mighty Acts

Following the Creation question, the next immediate concern in the conflict between gnostic and biblical religion is the doctrine of salvation. In biblical religion, salvation is related to the mighty acts of God: "In many and various ways God spoke of old to our fathers by the prophets; but in these last days he has spoken to us by a Son, whom he appointed the heir of all things, through whom also he created the world."[36] Here we have linked together the Father and the

Son, the Old Covenant and the New, history and nature, the past and the present. It is this connected data, this given reality, which is the object of knowledge in orthodox Christianity.

Not so for the Christian gnostic: "For Basilides the world and history were merely symbols referring to an inner process." Similarly, states Quispel, in Valentinian philosophy "the point of departure is always *man:* it is of man that we must think unremittingly. The center of gravity of this system is *our salvation*."[37] The stories of the Old Testament might have been of interest to most early Christian gnostics; the accounts of Christ's ministry, death and resurrection would have been considered vital, but only because they provided grist for the gnostic mill. As Quispel explains it in regard to Valentinus:

> But after all these influences (whether philosophic, Hermetic, Johannine, or Pauline) are not very important. Hippolytus declares that a vision of Christ was the impulse for the composition of the myth. On the whole this metaphysical poem seems inspired by *vivid emotions* and *personal experiences* . . . he expressed his tragic conception of life in the symbols of creative imagination.[38]

What we have then in gnostic thought is not imaginative interpretation of given material, but rather the imaginative treatment of a private vision.

As far as the gnostics were concerned, the "many" were overly fascinated by historical happenings, even by the historical events in the life of Christ. Elaine Pagels, writing on the ahistorical views of Heracleon, reports that he claimed

> that those who insist that Jesus, a man who lived in the flesh, is Christ fail to distinguish between literal and symbolic truth. . . . Heracleon goes on to say that those who take the events concerning Jesus "literally"—as if the events *themselves* were revelation—have fallen into flesh and error.[39]

Concern about the mighty acts of God in both the Old and New Covenants was from a gnostic perspective a lower stage in the development of an authentic Christian understanding. To *know* Christ was not in any sense to have knowledge about the "historical man of flesh and blood" but rather to be personally related to the mythical heavenly being who liberates humanity from historical concerns.[40]

This utterly different concept of what it is that is to be *known* caused an irreconcilable rift at the very center of the Church's life, namely, in the understanding of the eucharistic feast. Again Heracleon is quoted as saying:

> It is characteristic of psychics ("the many") that they mistake the images of spiritual reality for the reality itself. . . . They interpret the eucharistic "eating" as the recalling *anamnesis* of the Lord's death and parousia (I Cor. 11:23–26) . . . they worship in flesh and error.[41]

The reason for this totally different concern of the gnostics is their conviction that the root problem of humankind is *ignorance*. Judaism and Christianity in their orthodox expressions would understand the basic source of all our misery to be *sin,* humanity's failure to meet God's expectations or its own potential; gnosticism would see the human predicament as resulting from a profound blindness concerning the human situation. "Ignorance of the Father," states the Gospel of Truth, "brought about anguish and terror. And the anguish grew solid like a fog so that no one was able to see."[42]

With this understanding of the problem, *mea culpa* having been replaced by *mea ignorantia,* the function of the Gospel becomes solely that of enlightening the soul concerning what previously has been hidden. God the Redeemer who acts in history, who led the Children of Israel out of slavery into promise, and who raised Jesus Christ from the dead has been reduced to God the Revealer who uncovers what is to be *known* if we are to be saved. Scriptural passages such as, "No one has ever seen God; the only Son, who is in the bosom of the Father, he has made him known" or "And we know that the Son of God has come and has given us understanding, to know him who is true"[43] would be close to the gnostic heart. Similar texts, of course, can be found throughout the New Testament to give credence to the gnostic cause.

How then could the Church differentiate its own necessary thought patterns regarding salvation from gnostic patterns, especially when the two often sounded identical or, at least, very similar? First, there was on the part of the Church a clinging to Holy Scripture, primarily the Old Testament, as a revelation not of salvation techniques, but a revelation of God's mighty acts. Harnack—with his abiding Protestant suspicion of things Catholic—finds the only difference between the gnostic systems in their "acute" hellenization of Christianity and the Catholic system in its "chronic" hellenization of the faith to be that gnosticism rejected the Old Testament and Catholicism did not.[44] Even if that simplification were true, what a difference! By identifying itself with the Old Covenant, the Church, if nothing else, was retaining an Hebraic understanding of salvation *knowledge*. The Greek word, *ginoskein,* in the Septuagint usually represents the Hebrew verb *yada,* which denotes the act in which man comprehends the world, the people and the objective circumstances of his life. It has often been noted that the same word, *yada,* which is used to describe "knowing" God, is also used as a verb for sexual intercourse.[45] Knowledge of God in Hebrew thought thus implies an earthy relationship *with* rather than a cognitive apprehension *of* the divine. Knowledge of God in the language of Cana, as Bultmann points out, is not a "knowledge of God's eternal essence . . . On the contrary, it is a knowledge of His claim. . . . Above all, however, *yada* is used for acknowledgement of the acts of God."[46]

With this Old Testament usage in the background, the Church's general connotation of *ginoskein* would have been the ordinary Greek meaning, that is, "the intelligent comprehension of an object or matter." *Ginoskein,* in most instances, would have been used as a verb needing or implying an objective genitive.[47] To know is to know *something* and something specific. Perhaps that explains why within the New Testament itself we find already an attempt to distinguish between legitimate *gnosis* and false *gnosis:* "O Timothy . . . avoid the godless chatter and contradictions of what is falsely called knowledge [*pseudonumou gnoseus*], for by professing it some have missed the mark as regards the faith."[48]

The New Testament confining truth to the mighty acts of God as opposed to the gnostic using Scripture as a springboard for speculation, will be seen again in chapter 3 when we deal with legitimate gnostic motifs within the Church. What should be clear at this point is that the Church's stubborn adherence to Old Testament thought patterns has been essential in drawing a line of demarcation between itself and heretical gnosticism.

This line was drawn again by Irenaeus and became one of the bases for his battle against the gnostics. In his famous work, *Against Heresies,* Irenaeus interrupted his argument to pray:

> Lord God of Abraham, and God of Isaac, and God of Jacob and Israel, who art the Father of our Lord Jesus Christ, the God who, through the abundance of Thy mercy, hast had a favour towards us, that we should *know* Thee . . . give to every reader of this book to *know* Thee, that Thou art God alone, to be strengthened in Thee, and to avoid every heretical, and godless, and impious doctrine.[49]

Here is Christian knowledge: the knowledge of God in terms of His mighty deeds among men and women.

Salvation Through Escape Versus Salvation Through Pilgrimage

New Testament Christianity, feeding on its Old Testament roots, sees human existence as a lifelong pilgrimage. Yes, there will be an end to the trek through the desert—the Jordan will be crossed, the Promised Land attained; when Christ comes again this present struggle will be ended. For the time being, however, a Christian is a *homo viator,* a person always on the road. Paul confesses:

> Not that I have already obtained this or am already perfect; but I press on to make it my own, because Christ Jesus has made me his own. Brethren, I do not consider that I have made it my own; but one thing I do, forgetting what lies behind and straining forward to what lies ahead, I press on toward the goal for the prize of the upward call of God in Christ Jesus.[50]

This image of an earthly race to be run with patience and perseverance—unless there were some extravagant exegesis and sophisticated spiritualizing of it—would have been totally unacceptable to the gnostics. For the gnostic personality, religious knowledge (knowledge of God) could never be discovered in terms of earthly pilgrimage. Knowledge of God required the exact opposite, a turning away from this world. Again, Bultmann states, in his study of the word *gnosis,* that for the gnostics, "knowledge of the *kalon* [good] . . . does not serve the shaping of the world as in Plato, but rather aversion from it."[51] Even Plato, despite his suspicion of the material world, comes across as an earthy thinker when compared to the gnostic.

In gnostic thought, insofar as a person is spirit (*pneuma*), that person realizes that he or she does not belong in the cosmos. The *pneuma* originated or eternally existed in a transcendent world. There will be no consolation for the *pneuma,* no relief for the intense nostalgia for "home," so long as the *pneuma* remains in this abyss called cosmos. Goethe's Faust expresses the nostalgia as well as the struggle between the earthly nature of man and the divine nature:

> Two souls alas! are dwelling in my breast;
> And each is fain to leave its brother.
> The one, fast clinging, to the world adheres
> With clutching organs, in love's sturdy lust;
> The other strongly lifts itself from dust
> To yonder high, ancestral spheres.[52]

Gnosticism cannot possibly pursue God in terms of natural cosmos or historical cosmos because both nature and history are alien factors to the eternal in humanity. The natural, the historical and matter itself must be overcome. Basilides is said to have taught:

> Through Christ, the spiritual man is freed from matter and purified, the spiritual element is released from the great and formless mound of the immanent world, the great differentiation begins. And that is why Jesus is called "the initiator of the differentiation of confounded things."[53]

The office of the Christ becomes that of a spiritual filter that strains our spirits of matter.

When knowledge of God is thought to be *pure* knowledge (as in gnosticism) unencumbered by time, place, event, person or any other tangible ensnarement—that is, when knowledge has no object—then such knowledge of God requires a total escape from the world.[54] A modern poet aptly expresses the enticement of escape:

> We doctors know
> a hopeless case if—listen:there's a hell
> of a good universe next door;let's go[55]

Classical gnosticism, with much more anguish and no humor at all, was determined to step off into that universe next door. As Harold Bloom has argued, within the context of their own system the escape of the gnostics has been successful:

> It is a familiar formula to say that failed prophesy becomes apocalyptic, and that failed apocalyptic becomes Gnosticism. If we were to ask: "What does failed Gnosticism become?" we would have to answer that Gnosticism never fails . . . a vision whose fulfillment, by definition, must be always beyond the cosmos, cannot be said to fail *within* our cosmos.[56]

Though no failure is possible within these terms, it can also be said that, as with any escape from reality, neither is victory possible.

The Church was quick to recognize the no-win predicament of gnostic philosophy. The New Testament authors themselves began to ask what would be the result of gnostic spirituality. For St. Paul, for example, the real test was not how successful the ecstasy, but three other factors: faith, hope and love. Of these, love (*agape*) is the most determinative of all: "If I . . . understand all mysteries [*mysteria*] and all knowledge . . . but have not love, I am nothing. . . . as for tongues [*glossai*], they will cease; as for knowledge [*gnosis*] it will pass away. For our knowledge is imperfect."[57]

In a similar vein, it seems that I John is an answer to a heretical movement in the Church which has offered the pure love of God as an alternative to the difficult demands of communal life.[58] Against those who claim already to have escaped from this world's problems, the Johannine author writes:

> If we say we have no sin, we deceive ourselves, and the truth is not in us. . . . And by this we may be sure that we know [*ginoskomen*] him, if we keep his commandments. He who says, "I know [*egnoka*] him" but disobeys his commandments is a liar, and the truth is not in him.[59]

The commandments with which the author is preoccupied are, of course, the commandments of love. "If anyone says, 'I love God,' and hates his brother, he is a liar; for he who does not love his brother whom he has seen, cannot love God whom he has not seen."[60] Absolutely no escape from this tangible world of sensory perception is allowed. Salvation from the world by any other route than through the world will be called a fraud. The author is so adamant in this direction that he does not mention the love of God itself in a positive sense. The real test of the spiritual journey is this: "We know that we have passed out of death into life, because we love the brethren. He who does not love abides in death."[61]

The contrast between gnostic escape from the world and Christian pilgrimage through the world can be understood in terms of the conversion experience.

> The contrast is clear. Judaism and Christianity demanded renunciation and a new start. They demanded not merely acceptance of a rite, but the adhesion of the will to a theology, in a word faith, a new life in a new people. . . . A man used Mithraism, but he did not belong to it body and soul.[62]

In other words, whereas "one cannot be a Christian on the side," one can indeed "be a Mithraist on the side."[63] An identical distinction can be made between Christian gnosticism and Christian orthodoxy. When the gnostic *escapes* the world, it becomes very possible for him to be a Christian on the side, even in his spare time. But the Christian whose life has been transformed from aimless wandering to determined pilgrimage will find no respite. The Christian and the cosmos are inextricably bound together until death do them part.

Within orthodoxy, there will be but one release from this difficult pilgrimage—that of physical death. Christians who are suffering great distress cannot at times resist longing for that escape. "Wretched man that I am!" cried the apostle, "Who will deliver me from this body of death?"[64] And again he admits that if it were a matter of his own choice, "we would rather be away from the body and at home with the Lord."[65]

The Knowing Self Versus the Believing Community

The gnostics were able, at least to their own satisfaction, to accomplish in Houdini-like fashion a successful exit from the cosmos prior to physical death. In fact, all the promises that faith offers to the Christian are fulfilled for the gnostic here and now, though in a necessarily truncated form. For the escape the gnostic accomplishes is, in simple terms, an escape into the *self.* Knowledge of God involves the knower not in a further or more profound relationship with the world—nature and other persons—but rather in a disengagement from the world and a concentration on the self and the self's concerns.

The identification of *self* with God in gnostic wisdom is explained by Hans Jonas with his usual clarity. He states that because the gnostic sees humanity as partly divine, having this "transmundane element" within him, there is an "identity or consubstantiality of man's innermost self with the supreme and transmundane God, himself often called 'Man.' "[66] The search for God and the search for self, because of this ontological identification, become synonymous.

Escape into the self is psychologically motivated; it is a psychological technique. Whether the technique is valid or spurious depends on one's point of view. For Carl Gustav Jung, gnostic symbols of self-awareness are extremely helpful in the treatment of emotional illness. Modern life, Jung maintained, owed to the ancient gnostics and the medieval alchemists what he called "the process of individuation"—that which sets the individual apart from all others, the knowledge of himself as self. In Jung's gnostic image, the self is like "a young bird who picks its way out of an egg."[67] The eggshell that the gnostics pick their way out of can be nothing else but the cosmos itself, for the cosmos is what imprisons us—it is the wall that encloses us and denies us a vision of our true being. Jung's theory that the concept "God" is coextensive with the "collective unconscious" is, as Carl Raschke has shown, but another illustration of Jung's "propensity to claim an apotheosis of the self."[68]

On the other side of the psychological fence, Karen Horney argued that the desire to escape from the concrete into the fantasy of self-alone is always a futile attempt, symptomatic of the emotional illness itself. She, in fact, used the Faustian story, a gnostic legend, to describe the neurotic person. The neurotic, in order to gratify the self as self-alone, must agree to live a kind of half-life—a life realized in terms of the self rather than in terms of others—and to forsake all hope of wholeness and healing.[69]

Whether the flight to self is genuine or synthetic, helpful or hopeless, it would appear to be a continuing human drive "deeply rooted in the soul of man."[70] Thomas Mann referred to the gnostic vision as a "narcissistic picture, so full of tragic charm."[71] The focusing on God alone—God isolated from cosmos, God isolated from change, time, place, and fellow creatures—can reveal only a God who is a reflection of self or, more accurately, fantasized self. Though that reflection, finally, cannot save us from our plight, who could deny that Mann is correct? The picture is full of "tragic charm," even of enchantment. The enchantment lies in the fanciful nature of the vision. Bultmann observed that "[for the gnostic] all knowledge serves the knowledge of self . . . as reflection on one's spiritual endowment and abilities . . . by his vision he [the gnostic] is transformed from a man into God."[72]

As we have seen, salvation in gnostic terms is not salvation from sin but salvation from ignorance. The significance of the Gospel, then, becomes solely that of illumination. And what is illuminated is the true *self.* As A. D. Nock has understood, with this illumination, a man is able to return to his own true nature. Unlike the prodigal son who returns to the *other,* the gnostic who has wandered away, once he sees the light, is able to return to himself.[73] The gnostic illumination enables persons not so much to see their own reflection in the being of God, as to see the being of God in their own reflection: "As ye see yourselves in water or mirror, so see ye me in yourselves."[74]

The *Gospel of Thomas* contains several allusions to self-knowledge as a means to and even as identical to the knowledge of God. Note the sequence of the following: "When you come to know yourselves, then you will become known." On the other hand, "If you will not know yourselves, you dwell in poverty and it is you who are that poverty."[75] At one point, the disciples ask Jesus when he will be revealed to them and when they will see him, a question that in itself demonstrates a highly spiritualized concept of the Savior. Jesus answers: "When you disrobe without being ashamed and take up your garments and place them under your feet like little children and tread on them, then [will you see] the Son of the Living One, and you will not be afraid."[76] This is not an admonition to practice nudity, though some gnostics have been led to act out their innocence in that way; rather, the instruction is to expose the naked soul to the self and by knowing the self to know the divine. Near the end of the *Gospel,* the doctrine of self-knowledge is made explicit; Jesus is quoted as saying: "The heavens and the earth will be rolled up in your presence . . . whoever finds himself is superior to the world."[77]

The solitary nature of the religious quest is a continuing theme of gnostic literature. At times its peculiar thrust would seem to require a serious adjustment of the biblical tradition. Whereas Jesus is reported by Matthew to have said, "Where two or three are gathered in my name . . . ,"[78] a gnostic document offers this counter-report, "Jesus said, wheresoever there be two, they are not without God; and wherever there is one alone, I say, I am with him. Raise the stone and there thou shalt find Me, cleave the wood and there I am."[79] The author's aim clearly is to legitimize the private communion with God so dear to the gnostic soul. There is within this philosophy no real need for the *other;* the individual is a complete unit of faith and knowledge.

An alternate text, taken from the same papyrus, teaches that, "The Kingdom of Heaven is within you; and whosoever shall know himself shall find it."[80] With only a slight change in wording from a teaching of Jesus reported in all three synoptic gospels,[81] the gnostic text is able totally to transform the original idea into a persuasive appeal for self-awareness with nothing less than arrival at the Kingdom itself as the final reward.

These slight changes, a word substituted here or there, a phrase or two added better to complete Jesus' thought, make all the difference. Suddenly, we find ourselves not with a slightly altered gospel but with an anti-gospel. How radically it was anti-gospel can be illustrated by an observation of Quispel's: "It is most significant that Valentinus and Basilides, who wished to be Christians, who were well acquainted with the Bible and in particular with the Gospel of St. John, never said that God is love."[82] This is significant, but not surprising. When human beings are perceived in individualistic, nonrelational terms, not dependent on any other creature in their search for God, does it not follow that the God they find will also be isolated and nonrelational? If we find God only through self-awareness, how can the God we find be anything more or less than a reflection of ourselves? How can God be anyone other than the figure that fascinated the doomed Narcissus? And if the self we discover is filled only with *gnosis* and void of love, will the reflected One not be the same?

The Church could not help but be frightened by this extreme individualization of the faith, especially by the promise that the true God is to be discovered by an inner spiritual journey. Nothing could have been further from biblical religion. As Bishop Leslie Newbigin has written in answer to some contemporary exponents of individualistic Christianity:

> The object to which God's purpose of grace is directed is the whole creation and the whole human family, not human souls conceived as billions of separate monads each detached from its place in the whole fabric of the human and natural world.[83]

In reattaching these separate monads to humanity and to nature, one of the key strategies of orthodoxy would again be dependence on the Old Testament. In the Old Testament, Yahweh illuminates not simply by saying, "Let there be light," but also by ensuring that "there *was* light."[84]

The Old Testament certainly provides for meditation, but it is not meditation on the *self;* the blessed man will meditate on "the law of the LORD . . . day and night"[85] or "on thee [God] in the watches of the night"[86] or "on all thy [God's] work."[87] In each of these cases, the Hebrew word for meditate is *hagah,* the root meaning of which is to mutter or move the lips, which means that when the psalmist meditates there is a concrete memory in mind: a law, a deed, an event of God.

It is inconceivable that meditation would attempt to discover God through a discovery of self, because the God of Israel is Himself the discoverer: " 'A wandering Aramean was my father . . .' " and then an afflicted slave in Egypt " 'when the LORD heard our voice.' "[88] Later the Israelites were but another anonymous Middle Eastern nation with no future and no hope when the Lord said:

> I will have pity on Not pitied,
> and I will say to Not my people,
> 'You are my people.'[89]

It is Yahweh who has searched for and found Israel rather than the other way around. And Israel is not confused:

> O Lord, thou has searched me and known me!
> . . . Such knowledge is too wonderful for me;
> it is high, I cannot attain it.[90]

What the Old Testament person can know about God is not self-discoverable. It can be learned only through the community because only through the community has He revealed Himself. When Yahweh makes His presence known to Abraham, Isaac and Jacob, the purpose is not the enlightenment of those individuals. The patriarchs and prophets are those who are related to God on behalf of the community to which they, in turn, are related. In the case of Jacob, for instance, his very name, Israel, is synonymous with the community itself.[91]

The truth about this God is a truth that always involves His action, His word, His relatedness to Israel rather than some abstract knowledge of His being. And the truth is conveyed by the concrete methods of family nurture:

> You shall teach them [these words of mine] to your children, talking of them when you are sitting in your house, and when you are walking by the way, and when you lie down, and when you rise. And you shall write them upon the doorposts of your house and upon your gates.[92]

It is in this communal sense that Israel is to go about "loving the LORD your God, obeying his voice, and cleaving to him."[93] And it is in this sense of communal relatedness that men and women are able to enjoy life and length of days.

The Old Testament not only binds people to one another, but also to nature, to the good earth:

> You [Israel] shall no more be termed Forsaken,
> and your land shall no more be termed Desolate;
> but you shall be called My delight is in her,
> and your land Married; . . .
> For as a young man marries a virgin,
> so shall your sons marry you [the land].[94]

Within Yahweh's community, it is unthinkable for the individual to turn away from his people or from his world.

When we come to the New Testament, the theological limitations are not nearly so cut and dried. As we have seen, there were many opportunities within the early Church for interpretation and revision which would allow for gnostic inwardness and even for a narcissistic fascination with one's spiritual being. Nevertheless, the Church as a whole fought back in terms of its heritage in Israel and also its own emerging life and thought.

It is possible that the community of Jesus Christ would regard this very drive for self-realization as the root sin itself. Is it not the all-too-human fascination with self that the devil repeatedly brings to Jesus' mind in the wilderness? If Jesus is the Son of God, why should he bother to draw the masses to himself through love? Why should he not perform his own religious spectacular? And finally, the prototypical temptation of the Faustian legend: if Jesus will worship the devil, all his private fantasies—"all the kingdoms of the world and the glory of them"—will be fulfilled.[95] The outcome of the story is quite different from that of Faust: the protagonist refuses to succumb to the devil's destructive suggestions. The implication of the Gospel accounts is clearly, however, that if the Lord Jesus himself found self-fulfillment so attractive, how much more will his sinful followers. Is this narcissistic tendency not the most troublesome human problem?

The Four Gospels at various other points challenge the notion that salvation has to do with spiritual self-fulfillment. "He who finds his life will lose it, and he who loses his life for my sake will find it."[96] And also in the First Gospel, "If any man would come after me, let him deny himself and take up his cross and follow me. For whoever would save his life will lose it, and whoever loses his life for my sake will find it."[97] If we read into this recurring theme only a disregard for physical life and a call to sacrifice the physical body, have we not missed the point? Is it not preoccupation with self, both physical and spiritual, against which Jesus is issuing a warning?

The rich ruler asks Jesus the traditional question of spiritual self-concern, "Good Teacher, what shall I do to inherit eternal life?" Jesus' answer from the outset denies the validity of the question: "Why do you call me good? No one is good but God alone," at once putting the lie to any claim of inner righteousness or spiritual competence on the part of the ruler. When the ruler goes on to credit himself with having obeyed the commandments, Jesus has yet another obstacle to place in the way of this isolated search for salvation, "One thing you still lack. Sell all that you have and distribute it to the poor and you will have treasure in heaven."[98] In the story immediately preceding this incident, Jesus has said to the disciples, "Whoever does not receive the kingdom of God like a child shall not enter it."[99] Perhaps contrasting this very quality of unselfconsciousness and self-abandonment, so evident in small children, with the self-preoccupation of the rich ruler, is the purpose behind Luke's linking of the two events.

Many passages in the epistles are echoes of the Old Testament corporate view of God's people, "But you [plural] are a chosen race, a royal priesthood, a holy nation, God's own people. . . . Once you [plural] were no people but now you are God's people."[100] Within this context of God's people, how is it possible to concern oneself with an isolated search for self-knowledge, much less to hope for salvation through self-awareness?

Nor does St. Paul, who is often accused of having gnostic tendencies, ever indicate the slightest interest in an individual search for God. Even less does he offer any hope for locating God within the self. All along he maintains a staunchly corporate view of what faith is. Faith is the opposite of finding ourselves; it is being found by God: "God is faithful, by whom you [plural] were called into the fellowship [*koinonia*] of his Son."[101] *Koinonia* is a Pauline word used to describe the particular form of participation with one another by which Christians are bound together. In classical Greek usage, *koinonia pantos tou biou* (marriage) "is closer and more comprehensive than all other forms of fellowship."[102] It is in this spiritually intimate and physically interconnected sense that Paul wishes to state the participatory bonds that hold Christians together. In writing the Philippians, the Apostle is thankful for their *koinonia* in the Gospel from the first day until now.[103] And in the eucharistic meal, the participation of Christians with Christ and with one another is enhanced: "The cup of blessing which we bless, is it not a participation [*koinonia*] in the blood of Christ? The bread which we break, is it not a participation [*koinonia*] in the body of Christ?"[104]

The final word to the Corinthian Christians in the second letter of St. Paul has to do with the necessity of *koinonia* in which *koinonia* itself is said to *be* the blessing: "The grace of the Lord Jesus Christ and the love of God and the fellowship [*koinonia*] of the Holy Spirit be with you all."[105]

All of this is not to say that either the Gospels or the epistles are in these instances setting out to dispute gnostic claims or that there is always a conscious argument against gnostic individualism. It is simply to recognize that biblical religion is far removed from the kind of narcissistic concerns we find in gnostic writings. Little wonder that a canon of Scripture was to become a principal ally of the Church Fathers in their struggle against heresy.

In addition to the Scriptures of the Old and New Testaments, the Fathers also opposed gnosticism with the weapon of Church discipline. Individuals would not be allowed to define God in terms of their own self-discovery. Ignatius of Antioch was the first theologian to use the word *catholic* as a descriptive term for Christ's Church: "Where the bishop appears, there let the people be, just as where Jesus Christ is, there is the Catholic Church."[106] Clement of Rome (pope ca. 95–97) and Irenaeus (ca. 130–ca. 200), at this remarkably early period of the Church's life, would certainly have agreed that the pastoral office with bishops and presbyters is essential to the Church's united and faithful witness to Christ.[107] If the Christian faith were to be more than a collection of ideas from individual imaginings, then discipline and concrete structures were necessities.

A Spiritual Elite Versus Ordinary People

The gnostics would have considered bishops, presbyters, and other symbols of discipline quite acceptable, perhaps even necessary—for ordinary Christians. The idea, however, of the *gnostikoi* having to submit to such worldly trappings was not to be tolerated. These mundane, formalized, uncreative expressions of Christianity so carefully maintained by the orthodox Church were an embarrassment to the pneumatics within the Church. Some scholars even believe that the rapid growth of the gnostic movement can be explained as a reaction against the popularizing of Christianity. That is, as the Christian Church became universally accepted by the masses, its preaching adapted to the general public and its worship sometimes pro forma, the more enlightened Christians began to yearn for a kind of faith which was more intense, more spiritual—which called for more dedication. These persons were offended by being put in the same category with ordinary Christians who were operating on so low a level of intellect and spirit.[108]

Whatever the cause of the elitist sentiment within gnosticism, certainly it was there. The Valentinians found the preaching within the Church to consist predominantly of childish moralizing, offering nothing to challenge the enlightened ones within the congregation.[109]

The Church's sacramental life also, as we shall see, was an affront to gnostic spirituality. What the gnostics considered a base materialism was capturing ordinary Christianity.

Thus the gnostics felt compelled to separate themselves from the ordinary Christians. Probably most of them remained formally attached to some local Church, took part in some or all of its activities, but meanwhile operated, at least to their own satisfaction, on an entirely different level from the nongnostic members. The enlightened ones would be sustained by a pneumatic reading of Scripture as opposed to that proclaimed from the pulpit, being further aided at times by special literature and discovering through these writings more profound insights into Christian symbols.

The literature itself abounds with assurances that the *gnostikoi* are different from the run-of-the-mill Christians. In the *Gospel of Thomas,* for instance, Jesus said: "It is to those who are worthy of My mysteries that I tell My mysteries. Do not let your left hand know what your right hand is doing."[110] Many people can hear the word of Christ and go through the motions of worship, but only the worthy can really grasp the mysteries of true faith.

The gnostics often divided humankind into three categories. There were the somatic (*hylic*) ones who were content to exist on a bodily level: eating, drinking, defecating, sleeping, copulating, dying. There were the psychics who functioned at the level of mind, intellect, emotions—the commonsense types who composed the "many" in the Church. Finally, there were the pneumatics, or *gnostikoi,* who were worthy of understanding the mysteries. The first group, those without spirit who felt completely at home in the natural world, who had no transcendental nostalgia, no longing for an escape into the perfect world from which man originated, were quite simply beyond all help. Basilides, when asked if such persons could really be called men at all, categorically denied it: "We are men; all the others are pigs and dogs."[111] Man, in other words, is either spiritual man or he is no man at all.

This stratified view of humanity was held along with a strong belief in divine election. The *Gospel of Thomas,* which has Jesus telling his mysteries to the worthy, also introduces the idea of merit into the story of the lost sheep. The new twist in the Thomas version is that "one of them [one of the one hundred sheep], the largest, went astray. He left the ninety-nine and looked for that one until he found it. When he had gone to such trouble he said to the sheep, 'I care for you more than the ninety-nine.' "[112] In this variation on a Gospel theme, the gnostic author reverses the picture of Jesus the Good Shepherd searching for and finding the one lost sheep. In Matthew's account, the parable is introduced by the phrase, "see that you do not despise one of these little ones" and concludes with, "so it is not the will of my Father who is in heaven that one of these little ones should perish."[113] Luke's Gospel has the shepherd, when he has found his lost sheep, laying it on his shoulders—quite a burden were it the largest animal in the flock. But regardless of size, the Third Gospel's message coincides with that of the First Gospel, for the summation is, "I tell you there will be more joy in heaven over one sinner who repents than over ninety-nine righteous persons who need no repentance."[114] In both canonical Gospels reporting the story, the Good Shepherd elects to go after the one sheep because the one needs him, not because of any lack of concern for the flock as a whole. In the *Gospel of Thomas,* the shepherd goes after the largest, the most valuable, the one he *should* go after, the one he cares for more than the *many*.[115]

The pneumatics, according to gnostic wisdom, have been elected because they are worthy of election. Here, again, is a variation on a New Testament theme. No doubt, St. Paul's doctrine of election made a deep impression on Basilides, Valentinus and Marcion and endeared him to his gnostic readers over several generations. For the gnostics to make use of the Pauline doctrine, however, they had to amend it rather seriously:

> When the Apostle [Paul] speaks of the chosen people, he has in mind the historic people of Israel, of which the Christian Church is a continuation, while Basilides applies this term to the people, transcendent, i.e., nonhistorical, spirit. . . . all in all, the Gnostic election is . . . a mystification of the Biblical conception.[116]

In gnosticism, God elects, not a people, but individual persons: persons who have a nostalgic yearning for the higher life, persons who have some spiritual insight, persons who are creative enough to see beyond the written text a meaning hidden to the many.

This election resulted, negatively, in certain oblivion for the somatics, the mere animals who happen to be in human form.[117] Election guaranteed salvation to the pneumatics because they were worthy.[118] And the psychics, in the middle, could go either way. Through the help of a pneumatic, the psychic might be brought out of ignorance into knowledge and salvation. The evangelistic drive within gnosticism arises from the desire to help the otherwise lost psychic. It would be gratifying for the pneumatics to know that they have "brought many back from error."[119]

The elitest nature of gnosticism was perhaps its greatest threat to the orthodox Church. In any large religious organization, there will be, of course, many varieties of faith: individuals will hold unusual, even bizarre, beliefs concerning the given tradition or practice. Such individual expressions, even when considered erroneous, can often be tolerated or ignored by the corporate body. An elitest attitude, however, poses a real danger: it divides a congregation of believers into factions. In this instance, it divided Christians into a higher level of concerned, spiritual, creative Christians, on the one hand, and a lower level of apathetic, materialist, dull Christians, on the other. The division not only endangered the peace and unity of the Church, but also, from the orthodox viewpoint, struck at something very close to the heart of the Gospel.

As Max Weber noted: "From its very beginning, Christianity . . . took a position against intellectualism (gnosticism) with the greatest possible awareness and consistency . . . [against] the soteriology of the Gnostic intellectual aristocrats."[120] Weber's identification of gnosticism with intellectualism might be open to dispute. Certainly, it was a peculiar sort of intellectualism. His observation about the Church's reaction, however, is absolutely accurate: the Church came down with both feet on all those who would flaunt their own knowledge and spirituality while denigrating that of others.

Once again, the New Testament community drew great strength from the tradition of Israel. The people of God in the Old Testament had never *known* God through their keen intellect or spiritual insights. For the patriarchs and prophets, *knowing* God meant a practical recognition of God through confession, thanksgiving and daily life.[121]

> Did not your father eat and drink
>   and do justice and righteousness?
> Then it was well with him.
> He judged the cause of the poor
>   and needy;
>   then it was well.
> Is not this to *know* me?
>   says the LORD.[122]

The Old Testament God has secrets; even the prophets are not advised of all His schemes.[123] But God is constantly giving signs: "I will dwell among the people of Israel, and will be their God. And they shall *know* that I am the LORD their God, who brought them forth out of the land of Egypt."[124] In the sense that God is continually revealing Himself to Israel in historical event and in the traditions of His people, the prophetic promise is that

> The earth shall be full of the
> knowledge of the LORD
> as the waters cover the sea.[125]

Old Testament theology understands that the truths concerning God are the heritage of all the people of Israel: "The secret things belong to the LORD our God; but the things that are revealed belong to us and to our children for ever."[126]

That certain knowledgeable persons should have an inside track to the Almighty would have been out of the question. Job is chastised by Eliphaz the Temanite for claiming a wisdom beyond that of Israel:

> Are you the first man that was
> born?
> Or were you brought forth before
> the hills?
> Have you listened in the council
> of God?
> And do you limit wisdom to your-
> self?
> What do you know that we do not
> know?
> What do you understand that is not
> clear to us?[127]

The knowledge of God in the Old Covenant is *open* knowledge, available, at the very least, to all of Israel. For even though "thou art a God who hidest thyself," nevertheless says the Lord:

> I did not speak in secret,
> in a land of darkness;
> I did not say to the offspring of Jacob,
> 'Seek me in chaos.'
> I the LORD speak the truth,
> I declare what is right.[128]

The irony here is that though God himself cannot be known as pure Being, a knowledge which is not permitted in the theology of Israel, nevertheless, God's truth, His acts, words, laws, statutes, intentions and promises are a matter of public record and can be known by any sane person.

This open, non-mysterious understanding of religious knowledge stands behind much of New Testament thought, and the Old Testament, as its sacred literature, was securely a part of the New Israel's liturgical life. As such, it stood as a strong safeguard against any emergent elitism.

Israel's anti-elitist spirit is reflected specifically in some of the writings of the Apostle Paul. New Testament scholars are now largely in agreement that the theological opponents against whom Paul is writing often represent a form of early gnosticism. Rudolf Bultmann interprets Paul's prophesy recorded in the Acts of the Apostles to be a warning concerning the gnostics within the Christian community: "I know that after my departure fierce wolves will come in among you . . . and from among your own selves will arise men speaking perverse things to draw away the disciples after them."[129] Bultmann goes on to identify the "false apostles, deceitful workmen, disguising themselves as apostles of Christ,"[130] as those who have initiated a pneumatic-gnostic movement in Corinth.[131] And Schmithals further argues that Paul is writing against gnostics in the Corinthian letters, Galatians, Philippians, I and II Thessalonians and Romans.[132] Bornkamm, also, sees the gnostics as the Apostle's chief adversaries and in particular mentions Paul's having to deal with their elitism: "These fanatics boasted that they, and they alone, had already reached the state of 'perfection' and were in possession of 'spirit' and 'knowledge.' "[133]

If these interpreters are correct, then many of Paul's teachings can be understood as clear warnings against the prideful elitism of gnostic thought:

> We know that "all of us possess knowledge [*gnosis*]." "Knowledge [*Gnosis*]" puffs up, but love builds up. If any one imagines that he *knows* something, he does not yet *know* as he ought to *know*.[134]

> I think that I am not the least inferior to these superlative apostles. Even if I am unskilled in speaking, I am not in knowledge [*gnosis*].[135]

On several occasions Paul indicates that he, too, could be an elitist if he wanted to be, but intentionally, "I did not come proclaiming to you the testimony of God in lofty words or wisdom. For I decided to know nothing among you except Jesus Christ and him crucified."[136]

A striking example of a defense of the ordinary Christian against the claims of the *gnostikoi* is found in the section of I John dealing with those who have broken away from the Church: "They went out from us, but they were not of us; for if they had been of us, they would have continued with us."[137] The schism could have occurred because a group of pneumatic Christians were unable to accept the prosaic, seemingly uninspired spirituality or (in their eyes) lack of spirituality of the "many." This possibility becomes a probability when we see in the verse immediately following, this encouraging word to the "many": "But [despite their having left us] you have been anointed by the Holy One, and you know (*oidate*) everything."[138] You ordinary Christians may not know (*ginosko*) like the gnostics know, but you know (*oidate*) everything that you need to know. The Johannine author goes on to assure the ordinary ones that love of one another is the real test and that, in light of this love, they are to have complete confidence.[139] Their faith is validated not by esoteric knowledge but by public confession: "Every spirit which confesses that Jesus Christ has come in the flesh is of God."[140]

In the spirit of both the Old and the New Covenants, Irenaeus continues to attack any person or group claiming to possess a more profound understanding of the faith than that held by the orthodox Church. Against those who claim that the beliefs of ordinary Christians are merely shadows of much deeper insights held by themselves, the pneumatics, Irenaeus writes: "For we [the Church] possess the Lord of the law, the Son of God, and through faith in him we learn to love God with our whole heart and our neighbour as ourselves."[141] Here the bishop of Lyons is insisting that Christian faith is not dependent for its appropriation on the insights of some particularly gifted pneumatics, but rather on those realities of revelation and tradition entrusted to the safekeeping of the Holy Catholic Church. Anyone who clings to the Lord of the Church or to the Church of its Lord can *know* the truth.

Nor, for Irenaeus, can any doctrine of election obviate the freedom of the ordinary man or woman to understand the message of salvation: "It is within the power of all, therefore, in every church, who may wish to see the truth, to contemplate clearly the tradition of the apostles manifested throughout the whole world." Irenaeus even compares this truth, a gift of God, to the greatest natural gift of God: "As the sun, that creature of God, is one and the same throughout the whole world, so also the preaching of the truth shineth everywhere and enlightens all men that are willing to come to a knowledge of the truth."[142]

Divine election for the Fathers, as in biblical thought, pertains to the calling of a people, not to the singling out of gifted or worthy persons. In writing of the biblical and patristic tradition concerning infant baptism, Jeremias reminds us:

> The whole people of God were baptized when they passed through the Red Sea (I Cor. 10:lf.), the whole family of Noah was saved in the ark (I Pet. 3:20f.), the promise of the Spirit is referred to the "houses," "to you and your children" (Acts 2:39). They are seen as one unit in the sight of God . . . the universal character of Christ's grace reveals itself in that it is the "houses" which are summoned to believe and are baptized.[143]

The final decision by the Church Fathers for the universal acceptance of infant baptism was a strong move against spiritual elitism. The practice should have guaranteed that one brought to Christ in such fashion could take no credit for his or her election.

Athenagoras, an early apologist, offered this appreciation of those ordinary but holy people within the Church: "Among us you will find uneducated persons and artisans and old women, who if they are unable to prove in words the benefit of our doctrine, yet by their deeds exhibit the benefit arising from their possession of its truth."[144]

Selective Syncretism Versus Particularity

The gnostics, with their disdain for the faith of ordinary persons, felt that the orthodox Church was erroneously *bound* to materiality: water, bread, wine, the flesh. The pneumatics were bound to no *thing* in particular and open to all things in general so long as the objects were merely metaphorical and spiritually edifying. The gnostic appropriation of every useful symbol or idea is often referred to as the syncretistic aspect of the gnostic type.

Much has been made of this tendency within gnosticism. If the Apostle Paul, despite his profound intelligence and wisdom, "decided to know nothing among you except Jesus Christ and him crucified,"[145] the gnostics decided to know anything and everything that might abet their cause.

The gnostics were not alone in this sort of religious plagiarism.

As Frederick Grant noted, "The main characteristic feature of Hellenistic religion was syncretism: the tendency to identify the deities of various peoples and to combine their cults."[146] Christian orthodoxy, of course, shared this hellenistic propensity for the syncretistic.

The syncretism of orthodoxy, however, might well be called accidental; it occurred because Christianity absorbed what happened to be around it. Unfriendly critics might say that Christianity became absorbed in the world about it. Either way, the coalescing of Christianity and other religious expressions happened because the Christian faith always exists in a religious milieu of some kind or other, and the Christian faith, often unwittingly, adjusts to and compromises with that milieu. The mix takes place for purposes of apologetics, missionary outreach, or simply by accident of proximity.

The syncretism of gnosticism was purposeful. It appropriated to itself everything which could support the *gnosis* that no *thing* matters. If a particular myth such as the Christ myth tends to be more important than the others as is the case in the *Gospel of Truth,* it was only because the Christ myth better expressed for the gnostic the understanding that nothing in history and nature could make any real difference anyway. Hans Jonas has insisted that the syncretistic tendency within *gnosis* is quite purposeful; it is "not a directionless eclecticism."[147] The selection of material has to do with a "fallen God," "benighted creator," "sinister creation," "cosmic captivity," "acosmic salvation," "divine tragedy."[148] Is it not then the syncretistic purpose of gnosticism to gather to itself any material that can set the scene in a world other than this world? Would not any raw material be appropriate so long as it helped shift our concern from here to there? Such is the mistaken confidence of the gnostics that without the impedimenta of events, things, seasons or persons (i.e., without particularity) religious salvation can be achieved.

The gnostic rejection of particularity means that Christ himself becomes a vague spiritualized being. In *The Apocryphon of John,* the author is beset with an acute case of religious doubt concerning the resurrection of Christ. The doubt was supposedly prompted by the taunts of a Pharisee, but possibly had been lingering in his psyche because of overwhelming evidence to the contrary. Whatever the cause, John reports that while he contemplated these things in the desert, a youth stood beside him:

> While I looked [at him he became] like an old man. And he [changed his] form (again), becoming like a servant. There was [not a plural-

ity] before me, but there was a [likeness] with multiple forms in the light . . . [and] the likeness had three forms.

Nor does the ephemeral nature of Christ end there; the Christ says to John, "I [am the Father], I am the Mother, I am the Son."[149]

Now, perhaps, we are able to see more clearly the true nature of the contrast between orthodoxy and gnostic heresy. If St. Paul "decided to know nothing . . . except Jesus Christ and him crucified,"[150] and if that knowing can be considered shorthand for the Incarnation—for God's entire venture into time, place and history—then is not this material precisely what the gnostics decided not to know? Their syncretism was, in other words, a collection of data denying particularity.

The Manichaeans, a gnostic sect of the second century, offer a clear example of such a denial. Regarding this cult of which he had at one time been a member, Augustine explains that, for them, Jesus not only was revealed light, but was present everywhere: he signified "man's life and man's salvation hanging on every tree." That is why the Manichaeans had no special regard for the bread and the wine of the Eucharist.[151]

Christ as a divine being had to be, for the gnostics, anywhere and everywhere. What he could not be was *somewhere* and *someplace* such as at the eucharistic table. Ignatius of Antioch explains that "They [the gnostics] hold aloof from the Eucharist and from services of prayer because they refuse to admit that the Eucharist is the Flesh of our Saviour Jesus Christ, which suffered."[152] Irenaeus also finds his opponents to be contemptuous of the sacraments. Some gnostics, he wrote, "reject all these practices and maintain that the mystery as the unspeakable and invisible power ought not to be performed by visible and corruptible creatures."[153]

Like the Eucharist, baptism also was problematical for the ancient gnostics. Heracleon argued that only the lowest prophetic office should have "the duty of baptizing" because baptism is merely a bodily washing with water. He admitted that John the Baptist did, in his "external role," baptize. Inwardly, however, John did not baptize: "As 'voice' he offer[ed] not the physical act but its interior, ethical meaning."[154] The metaphor was acceptable; the actual event was an embarrassment.

The more inclusive issue was the gnostic denial that Christ was located in the Church itself. It was a scandal, in gnostic eyes, that what is divine should be attached in any sense to a particular people in time and space. At the Yale Conference on Gnosticism in 1978, Frederik Wisse, in discussing the so-called Sethite gnostics, said: "Regarding the reference to baptism [by John Strugnell]—I picture individuals leaving the Church and, like the desert fathers, trying to spiritualize the sacraments to remove any dependence on the Church."[155] If Bultmann were right in claiming that "gnosticism lacks the specific characteristics of Church-consciousness,"[156] it could also be said that gnosticism lacks it purposefully.

It is obvious that the orthodox Church could not accept the gnostic denial of particularity. Christianity, under these conditions, would have to forsake its Jewish heritage, and the essential role of the historical Jesus would fade into the mist of gnostic spirituality.[157] From the beginning, the Church faced this challenge and opposed any attempt to "tamper with God's word" in a way that would deny the historicity of Jesus the Christ or weaken the concreteness of his union with the Church.[158] Bultmann explains:

> Let it be granted that there is a difference between this [the cross event] and the salvation-occurrences related by the myth of the mystery-religions and by Gnosticism: Here [in the Pauline writings] the subject is an historical person, Jesus, and his death on the cross only a few years earlier is at the center of the salvation-occurrence.[159]

So the Christ is preached as one "born of woman, born under the law,"[160] "crucified in weakness,"[161] even though such preaching will be received as a "stumbling block" and "folly."[162]

In the age of the early Fathers, the battle line between orthodox particularity and gnostic purposeful syncretism was drawn on the issues of sacramental practice and Church discipline. If a person could not live with the particularity and materiality of baptism and Eucharist, presbyter and bishop, then neither could he or she follow the way of the cross.

Irenaeus held firmly that the infinite could be seen only in the finite, that, in fact, "in God nothing is empty of sense."[163] He also saw that "only in Christ is all creation gathered together and sacrificed to God."[164] Father Jungmann, commenting on Irenaeus's argument, observes:

> In taking a position against the exaggerated spiritualism of the gnostics, Irenaeus appears to be compelled to defend the worth of earthly creation. With clear vision he sees the symbolic meaning of what occurred at our Lord's institution of the Blessed Sacrament, when things of this earth of ours were so exalted that by the word of

> God, they became Christ's flesh and blood and were thus empowered to enter into the clean oblation of the New Covenant.[165]

The Fathers, that is, were no less spiritual than those who claimed a higher spirituality; what so radically distinguished them from their opponents was their determination to see the eternal through the God-given temporal gifts of creation.

The early Church's employment of ecclesiastical discipline against its heretical opponents is so familiar it needs little retelling. Ignatius of Antioch urged the faithful to "agree in one faith in Jesus Christ, who was of the family of David according to the flesh, the Son of Man and the Son of God, so that you obey the bishop and the presbytery with an undivided mind, breaking one bread . . . which is life forever in Jesus Christ."[166] Cyprian, bishop of Carthage (ca. 248–258) was so anxious to establish the connection between the divine Christ and the earthly Church that he advised Christians to "look to the bishop as to the Lord himself; do nothing without the bishop. The Church is established in the bishops and the clergy."[167]

A. D. Nock sums up the Church's overall strategy: "Against the individualism of the Gnostics stood the growing strength of episcopal organization, the idea of an apostolic succession of doctrine and the formation of the Canon of the New Testament."[168] With that strategy and with the will to employ it, the orthodox Church prevailed, at least for a season, against the formidable enemy within its gates.

CHAPTER THREE

Gnosticism Within the Orthodox Faith

CRITICS of orthodox Christianity are quick to point out that a great deal of what we have referred to as gnosticism has existed within the Church throughout its history. The world-denying, escapist, elitist themes have had their advocates in every Christian era. Are we not all aware of the Church's image of promoting otherworldliness, mortification of the flesh and denial of sexual pleasure, not to mention the Marxist taunt, "Pie in the sky by and by when you die"?

No one could deny that there is more than ample evidence to support such a critique. The Church has indeed sheltered gnostic individuals; it has, in some generations, been greatly influenced by them. The Church has, to a degree, been gnosticized as, in turn, it has been hellenized, Platonized, stoicized and romanticized.

The definitive question in heresy, however, is precisely this matter of degree. For heresy always involves a truth being carried to an illogical or dangerous degree. Heresy implies a lack of dialectical tension: speaking of good without speaking of evil or speaking of evil without speaking of good. In the case of gnosticism, it involves some of the oversimplifications we have examined: other world without this world, soul without body, self without Church, spirit without matter.

But what about the Church's handling of these necessary polarities—has there been a continuing orthodoxy capable of maintaining a precarious theological tension? Because we are living in an age that is quick to find fault with the Church's past performance and that is reluctant to credit Christendom with any positive contributions, it is important to look again at the various periods of Church history leading up to the present. A reexamination of the Church's response to gnostic tendencies within itself will help us answer the question of whether or not there exists a valid orthodoxy against which the contemporary North American scene might be compared and analyzed.

The New Testament Period: The Problem of Alienation

We have discussed the New Testament Church's reaction to the gnostic threat; we have also seen that on certain major issues, biblical faith and speculative gnosticism took widely divergent positions. To clarify the divergence, we have, for the most part, been looking at classical anti-gnostic texts.

On the other hand, some modern analysts of Western thought, among whom is Eric Voegelin, claim that there is a fundamental capitulation to gnostic thought even within the New Testament. Voegelin finds that the acosmic theology of later Judaism receives further articulation in Paul's writings and culminates in the Gospel according to John.[1] Although Professor Voegelin's assessment of prophetic, Pauline and Johannine theology seems to me to be quite inaccurate, he has correctly identified the point of affinity between gnostic and New Testament thought, namely, that gnosticism and the New Testament (not only Paul and John) share a distrust of cosmos. For both the cosmos is a place of utter darkness, in and of itself without hope.

Conzelmann has observed that the early Church's lack of ultimate faith in the Creation is shared with the prophetic tradition of the Old Testament: "As creation, heaven and earth are transitory, and they will pass away . . . in Judaism and Christianity, the original, Old Testament faith in creation has been changed into an eschatological hope."[2]

Gnosticism and orthodoxy sound so much alike it is easy, mistakenly, to confuse their intentions. Both wish to say that there is no hope in this present world, that given the condition of the Creation, humanity cannot be at home in this locale. Were Christianity to change that message, it would be offering what it would consider to be false hope. At the very outset of its theology, then, the New Testament Church was forced to be identified with the gnostics in their sense of alienation.

The affinity, however, was largely one of appearance. For the basis of the alienation and the end result of it were quite distinct. Christian orthodoxy, as we have seen, did not find fault with the prime Creation, but with the Creation as sinful humanity had distorted it. True, the Apostle Paul sees the world without Christ as a world in darkness,[3] and therefore the world *as such* has nothing to offer us: "For the form of this world is passing away";[4] "Why do you live as if you still belonged to the world?"[5] No doubt, Paul and all the authors of the New Testament would agree with John's sentiment that "we know that we are of God, and the whole world is in the power of the evil one."[6] Because the world offers us no permanent home and no present protection, "we look not to the things which are seen but to the things that are unseen; for the things that are seen are transient, but the things that are unseen are eternal."[7]

The Apostle Paul can even speak of God and man as "enemies"[8] and man as under the "wrath of God."[9] Yet, unlike the gnostics, who would continue to blame the enmity and the wrath on the Creator, Paul sees the Creation as the work of a loving God.[10] The fault is our own: "Ever since the creation of the world, his invisible nature . . . has been clearly perceived in the things that have been made. So they are without excuse; for although they knew God they did not honor him as God or give thanks to him."[11] Or, using the creation story from Genesis, Paul writes: "Therefore as sin came into the world through one man and death through sin, and so death spread to all men because all men sinned."[12]

Paul's position is that as a consequence of human sin, death has spread also beyond ourselves into the cosmos itself: "The whole creation has been groaning in travail together until now."[13]

In his Gospel, John also speaks of a Creation that has reverted to primal darkness.[14] The light of Christ has come into the darkness,[15] but "men loved darkness rather than light."[16] Humanity has a choice: it can sit in the darkness or walk in the light of the Word. But apart from the Word there is not so much as a glimmer.[17] The coming of Christ forces humanity into an irreconcilable conflict. Professor Painter has called John's "use of antithesis, light and darkness, truth and falsehood, flesh and Spirit, freedom and bondage, life and death, love and hate, . . . [a] crisis of decision."[18] Admittedly, John has employed a gnostic motif.[19]

With John as with Paul, however, it is sin, not a cosmic error, that darkens the otherwise brilliant landscape of the Creator. At the first recognition of Jesus as Word, John the Baptist proclaims: "Behold the Lamb of God who takes away the sin of the world!"[20] The mission of the Chosen One is neither to restore a disorder in the *pleroma,* nor to remove the ignorance of humankind—both gnostic solutions. The Lamb of God will be offered in life and death as a sacrifice for sin, indeed for the sin of the world.

In the presence of this One, announced by John, we are enabled to see that the present darkness of the Creation cannot thwart the good intentions of the Creator: "For God so loved the cosmos that he gave his only Son. . . . For God sent the Son into the cosmos, not to condemn the cosmos, but that the cosmos might be saved through Him."[21] This central theme of the Evangelist would hardly expose an acosmic theology.

"Chaos, Cosmos! Cosmos, Chaos!" shouts Tennyson in his poem "Locksley Hall." Whether these words are uttered in the first century or the nineteenth, within the context of Christian orthodoxy they constitute not a complaint against the Almighty but a lament over the unhappy state of God's good world.

The early Church, although engaged with gnosticism almost from its beginning on the issue of alienation, successfully differentiated itself through an unwavering belief in a good Creation. Following the course set by this thankful view of the world, the apostolic age went on to affirm "a new creation [in which] the old has passed away, behold, the new has come."[22] The mood, far from remaining pessimistic, has become so hopeful that "all the promises of God find their Yes in him."[23] And John, the most gnosticized of all New Testament writers, can joyously claim that "in him is no darkness at all"[24] and even that "the darkness is passing away and the true light is already shining."[25] Those modern detractors of John who still find him making alliance with the gnostics in his supposed overspiritualizing of the Gospel, should read the verse that follows: "He who says he is in the light and hates his brother is in the darkness still."[26] The light John sees is here on this earth; the path it lights leads us to one another.

The Catholic Church, Ancient and Medieval: The Temptation to Escape

If the point of contact between the Apostolic Church and gnosticism was their shared sense of alienation, the ancient and medieval Church was most tempted by the gnostic effort to *escape* the world. An asceticism which was conceived coincidentally with the faith itself blossomed in the Nile Valley among the Pachomian monks and bore fruit in the countless monasteries and nunneries throughout Christendom. From Simeon Stylites to St. Francis of Assisi to certain aspects of Calvinism, the aversion to this world with a desire to escape it has been one of the most prominent strands in the fabric of Christianity.

Where did this pessimistic view of the human predicament with its concomitant escapism originate? The answer seems to be—from many directions. Quispel has claimed that,

> late antiquity is a land of three streams in which Greek philosophy, Christian faith and Gnosticism flow side by side . . . the history of the Church is the Christianization of Greek thought and Eastern mysticism on the basis of the Gospel.[27]

The Christianization process always involves not only absorption, but also adaptation. In gathering these powerful forces to herself, the Church, quite naturally, made them a part of her being. Because gnosticism seems to have been present in both Greek and Eastern thought, how could Christianity help but be radically shaped by it? R. M. Grant expresses it well: "This kind of gnosis was in the air they breathed, and some of it entered their lungs."[28]

What entered those early Christian lungs, among other things, was a deep breath of dread, the feeling that unless some dramatic change occurred very soon, all would be lost. At the same time, because the evil of the world was so firmly rooted, so universal, so pervasive, how could the situation change other than by a self-conscious retreat from the world?

James Robinson described the "focus that brought the [Nag Hammadi] collection together" as

> an estrangement from the mass of humanity, an affinity to an ideal order that completely transcends life as we know it . . . it is not an aggressive revolution that is intended, but rather a *withdrawal from involvement* in the contamination that destroys clarity of vision.[29]

Something very much like that gnostic focus informed the Church's thought and lifestyle. Orthodox music, architecture, liturgy and theology all received a portion of inspiration from the felt need to withdraw from contamination. It is difficult to imagine a Christian piety which does not include the feeling behind Augustine's prayer: "Our hearts are restless until they rest in thee."[30]

Again, the problem is that although there is eternal truth in *gnosis,* gnosticism carried it beyond the acceptable confines of biblical religion. When the gnostics confessed that God is transcendent, orthodox Christians had to agree. And, within the context of the ancient and medieval world, when the gnostics saw the given world as a prison from which enlightened people must escape, orthodox Christians often could agree. By the thousands, Christian men and women did agree, to the extent of leaving family, possessions, everything behind, literally obeying the words of Jesus to his disciples, "Carry no purse, no bag, no sandals." Throughout the Middle East, North Africa, Greece and Europe, they were often "lambs in the midst of wolves." And given the miraculous growth of the Christian faith in a hostile, pagan world, Jesus' disciples rejoiced that "even the demons are subject to us in your name!"[31] Troeltsch's theory that "the real reason for the immense appeal of this ascetic ideal lay in the fact that the civilized world of that day was suffering from a nervous disease which sought purification and support in religious ideas"[32] does not begin to explain the phenomenon.

The ascetic drive within the Church received strong theological support from the Alexandrian school, especially its renowned thinkers, Clement and Origen. For both of these great teachers of the Church, *gnosis,* far from being a forbidden word, was a basic tenet of their system. Father Daniélou flatly states that "the word *gnosis* is the key to Clement's work,"[33] while for Origen a spiritual exegesis of the Holy Scriptures "constitutes the gnosis truly so called."[34] For the Alexandrians and all the early Church Fathers, a proper interpretation of Scripture could not help but urge the Christian to a life of *withdrawal* from the senseless struggles of this present world: for "flesh and blood cannot inherit the kingdom of God."[35]

Although it is possible to explain the strong gnostic flavor of Clement and Origen by the simple fact that these were men of their own time, inspired by a similar gnosticized atmosphere, there is also a more direct explanation. As so often happens in a sustained polemic, they unconsciously adopted many of their enemies' arguments in their struggle against heretical gnosticism. The Alexandrian school was indeed one of the historical moments of the Church's closest proximity to gnostic heresy; nevertheless, the distinction between Origen's mood of freedom and hope and his antagonists' sense of determinism and despair should not be overlooked.[36]

The theology of St. Augustine is another example of the orthodox Church—in its heated conversation with gnosticism—being led further down the gnostic path than otherwise it would wish to go. Augustine, of course, had come to his mature faith by way of Manichaeism and, therefore, was especially sensitive to the threat of that form of *gnosis*. For the Manichaeans, this world must be escaped because sin—the demonic, the evil, the deficient—exists as a physical reality which has entered the cosmos from the outside. Paul Ricoeur interprets this particular gnostic vision:

> This exteriority of evil immediately furnishes the schema of some thing, of a substance that infects by contagion. . . . The existential anguish which is at the root of Gnosticism is immediately situated in oriented space and time.[37]

Because of the Manichaean materialization of evil, "the evil which man confesses is less the act of doing evil . . . than the *state* of being in the world, the *misfortune* of existing."[38]

Despite his unhappy experience with the Manichaeans, Augustine, in response to his later adversaries, the Pelagians, resorted to a view of sin all too similar to that of the gnostics. It was Augustine, who in this circumstance, appended to the term original sin the words, *per generationem,* thus giving a literal interpretation to Paul's words: "And so death spread [through procreation] to all men."[39] Whereas the Apostle uses the sin of Adam and what followed in an illustrative sense, Augustine applies it literally and juridically. Ricoeur, commenting on the serious consequences of this theological commitment, does not hesitate to say "that from the epistemological point of view, this concept (*per generationem*) does not have a rational structure different from the gnostic concepts—Valentinus' fall prior to the Creation, the empire of darkness according to Mani, and so on."[40] If Ricoeur is correct in his assessment of the Augustinian doctrine of sin, it could help to explain many of the peculiarly Western forms of anti-physical, anti-body, anti-cosmic thought as well as the Western forms of world-escaping praxis.

It is true that Augustine opened a door for those looking for an excuse to escape the world, but he intended for the door he opened to lead to an earthly Church. This same Augustine spoke of Christ as having a triple mode of being: Christ the eternal Word of the Father, Christ the God-Man, and Christ the Church. The Church, according to Augustine, is *totus Christus:* he is our head and we are his body. Together, the head and the body compose the One Christ.[41] Against the Manichaean illusion that escape from cosmos meant escape from earthly dependencies, Augustine asserted, "I should not believe the Gospel, did not the authority of the Catholic Church induce me."[42]

The door from a hopeless world into a hope-filled *koinonia* was the only door that Augustine would open. Many of the other Fathers were more adamant than he on this matter and less reluctant to identify the *communio sanctorum* with the *externa communio*.[43] Cyprian, bishop of Carthage (ca. 248–258), put it bluntly:

> He cannot have God for his father who has not the Church for his mother. If anyone was able to escape outside Noah's ark, then he also escapes who is outside the doors of the church.[44]

When escape from cosmos is limited to escape into *koinonia,* that is, into an earthbound spiritual community, the escape is no longer escapist. It is, in fact, transformed into pilgrimage. Describing the difference between orthodox faith and that of the Docetists, Ignatius of Antioch (d. ca. 110) writes:

> They [the Docetists] have no concern for love, none for the widow, the orphan, the afflicted, the prisoner, the hungry, the thirsty. They stay away from the Eucharist and prayer.[45]

Bernard of Clairvaux (1090–1153), a medieval descendent of Augustine and recipient of his doctrine of sin, has had a continuing influence on the Western Church. Bernard spent a great deal of his energy combating gnosticism in the form of the Albigensian heresy. The Albigenses, or Cathari (the pure ones), were similar to the classical gnostics except that they existed in more definite sects outside the confines of the orthodox Church. They shared with the ancient gnostics a radical dualism of spirit and matter. For them, matter was evil; the world was composed of matter; therefore, the world was evil and must be escaped.[46]

Phyllis McGinley believes that St. Bernard's theology is another example of a prolonged polemic leading to absorption of the enemy's argument. While fighting the Albigensian virus, he picked up some of the infection.[47] Bernard, always conscious of the ultimate uselessness of matter, determined that it should play no bigger role than necessary in the life of the Church:

> Citeaux [Bernard's monastery] abhorred distraction. No more of the grotesque statuary which adorned—Bernard said defaced—the Romanesque Churches and abbeys! If the common folk must have

some external excitation, let them be pardoned, but those who have advanced upon the mystic way should rather gaze than gape. Stained glass windows were likewise deemed a distraction.[48]

Thus, even among the most solid leaders in the ancient and medieval Church, we find gnostic motifs. But what should not be forgotten is that teachers such as Origen, Augustine and Bernard were expounding many other doctrines as well, that they were aware of the necessity to present the Gospel in an honest and comprehensive way.

If Christianity can be said to have offered an escape from cosmos, it also provided a reentry into cosmos, cosmos reconsidered. Bernard, for example, continued to cling to the Eucharist. The mass itself, the voice of the whole Church, contained the words *per quem haec omnia semper bona creas* (through whom you always create everything good), which Jungmann explains as

> taking up again the antithesis against gnosticism and manichaeism . . . a statement of praise, proclaiming that the gifts which lie before us sanctified, are God-created, and that God always has done well in His creative labours, and continues to do so. This He does through the Logos, . . . the Incarnation itself was the grand consecration of creation.[49]

No doubt, the Church's suspicion of cosmos led to some unfortunate attitudes toward the flesh, human nature, and sexuality, as we shall see. But the beautifully simple understanding of Irenaeus that "the glory of God is a person who is fully alive" remained within the Church's consciousness. The otherworldly and escapist aspect of medieval Christianity has been exaggerated. One of the most respected authorities on the period, although asserting that "medieval thought in general was saturated in every part with the conceptions of the Christian faith," could go on to say that "in the Middle Ages the demarcation of the sphere of religious thought and that of worldly concerns was nearly obliterated."[50] Despite all the abuse heaped upon the Church of the Fathers and the society of the Middle Ages, both might have been closer to biblical thought than we have dared to imagine. Did they not to a great extent fulfill Jesus' prayer, "I do not pray that thou shouldst take them out of the cosmos, but that thou shouldst keep them from the evil one. They are not of the cosmos . . . [in the same sense that] I am not of the cosmos"?[51] The search for the Holy Grail did not lead Western man out of the cosmos; it led to new frontiers, through dense forests, beside undiscovered waters, to do battle with ever reappearing dragons.

The Reformation: Beyond a Knowledge That Saves

The familiar picture of the Protestant Reformers as anti-authoritarian, individualistic and puritanical is more caricature than characterization. Even so, at one critical point, the great Reformers seem very close to adopting a form of Christian gnosticism. This appears in the context of the issue of *gnosis* itself, what we have referred to as knowledge that saves.

Hans Jonas, in his important typological study of the gnostic phenomenon, described this form of knowledge as "secret, revealed and saving knowledge . . . it is of mysteries . . . not come by in a natural manner, and . . . its possession decisively alters the condition of the knower."[52] Jonas describes the content of the *gnosis* as that which is and always remains entirely transcendent. What is known may be expressed by a mythology of one sort or another, but the mythology only describes something that by its very nature cannot be known by ordinary means. The object of *gnosis* is simply unknowable:

> The transendence of the supreme deity is stressed to the utmost degree in all gnostic theology. Topologically, he is transmundane, dwelling in his own realm, entirely outside the physical universe, at immeasurable distance from man's terrestrial abode . . . he is naturally unknown (*naturaliter ignotus*), ineffable, defying predication, surpassing comprehension, and strictly unknowable.[53]

All of this sounds frightfully close to the description of the attributes of God listed in the Westminster Confession of Faith (1647):

> There is but one only living and true God, who is infinite in being and perfection, a most pure spirit, invisible, without body, parts, or passions, immutable, immense, eternal, incomprehensible, almighty, most wise, most holy, most free, most absolute.[54]

Do these similarities support the popular notion of the Protestant intention—that the Reformation attempted to remove Christianity from the realm of the natural and the historical and, in turn, attempted to spiritualize it, personalize it? Could Eric Voegelin be correct when he charges that whereas the Church throughout the Middle Ages "was occupied with the struggle against heresies of a metastatic [Voegelin's term for gnostic] complexion, . . . with the Reformation this underground stream has come to the surface again in a massive flood"?[55] Are those whom Irenaeus accused of "opening God like a book" and of placing salvation "in the *gnosis* of that which is ineffable majesty" once again in ascendency in the sixteenth century?[56] In Protestantism were the mighty acts of God being replaced by a knowledge that saves?

An ominous connection between medieval gnosis and the Reformation has been hinted at by some historians. Jonathan Sumption, for example, notices that "The Calvinism of the sixteenth century took root in regions which had been Cathar strongholds in the thirteenth."[57] Though he goes on to cast doubt on a historical continuity, the question remains: was Protestantism another instance of the gnostic tendency finally taking root at the proper season on inviting soil?

In the writings of the principal Reformers, we find what appears to be strong evidence in support of this contention. Certainly, for Luther, Calvin and also for Zwingli, there was a renewed preoccupation with the saving *knowledge* of God. The knowledge that preoccupied them, however, was not of an arcane nature, but rather an objective knowledge revealed through Scripture to the Church. Despite strong gnostic themes which would be taken out of context by later Protestantism and carried to dangerous extremes, Luther and Calvin in particular were able to maintain a dialectic that kept them and their generation solidly within historical orthodoxy.

Before we see how Luther was able to keep this theological tension through his ecclesiastical practice, it is important to look at his gnostic leanings, which provided the bases for later distortions of Christian truth. In Lutheran theology, the central theme of justification by faith, a recovery of a particular Pauline emphasis,[58] becomes the content of religious knowledge. The Old Testament and the New, the acts of God, seem to be important only because they all unveil the hidden God to the extent that He can be known as a gracious God. It is a grave error to categorize Luther as a biblicist; the Bible was essential for him only in that our justification is revealed through it. Because the Gospel of John and Romans do that most clearly, they are the "best and noblest"; and because James does not tell us about justification at all, it is "an epistle of straw."[59] Despite his own insistence on *sola scriptura,*[60] the authenticity of the text was determined by the evangelical nature of its content.[61] The Scriptures were preeminent for Luther insofar as they spoke to him of the gracious God. It is nowhere better put than in his most celebrated address before the Diet at Worms (1521): *"I am bound by the Scriptures I have quoted* and my conscience is captive to the *Word of God.* I cannot and I will not retract anything, since it is neither safe nor right to go against *conscience.*"[62]

If this use of Scripture and conscience had been carried to anything like a logical conclusion, it would have made of Christianity a highly personal religion open to an almost infinite number of personal interpretations. As Niesel sees it:

> Lutheranism's interest in personal salvation, and its one-sided preoccupation with the doctrine of justification, obscured the fact that the Christian message is primarily concerned, not with salvation of the individual man, nor, of course, even with the salvation of many men, but with the Saviour Himself and with the gracious rule He establishes among men, and therefore with His Church and its individual members.[63]

For Luther, salvation at this point comes dangerously close to dependence on a knowledge that saves, as opposed to a knowledge of the mighty acts of God.

The central importance of this unique saving *knowledge* strongly colored Luther's doctrine of the Church and his teachings about the sacraments. From the outset, it made him contemptuous of any faith that vests authority in the Church itself. In his sermon preached in Pleissenburg Castle (1539), he declared that with the Word of God and the love of Christ "you can answer the screamers and spitters who have nothing in their gabs but church! church!" Luther then proceeded to show that entrusting the Church with self-authenticating powers can and does lead Christianity into ridiculous claims:

> Tell me, dear Pope, what is the church? Answer: the pope and his cardinals. Oh, listen to that; you dunce, where is it written in God's Word that Father Pope and Brother Cardinal are the true Church? Was it because that was what the fine parrot bird said to the black jackdaw?

Luther concludes that these "human precepts" based on ecclesiastical authority have allowed "the miserable pope and his decretals [to make] of the church of God a filthy privy."[64]

For this self-authenticating Church, Luther would substitute a Church composed of those who hear and accept God's Word. He even held that the term "*kirche* should be discarded . . . [and] replaced by the word *gemeinde* [community, congregation]," the idea being that the authoritative institution would give way to a group of Christians who gather themselves about the Word. What is lost in this substitution is that a *kirche* or *ecclesia* is called together by God, whereas a community or congregation can be a voluntary association of like-minded believers.[65]

Within this new type of Church, saving *knowledge* would become the one test of authenticity:

> Whenever then you hear or see such a Word preached, believed, confessed and done something about, have no doubt that there must certainly be the same, a true, holy Catholic Church, a holy Christian people . . . and if you can find no other sign than this alone, even so it is nevertheless enough.[66]

Because the one mark of the Church is the validity of its saving knowledge, it becomes extremely important for Luther to distinguish between the true Church of the Word and the Church of mere outward form. Using the Augustinian formula of invisible Church as opposed to visible Church, the great Reformer is able to claim that "the essence, life, and nature of Christendom is not a bodily assembly but an assembly of hearts in one faith."[67] It would be difficult to imagine a more docetic view of the Church.

Luther's doctrine of the Church is to a great extent reflected in his view of the sacraments. Again, we have the preeminence of the Word: "For the sacrament without the word can be nothing, but indeed the word without the sacrament [can], and if necessary, one can be saved without a sacrament, but not without the Word."[68] Again and again we are presented with a dichotomy between knowledge and participation, and always knowledge is the indispensable factor—participation is only desirable. In referring to the Eucharist in particular, Luther approves the words of Augustine: "Why do you make your teeth and stomach ready? Believe and thou hast eaten"; he then goes on with the remarkable spiritualization of the Supper, "Thus I am able daily, indeed hourly, to have the mass; for, as often as I wish, I can set the words of Christ before me, and nourish and strengthen my faith by them. This is the true spiritual eating and drinking."[69] Were this all Luther had to say about the Holy Supper, we could safely assume that he had gnosticized it out of existence. Christians could receive spiritually through *gnosis* and save their teeth and stomach the effort. Had Luther carried his suppositions to a logical conclusion, the character of Lutheranism and Protestantism would have been quite different, something very much akin to the medieval Cathari.

Luther, of course, did not carry his ideas to logical or gnostic conclusions. The solid earthiness of his personality militated against a spiritualizing theology. That extra ingredient of humanity was continually being stirred into the Wittenberg stew. The Word of Grace involved a great deal more than *knowledge*. "It is the pure and inestimable grace of God," he confessed, "that He gives me, a completely wicked, blasphemous, and sacrilegious rascal . . . the knowledge of salvation, the Spirit, His own Son Christ, the Apostolate, [and] eternal life."[70]

No doubt, one reason for the anabaptist frustration with Luther was his adamant refusal to allow the Church to become in praxis what he had theoretically indicated it should become. Luther had no sympathy for the anabaptists because they sponsored the sort of voluntaristic religion he deplored.[71] Never could a Gospel faith lead individuals to concentrate their attention on the self:

> Some have held that God ought to deal with the individual and confer the Holy Ghost upon him by means of a special light and a secret revelation in the heart, as though the printed word, . . . Scripture, and the spoken Word . . . are not needed.
>
> Therefore we should know that God has ordained that no one is to come to a knowledge of Christ . . . without external and general means. God has deposited this treasure in the spoken Word of the ministry and does not intend to confer it privately or secretly in the heart.[72]

Far from being on his or her own, a naked soul before the Almighty, Luther's Christian is inextricably bound to the community of faith:

> You do not seek Him, He seeks you; you do not find Him, He finds you; for the preachers come from Him, not from you; . . . your faith comes from Him, not from you; everything that faith works in you comes from Him, not from you; . . . where He does not come, you remain outside.[73]

Thus the much celebrated individualism of Luther, in particular the individual religious knowledge of the believer, is always subject to the community as a whole. It is well expressed in his formula: "A Christian is a perfectly free lord of all, subject to none. A Christian is a perfectly dutiful servant of all, subject to all."[74]

Recognizing the grave dangers involved in an individual's appropriating the first part of the formula without the second, Luther continued to stress the uniqueness and the necessity of the Church, "[that] special community in the world, which is the mother that begets and bears every Christian by the Word of God."[75] In this regard, the rebel against Rome begins to sound more like Cyprian:

> Therefore, he who would find Christ, must first of all find the Church. How would one know where Christ and His faith were, if one did not know where His believers are? And he who would know something of Christ, must not trust himself, or build [his] own bridges into heaven through his own reason; but [he must] go to the Church, visit and ask of the same . . . for outside the Christian Church is no truth, no Christ, no salvation.[76]

Despite all implications to the contrary, the overall effect of Lutheran doctrine is a turning away from individual *gnosis* toward the action of God in the midst of his people. In his commentary on Psalm 143:5, Luther writes:

> The Holy Christian Church is the *principal work of God,* for the sake of which all things were made. In the Church, great wonders daily occur, such as the forgiveness of sins, triumph over death, . . . the gift of righteousness and eternal life.[77]

Irenaeus could not have expressed the place and the power of the Church in a more forceful way.

Nor was Luther in the least attracted to the anabaptist picture of a perfect Church, a *societas perfectionis*. "Farewell to those," he cried, "who want an entirely pure and purified church. This is plainly wanting no church at all."[78]

When it came to the practice of the sacraments, Luther really dug in his heels. For him the validity of baptism was not dependent on the faith of the individual, nor on the faith of the parents of that individual:

> I do not baptize it upon its [the child's] faith or someone else's faith, but upon God's word and command. In my faith I may lie, but he who instituted baptism cannot lie. [Therefore] . . . the children must necessarily be baptized, and their baptism is true.[79]

It was on the question of the Lord's Supper that Luther's anti-*gnosis* became most explicit. Any Christian who failed to recognize the centrality of the Table in his own life was blatantly offending God. After saying that attendance at the Eucharist is no longer compulsory, he went on to warn:

> What does it matter to me and the chaplains if you don't want to listen and receive the sacrament? You have four doors here—go on out! But he who is above says: If you want to be a Christian, if you want to have forgiveness of sins and eternal life, then come here! There stands your God; he offers you his body and blood . . . if you

> want to despise God and neglect the forgiveness of sins, then stay away.[80]

Any hope that spiritualists might have placed in the Lutheran doctrine of the Word would at the end of the day be dashed on the rock of Luther's obdurate eucharistic theology.[81]

John Calvin, according to popular wisdom, provides a more consistent example of gnosticized Christianity than Luther. Certainly, many secular students of the Reformation assume that Calvin carried the Protestant revolt at least a step further than the German reformer. Luther's Church, like the Anglican Church, still cherished many of the old forms and customs, whereas Calvin wanted to make a clean sweep of all Roman embellishments. Such is, at any rate, the prevailing contemporary view of the two principal reformers of the sixteenth century.

It is essential that we look at Calvin as carefully as possible because his influence on North American Protestantism has been of unparalleled importance. The influence of Geneva has either enriched or polluted our culture, according to one's point of view.

In our discussion of the gnosticizing trends in Calvin's thought, it is useful to postpone discussion of those elements which kept him within the orthodox camp. By suspending that side of his ingenious dialectic, one is better able to understand how his thought could have been so misconstrued by those who were to follow.

As we have indicated, the Reformers, especially Calvin, would intersect with gnostic thought most decisively on the issue of *gnosis* itself. The importance of knowledge for Calvin is evident in the priority given to the subject in his systematic work, *Institutes of the Christian Religion*. Book One is entitled, "Of the Knowledge of God the Creator"; chapter one of Book One, "The Knowledge of God and of Ourselves Mutually Connected—Nature of the Connection." And the very first words of chapter one are:

> Our wisdom, in so far as it ought to be deemed true and solid wisdom, consists almost entirely of two parts: the knowledge of God and of ourselves. But as these are connected together by many ties, it is not easy to determine which of the two precedes, and gives birth to the other.[82]

The apparent parallel between this interfused search for God and self and the gnostic search is striking.

Although Calvin's search does not lead him to criticize the Creator or to locate the fall prior to the creation, he does envision a Creator filled with disgust and loathing for his human creatures, and he does locate our corruption prior to our birth. As Wendel has observed, "Calvin had no very high opinion of humanity even before the original sin." He quotes Calvin:

> Even if man had remained in his integrity, still his condition was too base for him to attain to God. How much less could he have raised himself so far, . . . after staining himself with so many defilements—nay, even stinking in his corruption and all overwhelmed with misery.[83]

Is the knowledge of our humanity as Calvin would have us learn it, all that different from the gnostic understanding of physical man as an abortion, a deficiency? "The image of God," he tells us, has become "so deeply corrupted that all that remains of it is a horrible deformity," and therefore mortals "can do no more than crawl over the earth like little worms."[84]

According to Calvin, this knowledge of human depravity is for our benefit.

> Never would our heart knowingly school itself to desire and meditate upon the future life, without having first been touched by a contempt for the earthly life . . . wherefore, if we have any care for immortality we must diligently strive to disentangle ourselves from these sorry bonds.[85]

The first step in Reformed knowledge, the "very spring-head [of piety]" will then be "mortification of the flesh and newness of life."[86]

It would appear at first glance that the other part of "true and solid wisdom," the God connection, brings us to a similar intersection with gnostic thought. We have seen how for the ancient gnostics, *gnosis* pertained to the pure knowledge of God, the essence of God. Calvin gives every indication that this *essentia* will be one of the two subjects of his work. One of the basic reforming tenets would be the absolute transcendence of God. In explaining Calvin's intention, Wendel points out that as far as the Reformer is concerned,

> No theology is Christian and in conformity with the Scriptures but in the degree to which it respects the infinite distance separating God from his creature and gives up all confusion, all "mixing," that might tend to efface the radical distinction between the Divine and the human.[87]

For the author of the *Institutes* there is no other way of speaking of the essence of God than of God in majestic contradistinction to anything that is earthy, material, creaturely.

The discussion of God's essence would not, in fact, be undertaken by Calvin. He would follow in this respect an entirely different course from the gnostics. He does appear, however, to come dangerously close to *gnosis* in his views of the immortal soul and of Christ's dual nature as well as in his suspicion of the externals of religion, even the bread and wine of the Eucharist.

The original state of man for Calvin as for classical gnosticism was that of immortal soul. When the Reformer confines himself to "our nature in its original integrity," he argues that God "not only deigned to animate a vessel of clay, but to make it the habitation of an immortal spirit."[88] Even now, after the cataclysmic Fall, "still the light is not so completely quenched in darkness that all sense of immortality is lost."[89] When finally "the soul is freed from the prison-house of the body, God becomes its perpetual keeper."[90] In light of this *soul* we are to "regard a blessed immortality as our destined aim."[91] Valentinus would certainly be in solid agreement about the knowledge of "who we were, what we became; where we were, whereinto we have been thrown; whereto we speed."[92]

Furthermore, in his commentary on I John, Calvin comes close to espousing a docetic Christology:

> But no less frivolous . . . than impudent is the wickedness of Servetus, who urges these words (I John 1:1) to prove that the Word of God became visible and capable of being handled; he either impiously destroys or mingles together the twofold nature of Christ.[93]

Even if we are willing to admit that Servetus was a theological rascal, is he in this case saying anything more than the Apostle is saying? Even Wendel, who at most points is more than sympathetic to Calvin, could not help but wonder

> whether, by thus accentuating the distinction between the two natures, he did not endanger the fundamental unity of the person of Christ, and whether some of the affirmations he made would not tend toward somewhat unorthodox conclusions.[94]

This, indeed, is a restrained way of asking whether or not Calvin risks denying the Incarnation of Christ.

There is no doubt that Calvin's consistent fear of mingling explains much about his ecclesiology and his doctrine of the sacraments. In maintaining a distinct dualism between God and man, spirit and flesh, he would always be on guard against awarding too much dignity to the visible Church as Church, and he would always be suspicious of the externals of religion.[95]

It is common wisdom that Calvin would allow no images in Reformed churches. An entire chapter of the *Institutes* is devoted to the "impiety of attributing a visible form to God."[96] In this section, Calvin lashes out, "without exception, [at] all shapes and pictures, and other symbols by which the superstitious imagine they can bring him near to them."[97] Calvin's concern is based on his conviction that "men are so stupid that they fasten God wherever they fashion him."[98]

Calvin is so eager to devalue all paraphernalia that even the ancient symbol of the cross, when represented by the artisan, becomes an object of Calvin's scorn: "From this one doctrine [Christ's sacrificial death as in Galatians 3:1] the people would learn more than from a thousand crosses of wood and stone."[99]

It is easy to see how Calvin's suspicion of knowing God through material things would influence his sacramental theology. Although he makes every attempt to keep Word and Sacrament together, to handle them in a parallel way, there is never the slightest doubt in his mind as to which is preeminent. If necessary, the Gospel could stand by itself and indeed would do so were it not for our human weakness, which makes us dependent on these more primitive means of grace:

> Forasmuch as we are so ignorant, so given up to earthly and carnal things and fixed upon them, so that we can neither think, understand nor conceive of anything spiritual, the merciful Lord accommodates himself in this to the crudity of our senses.[100]

Nowhere are Calvin's spiritual antennae more alert than in his numerous debates over the Eucharist. He considers the "recent" Roman Catholic doctrine of transubstantiation beneath contempt, mere superstition and magic, a "fiction of the schoolmen."[101] Though he takes the Lutheran consubstantiation doctrine more seriously, he will by no means accept it:

> Let there be nothing derogatory to the heavenly glory of Christ. This happens whenever he is brought under the corruptible elements of this world, or is affixed to any earthly creatures.[102]

The most telling question to be asked of Calvin's doctrine of the Eucharist is that posed by Wendel:

> What exactly does the Supper give us that we cannot obtain otherwise? Under these conditions [preeminence of the Word over all material representations of it], is there still good reason for the existence of the Supper alongside the preaching of the Word? This problem touches the very nerve of the notion of the sacrament as it was elaborated by the reformers; and the mere fact that it can present itself shows that they did not manage to integrate the sacrament organically into their theological system.[103]

The possibility that Calvin left the Eucharist dangling, an inadequately attached appendage to his system, could explain what has happened to the Supper among the spiritual children of Geneva.

Now it is necessary to consider the other Calvin, the man hidden from popular imagination, the theologian who so valiantly attempted to say again, in a reforming way, what he believed the Holy Catholic Church to have always been saying. This exercise is necessary, not only to be fair to Calvin, but also to make sense of the positive streams that have flowed from this fountain.

On the critical issue of *gnosis* itself, Calvin's insistence on the utter transcendence of God rather than leading him in the direction of Valentinus, leads him toward a biblical theology perhaps more thoroughgoing than any since Irenaeus. Precisely because God is unreachable, beyond our realm, Calvin holds that

> the knowledge of God we are invited to cultivate is not that which, resting satisfied with empty speculation, only flutters in the brain, . . . [therefore] the fittest method is, not to attempt with presumptuous curiosity to *pry into his essence* . . . but to contemplate him in his works, by which he draws near, becomes familiar, and in a manner communicates himself to us.[104]

At any rate, "his essence, indeed is incomprehensible, utterly transcending all human thought."[105] And therefore Calvin quotes Hilary of Poitiers with approval:

> Leave to God the privilege of knowing himself; for it is he only who is able to bear witness of himself who knows himself by himself alone. And we shall be leaving him what belongs to him if we understand him as he declares himself, and ask nothing at all concerning him except through his word.[106]

Once again we are thrown back on whatever knowledge can be gained from the God who moves across the face of the deep, acts in history and allows these mighty events of nature and history to be recorded. "No one," writes Calvin, "can have even the least taste of sound doctrine and know that it is of God, unless he has been to this school, to be taught by the Holy Scripture."[107]

Unlike Luther, who tended to elevate those portions of Scripture most compatible with his own understanding of the faith, Calvin refrained from making qualitative distinctions between various texts.[108] Nor is Calvin a biblicist, approaching Holy Writ as the object of his faith. The Scriptures are a means of grace, the means to the knowledge of Christ: "Inasmuch as Jesus Christ is the fulfilment of the Law and the Prophets and is the substance of the Gospel . . . we incline towards no other end but to know him."[109] With this willingness to regard the Old Testament as evangelical, indeed equally as evangelical as the New, Calvin covered a multitude of his gnostic sins. For on many different issues, the Old Testament would keep his feet firmly on the ground. Like Irenaeus, whom he quotes often and always as a beloved father, he would be able, ultimately, with the same Old Testament, to oppose all acosmic presentations of the Gospel.

Attempts to know God apart from His mighty acts revealed in Scripture are bound to lead either to fantasy or failure: "For no sooner do we, from a survey of the world, obtain some slight knowledge of Deity, than we pass by the true God, and set up in his stead the dream and phantom of our own brain."[110] Through the knowledge we have in the Scriptures, we can know all that we need to know of God. On this point Calvin writes:

> Irenaeus says that the Father, who is boundless in himself, is bounded in the Son, because he has accommodated himself to our capacity, lest our minds should be swallowed up by the immensity of his glory (Irenaeus, Lib. IV, cap. 8).[111]

The fruit of this knowledge far exceeds the understanding of God derived from other sources, no matter how respectable. Though we cannot describe God's essence, we can speak of His attributes: "[The attributes] most necessary for us to know," Calvin says, "are these three: Loving-kindness, on which alone our entire safety depends; Judgement which is daily exercised on the wicked; . . . Righteousness, by which the faithful are preserved, and most benignly cherished."[112]

On the central issue we have raised, whether the Reformers were seeking a *gnosis* that saves or a *gnosis* of mighty acts, Calvin makes his own position abundantly clear. During his exchange with Cardinal Sadoleto, after the cardinal had urged the people of Geneva to remember their own salvation and thereby to return to the Holy Roman Church, Calvin responds with these remarkable words:

> It is not very sound theology to confine a man's thoughts so much to himself and not set before him as the prime motive of his existence zeal to show forth the glory of God. For we are born first of all for God, and not for ourselves . . . it certainly is the duty of a Christian man to ascend higher than merely to seek and secure the salvation of his own soul.[113]

So much for a *gnosis* whose only aim or even primary aim is personal salvation.

Instead, we are taught in the *Institutes* again and again that the purpose of knowledge is to overcome our self-concern through awareness of the majesty of God:

> Our breast cannot receive his mercy until deprived completely of all opinion of its own worth . . . for to whatever extent any man rests in himself, to the same extent he impedes the beneficence of God.[114]

Calvin's most eloquent appeal for self-abandonment and for a life given over wholly to the concerns of God is found in his "Summary of the Christian Life." Here he reminds us that

> we are not our own; therefore, neither is our own reason or will to rule our acts and counsels. We are not our own; therefore, let us not make it our end to seek what may be agreeable to our carnal nature. We are not our own; therefore, as far as possible, let us forget ourselves and the things that are ours. On the other hand, we are God's; let us therefore, live and die to him (Romans 14:8) . . . We are God's; to him, then, as the only legitimate end let every part of our life be directed.[115]

We have mentioned the Old Testament as an anti-gnostic force in Calvin's theology. Another factor that played a significant role in protecting him from an overspiritualized tilt toward *gnosis* was his high regard for the early Fathers and the Ecumenical Councils. Though he is unwilling to place their importance over Scripture or even alongside Scripture, he writes of the ancient councils, "I venerate them from my heart, and would have all to hold them in due honour."[116] And, more specifically, he writes:

> Those ancient Councils of Nicaea, Constantinople, the first of Ephesus, Chalcedon, and the like, which were held for refuting errors, we willingly embrace, and reverence as sacred, in so far as relates to doctrines of faith, for they contain nothing but the pure and genuine

> interpretation of Scripture, which the holy Fathers with spiritual prudence adopted to crush the enemies of religion who had then arisen.[117]

The Reformer's desire to conform his thoughts to the Church's ancient wisdom concerning interpretation of Scripture made him a careful self-critic, always alert for signs of heresy.

Calvin would be ever vigilant against the heretical claim to an individual *gnosis*. Religious knowledge, for Calvin, can lead one in no earthly direction but toward the Holy Catholic Church and its sacraments. The reverence which Calvin had for the Church during his Roman Catholic period remained intact through his reforming days. In a rare moment of self-disclosure, Calvin admits to Cardinal Sadoleto that in his younger days as a Roman Catholic

> one thing in particular made me averse to those new teachers [the Reformers], namely reverence for the Church. But when once I opened my ears and allowed myself to be taught, I perceived that this fear of derogating from the majesty of the Church was groundless . . . how great the difference is between schism from the Church, and studying to correct the faults by which the Church herself is contaminated.[118]

It is not by accident that Calvin devotes about one third of the *Institutes* to the doctrine of the Church. The doctrine of God, the Christology and soteriology all culminate in the mystical body of which Christ is the head.[119]

The close bond between his doctrine of Christ and his ecclesiology sounds alarmingly un-Protestant:

> Truly, it is a great mystery that Christ allowed a rib to be taken from himself, of which we [the Church] might be formed; that is, that when he was strong, he was pleased to become weak, that we might be strengthened by his strength.[120]

In his commentary on I Corinthians, Calvin notices an identification between Christ and Church:

> Because Paul calls the Church "Christ" this verse [I Cor. 12:12] is full of rare comfort. For Christ invests us with this honour that he wishes to be discerned and recognized, not only in His own Person but also in His members.[121]

And in one of his sermons on Ephesians, Calvin is bold enough to say that God is *completed* (*accompli*) through His Church.[122]

Because the Church is so inseparably connected to the Godhead, could there be any doubt about the necessity of the Christian being a member of it? Calvin affirms that

> There is no other entry into life, unless she [the Church] conceive us in her womb, bring us forth and nurse us, and finally keep us under her own care and discipline until, having put off our mortal flesh, we shall be like to angels.[123]

And again, simply, "They cannot be God's disciples who refuse to be taught in the Church."[124]

Calvin was a strong advocate of the Augustinian doctrine of a visible and invisible Church. However, it must be understood that regardless of how Augustine and Luther might have conceived of the distinction, for Calvin there could be in actuality only one Church under the Lordship of and in the service of Jesus Christ.[125] Those groups, like the anabaptists, who could not accept a partially imperfect Church would find no ally in Calvin. "It is a dangerous temptation," he warned, "to think there is no Church, where perfect purity is lacking." It is, after all, because of our impurity that all Christians are required to pray daily for forgiveness. "[In this life], it is enough if every day brings some nearer to others, and all nearer to Christ."[126]

Calvin, in fact, would offer no support to schismatics of any sort. The reason he took such pains to show that the Roman Church was no longer Church was to validate his leaving it. Had Rome been simply an impure expression of Christ's Church, there would have been not the slightest excuse for deserting her.[127] "We [the Reformed Catholic Church]," he wrote Sadoleto, "are assailed by *two sects,* which seem to differ most widely from each other. For what similitude is there in appearance between the Pope and the Anabaptists?" He then goes on to show how these "two sects" are birds of a feather in that by making extravagant claims on the Holy Spirit, both "inevitably tend to sink and bury the word of God, and to make room for their own falsehoods."[128]

The true Church, in which the invisible Body of Christ is becoming visible, in which "we see the word of God sincerely preached and heard, [and] . . . the sacraments administered according to the institution of Christ,"[129] must be adhered to and obeyed. With Calvin, the patristic principle of *extra ecclesiam nulla salus* remains firm: "Beyond the pale of the Church no forgiveness of sins, no salvation can be hoped for . . . the abandonment of the Church is always fatal."[130]

From a positive point of view, all of Calvin's theological efforts were aimed at the restoration of the Church. Again in his letter to Sadoleto he laments the present ecclesiastical state:

> I ask you to place before your eyes the ancient form of the Church as their writings prove it to have been in the ages of Chrysostom and Basil among the Greeks, and of Cyprian, Ambrose and Augustine among the Latins; and after so doing, to contemplate the ruins of that Church which now survive among yourselves. . . . Will you here declare one an enemy of antiquity who, zealous for ancient piety and holiness and dissatisfied with the corrupt state of matters existing in a dissolute and depraved Church, attempts to ameliorate its condition and restore it to pristine splendour?[131]

Contrary to the often held misconception of Calvin, the restoration of the sacraments to their proper place and dignity was essential to his reconstruction of the Church. As Father McDonnell has so aptly expressed it:

> Though Calvin did not consider the sacraments as necessary means of salvation, and though union with Christ was not considered as dependent on the sacraments . . . he did consider union with Christ as quite *unthinkable* apart from the sacraments.[132]

It is due to our "ignorance and sloth," our sinful humanity that the gracious God has deigned to grant us "another help . . . akin to the preaching of the Gospel."[133] Calvin continues, "He manifests himself to us in as far as our dulness can enable us to recognize him, and testifies his love and kindness to us *more expressly than by word*."[134] Again, Calvin agrees with Augustine's practical dictum, "In no name of religion, true or false, can men be assembled, unless united by some common use of visible signs or sacraments."[135]

Calvin's doctrine of baptism emphasizes the corporate nature of the sacramental blessing. For Calvin, a reformed church's view of infant baptism differentiated a church from a sect.[136] Baptism, for Calvin, is a highly objective act: "We ought to consider that at whatever time we are baptized we are washed and purified once for the whole of life. Wherefore, as often as we fall, we must recall the remembrance of our baptism."[137] He sees in the anabaptist strictures against paedobaptism a satanic plot to undermine our confidence in the divine goodness: "Here we may see how he [God] acts toward us as a most provident parent, not ceasing to care for us even after our death, but consulting and providing for our children."[138] In his attack on Servetus and the others who would "exterminate infants from the

Church" and make *gnosis* essential for salvation, Calvin argues, ". . . for regenerating us, doctrine is an incorruptible seed, if indeed we are fit to perceive it; but when, from nonage, we are incapable of being taught, God takes his own methods of regenerating."[139]

This affirmation of the objective reality of the baptismal act carries Calvin far beyond *gnosis,* for the gracious love of God is not restricted to our apprehension of it. It is the objective communal understanding of baptism which leads Calvin to forbid the medieval practice of private baptisms: "Whenever anyone is to be baptized, present him to the assembly of believers, and with the whole church looking on as witness and praying over him offer him to God."[140]

The centrality of the Eucharist in Calvin's thought has not escaped the Roman Catholic scholar, Kilian McDonnell. He is aware that Calvin refuses to accept the necessity of the sacraments in the Roman sense of God's being bound to that method of salvation. Though God is not bound, however, we Christians are bound: "For it would be of no avail to us that the sacrifice was once offered, if we did not now feast on that sacred banquet."[141]

Against Zwingli, and largely under the influence of Bucer, Calvin denied that the eating of the Eucharist is simply identical with faith. As McDonnell understands the conflict:

> Calvin is not insisting on a real distinction between the two [faith and eating] but he is insisting on what he considers a safeguard against a purely intellectual concept of faith . . . eating is an interpretation of faith insofar as it guards against an intellectualization of faith.[142]

At no point does Calvin become so explicit in his polemic against crypto-gnosticism as in his discussion of the Holy Supper. He expresses dissatisfaction with "the view of those who, while acknowledging that we have some kind of communion with Christ, only make us partakers of the Spirit, omitting all mention of flesh and blood." He goes on to inveigh against those "hyperbolical doctors who, according to their gross ideas, fabricate an absurd mode of eating and drinking, and transfigure Christ, after divesting him of his flesh, into a phantom."[143]

It was for similar reasons that Calvin was forced to distinguish the Reformed position from that of the Lutherans and to do so at great length. The Lutherans with their concept of ubiquity (the local presence of Christ existing under the elements) would seem at first glance to be making a strong anti-gnostic affirmation—Jesus himself present in the flesh in each particular parish. What could be more down to earth? Calvin, however, felt that Wittenberg had attached to the Supper

> an ubiquity contrary to its nature . . . what a door is opened to Marcion, if the body of Christ was seen humble and mortal in one place, glorious and immortal in another! And yet, if their opinion is well-founded, the same thing happens every day, because they are forced to admit that the body of Christ, which is in itself visible, lurks invisibly under the symbol of bread.[144]

What concerns Calvin is not the earthiness of the Lutheran conception, but precisely the docetic danger of denying the humanity of the Savior, even of the risen and glorified Savior:

> Let no property be assigned to his body inconsistent with his human nature. This is done when it is either said to be infinite, or made to occupy a variety of places at the same time. But when these absurdities are discarded, I willingly admit anything which helps to express the true and substantial communication of the body and blood of the Lord, as exhibited to believers under the sacred symbols of the Supper, understanding that they are received *not by the imagination or intellect* merely, but are enjoyed in reality as the food of eternal life.[145]

Even yet, Calvin has not finished with the Ubiquitists. And always his concern is the threat of gnosticism:

> Fool! Why do you require the power of God to make a thing to be at the same time flesh and not flesh? . . . I admit that they have the word [the literal word], but just as . . . Marcion and the Manichees had it when they made the body of Christ celestial or phantastical.

On the contrary, for Calvin, "the body with which Christ rose is declared . . . by the Holy Spirit to be *finite,* and to be contained in heaven until the last day."[146] In Calvin's theology, though there is nothing "derogatory to the heavenly glory of Christ," at the same time we are not allowed to forget that a *human being* is in heaven pleading our cause, exerting his exalted power on our behalf.[147] That the ubiquity issue should have occupied so much of Calvin's energy (fifteen out of fifty sections of chapter 17, "Benefits Conferred by the Lord's Supper") is indicative of his concern that the *Real Presence* of Christ not be confused with a sentimentalized, imagined or ghostly presence, such as that prompted by gnostic thought.

What the *Real Presence* of Christ was for Calvin is a matter of intense debate. His mind was so often occupied with the Holy Supper, not only as a doctor of the Church, but as a pastor, that he had occasion to write and speak often on the subject, and sometimes did so in seemingly contradictory terms. At times, he would appear to be holding an extremely spiritual understanding of Christ's presence, emphasizing the *sursum corda* (lift up your hearts) moment of the liturgy more than the *hoc est enim meam corpus* (this is my body). And yet, Calvin can also affirm that, through the Holy Spirit, Christ is truly present, in his humanity as well as in his divinity.[148] In his commentary on I Corinthians 11:24 he assures us that

> we possess him . . . when he dwells in us, when he is one with us, when we are members of his flesh . . . the body of Christ is given us really, as they say, that is, truly, to be a food healthful to our souls.[149]

Also, in answer to the Lutheran charge that he had overspiritualized the relationship between Christ and his people at the Eucharist, Calvin replied that "it is necessary for us to unite ourselves to him not only in the soul but *also in the flesh*."[150]

Despite the ambiguity of Calvin's doctrine of the Eucharist, any honest reading of his work will dispel the common notion that the great Genevan sponsored what later became a Protestant individualistic approach to the sacraments. It is ironic that a Benedictine scholar feels compelled to defend Calvin against the most respected of Anglican liturgical scholars, and in such strong terms:

> The corporate nature of the Eucharist is so clearly stated in Calvin—it was the sins of the Roman Catholics against the corporate and social character of the Eucharist which prompted much of his indignation—that it cannot be a matter of dispute among scholars. It is therefore painful and embarrassing to find a scholar of Gregory Dix's stature asserting: "The real Eucharistic action is for Calvin individual and internal, not corporate."[151]

Father McDonnell argues also that Calvin's desire for frequent celebration of the Supper was "an attempt to restore values which Roman Catholicism had obscured and neglected for centuries."[152] In the context of his plea for a simple celebration, Calvin expresses the fervent hope that once again, as in apostolic days, the Sacrament will be celebrated on every occasion when the Word is preached:

> All this mass of ceremonies being abandoned, the sacrament might be celebrated in the most becoming manner, if it were dispensed to the Church very frequently, *at least once a week* . . . thus we ought always to provide that—*no meeting of the Church is held* without the word, prayer, the dispensation of the Supper, and alms.[153]

Calvin's reforms went beyond sacramental concerns. His goal was the restoration of the Church to its "pristine splendour." He flung his genius and enormous energies into the upgrading of music and public singing; in the Genevan Church he employed the services of the musician and teacher, Louis Bourgeois, for nearly seventeen years.[154] Calvin also busied himself with the Christian education of young and old,[155] realizing that the Christian's restoration "is not accomplished either in a minute of time nor in a day, nor in a year . . . [but rather] little by little" so that all one's life is to be spent in penitence until our struggle ends at death.[156] His method was not the imparting of a secret *gnosis* but the painstaking nurture of the people of God. Church discipline was a major aim of the Genevan theology.[157] Though he rejected the Roman *required* confession, he urged his congregations to consult their pastors individually and to receive private absolution.[158]

Not even Calvin's severest critics could argue that his spirituality led to a disdain for worldly affairs. As Walker has indicated, "unlike Luther, who in practice handed poor relief over to the state, Calvin believed that social welfare is properly a concern of the Church."[159] And in a remarkable vindication of the magisterial office, Calvin wrote, "No man can doubt that civil authority is, in the sight of God, not only sacred and lawful, but the most sacred, and by far the most honorable, of all stations in mortal life."[160]

Far from hiding behind the cloud of an invisible Church and encouraging an individual *gnosis,* Calvin's set task was nothing less than to bring the invisible into visibility again.[161] The effort was, at least within his own generation, largely successful. "When I first came into this Church," Calvin recalled, "there was almost nothing there. They preached and that was all. They sought out the idols indeed, and burnt them, but there was no reformation. Everything was in tumult."[162] By the time of his death, a viable, international alternative to Rome had been established largely through his efforts. The alternative he offered was anything but a gnostic vision for private Christians; the Calvinist system was devised to provide a reformed theological structure for a reformed catholic Church.

The Early North American Puritans: Covenant with Church or Self? The Elect or the Elite?

We have concentrated on Calvin to the neglect of other Reformers such as Zwingli, Cranmer, and Bucer, not to mention the anabaptists, because for better or worse, in North America, the followers of Calvin have carried the day. Not only in the mainline Protestant churches, but also through the various sects, Calvinism has unquestionably exerted the dominant influence on the American scene.[163] And as Perry Miller and countless others have pointed out in different ways, Calvinism continues to have an enormous influence on American life even among people who have no knowledge of or interest in its creeds or intentions.[164]

The Calvinist influence in North America arrived, of course, with those resolute Puritans who brought to New England their English brand of the Reformation. Puritan Christianity attempted to be, certainly believed itself to be, faithful to the Calvinist vision. Despite the fact that they were in a new land, facing an utterly different challenge from that of their European comrades, the Puritans continued to take up what they considered to be the old Calvinistic weapons to assail the old Calvinistic foes, the papists and the anabaptists. American Puritans realized that in a new time and place Protestantism faced different problems. They did not, however, seem to be aware that they were making radical changes in Calvin's original strategy.

The Puritan changes often brought the New England theology perilously close to gnostic Christianity. Of particular concern is the Puritans' concentration on *self* and their tendency to regard humanity from an *elitist* perspective.

Something closely akin to Calvin's ecclesiology was carried across the sea to New England. The Puritan fathers retained the Genevan emphasis on the Old Testament; they identified themselves with the patriarchal family of Israel, with the pilgrimage of Israel into the Land of Promise, with the covenant transforming a small tribe into a mighty nation. All of these corporate images were close to their hearts.[165]

Perry Miller has done much to dispel the caricature of American puritanism as otherworldly, individualistic and irrational. Miller pointed out that the liberty of the individual was achieved "only upon terms." Theirs was no "me generation," but a group of neighbors who had covenanted with God and with each other to establish a holy society.[166]

The founding fathers of New England saw their prime obligation to be the preservation of God's true Church. As Robert Middlekauf has pointed out in his study of the Mathers:

> In its essence, the founders' thought remained always anchored to the Church. The Church in history, its form and membership and government, almost totally preoccupied them. . . . Their particular churches were a part of a larger institution and their purpose was to keep them—and it—pure.[167]

The existence of a hearty debate in the latter part of the seventeenth century concerning the nature of a catholic visible Church shows how far from individualism New England was, even at that time. On one side, Samuel Hudson argued that the word *Church* could only be used when all churches were visibly organized into a national confessing body. Thomas Hooker and Samuel Stone took the contrary position that congregational churches were valid expressions of Christ's Church. Stone's article in this exchange was entitled: "A Congregational Church Is a Catholike Visible Church."[168] The point is that all parties agreed that an identification of catholicity is important because they believed, as did Calvin, that the individual's salvation is dependent on the authenticity of the church of which one is a member.

Within the moderate wing of New England puritanism, a high view of the Church persisted well into the eighteenth century. Philip Greven writes:

> When moderates rose in defense of the standing churches [that is, inclusive churches that refused to make sharp distinctions between the converted and unconverted] . . . they believed that they were defending their churches, their communities, and their society as a whole against the seemingly corrosive individualism which they perceived at the core of the evangelical [extremist] spirit . . . they were convinced that individualism always needed to be balanced by the duties and obligations incumbent upon individuals as members of the larger community.[169]

During the early 1720s, John Trenchard and Thomas Gordon published a series of articles, popular among moderates both in England and New England, under the titles: *The Independent Whig* and *Cato's Letters*. Among their concerns was the threat to the community of faith posed by a radical individualism. "Bigotry," they said, ". . . being conducted by no Light but that of an *inflamed Imagination* and a sour, bitter, and narrow Spirit" was leading to every form of "Violence and Barbarity." While recognizing the rights of individuals, the authors insisted that "this Duty of a man to himself be performed subsequently to the general Welfare, and consistently with it. The Affairs of All should be minded preferably to the Affairs of One."[170]

This corporate view of life within puritanism was based upon the Calvinist conviction that all of life is *connected*. Greven has described this concept, termed "organicism," as "the belief that human society and institutions form a complex, interconnected whole, analogous to the human body, made up of indispensable but distinctive parts."[171]

There were and there remained within puritanism elements supporting a corporate understanding of the Church. Another stronger force was, however, finally to capture the field. Ernst Troeltsch, in his brilliant sociological study of Christianity, has clearly shown that

> the sect idea which influenced Calvinism a good deal from the outset became increasingly powerful as time went on, and finally prevailed. . . . [T]ogether [the sect idea and Calvinism] have developed into a force . . . called "ascetic Protestantism". It might also be called the "individualistic Protestantism of active-holiness".

Troeltsch went on to say that this individualistic interpretation of Calvinism was the "chief force in Protestantism, since it extends its influence far beyond the genuinely Pietistic and ascetic circles of 'earnest' Christians."[172] Even in these last decades of the twentieth century, Troeltsch's assessment holds true.

The transformation of Calvinism was not, as Perry Miller would have it, from a theology of unbridled, inscrutable divinity to that of the "chained God" of the covenant. The covenant or federal theology goes back beyond the Puritans, even beyond Cocceius, to Calvin himself.[173] The real transformation effected by eighteenth-century Puritan thought was the individualization of the covenant, the appropriation of a corporate Old Testament image to describe what became essentially a private psychological event. As Peter Bulkley, a later Puritan cleric, so explicitly stated:

> God conveys his salvation by way of covenant, and he doth it to those onely that are in covenant with him . . . this covenant must every soule enter into, every particular soule must enter into a particular covenant with God; out of this way there is no life.[174]

Rather than God entering into covenant with His people Israel or with His redeemed Church and the individual participating in covenant insofar as he is related to Israel or Church, under this new form of Calvinism, the individual makes a covenant with God directly; it is a one-on-one relationship. The influence on North American Protestantism of this theological shift has been enormous.

Closely connected to the conflict of corporate covenant with individual covenant was the Puritan preoccupation with the elect. Again, when the founders of New England society first landed, their Calvinism was pretty well intact. Thus, though their Church required a certain number of the intellectually elite to understand and convey the rather intricate dialectics of Reformed theology, the Church itself was not elitist, either from the point of view of intellect or of spirituality.[175] Church membership implied not a full understanding of particular doctrine but rather an appreciation of God's good will toward his people.[176] And most of the early Puritans in North America would have agreed with their mentor, Calvin:

> It is not our part to separate elect from reprobate . . . [but for practical purposes to employ] the judgement of charity, by which we acknowledge as members of the Church all who by confession of faith, regularity of conduct, and participation in the sacraments, unite with us in acknowledging the same God and Christ.[177]

Calvin and his immediate followers believed that "some men and angels are predestined unto everlasting life, and others foreordained to everlasting death,"[178] but they did not feel themselves required or indeed qualified to distinguish the one group from the other. Predestination was a matter of God's eternal decree and as far as the Church was concerned, must remain a "high mystery . . . to be handled with special prudence and care."[179]

This mood of charity prevailed in New England in the early days. As Greven has shown, "Church membership was synonymous with residence, with 'co-habitation', and came with the simple act of being born within the religiously defined community." Those who held to that founding tradition, the moderates, continued to envision and structure a local church "which ideally, included nearly everyone."[180]

Congregations like the Brattle Street Church in Boston opened their membership to all persons of sound faith and upright life. Its pastors and lay leaders refused to follow the growing practice of requiring from new members a testimony of their conversion experience. James W. Jones has described the partisans of Brattle Street as "men of catholic sentiments and charitable judgments [offering] no evidence that any deviated from the prevailing Calvinist orthodoxy."[181]

Despite its orthodox beginnings, however, New England and, finally, most of North American Protestantism was to fall into other hands which were neither catholic nor charitable. An evangelical elite was to gain ascendency and make the question of conversion the central question of Christianity. In 1750, Ebenezer Frothingham would charge:

> The Churches we have separated from generally hold, that external Morality is the Door into the Church, and the Lord's Supper is a converting Ordinance; or that all have a Right to join with the Church, that will make an outward public Profession of Christianity, altho' they be unconverted.[182]

Clearly Frothingham and his like-minded colleagues could never be satisfied until the sheep could be separated from the goats, the pure from the impure, the truly spiritual from the hypocrites, the converted from the unconverted. And they seemed to have no doubt that their own election qualified them for the necessary task of dividing humanity into flock of God and sheepfold of Satan. The development of Protestant elitism will be considered in chapter 8.

North American Liberals: A Simple Christianity or Religious Syncretism?

The narrow, self-righteous faith that flourished in eighteenth-century New England did not go unchallenged by more sensitive and creative Christians. In fact, those who did rise up to challenge the American form of Calvinism, displayed a courage and an intellectual openness which enabled them not only to change the religious climate in their own day, but to exert a continuing influence on North American Christianity for over two hundred years. Indeed the basic theological assumptions of the dissidents still inform and determine the shape of the largest part of North American Protestantism.

The revolt against a Calvinism gone awry came from what we now call liberalism. Liberalism, as opposed to New England orthodoxy, was not closed-minded, but open—open to fresh ideas, alien thought. Liberal thinkers would no longer be confined to Calvinism, the stated teachings of orthodox rationalism or even the Bible. The fresh air of open enquiry was blowing across the New World; Christians were able once again to breathe deeply, and the experience was exhilarating.

The religious revolt happened at roughly the same time as the political revolt. European ideas were invading North America and could no longer be ignored. Natural reason, natural law, natural rights were bringing into question the grace-alone, Scripture-alone, elect-alone doctrines that previously had been held sacrosanct.[183]

Perhaps it all began far back in the seventeenth century with the preaching of John Norton (1606–1663) who tried to reconcile the awful distance between God's election and man's freedom by asserting that God's will and righteous man's will are not necessarily contradictory, but can even coincide. "The Will [of man]," he wrote, "placed under this determining motion of God, inclineth itself freely to Act, and to that only where unto it would have inclined itself if . . . there were no decree."[184] James W. Jones has described the consequences of Norton's teaching as follows:

> It would not be long before the divine and human wills were totally identified, making it no longer necessary to speak of the divine will at all. The human will, then, stood virtually autonomous.

Norton, Jones feels, "opened a little breach in the wall."[185]

The little breach continued to widen with the help of Jonathan Mayhew (1720–1766) and Charles Chauncy (1705–1787), both of whom proclaimed the amiability of God and the vast potential of humanity.[186] Both were intellectually indebted to the natural law philosophy of Locke and Hobbes.[187] With the further aid of William Ellery Channing (1780–1842) and Ralph Waldo Emerson (1803–1882), the walls of American orthodoxy would come tumbling down.

One of the most frequent charges brought against liberalism—one which might raise the question of a gnosticizing tendency in that movement—concerns its syncretism. No doubt, liberalism is syncretistic in the sense that it is open to all sorts of data, regardless of the source. Perhaps no one expressed this openness better than Ralph Waldo Emerson, when he advised his fellow liberals that,

> no man could be better occupied than in making his own bible by harkening to all those sentences which now here, now there, now in nursery rhymes, now in Hebrew, now in English bards, thrill him like the sound of a trumpet.[188]

As we stated earlier, syncretism must be judged in terms of its purpose. When Christian thought draws into itself the philosophical, artistic and emotional expressions of the society for apologetic or missionary purposes or when it simply absorbs certain ideas or feelings from its surroundings by accident, such syncretism is natural and often necessary. Gnostic syncretism, on the other hand, believes everything in general for the purpose of avoiding a belief in something in particular. In the case of Christian gnosticism, what is being avoided is the particularity of the Gospel, that which is a "stumbling block to Jews and folly to Gentiles."[189]

There can be little doubt that initially the concern of liberalism in North America was to present the Gospel of Christ in an honest and attractive way. Indeed, its purpose went beyond apologetics or evangelism; the early liberals wished to *understand* the Gospel in a more authentic way. They set out to rediscover the ancient texts, to read the Bible as if it had not been interpreted by John Calvin. They were determined to see the beauty of Christ as he was before Jonathan Edwards distorted his features. Their abiding suspicion of traditional creeds did not imply a loss of confidence in Holy Writ. As Parrington has noted with respect to early Unitarianism:

> The Scriptures lie open and the heedful eye will discover God's revelation in their pages. The deeper spirit of Unitarianism is not inadequately embodied in the text, "Search the Scriptures, for they are they which testify of me." No abler or more devout Scripturists ever preached in America than the Unitarian ministers.[190]

Whether or not later liberals continued to be as biblically motivated and their syncretism still related to a respect for the particularity of revealed Scripture will be one of the concerns of part II.

Summary

From the New Testament writers to the early Church Fathers and the Reformers, there have been legitimate gnostic elements within the Christian faith. However, Paul and John, Clement and Origen, Luther and Calvin resisted oversimplification, kept alive a dialectic and, thereby, maintained a continuing orthodoxy within the context of the Church, the living body of Christ. The first North American Puritans and some early liberals were also able to sustain the precarious theological tension which is essential to true faith. Before we can examine what has happened to Christianity in North America, it is necessary to understand that there has been a valid orthodoxy throughout the history of the Church.

II

GNOSTICISM IN ASCENDANCE IN NORTH AMERICA

CHAPTER FOUR

Alienation: From Gratitude to Despair

AS WE have seen, the predominant religion in North America has been Protestant—that particular form of Protestantism which is rooted in the Calvinist branch of the Reformation. From the Low Church Episcopalians and Anglicans of Virginia and Canada, to Puritan New England, to the great churches of the frontier (the Methodist and the Baptist), the theological theme on this continent has been played in a Calvinistic key.[1]

Something drastic, however, happened to Calvinism in North America. By the middle of the nineteenth century it became apparent that a form of Christianity quite different from any known on the Continent or in the British Isles had not only asserted itself but had become the typical religion of North America. As early as 1800, Jedidiah Morse had exhorted his flock to "guard against the insidious encroachments of *innovation*—that evil and beguiling spirit which is now stalking to and fro in the earth, seeking whom it may devour."[2] Despite that warning and the famous boast of Charles Hodge that no new idea had ever originated at Princeton,[3] innovation was encroaching on every theological front, and new ideas, outside the precincts of Princeton, were out of control.

Following the Civil War, Henry Ward Beecher, the most prominent clergyman of that period, boasted: "This continent is to be from this time forth governed by Northern men, with Northern ideas, and with a Northern gospel."[4] This immodest claim would prove to be prophetic, for not only had the Union Army crushed the Confederacy, but also "Northern" evangelicalism in both its revivalistic and liberal forms would virtually annihilate any alternative spiritual expressions which tried to exert themselves in a public way.

Before Beecher's proclamation of victory, Philip Schaff, a church historian of the Mercersburg School, prophesied in more positive and less vindictive terms concerning the religion of his newly adopted nation. America, he wrote, is "destined to be the Phenix grave . . . of all European churches and sects, of Protestantism and Romanism." He referred to American Christianity as a "motley sample of all church history." In the American faith, "all the powers of Europe good and bad, are . . . fermenting together under new and peculiar conditions."[5]

In Part II we shall look at this peculiarly North American religious development—and especially its resemblance to another highly innovative theology which flourished during the early centuries of the Christian era. Despite the vast cultural differences between North American Protestantism and ancient gnosticism, the parallels between the two innovations can no longer be ignored.

Within biblical and orthodox thought, there is a consistent affirmation of the cosmos as the creation of a beneficent God. God is our Father, in that He redeems His people from slavery in Egypt and from their sins, but also He is Father, in that He is responsible for "our creation, preservation, and all the blessings of this life."[6] For our creation as well as for our redemption, "It is meet, right, and our bounden duty, that we should at all times, and in all places . . ." give Him our thanks.[7] The graciousness of God is shown to be united perfectly in the Christ, for "without him was not anything made that was made."[8] If the intention of the gnostics was to separate the act of creation from the Divine, the intention of orthodoxy was to connect so that, within orthodoxy, God is responsible for the Creation, even the Creation as we now find it in its fallen state. Certainly, God is not the author of evil, but God is ultimately responsible for evil, in that He takes it upon Himself to deal with it, overcome it and order the cosmos according to His ultimate design.[9]

John Calvin, the formative theologian for what was to become the prevailing Protestantism in North America, affirmed this essential connection between creation and redemption, nature and grace. Creation, for Calvin, was not a past event, but a present reality. "To make a Creator God temporal and of brief duration," he argued,

". . . would be a cold and meagre thing . . . for us, the virtue of God shines in the present, as much in the enduring state of the world as in its first beginning."[10] Human beings have not been *thrown* into a sinful, chaotic world, but *born* within a world that still remains the responsibility of its Creator. In 1559, Calvin wrote:

> When we speak of the providence of God, this word does not signify that he, remaining idle in the heavens, watches over what is happening on earth: rather is he like the captain of a ship, holding the helm in order to cope with every event.[11]

The gloomy mood often attributed to Calvin can certainly be found within his theology, but it is maintained in contrast to the gratuitous providence of God.

> If we consider to what end God created foods, we shall find that he wished not only to provide for our necessities but also for our pleasure and recreation. . . . With herbs, trees and fruits, besides the various uses he gives us of them, it was his will to rejoice our sight by their beauty, and to give us yet another pleasure in their odours. . . . Lastly, has he not given us many things which we ought to hold in esteem without their being necessary to us?[12]

It is obvious that the Reformer enjoyed the dappled, many-splendored things along with his glass of wine.

We have also seen how Calvinism, after it came to be replanted in North American soil, retained for many years its old world flavor. The Calvinistic affirmation of a beneficent providence remained for a time a central doctrine of the New World creed. The European celebration of a harvest thanksgiving festival was continued by the Puritan settlers and held special significance for them because of their temporal deliverance, despite the harshness of New England's climate and the hardness of its rocky soil.

Even Jonathan Edwards, a later son, who was to speak such frightening words about unredeemed humanity's alienation from God, was not unaware of the graciousness of the Creator. As a young man, he regarded the marvels of the natural world with both a scientific and poetic eye. He wrote of spiders as "these wondrous animals from whose glistening web so much of the wisdom of the Creator shines." While attending Yale at the age of thirteen, he even delighted in the scientific experiment of making his own rainbow by "spirting" water into the air![13]

According to William A. Clebsch, "the holiness of beauty" remained a determining factor in the theology of Edwards. The Christian's "proper relation with God," Clebsch writes, "allowed no bad relations with the world . . . Edwards came to be at home with God as a way of being also at home in the stark world of Massachusetts' western frontier." Sainthood implied "letting one's existence be made beautiful and enjoying the beauty of existence."[14] Ominously, however, Clebsch also asserts that, "[Edwards] stands as the last major American religious thinker who fully espoused an orthodox Christian world-view in all he thought and did."[15] Whether one can accept so positive a view of Jonathan Edwards or so negative a view of those who were to follow is a matter of strong contention. Most scholars, however, would agree that at about this point in the American story, a thankful view of the Creation was being replaced by something very different. The joyful hymn, "All people who on earth do dwell, / Sing to the Lord with cheerful voice" began to be sung with less confident voices and to fall on more skeptical ears. Many Christians would attempt to return to a purer, simpler appreciation of God and His Creation, but their efforts would require an unusual courage and would always be met by vigorous opposition. A sense of alienation had set in—a fundamental doubt as to whether the beauty of holiness and the holiness of beauty could be reconciled—and there was no turning back.

The problem seems to have stemmed from the old Calvinistic (initially Augustinian) doctrine of original sin. We have seen how St. Augustine in his polemic against the Manichaeans might himself have fallen into a gnostic trap. His interpretation of the poetic image of the Fall of humanity's original parents in a literalistic way and the extension of the consequences of that Fall to all persons *per generationem* left the Church with a theological formulation too close to gnosticism for comfort.[16] Some Calvinists, furthermore, were not content with the ambiguity of Augustine's and Calvin's wordings; they added the unambiguous doctrine of *total depravity*. The Synod of Dort (1619) had proclaimed that "the Fall has left man in a state of corruption and helplessness: his gleams of natural light are of no value for salvation."[17] The La Rochelle Confession of Faith (1571) had said it more explicitly: "We also believe that this [hereditary] vice is truly sin and that it suffices to condemn the entire human race, even infants in the wombs of their mothers, and that it is taken as a sin before God."[18]

So long as Christians are aware that language about original sin and total depravity is being used to describe an *imagined* world apart from the graciousness of God for the purpose of increasing the thanksgiving of the faithful, Christian thinking remains orthodox. As soon, however, as such language is no longer seen as a poetic suspension of the actual but is taken literally in the sense that evil is believed to have infused the cosmos from the outside, a barrier has been broken and those profound but perilous doctrines of the Church have become gnosticized.[19] As Ricoeur explains, when the source of evil is located entirely apart from ourselves, "the cosmos . . . is satanized and hence provides the human experience of evil with the support of an absolute exteriority, an absolute inhumanity, an absolute materiality."[20] Carried to this extreme, sin is no longer a matter of *mea culpa;* some other force is culpable.

This highly deterministic view of sin, a tenet of ancient gnosticism,[21] became a feature of the extreme form of puritanism that dominated American evangelical religion. Whereas the ancient heresiarchs had read God's words of creation, "Let us make man in our image, after our likeness"[22] as the mistaken and bungling act of the archons,[23] the New England theology concluded that these words were, apart from redemption in Christ, totally ineffectual. The end result is the same: in both systems, humanity finds itself thrown into a chaotic world, at the outset alienated from God, from fellow humans and certainly from the self. "This world is all over dirty," Jonathan Edwards observes:

> Everywhere it is covered with that which tends to defile the feet of the traveller. Our streets are dirty and muddy, intimating that the world is full of that which tends to defile the soul, that worldly objects and worldly concerns and worldly company tend to pollute us.[24]

Much can be said about the hearty earthiness of Puritan life and the good spirits of such churchmen as the Reverend Samuel Willard, who could remind his flock to

> see what an excellent being man was as he came out of the hands of his Creator . . . God made all things in wondrous wisdom but here was a result of all God's creating wisdom gathered together in one. There were many beams of his wisdom, power and goodness scattered among other creatures; here they are all contracted in this little model.[25]

Nevertheless, such sentiments of humanity's natural state became increasingly rare. And such sermons as "Sinners in the Hands of an Angry God," if an exception for Jonathan Edwards, too often were typical of many American clergy.[26]

What could have caused American religion to make this peculiar turn? Why did the extreme evangelical position, usually in a minority on the Continent and in Britain, become the dominant, established force in the New World? Could the answer be found in the same psychological and sociological factors which caused ancient gnosticism to develop the way it did? Hans Jonas, in attempting to find the reason for the ancient phenomenon, sensed that

> the Gnostic mood . . . has an element of rebellion and protest about it. Its rejection of the world, far from the serenity or resignation of other nonworldly creeds, is of peculiar, sometimes vituperative violence, and we generally note a tendency to extremism, to excess in fantasy and feeling.[27]

The close connection between the revolutionary spirit of eighteenth-century America and evangelical Protestantism has been noted by most historians of the period, whether writing from a secular or Church perspective. Philip Greven sums it up:

> To become a republican proved to be entirely consonant with the evangelical temperament, and republicanism in 1776 was to be virtually indistinguishable from evangelicalism as a political ideology.[28]

Starting with the Revolutionary period, there was such a strong feeling of alienation from the *given*—the British heritage, the historic Church, the world of nature, the self, the natural state—that it was generally believed that nothing much was to be lost in throwing off all these impedimenta.

There remains, however, the question of the origin of such a strong sense of alienation. From where does a metaphysical alienation arise that could cause the ancient gnostics to be repelled by the orthodox Church and the eighteenth-century Americans, by the European Christianity of their forebears? Again, Hans Jonas hints at an answer: "We suspect that the dislocated metaphysical situation of which gnostic myth tells had its counterpart in a dislocated *real situation:* that the crisis form of its symbolism reflects a *historical crisis* of man himself."[29] The historical crisis to which Jonas alludes could have been an ancient event such as the destruction of the Jewish Temple, the failing cultural cohesiveness of the Roman Empire, the delay in Christ's promised return—many suggestions have been offered for historical setbacks that could have caused early Christians to feel radically alienated from the real world in which they found themselves. The most likely explanation would seem to be that whatever event or events produced such an immediate effect, the principal cause was the Jewish-Christian preconception which would allow the event itself to embody such catastrophic significance. For example, if a Jew's apocalyptic hopes were entirely attached to the restoration of temple worship, the destruction of the Temple could represent the end of apocalyptic hope. Or if the Christian's faith were entirely pinned to the imminent return of Christ, the one-hundredth anniversary of the Resurrection could have signified the end of that form of faith.

On the American scene, the Puritan apocalyptic hope had been in the concrete establishment of a Wilderness Zion, a Holy Commonwealth. Ahlstrom describes the Puritan sense of mission:

> As a saving remnant they left England behind, to become a kind of Church of Christ in Exile, a "citty [*sic*] on a hill" for all the world to see, or even the final purification of church and state before the Last Days.[30]

It is easy to understand how those who were dreaming such dreams and seeing such visions were destined to have their hopes completely dashed on their own rocky soil. Alas, the antagonism, greed, apathy, jealousy of the Old World carried over to the New. The pilgrimage could take the people out of Europe, but it could not take Europe out of the people. More accurately, North America could not take humanity out of the people. The apocalyptic vision failed; an earthly hope which European Protestants had never entertained had been decisively destroyed by reality. From this disappointing experience, North American evangelicalism developed its own distinctive character, a chief ingredient of which was an abiding sense of *alienation*.

With the failure of the apocalyptic hope, the faith of the North American evangelicals, like that of Marcion, began to rest in an *alien* God: a God apart from Creation, apart from matter, apart from sinful humanity. American theology would not say with Marcion that the Creator-God was other than or opposed to the real God. Evangelicals knew enough Church history to avoid that blatant misconstruction. They were in fundamental accord with Marcion, however, in maintaining that the only real concern of religion has to do with the *Redeemer*-God whose intentions are made clear in Christ. And even the revelation of Christ pertains exclusively to the realm of the spirit, not to the kingdom of the flesh.[31] There is, then, nothing about the world, as world, in which to take pleasure. In fact, pleasure itself is suspect because it represents a misapprehension of the spiritual truth that the created world is worthless.

Protestantism in America has, of course, not been confined to theologians, philosophers of religion or the clergy. Martin Marty asserts, "Many a colonial theme can best be revisited not in Beecher or Bushnell but in Hawthorne and Melville."[32] The works of both of these literary children of Calvinism are especially revealing: although accepting a view of the world as immersed in sin—totally depraved—they continue to search for grace. They could neither avoid the darkness nor give up their longing for the light.

Ironically, it is Melville who describes Hawthorne as having "a touch of Puritanic gloom":

> This great power of blackness in him derives its force from its appeal to that Calvinistic sense of Innate Depravity and Original Sin, from whose visitations, in some shape or other, no deeply thinking mind is always and wholly free. . . . This black conceit pervades him through and through.[33]

Hawthorne himself confessed an inability to feel love for the place and time allotted to him. "Taking no root," he said, "I soon weary of any soil in which I may be temporarily deposited. The same impatience I sometimes feel, or conceive of, as regards this earthly life." On the basis of such consistently expressed feelings, Parrington was to see Hawthorne as "the extreme and finest expression of the refined *alienation from reality* that in the end palsied the creative mind of New England."[34]

What could be said of Hawthorne about darkness and gloom is true of Melville—in spades. Melville's severe combination of Dutch Reformed and Scottish Presbyterian upbringing had convinced him of one certain doctrinal truth, the sovereignty of God, which, to his mind, implied an absolute determinism. Self-reliance and personal assertion could not really be considered seriously by one who had taken an honest look at life and found humanity's fate almost wholly determined by exterior forces. In such a determined world and a world so pervaded by evil, as Melville understood it, either humanity was confronted by a malevolent Deity, in which case it was undone, or God was divided. If the latter were true, then the evangelical Christianity of his day had become obsolete; a new religious expression must be found.[35] Although Melville in his relentless search for an answer could come to no final conclusion on the matter, he was obsessed with the question in a way similar to that of the gnostics of old. His was a "quarrel with God," with the God of Creation. In his most famous work, which he termed his "wicked book," his object seems to have been to raise questions not only about the tyranny of Calvinistic evangelicalism, but about the tyranny of the Calvinistic evangelical God. Lawrance Thompson claims that

> Melville's underlying theme in *Moby Dick* correlates the notions that the world was put together wrong and that God is to blame; that God in his infinite malice asserts a sovereign tyranny over man . . . and heroic man will assert the rights of man and will rebel against God's tyranny by defying God in thought, word, deed, even in the face of God's ultimate indignity, death.[36]

Melville's complaint against his Maker was genuine and unresolved. His sustained outcry was against those who can simply acquiesce to an intolerable situation: "You fools! You flock of fools, under this captain of fools, in this ship of fools."[37] Had there been a resolution to this human-divine encounter, Melville might have found some inner peace. As it was, according to Parrington, "There is no other tragedy in American letters comparable to the tragedy of Herman Melville. . . . Like Jacob he wrestled all night with an angel, yet got no blessing from the touched thigh."[38]

Another quieter, but no less courageous victim of metaphysical alienation was the brave woman of Amherst, Emily Dickinson. Throughout her deceptively tranquil life, the poet waged a valiant inner battle against despair. Her rejection of New England theology was a primary necessity for her.

> Is Heaven a Physician?
> They say that He can heal—
> But Medicine Posthumous
> Is unavailable—
> Is Heaven an Exchequer?
> They speak of what we owe—
> But that negotiation
> I'm not a Party to.[39]

When we attempt to differentiate between those Protestant Americans who accept a primal sense of alienation and those who have struggled against that feeling, we discover some surprises on both sides of the fence. Tom Paine, the firebrand of the American Revolution, held a much more positive view of the Creator-God than did most of his contemporaries. Denouncing the anti-scientific, anti-natural preaching of the evangelicals, Paine held that the restoration of "true theology" could come about only with the overthrow of the unfortunate idea that God and His Creation are alien to one another.[40] Perhaps it is not so surprising to find Paine adamantly opposed to his fellow revolutionaries in his fundamental world view when we recall that he was a maverick in the anti-British cause and has always been an embarrassment to those whose support of the Revolution was based on theological grounds rather than on purely political, economic and practical grounds.

Theological liberalism has often attempted to break down the sense of alienation within American Christianity. Parrington says of Theodore Parker, a father of American liberalism, that "a metaphysical optimism throws a golden light on all his thinking."[41] Later, one of the principal reasons for Henry David Thoreau's revolt against New England religion would be its alienation from the created world, its refusal to celebrate the natural gifts of God. "Christianity," he wrote, "only hopes. It has hung its harp on the willows and cannot sing a song in a strange land. It has dreamed a sad dream, and does not yet welcome the morning with joy." It was in desperate retreat from the alienating preaching of the clergy and the alienated lives of their congregations that Thoreau was forced to worship elsewhere. "The Great God Pan," he proclaimed, "is not dead, as was rumoured. . . . Perhaps of all the Gods of New England and of ancient Greece, I am most constant at his shrine."[42]

Thousands of others were not as successful as Thoreau in finding a happier God; their different drummers could not lead them from the gloom of evangelicalism. Harriet Beecher Stowe understood the central theme of the New England psyche to be the "profound, unutterable, and therefore unuttered melancholy" that pervaded all things.[43] The vicar of Walden Pond, like Tom Paine, was the exception that proved the rule.

For those who could not carry on the *quarrel,* liberal theology continued to provide a more popular alternative to evangelical gloom. Liberal preachers, according to Fenn's *Religious History of New England,* categorically denied the existence of the God in whom the evangelicals believed:

> A God of election and reprobation, capable of dooming an entire race because its ancestors disobeyed a God of arbitrary will and discriminating grace—seemed to them simply an immoral being, and they frankly said so.[44]

Parker and those who followed him were certainly correct in their abandonment of the false, Marcion-like dichotomy between nature and grace espoused by the evangelicals. Temporarily, they brought relief, a sense of sanity, to American Christianity by once again preaching a positive doctrine of creation. Their positive view of the created world, however, was based on the theological premise that God is immanent in all things and all people. Whereas the evangelicals allowed God the Redeemer to eclipse God the Creator, the liberals did the opposite. The liberals made ample room for nature on their stage by moving grace into the wings. There remained in both camps a gnostic separation of Creation from Redemption.[45]

One of the hazards of this liberal form of separation was exposed when confidence in the immanence of God in nature became suspect. Once grace has been set aside, if God is seen as *absent* from the natural scene in any practical sense, then a new form of despair appears. Ralph Waldo Emerson was quick to notice this development in Protestant thought: "A new disease has fallen on the life of man . . . our torment is Unbelief." The founders of New England had gone to their graves obsessed by "the fear of Sin, and the Terror of the Day of Judgement." Now, however, "these terrors have lost their force," and in their stead, "our religion assumes the negative form of rejection."[46] When God is no longer felt to be the sustainer of the cosmos, liberal humanity finds itself like a child abandoned by its parents.

Whether or not Emerson himself was able to break away from the new terror or from the ancestral sense of alienation remains an open question. Certainly, the picture we are usually given of the great transcendentalist is one of self-reliance and unequivocal optimism. His optimism, however, does not apply to human beings in their natural state. "Human nature," he believed, "is as bad as it dares to be. . . . If it were possible to repair the rottenness of human nature it were well."[47] From one who has been described as the "flowering of two centuries of spiritual aspiration," one who embodied the "perfect fruition" of Roger Williams and Jonathan Edwards,[48] we might expect a more positive view of humanity.

In periods which afforded encouragement and hope, the good times between wars and depressions, American Christians found that the optimistic side of liberalism made a great deal of sense: God, after all, would seem to be immanent in all things when all things are going well. Prior to World War I, for instance, liberalism enjoyed much popularity. There seemed to be no reason to reject the argument that the "terror-filled surroundings" which had influenced the thinking of Augustine, Calvin and Edwards had now been overcome by human progress.[49]

With the outbreak of World War I, however, some prophetic spirits like Walter Rauschenbusch immediately began to express serious doubts about the liberal method of overcoming alienation. "History," Rauschenbusch warned, "laughs at the optimistic illusion that 'nothing can stand in the way of human progress.' It would be safer to assert that progress is always for a time only, and then succumbs to the inevitable decay."[50] By 1915, even George Angier Gordon, a leading Congregational preacher who only a few years earlier had insisted on optimism as a moral necessity for Christians, now admitted that, "Recent events have broken the opium pipe and dispelled the delusion."[51]

Those with less emotional involvement in the Protestant Church perceived an even more serious threat to the liberal alternative. Such diverse thinkers as George Burman Foster, Joseph Wood Krutch and Walter Lippmann could speak of the sense of loss in modern America as directly connected with loss of faith in God. In 1918, the year of his death, Foster saw that what was taking place in America as well as within himself was "the passing of theistic supernaturalism." Humanity was outgrowing theism "in a gentle and steady way."[52] The God who but a short time ago seemed to be everywhere, now could be found nowhere.

Much of liberalism's sense of alienation was, in part, the result of a new world-view initiated by modern science and by the social sciences. These disciplines seemed to be proving more and more that the Creation and human destiny were not under the control of a God but rather determined by an intricate interaction of biological, chemical, psychological, sociological and genetic forces that operated without rhyme or reason.[53] Albert Einstein's affirmation, "I refuse to believe that God plays dice with the world,"[54] would leave many Protestant Americans unconvinced. On the contrary, modern liberalism seemed to be saying that if God exists at all, He is probably playing some game of chance. The nineteenth-century scientific heritage had challenged the comfortable assumptions about a benevolent Creation: "Thought is merely an emission from the brain like urine from the kidneys"; there can be "no thought without phosphorus"; and even, "The soul is the sum of plasma-movements in the ganglion-cells."[55] Such pronouncements and their wide acceptance among even scientifically untrained people seemed to work against any sensible doctrine of creation.

A Humanist Manifesto (1933) took this scientific challenge into account in its attempt to make religious sense out of the given world-view. In their statement, thirty-four prominent American thinkers affirmed: "First: Religious humanists regard the universe as self-existing and not created." This radically altered doctrine of creation quite logically led to article five: "Humanism asserts that the nature of the universe depicted by modern science makes unacceptable any supernatural or cosmic guarantees of human values . . . religion must formulate its hopes and plans in the light of the scientific spirit and method."[56] If the cosmos simply *happened,* how could we expect history to unfold according to any particular form? If there were no Creator, how could there be a Sustainer? This neutralization of nature in modern thought recalls similar expressions in ancient gnosticism.

Many chaotic, anti-creational views have been brought forward since 1933; these make the world look even less "guaranteed" than it did then. Arthur Koestler, for example, sees the brain of man as an evolutionary "mistake;" in the transition from a bicameral to a unicameral system, a "flaw" occurred which is the source of man's pathological propensity toward violence. "We are a mentally sick race, and as such deaf to persuasion," Koestler laments. "The Promethean myth has acquired an ugly twist: the giant reaching out to steal the lightning from the gods is insane." This schizophrenia is built into the race because *homo sapiens* is a "biological freak, the result of some remarkable mistake in the evolutionary process. The ancient doctrine of original sin . . . could be a reflection of man's awareness of his own inadequacy, of the intuitive hunch that somewhere along the line of his ascent something has gone wrong." Thus, Koestler's only hope for the race is in universal tranquilizing by the treating of all drinking water.[57] One wonders how there can be mistakes and flaws if "the universe is self-existing and not created." However that may be, many people of today, perhaps all educated people, have had cause to wonder if the cosmos is really a well-planned gift or merely the remarkable by-product of astronomical and evolutionary occurrences.

The hidden influence of such thinking on Protestant Christianity, of course, has been enormous. No Protestant body would profess or even consider what the religious humanists said in 1933. Yet on a practical level, a metaphysical doubt is present. When the doubt remains unchallenged, it leads modern Christians into a position very similar to that of the ancient gnostics. If the heresiarchs devised archons to be responsible for the mistakes of the cosmos, thereby freeing God of responsibility, a scientifically oriented generation has interposed its own archons: the big bang, probability, evolution, all of which provide some distance between God and this deficient cosmos. And if Marcion "tore God the Creator away from God the Redeemer" by denying the kindness of the former, the same result has been achieved in our own day by denying the existence of the Creator. In both cases, humanity has been cut off from its origins, has lost the history of its existence and therefore cannot discover meaning within the context of the given universe.[58]

At the same time that the sense of metaphysical alienation was freeing the modernist spirit from any critical dependence on a doctrine of creation, a countermovement was responding to its own feeling of alienation in quite another way. Beecher's boast that the North American continent was destined to be governed by a "Northern" gospel became true, ironically, in the area most opposed to Northern thought, the Southern states. It was in the post-Civil War South that the evangelicalism of New England would be maintained in its most extreme form. Nowhere was the despairing aspect of Calvinism more evident than in the Bible Belt. "Among these fruits [of Reconstruction]," Martin Marty observes, "was the tragic sense of life which lived on in southern churches."[59] If the rest of the United States could feel the attraction of liberalism with its optimistic view of human progress, Southerners were still "born to lose."

In the South and within the North American movement which after 1910 became known as Fundamentalism,[60] the radical theology of New England was itself radicalized. Even the arcane doctrine of premillennialism, based on a literalistic interpretation of the Apocalypse, gained popular support. Among those who had no hope in the present cosmos and denied any hint of fulfillment within world history, the idea of a new cosmos under a new dispensation was quite appealing.[61]

The pessimistic mood of premillennialism was sustained by Billy Graham, America's most famous evangelist. In 1950, Graham prophesied: "I believe the judgement hand of God is about to fall upon you tonight . . . we may have another year, maybe two years . . . [and] it's all going to be over."[62] Graham, at times, became explicit concerning the hopeless condition of humanity. Unlike the idyllic Garden of Eden, he said, where there were "no union dues, no labor leaders, no snakes, no disease," the North Carolina evangelist saw the United States, "falling apart at the seams" as a result of deficit spending, "give-away" foreign aid programs, the influence of big labor, the "bungling" United Nations, and the "boring from within [of a communism] masterminded by Satan."[63]

The revival spearheaded by Graham reached its apex in the 1950s. Even though the revivalistic message denigrated the world and despaired of humanity, many American Christians outside the Fundamentalist fold nevertheless hoped that some spiritual gains might be made by means of it. By the 1960s, however, it became apparent that once again American Protestantism had been left more discouraged and confused after the revival than before.[64]

Secular writers were more discerning and more theologically accurate about the source of alienation than were the evangelists. Walter Lippmann wrote in his nationally syndicated column in 1964:

> The "virtual despair" comes from being uprooted, homeless, naked, alone and unled. It comes from being lost in a universe where the meaning of life and of the social order are no longer given from on high and transmitted from ancestors but have to be invented and discovered and experimented with, each lonely individual for himself.[65]

There continued to be, of course, positive forces at work, hopeful signs, prophetic voices. As early as 1927 Reinhold Niebuhr had observed, "a psychology of defeat, of which both fundamentalism and modernism are symptoms, has gripped the forces of religion."[66] Some Protestants, especially in the older liberal tradition, saw Niebuhr and the other proponents of what they called neo-orthodoxy only affirming a dark view of reality. The historian Winthrop Hudson finds the movement "preoccupied with the problem of the anxious and agonized conscience (the sense of guilt, estrangement, and frustration which once had been so prominently displayed in revival meetings)."[67] Although it is true that neo-orthodoxy, American style, did have much to say about the alienation of humanity from God, person from person, self from self, nonetheless, along with this negative analysis was a renewed interest in the world and in the task of the Church within the world. Secular literature, the plastic arts, music, economics, politics all became subjects of concern in a way they had never been before among American church people as *church* people. And if the Niebuhr brothers, Walter Marshall Horton, Paul Lehmann, and others painted the landscape with darker hues than those employed by traditional American liberalism, it was in order to produce a more realistic picture. Given their impassioned involvement in every aspect of the American culture, unlike the Fundamentalists, the neo-orthodox had found the landscape worthy of their undivided attention. Ahlstrom is accurate, it seems to me, when he concludes: "Despite all, however, Neo-orthodoxy was pervaded by a hopeful mood. It was neither cynical, pessimistic, nor nihilistic."[68]

Within a nation reared on revivalism, the neo-orthodox dialectics and social involvements could receive only limited support from Protestant Christians. Very quickly, in the 1960s, the old divisions of Fundamentalism and liberalism would reassert themselves and, seemingly, represent the whole of the Protestant scene. True, the liberals were a bit chastened by events as well as by Niebuhrian *realism*. John C. Bennett, for instance, had become "a changed liberal" and now could only profess to believe

> that it is possible on this earth to have a structure of society within which men can live together in an interdependent world without destroying each other, within which individuals and groups can rise to high levels and in which they can live without intolerable compromise.[69]

One would imagine that nearly any humanist not suffering from clinical depression could agree with that guarded statement. If it was in any sense typical of American Protestant thought, then this form of Christianity was no longer "dreaming dreams or seeing visions," and the prayer, "thy kingdom come on earth as it is in Heaven" had been scrapped. Like the world of the ancient gnostics "whereinto we have been thrown," the world of these modern Protestants seemed decidedly lacking in hope.

A serious attempt to deal with the scientific challenge to the biblical idea of a good creation has been made by contemporary Process theologians. Under the influence of the philosopher Alfred North Whitehead, theologians Charles Hartshorne, Shubert Ogden, John Cobb, and others have tried to show systematically that God, along with the Creation, is in the process of being created. Creativity is thus a force that underlies all beings and things. Here there would seem to be a close theological affinity to the ancient gnostics: by means of the Process model, obviously God is again taken off the creational hook. If He Himself has not arrived in Being, how can He assume responsibility for a few deficiencies in the cosmos?[70]

Harvey Cox, although not a Process theologian, shows some affinity to the Process school:

> Generations of biblical scholars, charmed by the spell of the Greeks, have overlooked or minimized the astonishing fact that creation is *not* completed by God in the Bible until after man is formed and begins to work as God's partner in ordering the chaos. This means, in effect, that creation is *never* really "complete."[71]

How could Protestants help but feel alienated from such a God, one who has not completed His creational task, who has not finally declared the world *good,* who has not yet found a solution for the chaos, who has not been able, on the seventh day, to rest and, therefore, who cannot allow His people to rest? How can Protestants help but feel alienated from the Father if they are indeed deprived children, bereft of all security and promise, left with only the Protestant admonition—to work!

Since the 1960s, the spirit of alienation, which from the eighteenth century had been a developing theme in American religion, has become a major motif. Every event and element detrimental to confidence seemed to coalesce during this period. At the zenith of its power and influence in the world, the United States was cursed with the assassinations of a president, a probable future president, and a spiritual leader whose message of hope had once again shown the power of Protestant Christianity to move the nation toward justice and reconciliation. By mid-decade, U.S. involvement in a war taking place in a nation that most Americans had not previously heard of had escalated beyond imagination. The younger generation, the minority groups and the poor—those elements of society which were to make the human sacrifice in that war—discovered that those in positions of military, governmental and corporate power seemed to be unresponsive either to their misgivings or later to their protests. Those in authority persisted in a course that further alienated the young from the old, the poor from the rich, the uneducated from the educated and the blacks from the whites. As if this tragedy were not enough, Vietnam was followed by Watergate, a political scandal that seemed to threaten the very democratic process on which the Republic had been founded.

In addition to these dashed hopes, defeat in war and humiliation at home, certain problems had become and remained chronic sources of anxiety: the poverty and poverty-related violence of the cities, the continued pollution of the environment and, above all, the threat of nuclear annihilation. For a people brought up on an American apocalyptic vision, these circumstances had been devastating. The dream had been, simply, lost. Lost was the mistaken faith in a God who guards the destiny of the United States of America, the God who acts in history in the cause of this particular style of democratic republicanism. The wilderness Zion had been exposed as a wasteland. The rising hopes of the new Republic had become the declining expectations of those who found themselves at the end of an age. Ahlstrom cautiously summarized the mood: "Americans, whether conservative, liberal, or radical, found it increasingly difficult to believe that the United States was still a beacon and a blessing to the world."[72]

When reality challenged the false apocalyptic dream, Americans turned in another direction. As Ahlstrom has observed, "otherworldliness arose in many new forms."[73] The door had been opened for a religious search quite different from that of traditional orthodox Christianity.

CHAPTER FIVE

Protestant Gnosis: From Holy Event to Private Illumination

THE difference between orthodox *knowledge* and gnostic *knowledge* has been described as the difference between open revelation and secret revelation. Although it is true for both faiths that the Holy Spirit is at work to open the eyes of the believer that he may *know* the truth, within orthodox thought the Holy Spirit's work takes place in the presence of, and in terms of, given historical data and within the context of the Holy Catholic Church. Thus, in the Apostles' Creed, the article affirming belief in the Holy Spirit is securely nestled between belief in the person and work of Jesus Christ and a willingness to learn from the Holy Catholic Church. That which humanity can and indeed ought to know—the data that bear the truth of God—is an open book. As Deutero-Isaiah assured Israel:

> He [the LORD] did not create it [the earth] a chaos,
> he formed it to be inhabited!
> "I am the LORD, and there is no other.
> I did not speak in secret,
> in a land of darkness;
> I did not say to the offspring of Jacob,
> 'Seek me in chaos!' "[1]

Here the prophet affirms not only the good order of the Creation, but the open revelation of Yahweh.

The New Testament writers follow this prophetic tradition when, on every occasion, they witness to "this Jesus . . . you crucified and killed by the hands of lawless men."[2] When Paul, after relating his conversion experience, is accused by Festus of being insane, the Apostle immediately establishes the basis of his faith:

> I am not mad, most excellent Festus, but I am speaking the sober truth. For the king [Agrippa] knows about these things [the events surrounding the crucifixion] . . . for I am persuaded that none of these things has escaped his notice, for *this was not done in a corner.*[3]

The *openness* of the revelation was a constant theme of Irenaeus in his polemic against the Gnostics. He argued:

> As the sun, that creature of God, is one and the same throughout the whole world, so also the preaching of the truth shineth everywhere and enlightens all men that are willing to come to a knowledge of the truth.[4]

The position that both Paul and Irenaeus felt they had to reject claimed an esoteric saving knowledge, a knowledge unrelated in any vital sense either to nature or to history. Because this knowing is secret and unrelated to history or to nature, an acosmic knowing, it is precisely not the worship of the Creator, precisely not the worship of the God of Israel, precisely not the worship of the God of the Christian Church.[5]

Over the centuries, Calvin has been accused of having intellectualized, legalized and doctrinized the Gospel to the point that the salvation of Christ became a formula, something held in the head rather than in the heart. This charge represents not only a gross oversimplification, but also a diversion from the real issue. The issue, certainly in North America, is not whether the Gospel is perceived by the head or by the heart, but whether the Gospel, however perceived, is an objective cosmic reality or a subjective knowledge (emotion) of the individual soul. On this question, Calvin is not in the least ambiguous. Everything for him rests on what God has accomplished in history. As to the individual's mode of grasping the event, Calvin is indifferent. Nowhere does he indicate that an experience of conversion is necessary for salvation. The marks of salvation are the same as the marks defining the Church itself: doctrine, sacrament and discipline.[6]

Very soon after Calvinism was transplanted to New England, however, the importance of *what* is to be known was eclipsed by the importance of *knowing*. In an attempt to defend the community against the threat of Arminianism (man's achievement of faith through his own will), the Puritans placed more and more emphasis on the direct, gracious act of God in converting the individual sinner. Cotton Mather, for example, considered any sort of preparation for salvation or any concept of stages of salvation a total capitulation to popery.[7] Jonathan Edwards, following this variation of Calvinism in one of his most significant sermons (delivered in Boston in 1734) expounded the idea of "a Divine and Supernatural Light, immediately imparted to the soul by the spirit of God, shown to be both a Scriptural and rational Doctrine."[8] With Edwards and the experience of the Great Awakening, the American preoccupation was dramatically shifted from the mighty acts of God to the religious experience of the Christian person. Edwards himself noted the shift, in his revealing statement:

> God has already put his honor upon the other continent, that Christ was born there literally . . . so as providence observes a kind of equal distribution of things, 'tis not unlikely that the great *spiritual* birth of Christ, and the most glorious application of redemption is to begin in this.[9]

Edwards's insight is an ominous harbinger of what, in fact, was to come about, namely the spiritualizing of Christ.

Although others such as Charles Chauncy were to oppose Edwards, warning that he and his fellow revivalists were leading New England into the very Arminian trap their forebears had so much dreaded, the warning had little effect. By the mid-1740s, William Livingston, a prominent clerical visitor from New York, could admit to a friend in Connecticut that he could not "boast that extraordinary divine illumination so common to your Country men."[10] In the United States the new grafting on the Calvinist tree was becoming the tree itself. What began in New England would be completed throughout the American colonies by Baptists, Methodists and Pentecostalists. For when it came to the imparting of saving knowledge, these latter churches could accomplish the task quicker and better. Although the Methodist and Baptist conquest of the frontier has often been related, historians have sometimes failed to note that by the period of the westward expansion the founding Colonial churches were no longer offering a theological alternative. The moment of truth, the inner feeling and the assurance of conversion had become the distinguishing features of the Christian person. George Ripley was to call for a completely new understanding of the nature of religion: "The time has come when a revision of theology is demanded. Let the study of theology commence with the study of human consciousness."[11]

This revision, which could almost be called an *inversion* of Calvinism, had come about largely through the influence of the eighteenth-century Enlightenment. Many scholars have emphasized the influence of Locke and Grotius on what had been a strong Calvinistic position. H. Richard Niebuhr has also observed that with the "blunting of the sharp edges of the doctrine of divine sovereignty" and the emphasis on salvation in terms of the individual experience of the believer, "the victory of the bourgeoisie over Calvinism" had been completed in America.[12] The strong ties between this highly adapted puritanism and the ascending middle class have been documented by Weber, Tawney and many other sociologists of religion. It is clear that an economic scheme based on individualistic achievement benefits from a religion based on the divine calling of the individual. Conversely, a theology based on acosmic and ahistorical revelation finds support in an economic scheme that frees the individual from natural and traditional obligations. Religion and ethics have both become a matter of private enterprise.

Having noted the historical development that elevated the conversion experience to such a position of importance and having recalled the now well-demonstrated socio-economic influences on this development, we cannot help but wonder again why American Christians have made such a radical departure from traditional Protestantism. Could another answer be that American Protestantism, like ancient gnosticism, fundamentally altered the faith by its understanding of the human predicament as ignorance rather than sin? When American Calvinism interpreted original sin and total depravity in such a literalistic sense that life became utterly *determined* by the caprice of God, it followed that humanity itself was no longer culpable. Despite all its talk about man as "sinful wretch" and "worthless worm," American evangelicalism, in the final analysis, did not hold man responsible for his sin. Ricoeur sees this as the reason why, for radical Calvinism,

> salvation comes to man from elsewhere, from out there, by a pure magic of deliverance, without any connection with human responsibility or even personality . . . because evil is thing and world, myth is knowledge.[13]

The identification of ultra-Calvinism with gnosticism is also substantiated by Hans Jonas, who tells us that the ancient gnostics un-

of personal *conversion* is more typical of American theology. The Gospel allows for "sweeping change in one's perception of self and world. . . . Obstacles to perception and to response are both removed. Man can now see what is happening in his world and react appropriately."[28] Though nothing has changed, at least individuals can see the situation in a clear light. *Gnosis* is the primary concern.

A similar note is struck in a recent publication by the World Council of Churches: *The Winds of God: The Canadian Church Faces the 1980s*. The author seems to be urging his fellow Canadian Christians to understand the Gospel in a more North American way:

> History seems to be telling us that such "faith" [in a God who *intervenes*] is a cop-out. God seems to be an incorrigible gambler who has decided that the potential benefits to us are worth the risk of the gift of human freedom. There is no evidence that God ever forced himself upon the human experience. Not even in Jesus. We are free to tell even him to go away.[29]

If God were really such an incorrigible gambler that he insisted on not interfering, what were the odds of the Passover experience being realized through natural causes, or of the Israelites crossing the sea dry-shod, or of Jesus being raised from the dead? And was Jesus not precisely forced upon everyone from his mother to Pontius Pilate? Was not the Crucifixion brought about for the very reason that the Jesus problem would not go away?

The Christ as revealer only for a great number of American evangelicals and liberals is a far cry from the Pauline assurance that "our gospel came to you not only in word, but also in power and in the Holy Spirit and with full conviction."[30]

Another way to shed light on the American tendency to regard Christ as revealer only, is to observe the American fascination with *technique*. For the evangelicals, conversion is a technique, a necessary one, for salvation. The history of Israel and the life of Jesus, which indeed were often spiritualized beyond recognition, were important only insofar as they could be employed to bring sinners to repentance. The "surprising conversions," which had begun during the time of the Tennents and Jonathan Edwards, within a short while would become the typical expression of American religion. "Revivalism," Mead tells us, "in one form or another became *the accepted technique* of practically all the voluntary churches."[31]

The more conversion as technique grew in importance, the less significant became the mighty acts of God. It has often been noted that the old colonial churches, which tended to stress the integrity of the Word of God itself, were eventually to lose out on the frontier to the "methodistic" types. The chief reason for their decline was that the traditional churches simply never mastered the technique. Their biblical witness could not compete with the simple conversion device of Billy Sunday, for example: "You are going to live forever in heaven, or you are going to live forever in hell. There's no other place—just the two. It is for you to decide. It's up to you, and you must decide now."[32]

Among the various Christian sects and cults that have flourished in America as in no other land—Christian Science, Unity, New Thought, Scientology—technique has entirely replaced any genuine concern for God's activity in human affairs. Their meetings have less to do with worship than with the direct acquiring of techniques of salvation.[33]

Horace Bushnell and others following his example made a concerted, but only partially successful, attempt to lead American Protestantism away from its fascination with revivalism and saving technique back to a genuine concern for God's saving action in history. Though Bushnell was considered by the evangelicals of his generation to be the arch heretic of all times, he saw his own work as a return to orthodoxy. After a thorough reading of the Church Fathers, he evidenced great surprise, stating, "I am so much nearer to real orthodoxy than I supposed, and . . . the New England theology, so called, is so much farther off." He added, "I really had done nothing more than to revive, in a modern shape, the lost orthodoxy of the Church."[34]

In pursuit of this herculean task, Bushnell had the temerity to tell Protestants that "knowledge by direct intuition is not possible, it must always have a physical base in what is already known." All language of spiritual things "must get its power to express the unknown by drawing images and figures from the known." Thus, for Bushnell, the stories of salvation history rather than the salvation techniques of the evangelicals were essential for Christians. Kirschenmann has commented, "It was a source of constant dismay to Bushnell that while it required an incarnate life for God to communicate Himself to man, New England divines were under the illusion that they could hold the truth of God in their tiny formulas." In Bushnell's most famous work, *Christian Nurture* (1847), he offered an alternative to revivalism, a restoration of genuine biblical education in the Church, a restatement of the preeminence of God's action over man's response. The majority of Protestants, however, considered Bushnell a dangerous radical. According to Washington Gladden, a leading proponent of the Social Gospel, "Bushnellism was a name with which no ambitious minister could afford to be branded."[35]

If the evangelicals were unwilling to accept Bushnell's restoration of Christian nuture, American liberals also shunned dependence on the mighty acts of God as the source of human redemption. From Emerson and the transcendentalist school, liberalism had inherited a strong faith in the immanence of God within the individual psyche. Emerson himself had made it quite clear that he did not believe in special grace, God's presence in particular events. At best, the biblical record could provide illustrations for truths that might otherwise be grasped by intuition and the intellect. Emerson was a true son of New England in believing that illumination comes from the work of the Spirit within rather than from some exterior source.

Following their Transcendental heritage, liberals have tended to regard the Scriptures as source material for ethical technique. The typical liberal sermon would concentrate on proper attitudes and proper behavior: techniques for living the Christian life were the means of salvation. We have seen how the ancient gnostics would interpret the Old Testament only allegorically. Modern American liberalism would do the same with the New Testament. The entire Bible was, for liberals, only a rich source of those truths that we, in our hearts, already know.

During the 1920s, the journalist Walter Lippmann, although admitting that he could not subscribe to Christianity, attacked Protestant liberalism for having abandoned belief in the very essentials of the Christian faith. Speaking against these liberals, he contended, "The historic churches . . . have founded faith on clear statements about matters of fact, historic events, or physical manifestations. They have never been content with a symbolism which the believer knew was merely symbolic."[36] Though it is possible that here was another case of the "children of this world [being] in their generation wiser than the children of light,"[37] the criticism had little effect, and the "historic events" and "physical manifestations" recorded in Holy Scriptures are still often regarded in mainline Protestantism as "merely symbolic" of truths we already possess by other means.

American liberals have almost universally accepted Rudolf Bultmann's demythologizing program. As opposed to Karl Barth's insistence that the word of God is inseparable from physical event, myth or holy act, followers of Bultmann contend that truth can be extracted from the myth and the myth discarded. Such demythologizing denies that the treasure carried in earthen vessels really requires the earthen vessels. This is also, in effect, a denial that "the transcendent power belongs to God and not to us."[38]

Gnosticism's knowledge is not knowledge in the usual sense. It is, as Irenaeus called it, pseudo-knowledge, an aberration of knowledge. Nowhere is this more evident than in American *gnosis,* for the end product of that *gnosis* is the profound and relentless anti-intellectualism that has plagued and continues to plague American Protestantism and indeed American life as a whole.

Popular revivalism not only was unconcerned with intellectual and cultural developments in the contemporary world, but, according to Ahlstrom, in the church life of revivalistic religion, "intellectualism was deprecated and repressed."[39] Any serious discussion of theology or doctrinal controversy was considered potentially devisive and thereby destructive of the evangelistic aim of converting sinners. Daniel Day Williams has shown that for many of the revivalists, the ultimate standard for judging every doctrine and every practice of Christianity was thus, "Will it help or hinder the salvation of men?"[40] With such a pragmatic standard, is it any wonder that serious students of Scripture and dogma have often suffered ridicule in local churches and even in seminaries?

Bishop Warren A. Candler of the Methodist Church was almost a caricature of revivalistic anti-intellectualism. He openly discouraged his clergy from theological studies for fear that they might become modernist. Congressman Hal Kimberly, during the same period of the 1920s, urged a tight restraint on reading: "Read the Bible. It teaches you how to act. Read the hymnbook. It contains the finest poetry ever written. Read the almanac. It shows you how to figure out what the weather will be. There isn't another book that is necessary for anyone to read."[41]

Not all Americans were prepared to give up the quest for a genuine knowledge. Emily Dickinson, from the sidelines of American Protestantism, had satirized its anti-intellectual spirit with her short verse:

"Faith" is a fine invention
When gentlemen can *see*—
But *Microscopes* are prudent
In an Emergency.[42]

There were also those within and without the evangelical tradition who followed the lead of Bushnell in accepting honest enquiry and biblical instruction as necessities of the Christian faith.

It is wrong to suppose that an American *gnosis* has flourished only among the revivalists, the more vocal advocates of "know nothing." From the development of transcendentalism and, later, modernism, to the present liberal ascendency in the Protestant Church, anti-intellectualism has been a powerful negative force. The reason is simple: if God is immanent, present within our psyche, if we already *have* the truth within, then why go through all the hassle of studying theology? If every well-meaning, right-living person has God at hand, apart from reports about holy events or miraculous happenings, then why burden children with details about the kings of Israel and Judah and the journeys of the Apostle Paul?

Religious sociologists have noted that since the various traumas of the 1960s, many cults have sprung up that claim special *gnosis* within their own membership. But along with this increasing anti-intellectualism on the fringes of the faith, there is within Protestantism itself a similar anti-intellectualism and at certain points a convergence of evangelicalism and liberalism in espousing a special religious knowing as opposed to a knowledge of discernable data.[43] Charles Glock and Robert Bellah make this cautious observation:

> Immediate experience rather than doctrinal belief continues to be central along all the religious movements, including the Jesus movements, and in the human-potential movement as well. *Knowledge* in the sense of direct first-hand encounter has so much higher standing than abstract argument based on logic that one could almost speak of anti-intellectualism in many groups.[44]

Americans in the two opposing strains of Protestantism, the evangelical and liberal, along with many adherents of Pentecostal and holiness cults, would agree that religious knowledge is special knowledge that cannot be taught or learned by ordinary means. This popular and widespread attitude cannot help but threaten a Christian orthodoxy which depends on the mighty acts of God. If it is because they "are surrounded by so great a cloud of witnesses" that Christians are able to "lay aside every weight and sin,"[45] what are they to do when the witnesses have been forgotten and only a cloud of knowing remains?

Christian orthodoxy, of course, does not overlook the power of the Holy Spirit in opening the minds and hearts of Christians to the truth of the Gospel, but, as Samuel Terrien observes of St. Paul's works on Christian growth (II Cor. 3:18): "Paul does not refer to an ecstatic vision or to an esoteric *gnosis*. Rather, he is concerned with the growth of a new being. He has in mind the constancy of the inner progress which, little by little, conforms the Christian to the *imago Dei*."[46]

The question of what constitutes genuine knowledge is a vital one for Church and society. Is what we have to know secret or open, based on immanent presence or on historical event, immediately discerned or painstakingly acquired by study and effort?

The foes of genuine Protestantism have been, to use Matthew Arnold's term, the philistines, middle-class Christians who have refused to take authentic knowledge seriously because they are certain they already know or else already feel whatever must be known or felt to accomplish their goal. What they, in fact, know or feel is very akin to what Irenaeus called *pseudo-gnosis,* a knowledge that appears to be what it is not at all. It is a kind of knowledge that involves escape from reality.

CHAPTER SIX

Modern Escape—from the Home of the Brave?

THERE are two instinctive human reactions in the face of danger: one is to fight; the other is to flee. At times, the only sensible solution seems to be escape from whatever threatens the life or well-being of the person.

When the world is seen as shrouded in dense fog and darkness, when evil is perceived to be the overwhelming force within the world (Calvin wrote that the "Manichees . . . made the devil almost the equal of God"[1]), when there is no hope for unalloyed earthly joy and love (and the gnostics were interested in no other kind), then obviously the desire to flee is very strong indeed.

Whatever can be said of the original Calvinism—and nearly everything derogatory has been said—in no way could it be accused of being escapist. Calvin's was no "pie in the sky by and by" faith. Alongside the ethic of St. Thomas, normative for the Roman Catholic Church, the Genevan ethic was proposed as a universal system, which like its counterpart would enable "the Christian to be active in the world with a good conscience and without a break between the Christian-ethical and the worldly ideals."[2]

For Calvin, the choice between flight and fight was clear:

> Anyone with eyes may perceive that it is not one flood of evils which has deluged us; that many fatal plagues have invaded the

> globe; that all things rush headlong; so that either the affairs of men must be altogether despaired of, or we must not only resist, but boldly attack prevailing evils.[3]

The bold attack, however, could not be sustained for very long, certainly not within North America. By 1730, according to Perry Miller, New England was "a parched land, crying for deliverance from the hold of ideas that had served their purpose and died."[4] The universal program of serving a sovereign God with His immutable plan and opposing evil on all fronts, regardless of the immediate outcome, had lost its appeal. Jonathan Edwards was beginning to speak of the great desire to "be as it were swallowed up in him [Christ] forever."[5] His wife, Sarah, seems to have achieved this goal for herself:

> My soul seemed to be gone out of me to God and Christ in heaven, and to have very little relation to my body. God and Christ were so present to me, and so near me, that I seemed removed from myself . . . the glory of God seemed to be all, and in all, and to *swallow up* every wish and desire of the heart.[6]

Surrendering, being swallowed up, melted, annihilated were images that increasingly expressed the deepest feelings of the American soul. Even Emily Dickinson, despite her immense personal courage, was to confess:

> I never hear the word "escape"
> Without a quicker blood.[7]

If the individual understands himself or herself to be a helpless captive within a hostile prison, what other course could there be but escape? Dickinson, however, would refuse the escape route which was mapped by the New England theology and which remains today the prevailing way of one strong segment of American Protestantism.

That route, the means of escape, became exclusively, for the evangelicals, the way of being born again. The concept of total rebirth, of the drowning of the old person and the rebirth of the new, had also held an immense appeal for the ancient gnostics. In the *Corpus Hermetica,* a non-Christian gnostic work, the spiritual teacher Hermes advises the young man to shun the temporal for the eternal, the "dissoluble" for the "indissoluble;" finally the teacher is able to say to his disciple, "now, my son, you know what the rebirth is."[8] Similarly, Jesus' words to Nicodemus recorded by St. John ("Except a man be born again, he cannot see the kingdom of God."[9]) became the key to the understanding of all faith and order. This one soteriological image, which is rarely used in Holy Scripture, became for many North Americans the theme of every sermon, the supreme test of orthodoxy, and in these latter days a label for the authentic Christian.

The typical sermon in American revivalism described the horrors of the world, humanity's alienation from God, the thrust of God's anger (hell fire) and then, the method of escape, "you must be *born again*."[10] The purpose of preaching was thought to be nothing other than soul-saving, persuading the hearers to *receive* the Lord, to be born again before it became too late.[11] If in ancient times, Plotinus had complained that the gnostics "say only, 'Look to God,' but they do not tell anyone where or how to look,"[12] much the same thing could be said of American revivalism. It was a call, almost totally lacking in content, to accept Christ, to surrender, to be saved. The same lack of content even today (from the evidence of radio and television) characterizes much of what might seem to be the predominant Christianity of modern America.

For the ancient gnostics, the desire to escape might have indicated a failure of nerve. A. D. Nock saw it as meeting a deep spiritual need, "a demand for something clear and dogmatic which explained the universe, and for an assured hope of immortality."[13] Escape always implies an escape *from* something. What are the realities from which American Christians have wished to be freed? When one, in revivalistic terms, comes to Jesus, what are the evils she or he hopes to leave behind?

Escape from Nature

Even Basilides, who was said to have been less radical than the other gnostics, displayed a profound distrust of nature, the created world. "Spiritual man," he wrote, "is abandoned like an abortion in the formlessness [of our sublunar world]."[14] For the gnostic Christians, the material world itself was part and parcel of the human tragedy. The cross became for them not a sign of triumph but of what Henry Chadwick has called "a negative evaluation of the created order." *Gnosis* understands St. Paul's words, "the cosmos has been crucified to me, and I to the cosmos," as nothing less than a condemnation of the entire created order.[15]

This spirit is the very opposite of biblical faith, which even from its beginnings in the cultic religion of Israel has understood humanity as having the closest connection with the natural world. Before the sacrifice was offered to Yahweh, the priest was required to place his hand on the head of the animal, thus identifying Israel with all other creatures.[16] Not only does Israel know that "you are dust,/ and to dust you shall return," but also that it is Yahweh's remembering "that we are dust" which evokes his fatherly pity for his children of dust.[17]

The later Puritan mind was not wholly satisfied with this close connection between natural world and spiritual humanity. Even their own children reminded evangelicals of the "indecent" bond between humanity and nature. Children were not received in the Puritan home as blessings from heaven. Rather, they were little savages whose natural wills had to be broken. John Wesley, whose advice on all subjects would be taken very seriously by American evangelicals, had observed, "Next to self-will and pride, the most fatal disease with which we are born is love of the world." The Father of Methodism went on to warn parents against indulging "the pleasure of tasting in their children" because pleasure in eating leads to lust and unlicensed sensuality of all descriptions. "Break their will," he admonished parents, "that you may save their souls."[18]

Jonathan Edwards had an even more frightening view of the natural child: "As innocent as children seem to be to us, yet if they are out of Christ, they are not so in God's sight, but are young vipers, and are infinitely more hateful than vipers."[19]

Some scholars have noted a similar attitude among North American evangelicals toward aboriginal people and blacks. Obviously, there have been strong economic motives behind the harsh treatment of native people and blacks. However, is it not possible that when a Pennsylvania judge, Hugh Henry Brackenridge, called for the "extermination" of "the animals vulgarly called Indians,"[20] he was voicing the embarrassment and fear felt by many Protestant Christians in the presence of human beings who were obviously close to nature? How could they regard the Indians as fellow humans without recognizing their own forgotten, repressed ties with the creaturely?[21] And could a parallel attitude toward blacks have developed for the same reasons? As Martin Marty has observed, because blacks were culturally untutored from a Protestant point of view, they called attention to a creation-human continuum that could only be upsetting and that had to be rationalized in one way or another.[22]

The evangelical view of children, native people and blacks serves to illustrate an understanding of the natural world as evil in and of itself. Apart from the order imposed by those who have been born again, there is only chaos. Any association with persons who, for any reason, are existing outside this fabricated order is threatening, unacceptable and calls for a solution. With some evangelicals, it amounted to "a paranoid vision of the outer world."[23]

This fear of the outer world has often led to a concentration on faith healing. Just as faith healing held an important place among the medieval gnostics of southern France,[24] it has also been a significant element in the more extreme sects of Protestantism. Since the advent of television, miraculous healing has become so closely associated with popular religion in America that its practice must be seen as a major characteristic of this religious type. The purpose of such healing is obvious: it is to prove that although nature is evil—crippling, blinding, deafening, deforming, killing—supernature is healing, restorative and saving. The Savior God is pitted against the natural (God), and before millions of television viewers the Savior God prevails.

The most radical form of anti-natural feeling is found among those few and scattered Fundamentalist sects in which the faithful handle poisonous snakes and drink "salvation cocktails" (thimbles full of strychnine). What is involved in these self-imposed encounters with death is a gamble for salvation; physical life is staked on the ability of the Savior God to triumph over nature, nature in its most terrifying and insidious forms.[25]

While the poor and ignorant act out in a literal fashion words from Mark's Gospel ("They will pick up serpents, and if they drink any deadly thing, it will not hurt them."[26]), more respectable Christians restrict themselves to less serious risks by acting out the biblical practice of speaking in tongues.[27] A similar concept is involved: the breaking of natural language barriers, the refusal to be bound by the linguistic rules of an earthly community.

The challenge to evangelicalism from the theological left has often been seen as a reaffirmation of nature, a new appreciation of natural beauty. Although nature was indeed celebrated by Emerson, the other Transcendentalists and the liberals who followed, it was in most cases a nature firmly in the hands of what Harold Bloom calls "the Central Man." Emerson's nature is a nature created by human imagination.

> Man is a dwarf of himself. Once he was permeated and dissolved by spirit. He filled nature with his overflowing currents. Out from him sprang the sun and the moon; from man the sun, from woman the moon. The laws of his mind, the periods of his actions externalized themselves into day and night, into the year and the seasons.[28]

For Emerson, the task of humanity, particularly of the poet, is to recover that sense of preeminence that properly belongs to humankind. Nature is beautiful so long as we can be free from it, so long as we know who is in charge here.

Unlike Emerson, Thoreau would not attempt to control or manage nature but would rather accept it as he found it:

> I wanted to live deep and suck out all the marrow of life . . . and if it proved to be mean, why then to get the whole and genuine meanness of it, and publish its meanness to the world; or if it were sublime, to know it by experience, and be able to give a true account of it in my next excursion.[29]

In Parrington's opinion, Thoreau "was at heart a Greek, with the delight in the simple round of the seasons and a responsiveness to natural beauty that belonged to the older civilization. Brought up under the 'pale negations' of Dr. Ripley's theology, he emerged a pagan."[30]

The pity is that this paganism had so little lasting influence on America's predominantly negative view of nature; the Emersonian desire to control or overcome nature still persists. In "Corson's Inlet," by A. R. Ammons, published in 1962, the writer states his poetic intention:

> I allow myself eddies of meaning:
> yield to a direction of significance
> . . . .
> there are dunes of motion,
> organizations of grass, white sandy paths of remembrance
> in the overall wandering of mirroring mind.[31]

It becomes Ammons's task, following the Emersonian tradition, to squeeze meaning out of nature, to bring nature under the control of mind. Harold Bloom, however, notes a significant difference of degree. In regard to "Corson's Inlet," Bloom comments: "I remember, each time I read it, that Ammons is a Southerner, heir to a darker Protestantism than was the immediate heritage of the New England visionaries or of Whitman. . . . [T]o a North Carolinian one hundred years after, Transcendentalism comes hard and emerges bitterly."[32]

In some later verses, Ammons seems to have reached the end of his search for meaning within nature:

> I do not speak to the wind now:
> for having been brought this far by nature I have been
> brought out of nature

and nothing here shows me the image of myself:
. . . .
. . . I touched the rocks, their interesting crusts:
I flaked the bark of stunt-fir:
I looked into space and into the sun
and nothing answered my word *longing:*
goodbye, I said, goodbye nature so grand and
reticent, your tongues are healed up into
their own
element
and as you have shut up you have shut me out: I am
as foreign here as if I had landed, a visitor:
so I went back down and gathered mud
and with my hands made an image for *longing:*
. . . .
. . . I returned to the city and built a house to set
the image in
and men came into my house and said
that is an image for *longing*
and nothing will ever be the same again.[33]

Here we have a description of man's alienation from nature and nature's refusal to provide any images for the unfulfilled visions of humanity. And we are confronted with our own escape from nature through the fabrication of meaning. Because an expression of *longing* is not present in the given, then *longing* must be fashioned by human hands. In desperation there can be only an imposed solution. In essence, the poet has shown us the American gnostic's escape from nature.

A similar escape has been effected within the thought and practice of much Protestant liberalism. What in Norman Vincent Peale in the 1950s had been condemned by thoughtful Protestants as an embarrassing misunderstanding of the Gospel, by the early 1970s had become accepted practice in thousands of liberal Protestant churches throughout North America. The human potential movement with group therapy sessions, massage workshops and marriage-encounter groups became and has continued to be a major part of the Protestant ministry to its own constituency as well as to the middle-class population as a whole. Like its precursor, the positive-thinking school of Peale, and, for that matter, the Christian Science of Mary Baker Eddy, the human potential movement involves an attempt to escape the power of chaotic nature through the development of psychological techniques. Nature cannot be broken or bent, but humanity can impose meaning on it by adjusting to its demands. It is a technique of mind over matter, an attempt to escape the uncontrollable aspects of existence through total control over one's reactions to the uncontrollable. Thus, unresolved psychological conflicts might be handled by the primal scream; sexual inhibitions, through nude-encounter groups; marital difficulties, through learning "the art of loving."[34]

In all of this there would appear to be very little interest in the natural condition of the human race. Perhaps because these programs are packaged for a white middle-class clientele, it can be assumed that the great majority of participants will not be suffering from malnutrition, racial injustice, unfair treatment in the courts or other genuine social maladies. For whatever reason, it is assumed that no natural event is so traumatic or problematical that it cannot be handled by technique. Even death itself, formerly considered to be totally unmanageable apart from the mercy of God, also now can be approached by means of technique. As marriage problems are conquered by the art of loving, death is overcome by the art of dying. When the proper steps are taken, even this last violent assault of nature can be typified and controlled.[35]

Nature as created world is also thought of as being entirely under human control. Certain American ecological movements give the impression that, failing the careful management of all fauna and flora by concerned study groups, all organisms are immediately doomed. Sensible efforts to bring a halt to corporate assaults on the environment, as in the case of acid rain, lose credibility because of the insistence of some ecological groups that all of nature must be brought under total control.

Escape from Time, History and Politics

Many students of ancient gnosticism have called attention to the gnostic revolt against time. Nothing is more frightening to the gnostic personality than the idea that this present world of decay, change, deficiency and death might have continuing significance. The gnostic hope is not that the clock will keep ticking, but that it will be mercifully stopped. Put another way, time and tide are yet other signs, incontrovertible signs, that life is beyond our control. That, for the gnostic, is an unacceptable aspect of life that must be escaped at any cost.

In a fascinating essay, Harold Bloom writes:

> Hating time, Gnosticism insists upon evading time rather than fulfilling time. . . . Evasion is in flight from or represses fate, and again, whether erotic, religious, or literary, the principle of evasion denies that existence is an historical existence.[36]

Ralph Waldo Emerson clearly states his own prophetic calling: "I am to invite men drenched in Time to recover themselves and come out of time, and taste their native immortal air."[37] Valentinus or Basilides could not have expressed the gnostic view of time any better.

An escape from time, of course, requires the rejection of history as a matter of serious concern in the present. In the *Gospel of Thomas,* Jesus is offended by the disciples' use of the prophets to substantiate his teachings. "His disciples said to him, 'Twenty-four prophets spoke in Israel, and all of them spoke in you.' He [Jesus] said to them: 'You have ignored the one living in your presence, and have spoken (only) of the dead.' "[38] It is unthinkable in biblical terms for the prophets of Israel to be spoken of as *dead;* they continue to be a living reality.

The Enlightenment spirit, as exemplified in the American revolutionary spirit, also held a disdain for history. "As to tradition," wrote Thomas Jefferson, "if we are Protestants we reject all tradition and rely on the scripture alone, for that is the essence and common principle of all the protestant churches."[39] Jefferson's confident oversimplification of Protestantism is typical of what the church historian Kenneth Scott Latourette has called the marked tendency of American Protestantism "to ignore the development which had taken place in Christianity in the Old World after the first century." Jefferson's statement also shows the extent to which, even among genteel Virginians, the left wing, the extreme anti-historical party of the Reformation, had won the field.[40]

Emerson was much more consistent in his rejection of history than was Jefferson. We have noted Emerson's challenge to time; in regard to history, he acknowledges:

> As far back as I can see the widening procession of humanity, the marchers are lame and blind and deaf; but to the soul that whole past is but one finite series in its infinite scope. Deteriorating ever and now desperate. Let me begin anew; let me teach the finite to know its master.[41]

Such a rejection of time and history has always had serious consequences in terms of politics, for attitudes toward time and history are worked out in the realm of political decisions. One of the central issues that divided gnostics and orthodox Christians in the early

Church was their understanding of the relationship between religion and politics. The Church Fathers accepted the political worldliness of the Jewish faith, contending that religion and politics are interconnected and inseparable.[42] The early Puritans and even Jonathan Edwards, following classical Calvinism, would have been clearly orthodox in this regard. The world of politics, of human institutions, was for them an essential locus of God's redemptive work.[43]

By Emerson's time, however, as a result of his rejection of history, the great transcendentalist could write, "Until men become wise enough voluntarily to cooperate to the common well-being, no good government is possible." Like many American religionists who were to follow, he was saying that political change can come about only through change in the hearts of individuals. In discussing his own unwillingness to involve himself deeply in the slavery issue, he explained, "I have quite other slaves to free than those negroes, to wit, imprisoned spirits, imprisoned thoughts, far back in the brain of man,—far retired in the heaven of invention . . . [they] have no other watchman, or lover, or defender, but I."[44]

Again, ironically, it was the anti-Church voice of Henry David Thoreau that cried out against any separation of Christianity and politics. Thoreau chided the faithful for not paying attention to their own Bibles: "I know of no book that has so few readers . . . to Christians no less than Greeks and Jews, it is foolishness and a stumbling-block." He recalls some of the hard teachings of Jesus such as the fate of the greedy farmer and then cries, "Think of this, Yankees! . . . Let but one of these sentences be rightly read from any pulpit in the land, and there would not be left one stone of that meeting house upon another." Thoreau went on to attack "the leisure of a slave driver, got by imprisoning his fellows in a treadmill." Of the factory system, he observed, "The principal object is not that mankind may be well and honestly clad, but, unquestionably, that the corporations may be enriched."[45] It is little wonder that the constables and bailiffs beat a path to his remote door and that Christians looked upon his exegesis with such disdain. For Thoreau was certainly guilty of sedition within a society trying to separate piety and politics. He was acting as an effective double agent for the God who will not be excluded from human affairs.

Within the orthodox Church, there were many examples of those who did support Christian involvement in politics. Horace Bushnell, the Beechers, and others would call for the Church to condemn slavery, for instance. But following the horrors of the Civil War and the realization that so little by way of justice seemed to have been realized by that awful experience, the cleavage between religion and political action had widened. Among the pious, the idea gained strength that little could be done to improve the world, that all efforts must be concentrated on the saving of individual souls.[46]

The American separation between society and the individual is often associated with Fundamentalism. Before we look at that phenomenon, however, we should be aware that long before evangelicalism had taken the turn away from societal involvement, liberalism had moved quietly in a similar direction. From the beginning, New England Unitarians did not expect their religion to interfere "seriously with the practical business of getting on in the world."[47]

As Max Weber has so brilliantly shown, there was a tight connection between the rise of capitalism and the Christian attempt to validate and thereby protect the system from ecclesiastical interference. In a letter to a friend, Weber called the second part of his masterpiece, *The Protestant Ethic,* "Protestant ascetism as the foundation of modern vocational civilization—a sort of 'spiritualist' construction of the modern economy." Later, Weber would say that "money is the most abstract and impersonal element that exists in human life."[48] Christians did not see in their support of capitalism any conflict between spiritual and earthly concerns, because a spiritualized economics could exist alongside a spiritualized Christianity without mixture or confusion between the heavenly and the earthly. Capitalism was an independent spiritual reality which could not interfere with a spirituality concerned only with soul conversion. The only possible threat to capitalism could arise from a religion firmly rooted in time and history. On the other hand, the only possible threat to a spiritualized Christianity could arise from an economic system based entirely on materialistic presuppositions.

Fernand Braudel has shown that the spiritualization of economics is a rather recent development. "Until the eighteenth century," according to his analysis "these two types of activity—the *market economy* and *capitalism*—affected only a minority and the mass of mankind remained encapsulated within the vast domain of *material life.*" With the Enlightenment, however, Braudel goes on to say:

> People believed, rightly or wrongly, that exchanges [commodity markets] play a decisive role as a balancing force, that through com-

> petition they smooth out uneven spots and adjust supply and demand, and that the market is a hidden and benevolent God, Adam Smith's "invisible hand," the self-regulating market of the nineteenth century and the keystone of the economy, as long as one sticks to *laissez faire, laissez passer*.[49]

If this is an accurate picture of the spiritualization of economics, it suggests that behind the Calvinistic-Puritan creation of, or complicity in, the origin of capitalism lies not only capitalism's need for ascetic Protestantism, but ascetic Protestantism's need for capitalism. Capitalism offered to a spiritualized, soul-saving faith a satisfactory explanation for the spiritual control of the material world. Of course, a gnostic God could not participate at all in such mundane affairs, but the "invisible hand" of capitalism freed the spiritualized Church of its worldly responsibilities and allowed it to concentrate entirely on the extramundane.

The alliance with capitalism has also allowed American Protestantism to move in a decidedly anti-institutional direction. Hospitals, schools, universities and libraries which had formerly been considered a Protestant responsibility, now, under a separate dispensation, no longer need concern the Christian conscience. With the assurance that wholly other powers are at work in those material areas, religion itself can remain "innocent of power and politics."[50]

Even Horace Bushnell, who in many respects wanted to keep Christianity in touch with the world, strongly urged the merchant to "do his trade by the strict law principles of trade, and never let his operations be mixed up with charities." Merchants were to reserve their charities, "all their sympathies, allowances, mitigations, merciful accommodations—for a separate chapter of life."[51] Bushnell's thinking was so typical of the time that historian Henry M. May could write of America's centennial year: "In 1876 Protestantism presented a massive, almost unbroken front in its defense of the social status quo." Martin Marty, supporting May's judgments, feels that the religious defense of the social arrangement was partly due to the frightening changes occurring at that time. Most frightening of all was the realization that the Western frontier had been settled; the wilderness and prairies no longer held out their promises; America had become in many respects merely another nation.[52] The last remnants of the apocalyptic dream were fast fading away. Under such conditions, at least the economy would remain under the control of "the invisible hand."

A non-escapist counter-opinion was to be offered by the Social Gospel movement. The quarter century prior to World War I brought forward men, like Washington Gladden, George Herron and Walter Rauschenbusch, who refused to observe the no-entrance sign on the doors of economic and social life. The social gospellers were appalled by the alienation and hopelessness sustained by capitalism. According to Rauschenbusch, capitalistic philosophy inculcated "a spirit of hardness and cruelty that neutralizes the Christian spirit of love."[53] The "invisible hand," far from guarding the people from harm, was snatching from the weak what was left of their joy and hope.

Despite the passionate advocacy of Rauschenbusch and his confrères, the social gospel remained a minority opinion within American Protestantism. Those who wished through their religion to escape the intricacies of history and politics and who were willing to leave mundane affairs in the hands of quite a different spirit from that of Christ still dominated the scene in North America.

Henry Steele Commager pondered the strange contradiction between American progressivism in the fields of science and technology and American Fundamentalism in the field of religion.

> Perhaps it was because religion meant, on the whole, so little; because, divorced as it was from the intimate realities of daily life and excused from active participation in the affairs of business, politics, or society, it could be regarded as a thing apart, not subject to the normal tests prescribed for secular faiths and doctrines. Fundamentalists resented a critical attitude toward their religion as they resented a critical attitude toward their mothers.[54]

Commager has discovered here the same phenomenon that A. D. Nock pointed out in the mystery religions, namely, a religion that could be practiced "on the side." Because the new American evangelicalism had no real interest in this world, and was, in fact, dedicated to escaping it, ordinary business life and political life could be carried on as if the Gospel did not exist.

That the function of religion was precisely that of escape could not have been better expressed than is was by one of the great heroes of the evangelicals. Dwight L. Moody, in a sermon, was to tell his audiences, "I look upon this world as a wrecked vessel. God has given me a lifeboat and said to me, 'Moody, save all you can.' "[55] It must be said that at this stage of American Christianity, a purely escapist, history-denying faith had triumphed at least in the Fundamentalist camp. For, with Moody and the lesser known evangelists of the day, salvation meant nothing other than salvation from the cosmos with all the promises and warnings of Christ to be realized in the next world, in the life to come.

This form of preaching, and the faith that it nourished, again jibed with the needs of a capitalist establishment. It was not by accident that the Fundamentalist movement, which began in 1909, was first financed by two California oil millionaires or that the political right wing continually poured money into the campaigns of Dwight Moody, Billy Graham and Jerry Falwell. As Martin Marty has shown, until very recent times, among the mass of the American people, "the preaching of otherworldliness alone remained a constant."[56] The alliance was firm: the spirituality of the eternal would be left to the religionists; the spirituality of the temporal would be left to the capitalists.

Among the evangelicals there are notable exceptions. The black church, though usually clinging to an otherworldly theology, has provided overall a clear witness to the transforming power of Christ in politics and human affairs. Martin Luther King, Jr. had been influenced at least as much by the Social Gospel movement as by evangelicalism. The fact that black evangelicalism was willing to be led by such a person is a sign that *political* escapism had not been a matter of conviction among blacks, as it was for their white counterparts, but rather a matter of historical necessity.

The Sojourners movement also represents a move away from traditional evangelical escapism. Influenced by a more or less literalistic interpretation of the New Testament, these evangelicals have seen the need for political involvement and have become passionately linked with the Latin American liberation theologians. Sojourners seems to be an authentic effort to state the Gospel in relation to political concerns, a more effective attempt than any being made from the theological left.

The politics of the Protestant left has, since the 1930s, been dominated by the Christian realism of Reinhold Niebuhr. Niebuhr, in many ways an heir to the Social Gospel thinking of an earlier generation, held that indeed Christians do have an obligation to be involved in the political arena. "The hope of a shepherd king," he wrote, "distinguishes Messianism as sharply from non-historical religions as from false interpretations of history . . . the fulfillment of life is sought in history and not in eternity."[57]

Niebuhr rejected the evangelical discontinuity between the salvation of souls and justice in the world: "We cannot build our individual ladders to heaven and leave the total human enterprise unredeemed of its excesses and corruptions." Yet, in Niebuhrian thought, a sharp division is still maintained between "moral man and immoral society." Whereas individual life can be lived in terms of the grace of Christ, political life will have to involve other considerations:

> The *history* of human life will always be the projection of the world of nature. To the end of history the peace of the world . . . [will not] be a perfect peace. But it can be more perfect than it is. If the mind and the spirit of man does not attempt the impossible, if it does not seek to conquer or to eliminate nature but tries only to make the forces of nature the servants of the human spirit and the instruments of the moral ideal, a progressively higher justice and more stable peace can be achieved.[58]

Obviously, the political world has to do with nature and, as far as Christian realism is concerned, will be affected only tangentially by the power of grace. Though with Niebuhr religion had moved with a vengeance into a mundane, the influence of an evangelical separation of spirit and matter was still evident.

However, the Niebuhrian position on political involvement—like the position of the earlier Social Gospel movement—has now become a minority opinion within American Christianity. Following the Vietnam War, the Watergate scandal and subsequent events, churches in the liberal camp have tended to turn toward personal growth and development. Neither the high idealism engendered by Dr. King's civil rights movement nor the tough ethics of Christian realism could sustain Christian people in this new age of cynicism. For a period, at least, it seemed that the evangelicals were moving closer to liberalism in their concern for the individual self-improvement of their constituents. And the liberal churches were asking themselves if the evangelical emphasis on another world might not after all have something to offer. Could it be that the Jesus people were right, that "after Jesus, everything else is just toothpaste"?[59]

Escape from the Body, Sex and Family

Irenaeus, commenting on the Incarnation, states that Christ

> did not despise or evade any condition of humanity, . . . but sanctified every age . . . He therefore passes through every age, becoming an infant for infants, thus sanctifying infants, a child for children, thus sanctifying those who are at this age . . . a youth for

> youths . . . and . . . because he was an old man for old people . . . sanctifying at the same time the aged also . . . then, at last, he came onto death itself.[60]

Elaine Pagels is quite accurate in arguing that "orthodox tradition implicitly affirms bodily experience as the central fact of human life. What one does physically—one eats and drinks, engages in sexual life or avoids it, saves one's life or gives it up—all are vital elements in one's *religious* development."[61] A Pauline passage often quoted by overly spiritualized Christians as a call to otherworldliness, in fact, concludes with the remarkable words, "You were bought with a price. So glorify God in your body [*soma*]."[62]

Gnostics of all eras have, on the other hand, maintained a most profound mistrust of the body, regarding it as the enemy *without* that constantly tries to undo the best efforts of the soul *within*. They regarded physical life as either an illusion or a distraction from higher purposes.[63] Their disdain for the physical led them to a docetic, disembodied view of Christ. In the *Acts of John,* one of the Nag Hammadi tractates, Jesus is seen on the shore by James and John first as a child, again as an older bald-headed man, and yet again as a young man "whose beard was just beginning." John further reports:

> I will tell you another glory, brethren; sometimes when I meant to touch him I encountered a material, solid body; but at other times again when I felt him, his substance was immaterial and incorporeal . . . as if it did not exist at all.

This gnostic John goes on to say that he looked carefully for footprints, but Jesus left none behind, nor was he ever observed to blink his eyes.[64] A docetic Christology has been developed out of a gnostic anthropology that will not have any part of the sanctification of flesh.

The Puritan divines were, of course, aware of the dangers of docetism and would not have been in the least attracted to the gnostic gospels. They seemed not to be aware, however, of how close they came to accepting a purely gnostic anthropology. "At the very core of evangelical experience," Greven declares, "the foundation on which piety was based, there existed a profound alienation of individuals from their own bodies and an intense hostility toward their own innermost natures."[65]

Runciman states in connection with the medieval Cathari: "There is one characteristic quality in any Dualist church. Man, to escape from the vileness of his body, must seek to make himself spirit as far as may be."[66] New England theology would certainly fit this dualist description. In 1723, Jonathan Edwards determined "to live in continual mortification, without ceasing, and even to weary myself thereby, as long as I am in this world, and never to expect or desire any worldly ease or pleasure."[67] And Edwards continued his mortification throughout his life.

After hearing a sermon by the Reverend Gilbert Tennant in 1741, Susanna Anthony was overwhelmingly convicted of her own total depravity: "I was ready to wish I never had been." As her sense of worthlessness grew, "the necessaries of life grew tasteless" and "though I took only enough to preserve life, yet every mouthful seemed to seal up my condemnation . . . my design was to mortify myself."[68]

The body for the evangelical was indeed a prison from which release was possible only through rebirth, the experience of conversion. New England theology did not approve of preparation for conversion, as being born again was wholly a matter of grace, but it was the duty of a Christian home to instruct children concerning their spiritual imprisonment. The wife of Thomas Hincksman "was first convinced of her estate by nature by means of her godly parent oft instructing of her and telling her what her condition by nature was and how to get out of the same."[69]

The imprisonment within the body was felt acutely in connection with the elimination of bodily waste. Greven observes that "urination and defecation were daily reminders of the inner corruption of human nature." Cotton Mather gives this account of his experience:

> I was once emptying the *Cistern of Nature,* and making *Water* at the Wall. At the same Time, there came a Dog, who did so too, before me. Thought I; "What mean and vile Things are the Children of Men, in this mortal State! How much do our natural Necessities abase us and place us in some regard, on the Level with the very Dogs!" . . . Accordingly, I resolved, that it should be my ordinary Practice, whenever I step to answer the one or other Necessity of Nature, to make it an Opportunity of shaping in my Mind, some holy, noble, divine Thought.[70]

Mather's resolution is, indeed, an extreme example of mind over matter. It is obvious that one of the leading fathers of American Protestantism rather than confessing his sinfulness is actually lamenting his humanity.

Jonathan Edwards is at least as explicit when he notes that "The inside of the body of man is full of filthiness, contains his bowels that are full of dung, which represents the corruption and filthiness that the heart of man is naturally full of."[71] Again, the human "machine" itself is a matter of shame and a persistent sign that our deficiency in large part stems from the fact that our spirit is embodied.

The history of American revivalism has often featured vigorous attacks against the flesh, flesh interpreted as body. Dancing, theater, the plastic arts were all forbidden or discouraged because they were correctly perceived as making a connection between the human spirit and the human body. This connection American evangelicalism was increasingly reluctant to admit.

Within Protestant liberalism, a revolt was mounted against this body-spirit duality. George Angier Gordon, for example, insisted that humanity's so-called animal nature could not be held culpable for what has gone wrong with humankind. Human reason and expecially "the idealizing faculty ha[ve] been to a painful extent the organ[s] of human selfishness."[72]

Among liberals too, however, a cleft view of man has been prominent and pervasive. The reluctance of liberals, for instance, to affirm the orthodox doctrine of a bodily resurrection and their preference for the more Platonic idea of survival of soul or spirit, is evidence of a strong sense of discontinuity between human body and human spirit. As Jürgen Moltmann has argued, the orthodox view expresses in symbolic language the inseparability of human life from bodily experience.[73] This inseparability, an essentially Hebraic, biblical understanding of life, has been and continues to be against the stream of American Protestant thought.

The novelist Walker Percy deals with the continuing problem of the sharp distinction between body and spirit in *Love in the Ruins*. His scientifically minded protagonist, Dr. Thomas More (!), has invented a new machine capable of restoring man's unity. More exults:

> Tomorrow-today I meet with the Director and hear the triumphant news about my lapsometer, the first caliper of the soul and the first hope of bridging the dread chasm that has rent the soul of Western man ever since the famous philosopher Descartes ripped body loose from mind and turned the very soul into a ghost that haunts its own house.

Even after the initial failure of his machine, the mad doctor is still hopeful: "Some day a man will walk into my office as ghost or beast or ghost-beast and walk out as a man, which is to say sovereign wanderer, lordly exile, worker and waiter and watcher."[74] In effect,

Percy longs for the day when the American man who walks in as a gnostic can walk out as a Christian.

The critical point in the division between body and spirit has been in the area of sexuality. For the ancient gnostic, sex represented everything fascinating and repelling about the human condition. Whether strictly forbidding sexual practice or in some rare instances encouraging sexual license as a kind of ritualistic catharsis of sexual drive, the gnostics consistently refused to accept sexuality as normal.

The precursors of New England puritanism, the European Calvinists, according to Troeltsch, held a similar view of sex. The Calvinists, writes Troeltsch, demand

> the excision of all those erotic and emotional elements which Catholicism and Lutheranism had always believed they ought to tolerate as the sensuality resulting from Original Sin. The sex life of marriage was to them *medicina libidinis*. Here, however, [in what Troeltsch calls "ascetic Protestantism"] . . . the life of sex is not to be used for enjoyment, but for the deliberate procreation of children.[75]

The American evangelicals were, then, following an already developed tradition in their attitudes toward sex. Here too, however, the negative side of their Calvinism was "writ large." Though the evangelical fathers sired many children, "their sexual repressiveness remained a potent source of inner anxiety, a deeply buried root of their profound hostility toward the body and the senses."[76] Cotton Mather, despite his large family, considered the sexual act itself to be mean and vile. In a fervent prayer for his own children, he confessed that he "ought to bewayl some inexpressible Circumstances of Meanness, relating to their Original, their Production and Conception." He continued, "I ought to obtain a Pardon thro' the Blood of that Holy Thing, which was Born of the Virgin . . . that so no Vileness of that Nature [the sex act] . . . may have any Influence, to render them abominable to Heaven, and cast them out of its favourable Protection."[77] One has the impression that Mather feels terribly contrite for not having found a more acceptable method of procreation. The medieval Cathari, when confronted with similar feelings of sexual shame produced an imaginative answer, at least in mythological terms: "God sent the Son [Archangel Michael]. . . . The Son entered the Virgin through her ear, took flesh there and emerged by the same door."[78]

The New England imagination could not rid evangelicalism of sexual shame. The young cleric, Michael Wigglesworth, in his diary, confesses a constant battle against carnal lust, especially as experienced in his dreams: "The last night some filthiness in a vile dream escaped me for which I loathe myself and desire to abase myself before my God." Nor did marriage assuage his guilt. Again in the diary, he noted that "carnal lusts [were] exceeding prevailing. Lord forgive my intemperence in the use of marriage for thy sons sake."[79] This exemplifies an attitude by no means atypical among evangelicals; the shame lies, not in a sinful illegitimate practice of sex, but in participation in sexuality at all. Semen is a "filthiness," sexual images are "vile," and marital conjugality a "perversion" of a higher humanity.

The revivalism and Fundamentalism which are so prominent in American religious life have continued to center moral attention on the sexual problem. Through the preaching of Moody, Billy Sunday and thousands of lesser lights, the sins of the *flesh* were identified with sexuality, and Protestantism often became indistinguishable from sexual repression, prudery and hypocrisy. When sexual passion erupted in certain individual scandals among the evangelicals, it was often received within non-evangelical circles as a sign that Melville was right in saying that "An uncommon prudence is habitual with the subtler depravity, for it has everything to hide."[80]

Many Protestant liberals made a genuine attempt to approach sexuality as a normal function of life, even as a God-given blessing to humanity. There was often in liberal churches great reluctance to speak openly of such matters, but the negative sexual focus of the evangelicals was, at least, clearly understood to be a distorted view of Christian faith.

With the new sexual permissiveness of the 1960s, liberal Christians felt the need for more explicit talk about sexuality. Bodily functions were essential; sexual needs had to be met; sexuality must be celebrated. Suburban churches introduced sex education into the church school curricula. The human potential movement dealt with sexual hangups. Women's Liberation and Gay Liberation groups were formed in local churches; women's caucuses became powerful in many Protestant seminaries. At last, it seemed that Protestantism was ridding itself of its sexual puritanism and that finally a great number of American Christians were coming down to earth and facing problems too long ignored by the church.

It should be remembered, however, that spiritualization can take many forms. The ancient gnostics were not unconcerned with sexuality; some of them also were anxious to celebrate it or ritualize it. What is unacceptable to gnostics of all ages is merely to *accept* sexuality as a gift among other gifts of creation and redemption. In *The Sociology of Religion,* Max Weber explains that highly spiritualized quests for salvation among classes of social privilege are often characterized by

> a disposition toward an "illumination" mysticism . . . associated with a distinctively intellectual qualification for salvation. This brings about a strong devaluation of the natural, sensual, and physical . . . the exaggeration and impressive *refinement of sexuality,* along with the simultaneous suppression of normal sexuality in favor of substitute aberrations . . . especially in the gnostic mysteries . . . [they] clearly appear to have been sublimated masturbatory surrogates for the orgies of the peasantry.[81]

Many elements of Weber's analysis seem to fit the current American scene. The American middle class, on a world scale, is certainly a people of immense social privilege, far removed from the mundane, in the sense of having to scratch out a living from the soil or struggling to provide a basic shelter for the family. If there is a need to escape the mundane, the need is felt in terms of either boredom or anxiety, often a combination of both. The escape takes place in the form of an enlightenment: education in the techniques of communication, of love making, of self-liberation, even of self-eroticism. Often the Protestant involvement in these areas seems like an attempt to lift its constituency above the frightening animal-like sexuality of the masses to a refined understanding of what sex is *really* about. That sexual union could be much the same for a Presbyterian stockbroker and his college-educated wife as for an ordinary blue-collar worker and *his* wife is quite unthinkable. If the sex act is to be acceptable to the children of puritanism, then first it must be removed from the realm of the temporal and given eternal significance. The natural, to be completely fulfilling, must be spiritualized.

Often the attempts of Protestant liberalism to come down to earth have had opposite results from those intended by Freudian psychology. If the Freudian goal is to enable people to perceive reality as it is rather than as distorted by infantile wishes and escape mechanisms, the human potential movement, on the contrary, often encourages its participants to act in terms of wish-fulfillment and escapism.[82]

Walker Percy longs for the day when the aberrations will no longer prevail, when a Christian sexuality may become normalized: "To bed we go," says Dr. Thomas More, "for a long winter's nap, twined about each other as the ivy twineth, not under a bush or in a car or on the floor or any such humbug as marked the past peculiar years of Christendom, but at home in bed where all good folk belong."[83]

It is precisely the normality of sex which is frightening to an overspiritualized Christianity, however, and nothing therefore is quite so frightening as sexuality within the context of family life, for the family regularizes and legitimizes sex and procreation. Among the ancient gnostics there were a variety of attitudes regarding the sex act, but gnostics would have agreed on one point, that the sex act leading to procreation *must* be seen in a negative light. Marriage, almost certain in ancient times to lead to procreation, presented a greater threat to the gnostic world view than did sexual license. As far as purity is concerned, gnostics could not, consistently, have accepted any distinction between casual promiscuous sex and long-term committed relationships. Both types of sexuality involve a participation in the material; one is as revolting as the other. It is reproduction, however, that offers a serious threat for the gnostic. "When Salome asked how long should death hold sway," an ancient gnostic gospel has Jesus answering:

> So long as ye women bring forth. For I came to end the works of the female. And Salome said unto him: I have then done well in not bringing forth? And the Lord answered and said: Eat of every pasture, but of that which hath the bitterness [of death] eat not. And when Salome asked when shall those things of which she had enquired be known, the Lord said: When ye shall tread upon the vesture of shame and when the two shall be one, and the male with the female neither male nor female.[84]

Obviously, woman presents a particular problem because she is able actually to bring forth further material life leading to further death. She, unlike the male, has the awful capacity to keep this thing going. There were some reports that the medieval Bogomils urged the castration of all believing males in order to put a stop to materiality.[85] But for the most part, gnosticism has placed the blame for childbearing and the burden of avoiding it on women.

Despite the strongly negative attitude of evangelicals toward the pleasures of sexuality, in early New England the family itself was held in high esteem. One of the great rewards of the Awakening, according to Jonathan Edwards, was that "it was a time of joy in families on the account of salvation being brought unto them."[86] The family, however, soon began to present problems to the evangelical conscience insofar as love of family was felt to conflict with love of God. Thomas Shepard, for instance, saw in the serious illness of his oldest child a sign that the Almighty was displeased with him because of his "immoderate love of creatures and of my child especially."[87] Jonathan Edwards also was aware of this conflicting loyalty. During a period of epidemics causing many deaths among New England children, he wrote, "May we not think the Design of God in the Great Sickness and Mortality there has been among Children to be a Testimony against our Immoderate Love to, and Doating upon our Children."[88] Needless to say, love between husband and wife was fraught with the same temptation to offend the jealous God by loving one's mate with an "immoderate love." George Whitefield, during his successful evangelistic tour of North America, determined not to marry at that point for fear of breaking his intimate relationship to Christ. He would entertain no real affection for anyone else. Later he declared, "I want a *gracious woman* that is dead to everything but Jesus . . . he daily grants me fresh tokens of his love, and assures me that he will not permit me to fall by the hands of a woman."[89] He, along with many other evangelical males, was intensely suspicious of women and feared their destructive powers.

It might well be argued that evangelicals could afford to warn of the dangers of "immoderate love" within the family because they could not envision the day when the family as institution would be in the slightest danger. At any rate, when Protestantism did begin to see the family unit imperilled by social change and scientific development, it immediately swung into action, defending marriage and exalting the home. Even denominations that were generally opposed to church involvement in politics were willing to concern themselves with laws dealing with the family. "The safeguarding of the home," the Rock River Methodist Conference of 1912 declared, "is the chief business of the state."[90]

The Church's support of home and hearth was often so sentimentalized that Christianity became associated with Mom, apple pie, and the supposed security of former days. After all, "the family that prays together stays together." Nevertheless, the Protestant Church's efforts to uphold the family, its cohesiveness and its influence within the society, has had a positive influence on American life throughout much of the twentieth century.

Recently, however, Protestantism's attitude toward the family has taken a sharp turn. When support for the nineteenth-century concept of marriage as a necessary social unit was felt to be no longer tenable, Protestantism seems to have unashamedly embraced the twentieth-century individualistic notion of family as a *convenient arrangement* for the *couple* who love one another. In such an arrangement, of course, rewarding companionship and sexual compatibility would be the major factors. The procreation of children and the security of members within the framework would be considered secondary.[91]

It is not, therefore, surprising that modern American Protestantism has moved away from its original opposition to birth control to become a chief sponsor of the planned parenthood movement.[92] The simplistic slogan, "No unwanted child should ever be born" captured the Protestant imagination. In the span of only a few decades, North Americans have moved from the false exaltation of *motherhood* to a recognition that the family can be a "baby trap."[93]

Neither is it surprising that when marriage and family are regarded merely as necessary arrangements for individual fulfillment, the differentiation between male and female roles within the home becomes a sensitive point of conflict. Thus, the Women's Liberation movement has at times gone beyond the concern for women's rights, beyond the legitimate protest against male tyranny and into a polemic against all differentiation. In some instances, there are striking similarities between the attitudes of the ancient gnostics and that of modern feminists. The *Gospel of Thomas* ends with these words:

> Simon Peter said to them [the disciples]: "Let Mary leave us, for women are not worthy of Life." Jesus said, "I myself shall lead her, in order to make her male, so that she too may become a living spirit, resembling you males, for every woman who will make herself male will enter the Kingdom of Heaven."

Furthermore, in the *Gospel of Mary,* Mary urges the disciples to "praise his greatness, for he has prepared us, and made us into *men.*"[94] Even Elaine Pagels, who finds some liberating words among the gnostics in regard to women, has noticed that "some extremists in the gnostic movement agreed with certain radical feminists who today insist that only those who renounce sexual activity can achieve human equality and spiritual greatness."[95]

There are those who, no doubt, would argue that the radical Women's Liberation and Gay Rights movements, with their emphasis on the body—the right of the woman to her own body, the rights of men and women to alternate sexual orientation—represent an extremely *this*-worldly, anti-gnostic ethical position within Protestantism. The persistent claim of these movements, however, is that a greater fulfillment can be achieved when one is freed from the mundane concerns of ordinary family life. The *Playboy* mentality, which sees females as bunnies, playmates or sensual toys, is unwittingly joined by feminists and gays offering an alternative to family life. The implication is that, beyond the merely physical chores of parents—childbearing, breast-feeding, dishwashing, laundering, baby-sitting, child disciplining, expense bearing (and, of course, the initial, most urgent of these tasks can be performed *only* by women)—there are latent spiritual profundities which are being suppressed by the entire enterprise of family life. And it is not only that alternative lifestyles to marriage and family should be acceptable, but more often than not there is the desire to embrace the alternative lifestyles as positively superior because they do not lock the human spirit into humdrum sex, unrewarding labor and the unexciting relationships that characterize family life.

In short, there are important forces within liberal American Protestantism that would like to escape the concerns of the physical body, of sexuality. Ironically, this movement reaches its culmination in the denial of the importance of the family, procreation and, therefore, of human life itself.

If, in the face of danger, there are two alternative instincts to be followed—one to fight and one to flee—the formative theologian of American Protestantism, John Calvin, chose to fight, launching a bold attack against all cosmic evils. His followers in North America have often chosen the opposite course—that of escaping the realities of nature, history and the body. That such an escapist faith and practice could have grown from Calvinist roots in the "home of the brave" must be one of the great ironies of Christian history.

CHAPTER SEVEN

Narcissism: From the Sacred Community to the Inner Self

TOLKIEN has eloquently defended the logic of escape—escape from the ugliness and sterility of modern life into the world of myth and fantasy. He makes an important distinction, however, between escape as a willful act of self-preservation and escape as desertion.[1] The former, escape into fantasy, music, and poetry, is not only an acceptable but a necessary aspect of our humanity. Gnostic escape, on the other hand, would fall under Tolkien's other category of *desertion* for two reasons. First, the gnostic does not retreat temporarily into a fortress of imagination for the regaining of sanity and strength with which once again to confront the world as it presents itself; he or she remains in the fortress of imagination. Second, the gnostic does not escape into another aspect of the world which has a tangible reality of its own to judge and direct his or her own psyche; rather, the gnostic escapes into the *self.* Within that secure realm of self, there can be no accurate scales of judgment and no precise charts for traveling. But once having entered this domain, the gnostic no longer needs those measured guides, for after the escape within, right and wrong turns are no longer being considered; the journey has ended.

When we discuss the journey into self, we are very close to the heart of gnostic thought. Quispel has described the *Gospel of Truth,* one of the most significant of the Nag Hammadi tractates, as "a summons to Introspection and Life, to that turning to oneself and to God *which is* Gnosis."[2] The turning to oneself and God in *gnosis* is always in that order. Often the first experience is so fulfilling that the second can be discarded.

As the gnostic teacher Monoimus told his disciples:

> Abandon the search for God and the creation and other matters of a similar sort. . . . Learn who it is within you who makes everything his own and says, "My God, my mind, my thought, my soul, my body." Learn the sources of sorrow, joy, love, hate . . . if you carefully investigate these matters you will find him *in yourself.*[3]

As we have seen, American Protestantism did not begin as a self-oriented religion. On the contrary, New England Calvinism, with its mentor's strong grounding in Old Testament theology, understood that the individual approached the holy God only as a member of the holy people. Philip Greven has shown that among the moderate elements of New England Protestantism, this communal spirit persisted for several generations to come. They insisted "upon the maintenance of the bonds and covenants that bound people together."[4]

How then did American Calvinism move from an essentially corporate understanding of Christianity to an emphasis on the self and an acceptance of individualism as a basic tenet of the faith? There are of course many reasons, some religious, some secular. Certain of these might be cited here as having been especially influential.

Religious Developments and Secular Influences

First, there is in Calvin's denial of the self, the possibility of a certain reverse concentration on the self. For instance, Calvin agreed with Augustine's advice to the Christian to "confess that you have all things from God, that all the good you have is from him, all the evil from yourself."[5] Were a sensitive person to brood about this distinction, in an introspective fashion, he could become quite preoccupied with separating the divine from the human initiative in any particular act or thought. This, in fact, seems to have been the reaction of many colonial Christians to their reading of Calvin. The preoccupation, at first, took the form of a "persistent and virtually inescapable *hostility* to the self and all its manifestations." Michael Wigglesworth cried out: "Behold I am vile, when thou showest me my face I abhor myself. Who can bring a clean thing out of filthiness."[6] Such unhappy thoughts before the mirror would seem to be a long way from *narcissism,* but are they? There is, after all, an affinity between hatred and love. And is there not a certain attraction to that which is utterly vile, abhorrent and loathsome?[7]

Karen Horney explains the connection between the denigration of self and the adoration of self. The self-disparaging subject, she observes,

> keeps reiterating the word "should" with amazing frequency. He keeps telling us what he should have felt, thought, done. He is at bottom as convinced of his inherent perfection as the naïvely "narcissistic" person, and betrays it by the belief that he actually could be perfect if only he were more strict with himself, more controlled, more alert, more circumspect.

She concludes, "He wavers then between self-adoration and self-contempt."[8] In her description of this neurotic type, Dr. Horney seems to be giving an accurate picture of the evangelical personality. It is easy to see that with only slight modification, such a personality could become narcissistic.

Nowhere has this concentration on self been more evident or more influential than in Protestantism's abiding faith in the *conscience*. Almost from the beginning, New England religion had been more concerned with the personal propitiation of an angry God than with any mundane obligations to neighbors.[9] Because conscience was held to be the voice of God within the self, the satisfaction of conscience became almost the sole criterion of ethics.[10] Jonathan Edwards would argue that the only assurance Christians have of their salvation is based on the good conscience which makes them *aware* that God is working savingly in their hearts.[11]

William Ellery Channing and Theodore Parker would contend that the conscience is the guide to theological understanding as well as to ethical behavior. "The only God," wrote Channing, "whom our thoughts can rest on, and our hearts can cling to, is the God whose image dwells in our own souls." And in his famous sermon, "On the Transient and Permanent in Christianity," preached in May 1841, Parker would call on Unitarian Christians to abandon supernaturalism and to adopt an "evolutionary theism," God speaking progressively through the awakening consciences of individuals.[12]

If "the Unitarians had pronounced human nature to be excellent; the transcendentalists pronounced it divine. . . . [Transcendentalism] refused to heed any other command save this inner voice of God."[13] This transcendentalist perception was to prevail across the board in American liberalism. As William Adams Brown of Union

Seminary, New York, assured his students, "What the theoretical reason cannot afford, the conscience and the religious experience provide."[14]

It would be refreshing to find expressed among Protestants of any stripe that suspicion of conscience so succinctly phrased by Mark Twain's Huck Finn:

> If I had a yaller dog that didn't know no more than a person's conscience does, I would pison him. It takes up more room than all the rest of a person's insides, and yet ain't no good, nohow. Tom Sawyer he says the same.[15]

There were also, of course, opinions contrary to the prevailing preoccupation with self. It has often been noted that within colonial Anglicanism, religion was more of a "public act than an inner preoccupation." It was generally assumed among Anglicans that the private interests of individuals must be subordinated to the interests of the public at large. In the diaries of genteel Christians such as William Byrd II there is little interest in the individual conscience or in any sort of introspection. Public events, the social world, the things of nature always took center stage.[16] Although closer to what European Christianity would consider orthodox, in the context of American religion this approach to faith would generally be regarded as eccentric.

Another religious development contributing to the focus on *self* arose from a significant change within Calvinistic ecclesiology. The change occurred because of the almost obsessive drive to establish a pure Church. Whereas Calvin had been convinced by the parable of the wheat and the tares as well as by the history of the Church that God's Church on earth will always be an imperfect organization—an admixture of saints and sinners—later Puritans were determined that the Covenant people would be free of mixture and error. They interpreted the parable of the wheat and tares as an admonition to "gather the weeds first and bind them in bundles to be burned, but gather the wheat into my barn."[17]

It was from this pressing concern for the purity of the Church that the Great Awakening and the revivals which followed were to receive their impetus. Out of the revivals came the view that a subjective experience of God's salvation was a required mark of a Christian.[18]

Whereas classical Calvinism had held that the Christian's assurance of salvation was guaranteed only through Christ and his Church, with his means of grace, now assurance could be found only in the personal experience of having been born again. This was a radical shift, for Calvin had considered any attempt to put "conversion in the power of man himself" to be gross popery.[19] Now with the ascendancy of revivalistic religion, conversion had certainly been put in the power of man. As Sidney Mead has recognized:

> *Conversion* tends to make man's initiative primary. Revivalism thus tends to lean theologically in an Arminian or even Pelagian direction with the implicit suggestion that *man saves himself through choice*. . . . In the hands of New England revivalists in the line of Timothy Dwight, Lyman Beecher, and Nathaniel W. Taylor, Calvinism was "modified" almost beyond recognition.[20]

Another way of understanding this not-so-quiet revolution within Calvinism—which, finally, was to create an anti-Calvinism—is to see that with the advent of revivalism, the Covenant itself had become individualized. Jonathan Edwards on 12 January 1723 "solemnly renewed" his personal covenant with God,

> So that I am not, in any respect, my own. . . . Neither have I any right to this body, or any of its members—no right to this tongue, these hands, these feet; no right to these senses, these eyes, these ears, this smell, or this taste. I have given myself clear away, and have not retained anything as my own.

In a similar way, Susanna Anthony renewed her covenant in February of 1757, concluding that, "there was not the least reserve; not the least iota, but was solemnly given up to God."[21]

What makes sense in terms of a corporate image, could become ludicrous in individual terms. The New Testament writers on several occasions referred to the Covenant People as the "bride of Christ," "a bride adorned for her husband."[22] In evangelical hands, however, the image became individualized so that each Christian person was held to be a bride of Christ. On 25 June 1741, Joseph Bean made a written covenant with God whereby he pledged, "[I] do hereby Solomly Joyn my Self in marige Covenant to him . . . I do here with all my power accept the and do take the for my head husband for biter for worse for richer for poorer for all tims and Conditions to love honour and obay the before all others and this to the deth." The Reverend Thomas Shepard, feeling a sense of alienation from Christ, lamented, "my widow-like separation and disunion from my Husband and my God." In a sermon preached in Philadelphia in the 1740s, George Whitefield proclaimed that the Lord Jesus "has made a Marriage Feast, and offers to espouse all Sinners to himself, and to make them Flesh of his Flesh, and Bone of his Bone. . . . Come then my brethren, come to the Marriage—Do not play the Harlot any longer.—Let this be the day of your Espousals with Jesus Christ, he only is your lawful Husband."[23] Not only does this strange application of the biblical conceit lead to sexual disorientation for members of both sexes, but theologically, it usurps the unique role of the Church as the true bride of Christ, changing the family of Christ into a vast harem of brides, all of whom on separate occasions have been to the altar with the same groom.

Such an individual attachment to the one spiritual husband led to a sense of profound loneliness and isolation, for these men and women "confronted their God and their fates directly and alone." The Reverend Ebenezer Frothingham, a supporter of Jonathan Edwards, spelled it out:

> If we rightly consider the Nature of Practice in Religion, on Obedience to God, we shall see an absolute Necessity for every Person to act *singly*, as in the sight of God only; . . . to bring the Saints all to worship God sociably, and yet have *no dependence one upon another*.[24]

This radical change in the understanding of God's relationship to humanity meant that nothing could be viewed in the same way as before. Now God and man, the family and society, nature and history would be seen from a new perspective, the perspective of the *self.*

Certain secular forces have reinforced this religion of the self. In the literary field, Harold Bloom offers the intriguing opinion that all recent poets have deliberately either *misread* or understood in an original, personal way the truth of their precursors:

> American poets, far more than British, have rebelled overtly against ancestral voices, partly because of Whitman's example, and also because of Emerson's polemic against the very idea of influence, his insistence that *going alone* must mean refusing even the good models, and so entails *reading primarily as an inventor*.[25]

Thus reading was regarded not as learning from another but as a purely imaginative exercise.

A good example of individualistic truth-making, according to Bloom, is Hart Crane's "The Broken Tower," in which the poet through the power of his own imagination constructs a new tower of the spirit, "healed, original now and pure," to replace the tower built by outside forces. This construction is possible by overcoming all previous worn-out conceptions in favor of a creation of the *autonomous mind*.[26] The influence of a poetic literature that understands the truth as a product of the creative self cannot be overestimated.

A philosophical romanticism has, at the same time, captured the thinking of North Americans: existentialism has been accepted as the unofficial philosophy of the mass media and popular literature. If existentialism is out of vogue among the academics, it has become an unrecognized orthodoxy, from *Time* magazine to rock music. Jean-Paul Sartre's statement that "the best way to conceive of the fundamental project of human reality is to say that man is the being whose project is to be God . . . to be man means to reach toward being God,"[27] strikes a responsive chord in contemporary America. In the wake of so many political defeats and disillusionments, this individualistic assertion seems almost irrefutable in the United States.

Another existentialist, Arthur Koestler, reminded his readers that the Greeks "bequeathed to us one of the most beautiful words in our language—the word enthusiasm—*en theos*—a god within . . . happy is he who has a god within, and who obeys it."[28] Such thinking would be purely gnostic if it were not thoroughly secular and antireligious. Existentialism has had so many champions in American Protestantism that it is impossible to enumerate them. Most significant, perhaps, is the continuing influence of Rudolf Bultmann among American New Testament scholars and theologians, not only in terms of his famous demythologizing of the New Testament, but also in regard to his grounding in philosophical existentialism. "The extent to which existentialism influenced Bultmann's Christology is evident in his astounding question about Christ: 'Does He [Christ] help me because He is God's Son, or is He the Son of God because He helps me?' "[29] Is it any real wonder that so many American preachers decided they preferred Bultmann to Barth because the former is so much more *preachable*?

The gnostic-like individualism of some modern psychiatry has been noticed by such scholars as Elaine Pagels and Gilles Quispel. Pagels asserted that "the gnostic movement shared certain affinities with contemporary methods of exploring the self through psychotherapeutic techniques" and that "both gnosticism and psychotherapy value, above all, knowledge—the self-knowledge which is insight."[30] Quispel draws a more precise parallel between the ancient gnostics and C. G. Jung. Jung was a student of gnosticism and an advocate of *gnosis* as a "religious form deeply rooted in the soul of man." For Jung, *gnosis* involved the uncovering of the positive imagery of the subconscious, the light and dark aspects of the soul.

He was confident that an acceptance of the soul as original and self-creating could lead eventually to health.[31] Much psychiatry is concerned with the necessary disclosure of the various dodges the human personality uses to avoid the crisis of healing—a clinical use of the Greek idea, know thyself—in order to free the patient from the chaos of self. The Jungian approach, on the other hand, encourages the patient to remain within the self. Clearly, Jungian psychology has had a formidable influence on American Protestantism.

In the field of education, the philosophy of John Dewey, though it has been challenged in many particulars, could nevertheless be considered normative in the United States. Dewey in his book, *A Common Faith* (1934), carried the philosophy of *self* to its ultimate secular conclusion, and the individualizing effect on several generations of school children can hardly be exaggerated. *Self-expression* and *self-fulfillment* were to be key words in a new American orthodoxy, and any form of social inhibition a heresy against the religion of individual freedom.[32]

The Radicalization of Self-oriented Religion

The significant alterations of Calvinist theology in conjunction with later secular influences would mean, ecclesiastically, that in the United States the conservative catholic-minded form of Protestantism had been overcome by the left wing of the Reformation. There would remain a core of Anglican, Reformed, and Lutheran church people dedicated to a more traditional European form of Protestant faith, but since the early days of the Republic, their story has not been the dominant theme of American Christianity.

The changes epitomized by the revival movement were not confined to evangelicalism. American liberals no less than evangelicals were children of the Great Awakenings. Following the revivals, many moderates and later liberals were to accept without question a highly individualistic understanding of Christianity. Charles Chauncy was typical of moderate opinion in holding: "self-approbation [is the] noblest kind of pleasure we are capable of."[33] It was from this love of self that all ethical incentives were to be derived.

Transcendentalism represented the apotheosis of individualism in American thought. Emerson, in particular, had no doubts about the place of the individual in the economy of God. The remedy for the ills of religion, he wrote, are "first, soul, and second, soul and evermore, soul."[34] "The master idea of the Emersonian philosophy is the divine sufficiency of the individual . . . each man is his own center."[35]

Emerson and the transcendentalists in general could have agreed wholeheartedly with this gnostic teaching from the *Oxyrhynchus:*

> The Kingdom of Heaven is within you; and whoever shall know himself shall find it. Strive therefore to know yourselves, and ye shall be aware that ye are sons of the Father, and ye shall know that ye are in the City of God, and ye are the City.[36]

The transcendentalists even came close to Mani's identification of the self as the Paraclete.[37] For, like Manichaeism, transcendentalism was not a philosophy but a faith. And it was a faith in a "mystical egocentric universe wherein the children of God might luxuriate in their divinity."[38] The transcendentalists believed strongly in the preexistence of the individual soul. As C. A. Bartol, one of the lesser lights of the movement, explained:

> Our soul is older than our organism. It precedes its clothing. It is the cause, not the consequence, of its material elements . . . it is the immortal principle. It is an indestructible essence. It is part and parcel of the Divinity it adores. It can no more die than he [God] can . . . it is the kingdom all things will be added to.[39]

Henry David Thoreau even had the temerity to question the Westminster Confession of Faith, asking if his forebears "*somewhat hastily* concluded that it is the chief end of man here 'to glorify God and enjoy him forever,' "—implying that glorifying the self and enjoying oneself might be a better occupation.[40]

Elder Henry James by 1847 was to see that Protestantism "as at present constituted, . . . is the citadel and shield of individualism, or the selfish principle." Thirty years later, his opinion was unchanged; he referred to Protestantism's "insane habit of regarding human life as *personally* and not as *socially* constituted."[41]

Within the Protestant establishment itself, individualism, though more restrained, was certainly pervasive. Perry Miller claimed that in the theology of Horace Bushnell, "Calvinism itself was, as it were, transcendentalized."[42] Bushnell's answer to rationalistic attacks on the dogmas of Christendom was an assertion of the reliability of the individual heart: "My heart wants the Father; my heart wants the Son; my heart wants the Holy Ghost. . . . My heart says the Bible has a Trinity for me, and I mean to hold by my heart. I am glad a man can do it when there is no other mooring."[43]

Sailing forth from this new mooring, Protestant liberalism was to become at least as individualistic as its evangelical counterforce. Octavius Brooks Frothingham, a popular liberal preacher, was to recognize "the *divine* character of the heart's affections, the *heavenly* illumination of the reason [and] the truth of the soul's intuitions of spiritual things." He expressed the need for "a deep faith in the soul's power to take care of itself."[44]

There were efforts among liberals such as Theodore Munger, a renowned New Haven preacher, to replace an "excessive individuality" with "a truer view of the solidarity of the race."[45] The rare social type was to assert itself vigorously in the Social Gospel movement. In 1913 Josiah Strong, a leader of that movement, noted with acute historical insight that "there are two types of Christianity, the old and the older. The one is traditional, familiar, and dominant. The other, though as old as the Gospel of Christ, is *so rare* that it is suspected of being new, or is overlooked altogether. . . . The one is individualistic; the other is social."[46] Walter Rauschenbusch insisted that in the Bible "personal religion was chiefly a means to an end; the end was social." The advocates of Christ's social ministry would argue that the goals of Christianity could not be achieved "if the Church continued to fix its attention on saving sinners one by one."[47]

The Social Gospel movement, though, was short-lived and had relatively little impact outside the seminaries and denominational bureaucracies. In academic circles and among church leaders, a great deal of lip service was given (and continues to be given) to Christianity as a corporate faith, but for the average person of the pew, Protestantism remained a very *private matter* between the individual and his God. The social message that spoke more convincingly to most was that of Charles M. Sheldon's *In His Steps*—collected narratives of faithful persons who solved their ethical dilemmas by asking the question, "What would Jesus do if he were in my shoes?" This individualistic formula, applied to individual crises, so captured the American Protestant imagination that from 1897 to 1965, *In His Steps* sold over eight million copies, a sales record surpassed only by one other work of fiction, *Peyton Place*.[49]

Following the agonizing experiences of the Great War and the Great Depression, many Americans became disillusioned with the easy private religion of Protestant liberalism and with the optimistic belief of the social gospellers that society could be easily Christianized. In the early 1930s, Barthianism was to have a brief day in the American sun. It became fashionable for a while to question, even to ridicule, the individualistic assumptions of Protestant Christianity.

Reinhold Niebuhr, though rejecting the Barthian approach, championed a qualified corporate understanding of the faith which was more palatable to Americans. Niebuhr still considered Protestant liberalism's *outstanding achievement* to have been the "discovery and affirmation of the rights of the individual."[50] The problem, in his opinion, was that individualism had gotten out of hand. "The modern sense of individuality," he said, "thereby begins on the one hand in Protestantism and on the other hand in the Renaissance. . . . The real significance of the two movements lies in the fact that one represents the final development of individuality within terms of the Christian religion and the other an even further development of individuality beyond the limits set in the Christian religion, that is, the development of the 'autonomous' individual." For Niebuhr this development "destroys the Christian basis of individuality" and brings about "the loss of self."[51] Although it must be noted that Niebuhr clearly endorsed "the development of individuality within terms of the Christian religion," nevertheless, through his voluminous socio-political writings, he was probably the most popular and effective countervoice to rampant individualistic Protestantism to be heard in the United States.

It is interesting that so many of the countervoices—Philip Schaff, John W. Nevin, Walter Rauschenbusch, the Niebuhrs, and Paul Lehmann—have been either immigrants or second-generation Americans with a more European, corporate understanding of the faith. Americans growing up in the peculiar American milieu seemed unable to understand individualistic Christianity as anything but normal. After all, personal faith is "that old-time religion"; if it is not "good enough for me," then the burden of proof is to show why not.

In liberal circles, the "old time religion" retained its revivalistic spirit through a concentration on individual growth. Norman Vincent Peale, though he had no evangelical message, continued to preach, with evangelical zeal, the gospel of self: "Make your life what you want it to be through belief in God and in yourself"; "Think, believe, visualize success"; "Think big, believe big, pray big, act big. . . . First thing every morning before you arise say out loud, 'I believe,' three times." Unless the last admonition is meant to show deference to the trinitarian formula, Pealeism had little relation to orthodox Christianity. Yet Peale supported the Graham campaigns and Graham considered Peale a born again Christian.[52]

During and following the Vietnam conflict, Pealeism came to be more and more respectable among liberal Christians in the various forms of the human potential movement. The movement, actualized in thousands of local churches through touch therapy and "I'm OK, you're OK" sessions, attempted to bring about the personal growth of individuals. Growth was to be realized by the use of various techniques to enhance self-consciousness, to allow the deep feelings and fantasies of the individual to surface so that the individual might be put in touch with the self. As John E. Biersdorf put it:

> The deep exploration of one's *own inner space* often leads to experiences which seem to be similar to those reported by followers of the great religious traditions. And interpersonal intimacy sometimes leads to intimacy of love and grace that, for want of better words, have been called "transpersonal."[53]

At times, it seems, certain interpersonal miracles can occur, but those occasions are spin-offs of the primary purpose, namely, the enhancement of the *self*. What was being advocated, in the name of Protestant Christianity, was an ethic of unbridled individualism. Life must be seen, the theologian Harvey Seifert wrote, as "an arena for enjoyment."[54] Lest it be thought that Seifert was promoting mere earthly joy, however, he insists that it is "transcendental joy" he has in mind—a distinction that makes his position more clearly gnostic. If, as Thoreau suggested, our forebears had "somewhat hastily concluded that it is the chief end of man here to 'glorify God and enjoy him forever,' " it seemed that the situation would soon be rectified by the human potential and personal growth movements.

Christian advocates of the human potential movement often make the claim that they represent the exact opposite of a gnosticizing trend. They are, they would say, calling the Church away from its otherworldliness to an appreciation of earthly realities. Donald Berry writes: "The antidote for such a 'theology of the infinite' is one that deals with the finite—sex, dying, anger, commitment, love, anxiety, rebirth, or reshaping of the self." While claiming to oppose gnosticism, he falls into the gnostic habit of seeing religion's purpose in terms of getting in touch with the self. Even though he tries to understand the self through other people, he concludes: "The mystery of human selfhood, with its connection to, but also its freedom from, the body is the best evidence I know for the presence of transcendence in our world."[55] Does this partially embodied, partially disembodied theology really describe the mystery of the Word made flesh? I doubt it.

Tom F. Driver, in identifying "human experience as Word of God," discovers divine grace in the bathtub:

> He [the theologian] proceeded to his neck, arms and shoulders. Here the contours were broad, his instinct to love uninhibited, the same reaction to his own body that he had to others'. He went on to his chest and stomach and all the way down his body. He washed his abdomen, his groin, and his genitals with mild erotic pleasure . . . to all this care his body responded. He could feel life stirring within him. . . .
>
> He put his hand once more upon his leg.
>
> They say that the divine antidote for sin is forgiveness. He thought this wrong, or beside the point. The real point, he believed, is love. What removes sin is not its being forgiven but the sinner's being loved. At any rate, he had not to "forgive" his thighs, much less imagine God would do so. What they wanted was care, attention, a certain honor—the opposites of shame, the attitudes of love. His hand resumed the caress. He opened his nerves to sense what the thigh felt like. What does my hand find when it touches this flesh? What is here of attraction and repulsion? He would invite to consciousness the suppressed sensations. No other way to love.[56]

In this unashamedly narcissistic account of auto-erotic bathing, the Paul J. Tillich Professor of Theology and Culture at Union Seminary unveils the startling theological discovery that the equivalent of what the Bible calls "forgiveness" is received not from the Almighty or from any of his agents, but from the *self.* Self loving self is the primary pattern of grace. When such eternal significance is given to a narcissistic "human experience" and we see such implicit gnosticizing of the human personality, we can only say what Irenaeus in exasperation was forced to say of Valentinus: "Iu, Iu, Pheu, Pheu!"[57]

In the evangelical camp, revivalism would remain endemic to the faith. The words Robert Baird had written a century before held true during and beyond the Eisenhower years, "[All] agree that . . . a revival is an inestimable blessing: so that he who should oppose himself to revivals *as such,* would be regarded by most of our evangelical Christians as *ipso facto,* an enemy to spiritual religion itself."[58] Therefore, Protestant clergy were expected to take part in the campaigns of Billy Graham, Incorporated. If they chose not to cooperate, the burden was on them to justify their decision.

Assassinations, the Vietnam War and the Watergate scandal accelerated the various individualizing, narcissistic impulses of the American people. Up to this time, common sense had continued to infuse Protestantism with some degree of communality. After all, the family, the congregation, the community and the country had to be preserved. With a massive loss of faith in the value of politics, the family, and any sort of communal activity, there seemed to be only one direction to take—the way of a radical gnostic narcissism.

Writing about the religious spirit on the college campuses across America, a surprisingly accurate bellwether of the nation at large, Barbara Hargrove explains that after the turbulence of the 1960s, "the quest had turned inward, to Eastern religions, to the Fundamentalist Protestantism that campus ministers had early set out to help students grow beyond."[59] In universities where students had only recently been in open political revolt against the Vietnam War, this was indeed a radical shift. Hargrove asserts that "the radicals went underground, went straight or became religious in non-American, non-Protestant ways."[60] But what could be more American or more Protestant (in an American sense) than the worship of God in an individualistic, inward way?

The Jesus People materialized, a new generation of Fundamentalists who worshiped Jesus as "Jesus the experience." Unlike the older generation of evangelicals who had always *enjoyed* Billy Graham, here were young people who were at last taking the Billy Grahams seriously. Otherworldliness, biblical infallibility, a literal view of the Genesis creation story, a rather austere personal ethic, and born again experience were accepted as synonymous with Christianity.[61] Any person or church not accepting these "basics" of the faith were, of course, not Christian at all. The Jesus People were often persons who had recently been turned on to drugs, but now were turned on to Jesus. The older evangelicals would have been delighted with this strange new development except for the fact that the Jesus People, for evangelicals, often followed rather strange lifestyles. Long hair, dressing down, rough language, tobacco and moderate drinking were sometimes allowed in such groups. All these practices were threatening to traditional Fundamentalism. Perhaps the most lasting effect of the movement will prove to be the number of young people who have taken that route into the Protestant ministry.

During this post-Vietnam period, a strange détente occurred between evangelicals and liberals. Many representatives of both sides could now agree that Christianity is a spiritual faith holding out no real hope for political or social progress in this world. Evangelicals were, for the most part, willing to give up their interest in theological doctrines, whereas liberals were losing interest in secular matters. Both sides could enthusiastically endorse a recognition that religion is a very private matter, that God speaks to each person through some point of contact within the person and that the aim of religion is enlightenment, the rebirth of the individual. For the time being, at least, there would be few arguments about what rebirth meant and what it led to.

The new détente received some support from academics. Herbert Richardson, in 1967, had already proposed a return to a religion of personal experience. Opposing Barth, Brunner, and the objectivity of that older generation, Richardson claimed that "the analysis of religion by modern theologians tends toward the following consensus: that an irreducible element in 'true religion' is a certain affection, or feeling."[62] In his attempt to move "toward an American theology," Richardson was certainly walking in the well-worn American path toward a theology of *self*.

Harvey Cox, although warning against the possible misuses of Eastern mysticism and the "naked revival," nevertheless endorsed the general move toward a more spiritual understanding of the faith. "The sickness of our time," he wrote, "is not the movement toward interiority but the disappearance of it." Cox spoke as well of the human need for a web of relationships: "We need a new web."[63] It is interesting to note that, despite himself, Cox has here chosen an individualistic image. The Christian does not require a new colony, den, hive or flock, but a new web for holding the self up. All other persons and relationships exist only as a part of the system designed for this individualistic purpose. I may exist as part of my neighbor's web or system, but at no point in this image are we fellow humans, brothers and sisters in mutual need of a more helpful spiritual locale.

Many contemporary theologians have stressed the need for a renewed appreciation of the work of the Holy Spirit, a recovery of the emphasis allegedly neglected during the Barthian period. What was recovered, however, was not an understanding of Spirit as "event . . . something which happens to man . . . sweeps man where it will, and then storms on into the world" as Buber described it. Rather, the renewed understanding, again in Buber's words, has been of the spirit that "can now no longer exist as an independent essence. There now exists only a product of human individuals called spirit, a product which they contain and secrete like mucus and urine."[64]

The Rejection of the Church

New Testament scholar Helmut Koester has declared that "the test of orthodoxy is whether it is able to build a *church* rather than a club or school or a sect, or merely a series of concerned religious individuals."[65] We have seen how, for the ancient gnostics, the Church had value only insofar as it could assist individuals in their search for *gnosis*. Even that function was a temporary one, for as the gnostic teacher Heracleon explained, "People at first are led to believe in the Savior through others," but once they are in contact with the source itself, "they no longer rely on mere human testimony."[66] Gnosticism, then, would see any sort of ecclesiastical organization to be, at best, a necessary evil.

Calvin insisted that without the Church there is no truth, "God is a liar, and . . . everything contained in his word is false."[67] In his comment on Ephesians, he taught that "he errs who desires to grow by himself. . . . Just so, if we wish to belong to Christ, let no man be anything for himself: but let us all be whatever we are for each other."[68] Abraham Kuyper, however, in his famous *Lectures on Calvinism,* interpreted Calvinist ecclesiology in a wholly different way. "Calvinism," said Kuyper, "by praising aloud liberty of conscience, has in principle abandoned every absolute characteristic of the visible church." This is "a liberty of conscience, which enables every man to serve God *according to the conviction and the dictates of his own heart.*"[69]

On the theological left, Adolf von Harnack took the position that the authentically spiritual is composed of those things that are inward, spontaneous and ethical as opposed to the outward, organized, ceremonial and dogmatic. The development, for instance, of a regular official ministry as an essential element of Christianity was, for Harnack, a step in an anti-spiritual direction.[70]

Among evangelicals in the United States, the type of Calvinism espoused by Kuyper was to prevail; among Protestant liberals, the individualistic view exemplified by Harnack was to predominate. Both parties were united in a religion with little regard for Church.

W. H. H. Murray, a prominent revivalist, said in 1870 that "undue importance . . . is attached to the connection of Christians one with another, and to the good or bad effect such connection has upon individual growth."[71] Daniel Dorchester, a Methodist church historian, was able to overlook what slight *connections* there were between American Christians and to be warmly grateful that "under Protestantism religion became purely a personal thing, passing out from under the exclusive control of the sacraments."[72]

This prevailing American suspicion of the churchly and the sacramental led to the rising influence of anti-churchly and anti-sacramental types of Protestantism. In his delineation of the sect-type as opposed to the church-type of religious organization, Troeltsch proposed this description:

> The essence of the sect does not consist merely in a one-sided emphasis upon certain vital elements of the Church-type, . . . [rather, within the sect-type] there is a full recognition of the value of *radical individualism* and of the idea of love. . . . The sect does not live on miracles of the past, nor on the miraculous nature of the institution, but on the constantly renewed miracle of the Presence of Christ, and on the *subjective reality* of the *individual mastery of life*.[73]

Troeltsch's typology helps to explain the historical fact of the Methodist triumph on the Western frontier. "After all, Methodism," H. Richard Niebuhr reminded us, "represented the religious aspect of that great revolutionary movement of the eighteenth century that placed the individual at the center of things and so profoundly modified all existing institutions." The growth of Methodism was significant not only as the success of a particular denomination, but more importantly, as embodying the success of the denominational concept, for Methodism was manifestly a denomination. The colonial churches—Episcopalian, Congregationalist, Presbyterian—retained for a while the old European memory of Church as elected people of God. That memory would disappear when all churches became mere denominations, that is, persons called by the same name.[74]

Sidney Mead has identified the central, unique feature of American Christianity as the *denomination,* which he defined as "a voluntary association of like-hearted and like-minded individuals, who are united on the basis of common beliefs for the purpose of accomplishing tangible and defined objectives."[75] The key word here is *voluntary*. No longer would it be possible for Protestants to relate to Jesus' words, "You did not choose me, but I chose you."[76] With denominationalism, it has become quite obvious that individuals not only do choose Jesus, but choose him on their own terms.

The first genuine history of American Christianity, *Religion in America* by Robert Baird, published in 1844, selects *voluntarism* as the "central motif marking religion in America."[77] Nothing has happened to challenge Baird's insight. For whether evangelical or liberal, American denominationalism has emphasized the personal, private vision and commitment of the individual believer. As Troeltsch said of the sect-type religion, "It tries to transform these groups [churches] from confessional unities into mere organizations for administration, offering a home to very varying minds and energies. It is opposed to the ecclesiastical spirit by its tolerance, its *subjectivism* and symbolism, its emphasis upon the ethical and religious *inwardness* of temper, its lack of stable norms and authorities."[78] The *normal* religion in America became denominational religion, which people "affiliated" with, had "preference" for, "joined" in the same way that they became affiliated with the Elks Club, preferred the Republican Party and joined the Masonic Order.

In the evangelical camp, there is continued interest in revivalism with more and more emphasis on the radio-television "ministry." This disembodied appeal to the individual's emotions requires no corporate response to the evangelists' appeal. Whereas previously the sinner had to "hit the sawdust trail" and confess the Lord Jesus before men, today the only sign of a person's conversion is to "keep those cards and letters coming." There is also in the electronic church a suspicion of all things ecclesiastical. The World Council of Churches continues to present a threat to the evangelicals, in part because the very existence of the body implies that many millions of Christians take the *visible* body of Christ seriously and even claim that the *visible* body has some theological significance. Sporadic attacks are launched against the Council and against ecumenism in general within the evangelical journals as well as in that guardian of all American values, the *Reader's Digest.* Ostensibly the World Council is accused of theological and political errors, but in reality any ecclesiastical organization whose interests go beyond that of individualistic conversion is a threat to the established piety of Protestant narcissism.

It is easy for evangelicals working with denominational Protestantism to make common cause with the church management and church growth movements. Evangelicals and many liberals alike can become enthusiastic about taking surveys to discover "what the people want" and then proceeding to accomplish those popular objectives. After all, the Church, like the Kiwanis Club and the Rotary International, is an organization of and for individuals. And the Growth Movement is but a more sophisticated form of old-fashioned soul winning and head counting.

Nor is there much support for a corporate-minded theology in liberal circles. For decades now, liberal theologians and, ironically enough, denominational bureaucrats, have been criticizing the Church for its irrelevance, lack of commitment, love for buildings and concern for its own institutions. The perpetual scapegoat of this sustained critique has been the local parish church, which, unlike the seminary and the denominational home office, is supposedly the seat of all religious irrelevance. Though, no doubt, there is ample justification for disapproval of parish attitudes and practices, the overall effect has been to cast suspicion on the one and only corporate expression of Christianity left to Protestant Christians.

Harvey Cox, for example, was extremely critical of what he called, "the residential parish," which he claimed originated during the era of "town culture" prior to urbanization. He suggested that the old pattern of Christians being united in one congregation because of the accident of common residences should be replaced by the formation of "communities of need." The latter would be constituted "with reference to such social crises as race, poverty and war."[79] It would seem that this last vestige of non-voluntaristic religion in America, the parish church, is an offense to liberal Protestantism. Could it not be replaced by organizations of our own choosing, fellowships of like-minded people? How else to ensure that the Church will be what we want it to be but by forming it ourselves to answer our own questions and to meet our own needs?

Ancient gnosticism loathed the patriarchal and authoritarian qualities of official Christianity. From the gnostic point of view, the structure and discipline of the Church stifled the spirit.[80] Much of Protestant liberalism's criticism of the Church has been along this line: the Church is unimaginative, repressive, unartistic, indistinguishable from the society as a whole. Without question all of these accusations and many more are true about the "residential parish" and the larger church units as well, but rather than attempting to *reform* the structures and practices of the Church, liberalism wishes to escape them in favor of a more thoroughgoing individualism.

Herbert Richardson, taking a sweeping anti-Church position, finds that there is no real justification for the uniqueness of the Church because the *holiness* of God is "an incommunicable attribute." He cites Paul Tillich's affirmation of the incommunicability of holiness as the "*Protestant protest* against every claim that holiness is communicated to a created reality."[81] One "created reality" to which Richardson and Tillich refer is, of course, the Holy Catholic Church, "a chosen race, a royal priesthood, a holy [*hagios*] nation, God's own people."[82] The end result of such a protest against the "holy nation" is the enhancement of individual autonomy.

The radical theology of Thomas J. J. Altizer offers still further support for individualistic Christianity. Altizer feels that Barth would have been a true biblical theologian had he not surrendered to the authority of the Church; Altizer himself is determined to understand the Bible apart from the Church and apart from tradition.[83] Is it any real wonder that, apart from the influence of the Church and tradition, an individualistic reading of the Gospel could perceive the Crucifixion event as "the death of God"?

Peter Williams has noted that this anti-Church religion became normal for American Protestants. He comments:

> A reticence about public discussion of religious matters became an increasingly important part of middle-class genteel reserve, and religion thus became even more relegated to the private sector. For many of the "comfortable" middle class, the force of Protestantism as a communal bond and as an "inner gyroscope" gradually evaporated. What was left was an emphasis on the individual, alone with his family to contemplate eternal things.

Thus, Williams concludes, "the new religiosity that was beginning to emerge . . . was characterized . . . by an in-turning and a passivity."[84]

The development of Hare Krishna, popular Zen and other non-Christian gnostic cults has been well explicated by Carl Raschke, among others. But these gnostic religious expressions are but caricatures of the more subtle gnosticism within the Protestant Church itself. The danger, as Raschke has noted, "is that we are all becoming gnostics of a sort." He goes on to warn that "the enthusiasts of the 'new consciousness' " will not see it as a danger, but only "as evidence of the widespread recognition of the tremendous potential of individual consciousness."[85]

It would of course be unfair to North American Protestantism to indicate that there have been no voices defending the Church against rampant individualism. There was the remarkable Mercersburg theology of John Williamson Nevin (1803–1886) and Philip Schaff (1819–1893) which saw North American theology as having abandoned the rich sacramental heritage of Calvin.[86] There has been the continuing European spirit of Canadian Protestantism which, in the words of Robert Handy, "preserved churchism."[87] And there was Walter Rauschenbusch with his emphasis on "kingdom of God" and "body of Christ."[88] More recently, Paul Lehmann, the preeminent Protestant ethicist of this generation, has attempted to place many of the concerns of the Social Gospel movement on a more solid theological base. While offering a Christological corrective within American social Christianity, he has also propounded an ecclesiological corrective. Not only does Lehmann state that "Christian ethics, as a theological discipline, is the reflection upon the question, and its answer: What am I, as a believer in Jesus Christ *and as a member of his church,* to do?" but also he proposes that "it is from, and in, the *Koinonia* that we get an answer to the question." And "just as there is no Messiah without his people, so there is no real presence of Jesus in history without or apart from the true people of God which as the work of the Holy Spirit is always at the same time a spiritual and visible reality."[89]

If Lehmann's corrective and those of his precursors are having an effect in contemporary Protestant America, however, they must be in the nature of the leaven "hid in three measures of meal,"[90] because what is happening on the surface in North American Protestantism would seem to be the restatement of anti-Church individualism in a less restrained way than ever before.

CHAPTER EIGHT

Elitism: From the Many to the Few

A PRIVATE, anti-Church view of Christianity of necessity correlates with religious elitism. When the self effectively becomes the center of God's activity in the world, then the self must be seen as holy, set apart from all common, unworthy selves. When the self is thought to have attained special knowledge, then the self must be distinguished from those quite different others which have not attained special knowledge. " 'Knowledge' [*gnosis*] puffs up, but love [*agape*] builds up," writes the Apostle Paul.[1] Already, the New Testament had found itself having to oppose gnostic elitism.

The early Church Fathers continued to resist any elitist attempts to separate the pneumatics from the psychics or the *gnostikoi* from the ordinary Christians. Although the gnostic *Gospel of Philip* was concerned that many baptizands "go down into the water and come up without having received anything," orthodoxy maintained that all those who had received baptism, confessed the creed, participated in the Eucharist and agreed to obey the Church were *Christians*. As Elaine Pagels has observed, "To become truly *catholic*—universal—the church rejected all forms of elitism, attempting to include as many as possible within its embrace."[2]

Irenaeus made it quite clear that an ignorant man of God is superior in the eyes of the Church to an arrogant heretic, be the latter ever so learned.[3] The strength of the Church was in the ordinary farmers and their wives who regularly attended the Eucharist and struggled to live in harmony with the Gospel of Christ.

It was, as we have noted, this very ordinariness that was repugnant to the gnostics. As spiritual people, they were not willing to be categorized with seemingly non-spiritual people. As Christians who *knew* what they believed and why, they were not content to be counted with nominal Christians, who simply attended public services but were too ignorant to speak meaningfully about their faith. The more popular Christianity became among the masses, the more determined the gnostics were to be differentiated from the herd.

The *gnostikoi* also found orthodoxy boring. The rituals of Baptism and Communion, which like all rituals were sometimes performed in a perfunctory way, were offensive to their spirituality. The sermons, simple expositions of the biblical texts for an uneducated audience, were an insult to their intelligence. So the gnostic personality cried out, "You mean this is it? This is all there is? No mystery, no arcane knowledge, no inner light, just these surface things that can be understood by that rude peasant and his unattractive wife?" Such a religion was impossible to accept, at least on the popular level.

In its long struggle with gnosticism, it must be admitted that the Church has made some damaging concessions to gnostic elitism. Augustine, for example, though he broke with the Manichaeans and vehemently opposed them on behalf of the orthodox cause, retained their underlying conviction that a very *few* were elected to salvation, whereas the great mass of people were destined for eternal damnation.[4] There is little doubt that Calvin, among other Reformers, was strongly inclined toward Augustinian elitism in his suspicion that the great majority of humanity would suffer damnation.

It is certain, however, that Calvin was aware of the dangers of spiritual pride. The famous doctrine of election was intended to serve as a bulwark against religious pride. Ignorance of the doctrine, Calvin warns, "pluck[s] up humility by the very roots," begets and fosters pride. There is "no other means of humbling us as we ought, or making us feel how much we are bound to him."[5]

And yet, as Calvin noted, it is necessary to handle the doctrine of election with extreme care. If it can be argued that Calvin himself did not always heed his own warning, it can be asserted without fear of contradiction that his followers often threw caution to the wind. The Westminster divines, in 1647, confessed,

> As for those wicked and ungodly men, whom God as a righteous judge, for former sins, doth blind and harden, from them he not only withholdeth his grace, whereby they might have been enlightened in their understandings . . . but sometimes also withdraweth the gifts which they had, and exposeth them to such objects as their corruption makes occasion of sin.[6]

With such a determined view of the fate of the damned, it is difficult to see how these followers of Calvin could be other than elitist. Unless a person considered himself a reprobate, he would certainly want to establish as much distance as possible between himself and the "wicked and ungodly." In fact, what so often happened, as Troeltsch explained, was that "against a background of the severest self-condemnation there stands out in clear relief in Calvinism the sense of being a spiritual aristocracy."[7]

New England Calvinism, almost from the beginning, saw itself as a spiritual aristocracy. Cotton Mather was appalled by the Arminian notion that Christ died for the sins of all people: "The Satisfaction of our Lord Redeemer, was not intended by Him, for the Redemption of all mankind; nor was it intended any further than His intercession is, which reaches only to the Elect of God."[8] Mather described the elect as people of "good character . . . Courteous and Sweet-natured people," who accomplish a "profitable employment of time."[9] Obviously, the riffraff could not be numbered with such saints.

In the writings of Jonathan Edwards, there is an even clearer distinction between those who have seen the light and those who have not: "He that sees the beauty of holiness . . . sees the greatest and most important thing in the world, which is the *fullness* of all things, without which the world is empty, yea, worse than nothing."[10] The glimpse of the *pleroma,* so important to the ancient gnostics, was also the decisive factor in New England.

Edwards demanded that only *visible* saints be accepted as members of visible churches. It was his fond hope that the Awakening would destroy the disparity between those who *possessed* saving faith and those who only *professed* it; the preaching of conversion would either bring the subject into true saving faith or else drive that person out of the community of faith. For Edwards there could be no "middle sort of persons with . . . such a common faith as is consistent with loving sin and the world better than Christ."[11] Instead of a Church populated by *middle sorts* and reprobates as well as by saints, Edwards longed for a smaller society of Christians whose outward lives were marked by the "beauty of holiness." Outside this small group, this remnant, all would be lost to the powers of darkness.[12]

Evangelicals have often retained Edwards's sense of exclusiveness in regard to the faith. Those less rigid, more catholic, different from themselves could not be tolerated as fellow Christians. The very word *moderate* was employed by evangelicals as a term of opprobrium to describe those less zealous than they. Charles Chauncy, a leading Old Light Calvinist and opponent of the evangelical revivals, charged that, "a grand discriminating Mark" of revivalism was "that it makes Men spiritually proud and conceited beyond Measure, infinitely censorious and uncharitable, to Neighbours, to Relations, even the nearest and dearest; to Ministers in an especial Manner; yea, to all Mankind, who are not as they are, and don't think and act as they do."[13]

This account of the discriminating marks of early revivalism could be used to describe the revivalistic movement throughout American history, including its expression in contemporary America. With few exceptions, revivalists have attacked churches not strict enough for their tastes, branded non-revivalistic clergy as "unconverted" and, at last, have succeeded in the United States in capturing the term, *born again Christian,* for themselves and their adherents. In common parlance, it is accepted that a born again Christian is a Protestant who has had an *experience* of some sort and who takes his or her religion seriously, unlike the ordinary folk who have merely been baptized, attend Sunday services and call themselves Methodists, Episcopalians, Lutherans or Baptists. Thus we are informed that certain athletes, movie stars, and even a recent president of the United States are born again Christians. To say, "I am a born again Christian," is to ask others not to confuse you with the pseudo-Christians who compose the greater part of North American humanity. "They call us," said Irenaeus, " 'unspiritual,' 'common,' and 'ecclesiastic.' "[14]

Even Donald Bloesch, a sophisticated spokesperson who would wish to distinguish American evangelicalism from mindless Fundamentalism, finally advocates dividing the churches in order to rid them of liberals and social activists. Bloesch is true to American evangelicalism in calling for a purified Church, regardless of the cost.[15]

Although the elitism of evangelicalism is well known in North America, there has been a more subtle and perhaps more insidious form of this spiritual pride developing in a quite different theological direction. An ancient gnostic writer proclaimed, "the end of [*gnosis*] makes the man king of himself, and then master of gods and men; thus is he at peace."[16] The elitism of the self-accomplished and self-contained, of those superior creatures who have conquered their human frailties—that is the form of gnostic pride adopted by American liberalism.

Unitarianism, as the foremost early opposition to Calvinist thought and the primary advocate of an Enlightenment faith, was always recognized as the religion of the *few*. The masses might be swayed to and fro by the vulgar appeals of the revivalists, but the proper Bostonians and their spiritual neighbors were able to handle their own thoughts and feelings, and quite well.[17]

A later Bostonian, Ralph Waldo Emerson, did not attack evangelicalism for its elitist tendencies but rather offered an alternative form of elitism. The new elite would not consist of born again Christians who, given the success of the various revivals, were not a very exclusive group. The elite, now, would include only those rare souls who had a profound understanding of themselves. "Very faint and few," Emerson wrote, "are the poets or men of God." But those who do exist, are unconcerned with the ordinary ties and friendships of the *many*. "They [the spiritually awake] are never so fit for friendship, as when they have *quitted mankind,* and taken themselves to friend."[18]

If Emerson were known as the great optimist, that optimism had to do with his high hopes for his own spirit and the spirits of those in his immediate circle. Of Boston, that center of American aristocracy, he wrote, "In Boston is no company for a fine wit. There is a certain *poor-smell* in all the streets, in Beacon Street and Mount Vernon, as well as in the lawyers' offices and the wharves." And even Harvard College was, in Emerson's eyes, "a tool of the Boston counting-houses."[19] The only valid and hopeful Christianity that existed, as far as the transcendentalists were concerned, was that which was "personally differentiated," an "entirely inward spiritual religion."[20]

A more Church-oriented liberalism was to follow Emerson's lead in locating true Christianity only among the enlightened few. For Lyman Abbott and the liberals of his persuasion, religion was defined as "the gradually developed experience of *men who had some perception of the Infinite* in nature and in human life."[21] There is, in Protestant liberalism, a certain underlying assumption that, among the spiritually discerning, there is an access to the truth of God, which is hidden from the masses. The unspoken creed of the liberal might be stated like this: what we *know* is not a result of our having been born again, but simply of our being spiritually discerning people; we have learned much from God and we can learn much more because we are, religiously speaking, astute.

Against the Calvinist doctrine of election, liberalism fostered a voluntaristic religion. Such religion is, by definition, elitist. If the Church has been conscripted, as was the case of ancient Israel, catholic Christianity and even reformed Christianity, there is no legitimate room for pride. In an army of volunteers, however, only the noblest and best who are of one mind and heart will hear the call. Lyman Beecher understood this distinction when he spoke of the various branches and organizations of Protestant Christianity as "voluntary associations of the wise and good."[22]

Eric Voegelin has recognized this development as a gnostic "derailment" of true religion. For, "when the *scientia dei,* which includes God's foreknowledge of man's eternal destiny, was immanentized into man's foreknowledge of his destiny, the foundation was laid for separate churches of the elect down to the contemporary degeneration into civic clubs for socially compatible families."[23]

At certain points, evangelicalism and liberalism have come together in their separate elitist attitudes. Nowhere has this been more evident than in their class understanding of Protestant Christianity. Max Weber, in his authoritative studies of religious sociology, has demonstrated the firm alliance between later Protestantism and the bourgeoisie. Of particular significance to the American situation is his comment, "Sect membership meant a certificate of moral qualification and especially of business morals for the individual. This stands in contrast to membership in a 'church' into which one is 'born' and which lets grace shine over the righteous and unrighteous alike."[24] It is easy to see how, in a sectarian society, grace will be provided only to those who voluntarily offer themselves for bourgeois certification.

A sign of this proper certification, as Weber has taught us, is the Protestant understanding that a certain amount of wealth or, at least, economic respectability accompanies religious grace.[25] In America the various denominations have become differentiated, not so much along theological lines, but along socio-economic lines. Therefore, within the Protestant spectrum of churches there are subtle shades of grace determined by prosperity. Nowhere has the caste system of American Protestantism been more clearly exposed than by H. Richard Niebuhr in his still valid study, *The Social Sources of Denominationalism*. Despite the shadings, however, Niebuhr also exposes the mind-set of middle-class Protestantism as a whole, which is united in the conviction that "success in the world is . . . a clear evidence of the presence of virtue and failure almost a certain symptom of vice."[26]

Henry Ward Beecher, one of the most popular preachers of his day, was quite in line with later Protestant thought when he declared, "looking comprehensively through city and town and village and country, the general truth will stand, that no man in this land suffers from poverty unless it be more than his fault—unless it be his *sin*." It is little wonder that in 1874 Beecher could say, without embarrassment, "our churches are largely for the mutual insurance of prosperous families, and not for the upbuilding of the great underclass of humanity." In the same year, the Rev. Charles Wood with similar indifference, observed, "The poor are not provided for, nor are they wanted as a part of the congregations which worship in the majority of our city churches."[27]

Even though the social gospellers made a valiant effort to swim against the middle-class stream in Protestantism, their movement had little effect. During the struggles of organized labor in the 1920s, both the friends and foes of corporate management recognized that "management was in the Church and labor was out of it."[28]

It might appear that the elitism of the Churches is but a reflection of the elitism of the middle class. The Canadian novelist Margaret Laurence, in *The Diviners,* sees the Protestant Church as a microcosm of the social order. Her heroine, Morag Gunn, worshiping with her guardian, Prin, the town scavenger, realizes, even as an adolescent, that the Church is no different from the culture as a whole. The hymns have to do with classless unity, but have nothing to do with the attitude of the worshipers: "When church is over . . . no one will say *Good Morning* to Morag and Prin. Not on your life. Might soil their precious mouths." "Morag loves Jesus. And how. He is friendly and not stuck-up, is why." Finally, however, with the help of Christian townsfolk, she concludes that God "is mean" and she "wouldn't trust him as far as she can spit."[29]

Whether the Protestant churches acquired their social elitism from the bourgeois society or the other way around remains a moot point. What is incontestable is that American Protestantism still accepts and practices a social exclusivism on behalf of the privileged and that the lower strata of society have been psychologically, intellectually and ethically excluded from the fellowship.[30] Social elitism is an insidious form of elitism and its presence seriously separates

American Protestantism from catholic Christianity. But there are other, more subtle forms of gnostic elitism within Protestantism.

According to Hans Jonas, one of the delineating characteristics of gnosticism is its propensity to oppose nature and history with spiritual power. Because the gnostic sees "the created world as a power system directed at the enslavement of this transmundane self,"[31] he or she is convinced that only an ideal, highly spiritualized politics could have any effect in overcoming this created world.

A form of spiritualized politics came to America by way of a radical Calvinism which held that it was God's will for "religious virtuosi" to dominate "the sinful world, for the purpose of controlling it." Weber found this view "fundamental in the theocracy of New England."[32] Even though the world is not to be trusted, nor the kingdoms thereof, an ideal government devised by a spiritual elite can be trusted. Thus, Timothy Dwight, president of Yale College, could prophesy in 1783:

> Here Empire's last, and brightest throne shall rise;
> And Peace and Right, and Freedom, greet the skies.[33]

And Horace Bushnell was not ashamed to boast: "We are the grand experiment of Protestantism! Yes we—it is our most peculiar destiny—we are set to show, by a new and unheard of career of national greatness and felicity, the moral capabilities and all the beneficent fruits of Christianity and the Protestant faith."[34] The fact that these words were written soon after the termination of the bloodiest, bitterest war in the history of our continent is evidence that Bushnell's vision pertained to the ideal rather than to reality.

The conviction that the salvation of souls throughout the world depends on the salvation of the American soul has been a continuing evangelical theme. Thomas Skinner, Presbyterian clergyman and professor of homiletics, declared in 1843 that "the moral condition of the United States is to decide that of the world."[35] President Woodrow Wilson, despite all that had taken place since Skinner's time, could still affirm: "America was born a Christian nation for the purpose of exemplifying to the nations of the world the principles of righteousness found in the Word of God."[36]

That America is a "nation with the soul of a church"[37] is a well-established theme among historians. What is often overlooked by historians is the extent to which Protestants of all stripes have offered support to the essentially elitist notion that Americans are God's chosen people. Speaking of Reinhold Niebuhr, for instance, Marty blithely declared, "He represented a turning point as had Edwards, Bushnell, and Rauschenbusch before him. He was the *only one* of these who did not share a kind of postmillennial chauvinist view of the American Protestant empire."[38]

The claim that Niebuhr took a different course from his predecessors on the matter of America's unique role in the world would be contested by the liberation theologians. In fact, from their perspective, the heart of Niebuhr's international political ethic had to do with the responsible use of American power in the world. In 1947, he was chosen by George C. Marshall to join the U.S. State Department's Policy Planning Staff. That blue-ribbon committee, composed of such notables as George F. Kennan, Paul H. Nitze, Louis J. Halle, Dorothy Fosdick and Hans Morgenthau, became known as the *realist* school of American foreign policy and Niebuhr, as the father of American *realism*. The underlying conviction of the group was that America could provide a responsible *hegemony* for the free world. With the collapse of the great colonial empires of Spain, Portugal, Holland, France and Britain, the United States had the obligation of moving into that vacuum lest the world fall under the domination of a monolithic Soviet tyranny.[39] Whether called "manifest destiny" or "American hegemony," it amounts to the same thing. American Protestantism feels that the United States is a chosen nation with the burden of the world on its shoulders.

In recent years, this national elitism has received refinement and sophistication from a leading religious sociologist. Robert Bellah, in an influential essay, sees "American civil religion . . . not [as] the worship of the American nation, but an understanding of the American experience in the light of ultimate and universal reality." Bellah admits the need for a *reorganization* of the American religion along universal lines; however,

> the reorganization entailed . . . need not disrupt the American civil religion's continuity. A world civil religion could be accepted as a fulfillment and not a denial of American civil religion. Indeed, such an outcome has been the eschatological hope of American civil religion from the beginning. To deny such an outcome would be to deny the meaning of America itself.[40]

Bellah is affirming the legitimacy of American apocalypticism, its faith that the best of America would finally be recognized as essential for all the peoples of the world. He, like Reinhold Niebuhr, is a revisionist of Protestant American elitism but at the same time a strong advocate of its validity.

It is painful to recognize any similarity between serious social critics such as Niebuhr and Bellah, on the one hand, and fanatical America-firsters such as Jerry Falwell, on the other. It must be admitted, however, that both points of view are informed by national elitism. Both would see America as the spiritual source capable of delivering humanity from its misery.

Ironically the determinative difference between the two, lies in the fact that Christian realism is basically conservative in outlook, whereas the Moral Majority is radical, extremist, revolutionary. The realism of Niebuhr would be practiced according to rational goals and long-established arrangements. The Falwell forces are in the same evangelical tradition that drove the Loyalists out of the United States back to England or up to Canada. As the Revolutionaries "sought to separate the virtuous members of the new republican community from the corrupt and unregenerated adherents of the ancient monarchical order,"[41] so the Moral Majority is intent on separating the virtuous (rigid, laissez-faire, capital punishment-adhering, born again Christians) from the unregenerated (flaccid, socialistic, criminal-coddling, ordinary Christians). The *New Right* is, in fact, not rightist , in the sense of conservative, at all. It stands for the overturning of long-established social agreements. As Philip Greven observed regarding the evangelical contribution to the spirit of 1776, "the evangelical impulse was not conservative in any sense but truly radical, not moderate but extremist."[42] This most recent expression of national elitism is symptomatic of a theology that sees the created world along with all its natural and historically developed systems as "directed at the enslavement of [the] transmundane self."[43] According to such an understanding, the elite, whether a small remnant or a *moral majority,* serve the purpose of freeing individual selves from *all systems.*

There have been and continue to be Protestants who recoil from an elitist interpretation of Christianity. Even though the predominant mood of evangelicalism became that of "excluding from their own ranks the imperfect as well as the unregenerate," many moderate churchmen and moderate congregations have been "content to live with imperfection."[44]

There were also those who refused to accept social elitism within the Church. Theodore Parker in "A Sermon on Merchants" preached in 1846, observed that "this class is the controlling one in the churches . . . in the . . . way it buys up the clergymen. . . . The clergymen will do its work, putting them in comfortable places." In no country in all of Christendom, said Parker, had life become so insecure for the masses, "so cruelly dashed away in the manslaughter of reckless enterprise." Whereas, he reminded the congregation, Jesus had taught, "the greatest of all, must be most effectively the servant of all," the whole ethos of evangelicalism supported those who diametrically opposed the Gospel teaching. The Church had become "the resort of rooks and owls."[45]

A later liberalism following Parker's lead continued to oppose evangelical elitism. If the revivalistic spirit seemed to be concerned only with those who "make their decision for Christ," many liberals insisted that Christ's life and death had to do with all humanity. As Christ had become the brother of all people, his Father was offering forgiveness and the "chance of salvation to all persons and not merely to a fortunate *cognoscenti*." Theodore Munger, for example, was concerned that the new liberal theology be of benefit to "ordinary believers who had been left bewildered, even if relieved, by the loss of traditional doctrines."[46]

Walter Rauschenbusch's egalitarianism went beyond the usual liberal concern for *communicating* the Gospel to those outside the churches. A Christian social gospel, Rauschenbusch insisted, will want Christ's Gospel to effectuate benefits for all people, whether Christian or not:

> An un-Christian social order can be known by the fact that it makes good men do bad things. It tempts, defeats, drains, and degrades, and leaves men stunted, cowed, and shamed in their manhood. A Christian social order makes bad men do good things. It sets high aims, steadies the faint impulses of the weak, trains the powers of the young, and is felt by all as an uplifting force which leaves men with the consciousness of a broader and nobler humanity as their years go on.[47]

The anti-elitist spirit within liberalism, however, has not generally prevailed. According to the distinguished church historian, Sidney E. Mead, "Few theologians today are practising and responsible churchmen. Most appear to belong to the highly abstract and conveniently invisible church whose fulfillments are 'beyond history' and not of this world." Mead goes on to say that most American theologians are either barely tolerant of, or contemptuous of, the "actual institutional incarnation" of the church. As a result, "much of their written work is addressed only to their fellow denizens of the self-made ghetto in which they live, and is almost totally unrelated to the experienced order of the mill run of pastors and church members." Mead, in this connection, quotes his colleague, Martin Marty, as having observed that one is able to "attend a discussion of theological educators talking about improving the ministry" and realize that "they can talk for a week and not mention preaching and parish routine."[48] There exists, in other words, in theological circles, an elitism that regards Christian higher learning as unrelated, not only to the masses, but even to the clerical and lay leaders of the Church. The burning questions of theology, apparently, are of concern only among the professionals. Max Weber was probably oversimplifying when he claimed, "Manicheanism and Gnosticism, the salvation religions of the Near East, are both specifically religions of intellectuals."[49] Most students of gnosticism would insist that if the ancient heresiarchs were intellectuals, it was a very peculiar intellectualism. Weber's description might still apply to many contemporary Protestant scholars, however, for their intellectualism would also seem to be of a very peculiar nature.

If some American theologians have been negative about the possibilities of an institutional Church composed of ordinary Christians, they have often been enthusiastic about "a few men and women scattered across the country—or around the world—[who] become aware of their shared commitment to create a new world, and begin to build a network of communication and solidarity with each other."[50] Harvey Cox, along the same line, sees the local church as a historical anomaly arising out of a "pre-urban ethos." The authentic Church, he claims, is not the "residential parish" but rather "God's avant-garde," those people of God who have the insight and the courage to be first on the scene, where God is in action in the world. Such persons will seek one another out, form "communities of need" and as a wholly voluntary community based on "free choice and not on blood ties or ethnic consanguinity" serve as God's avant-garde corps in the world. Meanwhile, Cox is condescending enough to allow the "residential parish" to exist in a truncated form: "Relieved of the necessity of being all things to all men, of pretending to 'serve the whole man' they can begin to concentrate on those areas of concern in which they really have some kind of entrée. Family problems, residential issues, and adult education seem to be among the things a local parish can deal with."[51] That is, while God's elite corps are engaged in the critical battles of politics and social action, the drones can meet to discuss marriage enrichment, zoning bylaws and the journeys of the Apostle Paul.

Nor has Cox essentially changed his mind about the authentic Church being the "avant-garde corps": only the terminology has been altered. Now the source of a genuine "postmodern theology" will emerge from the "bottom and the edges":

> Once again, on the edges and not at the centers of religious and political power, an energetic source of renewal is appearing, one that might do for a waning modernity what the monastic movement and its later descendants, the heretics and schismatics, the Waldensians and radical Franciscans, the Diggers and Anabaptists—did for previous failing eras.[52]

In the new religion of the secular city, the ordinary people of ordinary churches will not play a significant role.

It has often been noted that the early gnostic teachers could accept orthodox formulations only as a sort of primer for the real faith or, perhaps, as a continuing textbook for those primitive types who could not understand the profundities of genuine faith. For these teachers, Christ as the historical Son of God had been superseded by Christ the mythical heavenly being, the symbol of cosmic dimensions. Not only was the Old Testament rejected out of hand, but also the New Testament, as historical revelation, was not taken seriously.[53] Protestant liberal academics have had a similar elitist influence in their own theological disciplines.

The Process theologians, in regarding biblical religion as a sort of step along the way to the ultimate, seem to be going in a gnostic direction. According to Schubert M. Ogden, for example, the New Testament with its mythological conception of God's activity in the world is no longer intelligible to modern secular men and women. Carrying Bultmann to what he believes to be a logical conclusion, Ogden understands the theological task to be that of translating the biblical myth into the truth which humanity already knows through experience in the world to be the truth.[54] Not everyone, obviously, can properly discern this truth in experience. Whereas in orthodox Christianity revelation is held to be an act of divine grace whereby the simple can be as enlightened as the sophisticated, Process theology requires of the seeker for truth acute powers of observation and discerning mental faculties. As Colin Gunton has observed, "Revelation . . . [becomes] a function of the human mind and not of God" and "Man's mind takes the place of the Holy Spirit." Because of this dependence on human spiritual capacities, "Process theology," Gunton charges, ". . . in the works of Hartshorne and Ogden, is a system of gnosticism, with all the attendant intellectualism and elitism. The enlightened ones are those with the intellectual power to think themselves into the circle of belief."[55]

An understanding of Scripture similar to that of Ogden was held by Paul Tillich, whose immense influence on American thought is still being felt. Tillich, unlike Ogden and other Bultmannians, was unwilling to speak of *de*mythologizing the New Testament because symbols and myths are the necessary "language of faith" apart from which the Gospel cannot be received. Though, for Tillich, the myth must be "broken," taken apart in order to be understood, at the same time it cannot be discarded. A. J. McKelway has pointed out that whereas this "makes Tillich appear almost conservative in contrast to the radical nature of Bultmann's criticism," in reality,

> Bultmann at least keeps Jesus as a historical fact and event at the center of the Christian message. If all the myths were struck away, there would still remain a message and a man. But Tillich is not so sure that the man would remain. He can seriously consider the meaning of the Christian message apart from Jesus. It is the New Being, expressed in, but transcendent to, Jesus as the Christ, that is the subject of the saving act of God and which therefore, is the *sine qua non* of the Christian faith.[56]

The Tillichian mode of interpretation certainly comes close to expressing the gnostic conviction that the *real meaning* of Scripture lies hidden in Scriptural accounts of Jesus' life until the discerning, spiritual person uncovers the meaning and plucks it from the obvious.

Elaine Pagels, quoting from the *Gospel of Philip,* illustrates the gnostic drive to get behind the Church's *terms* to "the depth" of meaning behind the terms. Names, warns the *Gospel of Philip,* can be "very deceptive, for they divert our thoughts from what is accurate to what is inaccurate. Thus one who hears the word 'God' does not perceive what is accurate, but perceives what is inaccurate." Pagels goes on to observe, "The Protestant theologian Paul Tillich recently drew a similar distinction between the God we imagine when we hear the term, and the 'God beyond God,' that is, the 'ground of being' that underlies all our concepts and images."[57] In this distinction, just as in his biblical interpretation, Tillich describes two levels of understanding, one for the ordinary Christians who accept the conspicuous aspects of the faith and are, thereby, misled, and those, on the other hand, who have the intellectual and spiritual acumen to grasp "the depth" of meaning.

The particular level of understanding can be determined by social and economic realities. Max Weber maintained:

> The salvation sought by the intellectual is always based on inner need, and hence it is at once more remote from life, more theoretical and more systematic than salvation from external distress, the quest for which is characteristic of nonprivileged classes.[58]

Could it be that the "remote from life" form of intellectualism has led some liberal Protestants to a rejection of Liberation theology? Could their understanding of the Latin American theology as "simplistic" and "literalistic" be yet another example of a subtle elitism, an unwitting alliance with the established forces of Western society against the "wretched of the earth"?[59]

Many liberal Protestants seem confidently to accept the notion that because the New Testament authors were unenlightened in regard to modern science, technology and psychology, their understanding of life must have been vastly inferior to our own. They also assume that because of the great intellectual breakthroughs of recent times, intelligent Christians are faced with contradictions concerning the Scripture which have never had to be faced before. Actually, Irenaeus confronted a similar attitude in his generation:

> They [the gnostics] consider themselves "mature," so that no one can be compared with them in the greatness of their *gnosis,* not even if you mention Peter or Paul or any of the other apostles. . . . They imagine that they themselves have discovered more than the apostles, and that the apostles preached the gospel still under the influence of Jewish opinions, but that they themselves are wiser and more intelligent than the apostles.[60]

CHAPTER NINE

Syncretism: From the Particular to the Nebulous

THE ancient gnostics did not find it acceptable to confine themselves to the intelligence of the apostles. They were not at all prepared to place all their eggs in such a small basket. For gnosticism by its very nature is syncretistic: it accepts the "intermingling of given ideas and images"[1] as normal and necessary for faith.

Christian orthodoxy is syncretistic by accident. As we have seen, in its missionary zeal and in its interaction with neighboring religions, the Church has been inadvertently influenced by many other faiths. Orthodoxy, however, in all its twists and turns, is pointed in one direction, that of Jesus Christ the incarnate Son of God. The one direction is guaranteed through the orthodox community's regular celebration of Word and Sacrament.

Gnostic syncretism could not accept the one direction. How could its multiple agenda be realized through the Crucified One? In fact, the Christ present at his Eucharist, as a single focus, denied what *gnosis* considered to be the supreme goals of religion: alienation from the world, secret knowledge, escape from the world, escape into the self and special status for the knowledgeable ones.

Syncretism is not like the other categories delineating gnostic faith; it is not an object of faith but a method. It is the method of achieving the various gnostic goals. Gnostic faith can exist within Christianity, indeed can thrive within Christianity, so long as the Incarnation is accepted as only one image among many. Through purposeful syncretism the one image becomes diffused, a mere element in the gnostic mix. In this sense, gnostic syncretism involves not only an acceptance of many beliefs and practices, but a denial of the particular belief and the particular practice that make Christianity, Christianity. Many ideas, all lacking in subordination, aid and abet the gnostic cause; particularity, a single focus, represents a threat to the gnostic thought pattern.

It is difficult to see how American Protestantism, deeply rooted in Calvinist theology, could have moved in the direction of syncretistic religion. Calvin himself was quite clear about the single focus of the faith. McDonnell, a modern Roman Catholic scholar, argues that for Calvin "the unity of Head and members effected by the Holy Spirit is not a metaphorical unity but that of a body which is none other than the body of Christ."[2]

How then could what began with definite concepts of event, means of grace and sacramental life have become transformed into the present Protestantism, often so indefinite and nebulous? Is it possible that Calvin himself unwittingly left a loophole for gnostic misinterpretation and even for gnostic syncretism?

Even Wendel, the great student and advocate of Calvin's theology, conceded that there was room for ambiguity in Calvin's doctrine of the sacraments. He understood Calvin as believing that "we may attain to it [union with Christ] by other means, such as preaching, the reading of the Bible, or prayer,"[3] that is, by other means than through the sacraments. This open question was to lead his North American followers onto a lonely road and, finally, into a gnostic way far removed from "the ancient paths, where the good way is."[4]

The Puritan followers of Calvin heard their teacher loud and clear on the matter of the sovereignty of God. Because God is sovereign, He has no obligation to use the sacraments. If God wishes to cleanse us by other means than by baptism, He can. If He chooses to nourish us by other means than by Holy Communion, He certainly can.[5] They began to infer from this premise that God does *not* choose such means to save us. And because God is not bound to employ the Church itself to do His work, the Church does not occupy an essential role in redemption. Within puritanism, however, no syncretistic religion would have been tolerated. At least in theory, the Incarnate Christ still held center stage. What was being lost during this period was the single focus of Christ within his Church, Christ as he presents himself in Word and Sacrament. What was slipping away was a unified view of the world guaranteed by a particular means of grace.

Left with no definite means of grace, no certitude or even comfort, the Protestant individual found the Calvinistic doctrine of election to be a monstrous threat. The sinner was left to the caprice of the infinite God who despises finite means. Max Weber has perfectly captured the mood of this later Calvinism:

> In its extreme inhumanity this doctrine [election] must above all have had one consequence for the life of a generation which surrendered to its magnificent consistency. That was a feeling of unprecedented inner loneliness of the single individual. . . . No one could help him. No priest, for the chosen one can understand the word of God only in his heart. No sacraments . . . they are not a means to the attainment of grace, but only the subjective *externa subsidia* of faith. No Church . . . [because] the membership of the external Church included the doomed. . . . Finally, even no God. For even Christ had died only for the elect. . . . This, the complete elimination of salvation through the Church and the sacraments . . . was what formed the absolutely decisive difference from Catholicism.[6]

Grace had become unspecified, generalized and was, therefore, unrecognizable and unable to offer any real comfort or confidence.

Human beings can, of course, live only so long without comfort. Some poetic souls within American puritanism reacted negatively to a graceless Church. "The reason the mass of men fear God," Herman Melville wrote his friend Hawthorne, "and at bottom dislike Him, is because they rather distrust His heart and fancy Him all brain like a watch."[7] How could one help but resent a God who refuses to put His heart into His creation and who leaves His creatures alone and afraid without access to Himself? Emily Dickinson, in her desperate search for concrete grace, kept the Sabbath "staying at home" because there was more beauty to be found in nature than in Church. She continued, however, to look toward the Puritan Savior for help:

> At least—to pray—is left—is left—
> O Jesus—in the Air—
> I know not which thy chamber is—
> I'm knocking—everywhere—
> Thou settest Earthquake in the South—
> And Maelstrom, in the sea—
> Say, Jesus Christ of Nazareth—
> Hast thou no Arm for Me?[8]

"Knocking everywhere" but nowhere in particular, she makes the frightening discovery that grace is nowhere. The gnosticized Jesus "in the Air," now disconnected from his Church and his sacraments, will not or cannot help.

The theological protest against a graceless, anti-sacramental Church took the form of liberal syncretism. It has been said of Theodore Parker: "His mind was like the republican idea itself; it could afford to be hospitable, but could not afford to be exclusive."[9] Ralph Waldo Emerson, who was to carry liberalism into a new almost unbounded dimension would ask, "What is the scholar, what is the man *for,* but for hospitality to every new thought of his time?"[10] On the other hand Emerson's hospitality did not extend to Church and sacraments. These particularities were, to his mind, superstitious and offensive, a judgment consistent with his "perennial condemnation of the material."[11] With Emerson there was introduced that which later was to become a Protestant principle, namely, the rejection of all structures and outward forms as corruptions of the Gospel. If Calvin had unwittingly left ajar the door leading to a churchless and sacramentless Christianity, Emerson had opened it all the way, entered himself, and invited the rest to follow. It must be remembered that from an American point of view, Emerson and his friends were, in the words of Perry Miller, "Protestant to the core."[12]

The purposeful syncretism of the transcendentalists, with its "hospitality for every new thought" and its concomitant rejection of particularity—Church and Sacrament—could also be observed within mainline Protestantism. A later American liberalism was to be strongly influenced by G. W. F. Hegel, who proudly proclaimed Protestantism to be identical with "universal insight and education . . . our universities and our schools are our churches." For Hegel therein lay "the essential contrast with Catholicism."[13] Nowhere would the difference between Protestant and Catholic styles be more evident than in North America. Catholicism continues to be symbolized by the large, richly decorated church or cathedral, where worship is always circumscribed by the Eucharist. Protestantism is represented by the colleges and universities, even by the public school system; certainly, it is not concerned with religious things approached from a religious perspective. For Protestants, religion in the Catholic style confines, limits, narrows the mind to a contemplation of the definite. Religion in the Protestant sense has "hospitality for every new thought" but always with the unspoken understanding that the concrete, the definite will not be taken seriously.

American Protestants have been aware of the difficulty of their position. How can Christianity be open to all things and at the same time be in any sense historically Christian? How can the churches affirm that God is everywhere and anywhere, identical with the natural order of things and infused in historical progress, while still proclaiming the uniqueness of the Christian revelation—"In Christ God was reconciling the world to himself"?[14] William Wallace Fenn, Dean of Harvard Divinity School in 1910, was concerned by the lack of concreteness in his own liberal tradition. Liberalism, he said, had failed to fulfil two basic theological requirements: first, to fit thought to the *fact* and words to the thought; second, "to *distinguish between things that differ.*"[15]

Dean Fenn's observations were, of course, no news to the evangelicals. Benjamin Warfield, an eminent Princeton theologian, found the liberals weary of "thinking, distinguishing, defending"; they had become a "structureless, homogeneous mass." Billy Sunday was less restrained in his attack on modernist syncretism: "Lord, save us from off-handed, flabby-cheeked, brittle-boned, weak-kneed, thin-skinned, pliable, plastic, spineless, effeminate, ossified three-karat Christianity."[16] More thoughtful evangelical critics than Billy Sunday were also concerned about the liberal Sunday School. It seemed to be a place where everything of a religious nature was being taught, but not much that could be considered uniquely Christian. Henry C. Minton, also of the conservative Princeton school, demanded in exasperation, "Just exactly what is it that is to be studied in the Sunday-school?"[17] The criticisms from within and from the evangelical right were quite accurate. Liberalism had become an amorphous collection of religious ideas in general.

Valiant attempts have been made to reconnect Protestantism with its necessary particularities. As Ahlstrom has recalled, American theologians influenced by Karl Barth did try to restore "the doctrine of the Church, so slighted by liberals and fundamentalists" to a central theological position. Ahlstrom also recounts "Neo-orthodoxy's own critique of culture-protestantism and its demand for a prophetic church that would recognize its continuity with the New Testament community and, therefore, its *distinctness* from the world in which it proclaims the Word and to which it ministers."[18]

To date, American Protestantism has refused to take seriously the ecclesiological concerns of Barth and his followers. The particularity of Christ himself has remained an unacceptable scandal. "I am not prepared," pronounced Dean Willard Sperry of Harvard Divinity School, "to identify the case for religion solely with the revelation in Christ."[19] Harvey Cox was delighted that man had come of age and freed himself of the need for both magic and traditional Christianity. When Max Weber simply reported as a historical fact that Protestantism had accomplished "the complete elimination of salvation through the Church and the sacraments" and described this as "the absolutely decisive difference from Catholicism," Cox hailed that accomplishment as a step in the right direction. Cox was enthusiastic about the overcoming of all distinguishing particulars in the Church. He regarded it as spiritually beneficial that the Church is totally invisible: "*only faith can discern the Church of Jesus Christ.* It is not an entity which can be empirically detected and located by a bulletin board or a sociological survey."[20]

A syncretistic view of theology itself is given support by Frederick Herzog. In a *Christian Century* article, he argues that

> a sort of laissez faire mentality forces on us the competition of various systems in the free market of ideas. We are left with more or less free wheeling faith explorations. . . . [F]or that reason it is helpful to drop the word theology for the time being, and the demand for theological excellence as well. Sound teaching today stands for the great reversal of the sequence, from theory to practice.[21]

It would seem that because the Church has somehow been forced into the competitive marketplace of ideas, like other competitors in advertising and merchandising, it must abandon clear thinking. Rather than the Church acting on the basis of what it is taught through Christ, the Church's teaching is based on what it is, in fact, already doing. Given this new sequence, it is difficult to understand how Protestantism is to experience anything which could be called a *reformation*.

The Process school also refuses to be confined to Christian particulars. According to Colin Gunton, "In Process theology, the world takes the place of the Son . . . man comes to know God directly without the mediation of Jesus Christ." The recorded acts of God become little more than illustrations of the truth already at hand. "God," writes Gunton, "is essentially the one who accepts meekly into his memory all that man does. . . . God becomes little more than the one who validates human life as it is, a divine pat upon the human back."[22] Such a formulation could, of course, incorporate anything into faith, while depending on nothing in particular.

The other side of the syncretistic coin is an aversion to the particular. Within American Protestantism that aversion has been felt especially toward the particularity of Church and sacraments. For it is the Body of Christ that continually focuses attention on its Head, whereas the specific sacramental events demand that all words, music, art and thought be concentrated on the One Lord of the One Church.

Protestant rejection of Church and sacraments has been varied. William Newton Clarke, a liberal Baptist theologian, managed to write a five-hundred page outline of theology without discussing the Church and its ministry. William Wallace Fenn would say with determined pride that "the Liberal has no inclination to return to traditional Christianity, still less to the Church." And Washington Gladden simply wrote off the entire history of organized Christianity as "a signal and dismal failure."[23]

Unfortunately, the critique of liberal syncretism has come and continues to come chiefly from an evangelicalism which has an equal disdain for anything concrete in the Christian faith. If possible, the evangelicals were more suspicious of the sacraments than were their liberal opponents. Using the argument that a too frequent celebration of Holy Communion would detract from proper reverence for the event, most evangelical churches ministered the Supper no more than four times a year. This quarterly celebration has become so general a practice that it is often thought of as the normal Protestant tradition. Evangelicals would be loathe to acknowledge that this infrequent practice of the Eucharist was first suggested by a Roman Catholic theologian, Peter of Blois (d. 1204),[24] and that its rationalization bears a passing resemblance to the Roman notion that a frequent gazing upon the Eucharist could replace the actual reception of the elements. The Protestant custom is in effect a sort of spiritual reservation of the host. It is probable that spiritual reservation is rooted in the prevailing Protestant fear of *things* and founded on the logic that because God does not require particular objects to effect His salvation, neither do we require them to receive His salvation.

Walker Percy pinpoints the modern Protestant attitude toward the particular in *Love in the Ruins*. Dr. Tom More, Percy's Catholic protagonist, is having some conflict with his Protestant wife, Ellen, on the matter of his religious practice:

> What she [Ellen] disapproves is not that I am doing public penance. No, what bothers her is an ancient Presbyterian mistrust of *things,* things getting mixed up with religion. The black sweater and the ashes scandalize her. . . . What have these *things,* articles, to do with doing right? For she mistrusts the Old Church's traffic in things, sacraments, articles, bread, wine, salt, oil, water, ashes. Watch out! You know what happened before when you Catholics mucked it up with all your things, medals, scapulars, candles, bloody statues![25]

It is significant that in the doctrinal tests so important to American fundamentalists for distinguishing between authentic Christianity and liberal heresy, the sacraments are never mentioned. Sacramental theology, so critical to Roman Catholic and Eastern Orthodox Christians as well as to some Lutherans and Anglicans, is not of concern. For most American Protestants, it is a neutral area, an extinct volcano representing no threat to either side. American Protestantism has to a great degree become de-sacramentalized.[26]

Though the sacrament of Holy Communion is still being practiced in Protestant churches, however infrequently, the symbolism of the Supper has been truncated and even distorted. Calvin's strenuous objection to the Roman refusal to minister the cup to the people has been answered by the serving of grape juice. During the political drive for Prohibition in the United States and Canada, it was thought incongruous to have prohibitionist Christians indulging in a symbolic celebration with an alcoholic beverage. That Christ himself had blessed the fruit of the vine in his first miracle and commanded wine to be used as a memorial to him until his coming again was of small import beside the larger ethical issue. Calvin criticized the papists for having "placed the vessel of their salvation in this fatal vortex" of a gold cup, making a mockery of the simplicity and humility of the meal;[27] North American Protestants have chosen to confine the wine, or rather grape juice, in the fatal vortex of the individual cup, destroying the memory of the Passover feast of the people of God. Jungmann reports that within the early Church, "under pressure from gnostic circles that rejected all wine drinking, there was a trend here and there to replace the wine entirely by water."[28] It was a later gnostic influence, however, that led the Church to serve its unexhilarating element in a personal anticommunal cup.[29]

The depreciation of the Eucharist is but one aspect of the erosion of the Church itself within modern American Protestantism. For the Eucharist and the Church are intrinsically bound together. As Paul Lehmann put it, "The *koinonia* is either a eucharistic achievement or a conjurer's trick."[30] Without the particularity of the meal and without the particular Host who presides at the meal, the Church's agenda becomes something quite different from that assigned it in the New Testament, through the tradition of the Fathers, or even by the Protestant Reformers. The Church without sacraments exists for the purpose of accomplishing certain self-imposed goals which have at best only a tangential connection with the Gospel.

Paul Tillich noted "the death of the sacraments" in non-Roman Christianity and spoke of the need for the sacraments to be understood as symbols rather than as mere signs. He nevertheless believed that "the sacramental consecration of elements of *all of life* shows the presence of the *ultimately sublime in everything* and points to the unity of everything in its creative ground and its final fulfillment." And though, unlike Cox, Tillich still accepted the importance of a "manifest" Church, he also perceived a "latent" Church, a spiritual community not to be identified with churches.[31]

Herbert W. Richardson is delighted that "in American religion, the Sabbath replaces the Christological sacraments characteristic of European Christianity." This theological advance, he tells us, "involves a new conception of the 'marks' of the true Church. In European Protestantism, the marks of the Church include preaching and administration of the Christological sacraments. . . . This new sacrament of American Christianity is not *Christological* but *theological*. It focuses not upon the death of Christ but upon the theocracy of God, who is sanctifying His creation through His providential works."[32] There could not be a clearer statement of the syncretistic thrust of this kind of Protestantism; it refuses to confine Christianity to Cross, Supper, Church—anything in particular—in order to open it up to everything in general. The practical ecclesiastical result of this rejection of the Christological sacraments becomes clear in Richardson's observation that "in Europe the Church ceases to exist because 'the world comes of age' and no longer needs it; in America, the Church ceases to exist because it fully embodies its spirit in all the other institutions of life."[33] If the European Church can be accused of being irrelevant in the modern world, is it not perhaps a more serious indictment that the American Church has become diffused throughout everything—from the Dallas Cowboys to the American Defense Department? Despite the sophistication of Richardson's attempts to lead us "toward an American theology," what finally is the qualitative difference between his theology and Eisenhower's 1954 statement of belief: "Our government makes no sense unless it is founded on a deeply felt religious faith—and I don't care what it is"?[34]

At the end of his study of American Protestantism, Winthrop S. Hudson could find only "the form of surviving memories and a lingering identification with the resources of historic Christianity."[35]

III

GNOSTICISM ESTABLISHED WITHIN NORTH AMERICAN PROTESTANTISM: RESULTS AND REFORM

CHAPTER TEN

Results of a Gnosticized Protestantism

Rejection of the Good Earth: Ecology and the Bomb

THE decline of an authentic Protestantism and the ascendancy of gnostic Christianity in North America has wrought horrendous results and threatens even more tragic consequences in the future. If G. K. Chesterton was right in describing America as "a nation with the soul of a church," that is one thing, but when America becomes a nation with the soul of a *gnostic* church, that is quite another.

The sense of alienation felt by many Christians today is similar to that expressed in the mandalas of some Christian gnostics of the early Middle Ages. In some of their circular drawings or unifying symbols connecting male and female images, good and evil figures, there is no center. Those mandalas lacking a center, in which "no trace of divinity is to be found," signify according to Jung that the creator of the mandala has found a center within the self. "The place of the deity," Jung believes, "appears to be taken by the wholeness of man."[1] Although such a substitution of self for God can be and has been looked at as a positive step, humanity's "coming of age," the human race being now responsible for its own destiny or other bold assertions of emancipation, the place in the center remains empty: God's place has been filled with—a void.

This empty theology provides for the gnostic Christian a certain unity of the "eternal" present. In that present, a type of circular life is possible. Within a context in which male and female, good and evil, are interchangeable and all things are lacking in subordination, it is quite conceivable that one can make the daily rounds. What is totally denied by such a theological pattern, however, is a grounding in the past and any genuine hope for the future.

Nature itself in such a scheme is not a gift from the past, but merely the environment of the present. The Puritan spirit that led Jonathan Edwards to regard nature as an evil mother—"[who] hungry for the flesh of her children . . . swallows up mankind, one generation after another" so insatiable is her appetite[2]—has in the twentieth century been transformed into a notion of nature as totally indifferent. From a gnostic perspective, if the natural order is indifferent toward the spiritual person, treating that person like any other creature, why should the spiritual being have any regard for it? Nature becomes then that force which must be opposed and overcome.

Margaret Atwood claims to have noticed a distinct difference between American and Canadian attitudes regarding nature. Whereas Americans feel compelled to pit themselves against their natural environment and win a victory, Canadians "both English and French" are satisfied, with "Survival, la Survivance." In fact, Atwood continues, "Our [Canadian] stories are likely to be tales not of those who made it but of those who made it back."[3] Whether or not that distinction is valid, it is certainly true that in American life the evangelical tradition has founded and sustained a culture that regards nature as an adversary to be exploited.[4]

These attitudes have found public expression in the policies of an American Secretary of the Interior. After several official moves to ease strip-mining regulations, to open up more federal land to mining and logging, and after threatening to sell park lands for private exploitation, reporters asked the secretary if he were not worried about future generations and their right to enjoy the benefits of the land. As the *Wall Street Journal* reported: "Reverting to the stark religious symbolism that forms the foundation of his born again Christian faith, Mr. Watt calmly explained: 'I do not know how many future generations we can count on before the Lord returns.' "[5] Earth, air, water are of very little interest because there is no lasting material future. Meanwhile, within the "eternal" present, there is money to be made.

This attitude toward nature in general leads to a similar attitude toward human nature in particular. In Margaret Laurence's story "The

Merchant of Heaven," an American missionary, Brother Lemon, preaches a frenzied sermon to save African souls. Danso, a native artist, reacts with outrage to Lemon's sermon:

> Listen—he is telling them that life on earth doesn't matter. So the guinea worm stays in the flesh. The children still fall into the pit latrines and die with excrement in their mouths. And the women sit for all eternity breaking buildingstones with hammers for two shillings a day. . . . . . It must be quite a procedure—to tear the soul out of the living body and throw the inconvenient flesh away like fruit rind.[6]

In that incident, as in many of her other works, Laurence's attack on faith is directed at the gnosticized Protestantism of North America, which, both at home and abroad, denies the validity and the possibility of human life as it really is.

Nowhere is the denial of nature, of human nature and of a future for humanity more evident than in the nuclear arms race. George F. Kennan, the distinguished American diplomat and student of international relations, is almost incredulous that rational leaders in the United States can have employed nuclear weapons as the principal defense of Western civilization. In a speech delivered at Princeton Theological Seminary on 27 April 1982, Kennan asks,

> Must we not assume that the entire human condition out of which all this has arisen—our own nature, the character of the natural world which surrounds us . . . the entire environmental framework . . . in which the human experiment has proceeded—must we not assume that this was the framework in which God meant it to proceed—that this was the house in which it was meant that we should live—that this was the stage on which the human drama . . . was meant to be enacted? Who are we then, the actors, to take upon ourselves the responsibility of destroying this framework, or even risking its destruction?[7]

I would suggest the answer that only actors who have no regard for the scenery could possibly consider such a risk. In fact, only those who have come to accept a gnostic view of the world could even entertain the notion of defending anything by annihilating everything. Whether or not the holocaust actually occurs, the balance of terror itself is the result of a heresy, a circular heresy, with no respect for the past, no hope for the future and no real God at the center of its present.

Rejection of Biblical Boundaries: The Triumph of Private Vision

Ernst Troeltsch found that the liberal Protestantism of his day advocated a "theology of subjective experience in contrast to the theology of objective revelation; the sole value it assigns to Jesus is that of serving as the original stimulator of the religious consciousness."[8] This description could be applied accurately to many mainline churches in North America. The story of Israel, the life of Christ, the experiences of the New Testament Church are all accepted as interesting paradigms of universal truths which, in a limited way, can help us understand our own situation more clearly. Liberal American Protestantism, however, becomes embarrassed at the thought of being confined to objective revelation.

A prominent American liberal, Octavius Brooks Frothingham, was anxious to free the Christ from the particular person, Jesus of Nazareth: "To try to crowd the attributes of the theological Christ into the personality of the historical Jesus, is to plant a whole forest in a porcelain vase." Although such a suggestion properly understood the narrowness of the evangelical view of Jesus, it robbed the "theological Christ" of definite content. In fact, Frothingham would place himself "beyond Christianity" and deny the finality of the Christian religion.[9] American liberalism requires secret *gnosis* to understand the workings of a nebulous, disconnected-from-Jesus Spirit. Evangelicalism also requires secret *gnosis* because, despite all its repetition of the Lord's name, the content of the evangelical Christ remains undisclosed. One is to be converted to Christ, to come to Christ, to love Christ, to bring others to Christ, but the purpose of this Christ in the world is a mystery, except perhaps to those who have been born again.

e.e. cummings picks up the mood of this mystifying religion in his lines:

no time ago
or else a life
walking in the dark
i met christ

jesus)my heart
flopped over
and lay still
while he passed (as

close as i'm to you
yes closer
made of nothing
except loneliness[10]

The poet has caught the emptiness of modern American Christianity that offers no hope to the person "walking in the dark" because its Word is formless and void, "made of nothing except loneliness."

If the Christian faith is a secret *gnosis* without definite content, then the place of the Christian Church and the task of Christian people in the world will be very nebulous indeed. If, in the political sphere, the Spirit is at work apart from Christ or if Christ is understood apart from the humanity revealed in Jesus of Nazareth then, of course, anything goes. The Spirit could be for abortion—or against it. The Spirit could be for capital punishment—or against it. The Spirit could be for nuclear armament—or against it. Who is to say? Anyone with *gnosis* can make a personal judgment.

It was in such a confused religious atmosphere that America became involved in a war in Southeast Asia. In a world in which Christ has been assigned the limited role of persuading people to be caring and sharing and in which the purpose of God is unknown, the Protestant ethic regarding Vietnam was anyone's guess. Thus during the 1960s, until the anti-war movement had become a strong secular force, most Protestant church people were unable to consider the distant war a matter for Christian concern. It was generally understood that Christians were to treat other people in a kindly fashion, as Christ had clearly taught. But in international affairs, the undefined Spirit was at work, the Spirit not known through Christ. What right did the Protestant churches or Protestant people have to interfere with that work?

Even after some Protestant leaders did join with student groups and others in opposing American aggression, nearly always the Protestant message was an appeal to Christian kindness and charity (noblesse oblige) toward the Vietnamese. Rarely were prophetic voices heard warning the president and the Congress of the judgment of God against those who murder the innocent ones of Christ. Rarely were the taxpayers reminded of their complicity in the burning of villages, the napalming of children, the destruction of rice fields—all in rebellion against the will of Almighty God as he has *publicly* revealed Himself in Christ. Rarely were Protestants in positions of power able to say, "No, I resign; I cannot take part in such deeds because I am a Christian, and the teaching of Christ is clear." Rarely were preachers heard prophesying defeat and punishment for the American nation as a result of such blatant cruelty and injustice: "God is not mocked, for whatever a man sows, that he will also reap."[11]

The miscalculation that led to the American defeat in Vietnam was based not on military error alone, but also on a serious theological error which failed to account for the intervention of Almighty God on behalf of justice in the world.

Similar miscalculations are being made in Central America and will continue to be made elsewhere so long as the theology that undergirds American life fails to understand the nature of the biblical God and so long as Protestant Churches neglect to warn their national leaders of "the fury of the wrath of God the Almighty."[12] Lacking a theology rooted in "the mighty acts" of God, it is little wonder that Protestantism has been ineffectual in discovering an ethical direction different from that of American culture as a whole. Protestantism's "secularized and innocuous" bearing is a natural consequence of its gnostic view of history.[13]

Religion as a Category Separate from Life: Escape from Social Ethics

Insofar as North American Protestantism functions as an escapist religion, refusing to come to grips with nature or history, it promotes the practice of religion as something that can be done "on the side." Human beings, after all, can effectively escape reality on one level, but eventually at some time and place food must be supplied, bills paid, waste disposed of, laws passed, and animosities resolved. The practitioner of an escapist religion, then, is forced to conceive of religion as one category of life similar to categories such as economics, sex, music and sports. Often, in fact, American Protestant Christianity, along with another national institution, has become merely "a great American pastime."

Evangelicals gain from their religion feelings of comfort and assurance regarding their eternal salvation along with emotional evidence that, unlike the common herd of humanity, they have not been abandoned in this present earthly struggle. Liberal Christians find in their faith self-understanding and confidence and perhaps even some intimation of the meaning of their existence. In practical matters, however, in regard to those persistent phenomena such as economics, politics, disease and war, a second, more practical faith has been employed. That practical drive of modern gnosticism must now be investigated.

Medieval scholars often noted the apparent contradiction between the otherworldly theology of the gnostic Cathari, on the one hand, and their aggressive political ambitions, on the other. Runciman tells us that it was this strange combination of otherworldly religious fervor with "the swords of the nobility" that made the heresy such a formidable danger to the Catholic Church.[14] In a similar way, it might seem surprising that Dr. Billy Graham, who so often dismissed the need for prophetic preaching on the grounds that only the conversion of individuals could save the world, at the same time urged America in 1952 to "maintain strong military power for defense at any cost."[15] In the 1980s there has been a significant change in the preaching of Dr. Graham; he has shown courage in freeing himself from the American military position and in moving toward a more socially responsible preaching of the Gospel. It is noteworthy, however, that the evangelist's earlier sermons have enjoyed a far greater popularity and exerted a much stronger influence on American society than have his later ones. Many American Fundamentalists, while preaching about the love of God toward His elect, His graciousness in giving His Son for the redemption of sinful individuals, at the same time call upon the military with its nuclear arsenal to provide security against Communist aggression; support the dismantling of social welfare programs which provide for the unworthy; and demand the reinstatement of the death penalty for murderers. The religion of love, in other words, is something one escapes to, out of the horror of mundane life. Christianity is a faith practiced on the side. To cope with that world, which in practical terms cannot be escaped, Fundamentalists are often in support of capitalism, a capitalism in its most uncharitable form. Though such a course might appear to be contradictory, it follows quite logically from an escapist theology. For just as the evangelical soul escapes responsibility when entering the realm of religion, so also the evangelical soul escapes religion when entering the realm of responsibility.

The rise of Falwell and the Moral Majority does not represent a real deviation from evangelical otherworldliness. Far from being a sign of a new willingness on the part of the Fundamentalists to involve themselves in the political process, this type of involvement is but another example of their insistence on keeping the Gospel of Jesus separate from the mundane. Although it is proper, they are saying, to speak of love and forgiveness at evangelistic rallies when the subject is confined to religion, it is quite improper even to think of such matters in regard to the Russians or to nuclear disarmament. Thus the "freezeniks" must be opposed, and in the Reverend Falwell's words, "The first order of business is coming back to [military] equality with the Soviet Union."[16] At all costs, the two spiritual kingdoms must be kept apart. Whether the first priority for the new evangelical right is to maintain Christianity as a religion of pure escapism or to sustain capitalism as the sole spiritual guide to the temporal order is an open question. What is certain is that both items are on the agenda.

In the case of liberal Protestantism, escapist tendencies have been more subtle, and the distinction between religious life and secular life is often not evident. In fact, the strong point of American liberalism has been its sustained effort to be relevant to the contemporary scene. It is in this very struggle for relevance, however, that we find the liberal weakness. What is escaped in liberal Protestantism is the embarrassing humanity of Jesus, the confining physicality of his ministry, the witness of his poverty, the earthly failure of his mission, the even more discomforting presence of the Church he established. In breaking away from the bondage of the earthly Jesus Christ and his earthly Church with its earthly sacraments, liberals have been enabled to escape the reality of the world as it has been exposed by the humanity of Jesus.

The Hartford Appeal of 1975 justifiably repudiated the idea that "the world must set the agenda for the Church." Hartford further rejected the notion that "social, political, and economic programs to improve the quality of life are ultimately normative for the Church's mission in the world."[17] From an orthodox point of view, as explicated by the Appeal, the Incarnation of Christ must set the agenda for the Church and ultimately, through the Church, for the world.

The escapism of American Protestantism has been aided by an anti-intellectualism unfriendly to biblical preaching, serious theological dialogue, or liturgical practice that does not coincide with the *zeitgeist*. Thus in Sidney Mead's words, "the American denominations have successively leant themselves to the sanctification of current existing expressions of the American way of life."[18]

Nor can the new effort by Mead, Bellah and others to locate a genuine *civil religion* that is prophetic and self-critical avoid this pattern. Regardless of how lofty the ideals or how universal the goals of such a religion, nevertheless, what is prophesied is a lofty and universalized Americanism, which is in its own way, a spiritualization of biblical Christianity.[19] Evangelicalism's escapism often leans toward an affirmation of nationalistic capitalism; Protestant liberalism's escapism culminates in an allegiance to a refined, enlightened but nevertheless American way of life.

Worship of the Self

Even Protestant individualism can, on a private level, be accepted as a relatively benign development. Louisa May Alcott's sentiment,

> A little kingdom I possess,
> Where thoughts and feelings dwell,
> And very hard I find the task
> Of governing it well.[20]

could be seen as nothing more than a bland Victorianism so long as it harmed no one but herself. Protestantism's rampant individualism and recently its narcissism, however, have injected some poisonous elements into the American bloodstream.

Tom Wolfe, the journalist-essayist, was one of the first to notice that American individualism had reached gnostic proportions. In his essay, "The Me Decade and the Third Great Awakening," Wolfe recalls that until very recent times, humanity has shared a "belief in serial immortality." Whatever persons might believe or not believe about personal survival after death, "they have seen themselves as inseparable from the great tide of chromosomes of which they are created and which they pass on. The mere fact that you were only going to be here for a short time and would be dead soon enough did not give you the license to try to climb out of the stream and change the natural order of things." Wolfe, with his penetrating eye, sees that these beliefs have been overcome in modern America. Those imbued with the new religious consciousness have arrived "at an axiom first propounded by the Gnostic Christians some eighteen hundred years ago: namely, that at the apex of every human soul there exists a spark of the light of God." Salvation, for present-day gnostics as for ancient gnostics, can be found only through discovering the spark within. That search entails the willingness to separate the self from all binding earthly ties. The method of separation might vary from LSD to sexual ecstasy to Hare Krishna to Jesus. Regardless of the method, however, there has occurred, writes Wolfe, a "Third Great Awakening" in North America, paralleling that of Jonathan Edwards's era in the 1740s and the Second Great Awakening from 1825 to 1850. This Third Awakening, according to Wolfe, "has the mightiest, holiest roll of all, the beat that goes . . . Me . . . Me . . . Me . . . Me . . . " It is the fulfillment, Wolfe claims, of de Tocqueville's dire prophecy of America's future: "Not only does [American] democracy make each man forget his ancestors, it hides his descendants from him, and divides him from his contemporaries; it continually turns him back into himself, and threatens, at last, to enclose him entirely in the solitude of his own heart."[21]

Support for such gnosticized Christian expressions has been supplied by certain developments within modern theology. Rudolf Bultmann, for example, whose influence on contemporary American Protestantism has been immense, consistently interpreted the New Testament along individualistic lines. The importance of the Resurrection accounts, in Bultmann's hermeneutic, consists almost entirely in its importance to the individual Christian. Does Christ's being raised from the dead raise me to new life? The reality of the event depends on the answer one gives to that question.[22]

Herbert Richardson, in his attempt to justify an American homegrown theology, refuses to accept Bonhoeffer's critique that "God has granted American Christianity no Reformation." Instead, Richardson takes pride in the fact that America has offered shelter to those spiritualist elements expelled from Europe. He is grateful for what Bonhoeffer saw as the spiritualists' "disproportionate formative influence on American religion," and as a result, Richardson becomes an apologist for the American religious emphasis on the sanctification of the individual.[23]

Even though Thomas J. J. Altizer and the death-of-God school have been largely discredited as sensational and extremist, one cannot help but wonder if such reasoning as theirs is not the natural outcome of the American Protestant emphasis on disembodied Spirit and individual experiences. If experience of God's presence is the source of evangelical faith, then why would not experience of God's absence be the source of a new and very different sort of faith? And if the feeling of the presence of God testified to the redemption of the individual, why could not the feeling of the absence of God validate the omnipotence of the individual? There is, after all, a great advantage for American individualism in the death of God, for obviously the beneficiary of the deceased is none other than the spiritual, now wholly emancipated person.

Popular preachers have, of course, had a more direct influence upon the people than academic theologians. And among these none have made such consistent impressions as Billy Graham and Norman Vincent Peale. It is ironic that Graham, an evangelical, and Peale, a liberal, should have so often attracted the same audience, had so many complimentary things to say of one another, and finally, proposed similar solutions regarding social ethics. What do Graham the evangelist and Peale the proponent of positive thinking have in common? Simply that, for both of them, Christianity is understood from a gnostic point of view. Faith for them, as for so many Americans, has to do with the relationship between the individual and God, one on one. For both Graham and Peale, the world itself and its various communities are, at best, neutral. The real world with which religion has to do is the world within. Along with the great majority of popular religious leaders, both Graham and Peale would uphold the status quo and strongly support the entrenched American way of life, because any progressive social program would indicate that human welfare can be improved on a corporate, nonspiritual level. Happiness, even physical happiness, is acceptable as a legitimate goal. Indeed, in Peale's preaching, it is almost the only goal; but according to the prevailing rules of the game, the pursuit of happiness is confined to the single competitor and the finish line crossed only by the one who has run on a spiritual course. Such preaching has accomplished nothing in terms of gathering a Christian consensus for social justice or for international understanding. In fact, the results have been quite the opposite. The individualism and hyper-spiritualism of the popular Protestant message have helped to forestall gun control, medicare, nuclear disarmament and environmental responsibility. Anything that smacks of corporate compassion and social hope is highly suspect within popular American Protestantism.

The fruits of such an individualistic understanding of religion are not unique to modern America. Jeremiah had observed of his own day that the children of Israel had forsaken true religion, saying: "That is in vain! We will follow our own plans, and will everyone act according to the stubbornness of his evil heart." As a consequence, "they have stumbled in their ways . . . and have gone into bypaths, . . . making their land a horror, a thing to be hissed at for ever."[24]

Despite the failure of American Protestantism to develop a positive social program, it could be said that throughout most of American history the Protestant faith has had a beneficial influence on family life. It is almost as if American individualism had qualified itself with an amending clause excluding the family from its otherwise consistent preoccupation. So, even though individuals should do their level best to secure their own salvation at whatever social cost, nevertheless, certain obligations were owed to the family.[25] Recently, however, with the radicalization of the individualistic quest aided by the sexual revolution, the family clause has been repealed.

Rosemary Ruether, among others, has correctly discerned that the sexual revolt against home and hearth originated as a masculine attempt to overcome nature. Ruether finds the roots of such rebellion in Plato, where "the salvation of the liberated consciousness repudiates heterosexual for masculine love and mounts to heaven in flight from the body and the visible world."[26] The Puritan mind, despite its strong familial regulations, had retained the Platonic feeling that all human relationships, especially those tinged with sexuality, could never be allowed to have more than penultimate significance.

Tom Wolfe, moreover, has observed that in the 1960s and 1970s, the American male, in search of ultimate meaning in terms of the self, discovered that it was quite possible to "shuck" his wife and family in order to reach the goal. As Wolfe has so acutely concluded, the sexual revolution itself has been a religious search, a way of finding the self—apart from binding relationships or social constrictions—in terms of a pure sexuality. It has not been, writes Wolfe,

> a hypocritical coverup. It is merely an example of how people in even the most secular manifestation of the Me decade . . . are likely to go through the usual stages . . . Let's talk about Me . . . Let's find the Real Me . . . Let's get rid of all the hypocrisies and impedimenta and false modesties that obscure the Real Me . . . Ah! At the apex of my soul is a spark of the Divine . . . which I perceive in the pure moment of ecstasy (which your textbooks call "the orgasm," but which I know to be heaven).[27]

Only after the assault against home and hearth had been initiated by men did women begin their own revolt. Only after the husband walked out to "discover himself" apart from familial sex did the wife begin the attempt to "save her own life" in terms of casual sexual experiences.[28] The social results of the male quest for individual self-fulfillment and certain concomitant aspects of the Women's Liberation movement have been disastrous. The frightening rise in the divorce rate, the disregard for the psychological security of children, the normality of abortion, the fear of young people to become involved in lasting sexual unions—all are indicative of a society which is becoming unglued in its most essential elements. When individualism drives a wedge between male and female to the extent that even the commandment to be "fruitful and multiply" is threatened, then, obviously, a society is being gnosticized out of existence.

In William Faulkner's *The Wild Palms,* the author depicts a world to come, now already achieved, in his story of Charlotte and Harry. On a superficial level, this couple seem to be liberating themselves from a bourgeois lifestyle, courageously striking out on their own, bound by none of the sentimentality of past generations. Beneath the surface, however, their relationship is the epitome of the bourgeois way: it is, in fact, a nonrelationship, an alliance between two narcissistic souls. When Charlotte becomes pregnant, she persuades Harry to perform an abortion; she is frightened of having a child because "they hurt too much." The real hurt she fears is that of having the attention of life shifted from herself to another. Harry botches the operation and Charlotte dies. As Jim Gardner concludes in his critical essay, "Narcissism in Contemporary Literature," "in *The Wild Palms,* Faulkner shrewdly anticipates the abortion issue, which cannot be considered apart from its relation to narcissism. The attitude that if human life is an obstacle to individual goals then it can be obliterated is frighteningly narcissistic."[29]

Meanwhile, liberal Protestantism has been more concerned about "planned parenthood" than about abortion, about day-care centers than about divorce, about gay rights than about family survival. As the Roman Catholics man the barricades in defense of the home, Protestants seem to be satisfied that any step toward the liberation of the individual will be in accord with the Gospel. The liberal Protestant openness to sexual liberation coupled with its continued aversion to unrestrained childbearing presents one of the most striking and frightening parallels to ancient gnosticism. Although gnostics were divided in their attitudes toward sexual practice, some being very puritanical, others libertine, all gnostics were united in their ingrained suspicion of procreation. It is not necessary to be opposed to birth control, or to reject all instances of abortion, or to discredit the legitimate claims of homosexuals, to notice that Roman Catholic interests are predominantly communal, whereas Protestant interests are for the most part individualistic.

Religious sociologists as well as Church historians have often observed within American Protestantism a developing emphasis on economic individualism. In this development, the secular economic theory of free enterprise becomes almost an article of Christian faith. So long as the free-enterprise philosophy is understood as merely a capitalist device, an excuse for profit and unbounded greed, we cannot begin to understand its power. Max Weber's classic work, "The Protestant Ethic and the Spirit of Capitalism," brilliantly traces the progress of the spiritualization of economics. The essence of Weber's argument is that later Calvinism's rejection of a corporate covenantal relationship to God and its individualistic search for salvation led to a parallel individualistic search for economic prosperity. As the lonely, self-centered asceticism of Protestantism could lead to spiritual redemption, a similar lonely, self-centered effort could also lead to economic well-being.[30]

In the United States, this parallel movement of spiritual individualism and economic individualism was aided by the popular understanding of Darwinism and its "survival of the fittest" philosophy. "This anti-social teaching," Marty explains, "individualized the old Puritan-evangelical ideas about 'election,' ideas which were previously seen in the context of a covenanted community, and used them to justify personal economic competition."[31] According to Sidney Ahlstrom, the free-enterprise ethic has taken on new dimensions in America; he classifies it along with racism as one of the two root systems nourishing American social evils. He declares:

> The other [historical root] *is endemic in the United States of America as in no other land, . . .* and it may be called rampant anarchic economic individualism (RAEI) which destroys our sense of community by keeping human beings in a perpetual state of competition and instability from kindergarten to cemetery, and which also by the creation of corporate "persons" keeps cities, states, suburbs, regions, and neighbourhoods in destructive contexts of unnecessarily rapid social change, which in turn conduces to immeasurable amounts of human woe and to the general institutional instability and insolvency.[32]

While the support of laissez-faire economics by evangelical groups is a well-known and incontestable fact, the complicity of liberal Protestantism in this regard is not so widely recognized. Yet, by its relentless attack on anything traditional, inefficient or retrogressive, liberalism has provided the strongest possible backing for the acceptance of the present economic formula as an article of American faith.[33] Thus, though many liberal Protestants would be strong advocates of social welfare programs to care for the various victims of rampant capitalistic economics, no serious Protestant challenge to the basic system has been forthcoming. Certainly, nothing comparable to the Canadian New Democratic Party, a social democratic movement originating from Protestant and Pentecostal Christianity, has met with any success within the United States. Instead, there would seem to be a general acceptance among American Protestants that non-communal capitalism, which provides immense opportunity for the favored at the expense of the unfortunate, is a realistic and undebatable fact of life.

Meanwhile, the often maligned Walter Rauschenbusch remains one of the few prophetic voices raised in protest. In contrasting capitalism to the "organismic character" of Christianity, the great social gospeller attacked the free-enterprise spirit as "antagonistic to the spirit of Christianity, . . . [as having] a spirit that sets material goods above spiritual possessions." Worse still, capitalism "tempts, defeats, drains, and degrades, and leaves men stunted, cowed and shamed in their manhood."[34] Despite the material gains accomplished by social welfare programs since Rauschenbusch's day, the spiritual condition he described remains virtually unaltered.

C. G. Jung, consistent with his admiration of gnostic religion, believed that certain narcissistic attitudes were necessary for psychological healing. If reality is too awful to be faced, Jung argued, then reality must be escaped through the type of fantasy or religious symbolism that could lead one to a concentration on and acceptance of *self.* Freud and his school, on the other hand, considered a thoroughgoing narcissistic attitude as an almost impossible obstacle to therapy. Karen Horney, for example, speaking of escape into the self as "idealized image," insisted that such a psychological move is not only non-productive but positively dangerous. The concentration on self as idealized image occurs because one "cannot tolerate himself as he actually is." Although Horney admitted that "the image apparently counteracts this calamity" of self-rejection, the narcissistic personality once "having placed himself on a pedestal, . . . can tolerate his real self less and starts to rage against it, to despise himself . . . he wavers then between self-adoration and self-contempt."[35] On an individual level, such fantasizing about the self, can, as Horney was aware, make the task of the therapist extremely difficult, for the neurotic patient is apt to understand healing only in terms of the realization of the idealized self, an impossible goal.

On a socio-political level such fantasies can have horrendous consequences. In recent years, they have led to a politics not based on the needs of the commonwealth or even on the best interests of certain groups within the commonwealth, but a politics based on the fulfillment of *idealized selves*. Any understanding of American politics merely in terms of corporate greed, the profit motive, the maintenance of comforts for the middle class at the expense of the Third World or anything of this sort, is bound to fall short of the truth. For the real question before recent governments in the United States has not been the pragmatic one—how best to get the job done, whether it be concerning national health, the economy, unemployment, crime—but rather the spiritual one—what best allows me (all the me's) to keep the ideal image alive? Which social policy best promotes my image of myself as an autonomous unit, not dependent on man or God, living in a world of autonomous units? Obviously, it will be a social program in which I provide for my own medical costs, am allowed to own my own rifle, and decide about my own abortion. Any social program which implies that the family or the community is a more significant unit than the individual person, is foredoomed.

In regard to the all-important field of foreign affairs, the same non-pragmatic interest prevails. In this matter, the one overriding objective becomes to crush the world symbol of anti-individualism, namely Marxism. For example, though all parties agreed that the United States had no genuine vital interest in Vietnam, still great sacrifices were made, humiliation sustained and the economy seriously damaged, all to oppose what was perceived to be the most awful monster imaginable, an anti-individualistic economic philosophy. In Central America, though economic interests are at stake, the real reason behind a military rather than a political solution to the conflict, is that political accommodation would imply that the idealized image of self-alone is negotiable. Also in Central America, as in Southeast Asia, all other ethical guidelines—strictures against torture, the bombing of civilian populations, the destruction of life-giving crops—are suspended in deference to the theologically based ethic to protect the truth at all costs—the truth of an autonomous *self*.

This truth is ultimately guarded by a defense strategy which is willing to employ a civilization-destroying weapon to halt a Communist aggressor, for more important than everything received from the past and everything that could be bequeathed to children is the image of the independent *self*. More important than the cosmos itself is the theology of a self-centered universe. Love of nature, humanity, family, community, custom, culture—all are overridden by the accepted need to defend "the American way of life," and that way of life is the way of idealized self. If, in fact, the world must be destroyed in order to protect that fundamental truth of *self,* then the nation with the soul of a gnostic church will merely have been "standing tall."

Equality for All?

From early days, the American evangelical experience has required an elitist self-understanding. Although the unredeemed are by their very nature "immersed in materiality," "swallowed up by sin," those who have been born again have been freed of material concern. During periods of social turmoil and danger, it becomes even more important to be in that elite group which is free of material concern. Is there any real wonder that Americans, who have witnessed the assassination of three major political-spiritual leaders, defeat in war by a Third World nation, and the scandalous exit of a president, have turned in such numbers to an elitist born again Christianity? Or that a "defense" policy based on obliterating Western civilization has engendered a Third Great Awakening? For when a person is able to accept the gnostic vision, all temporal concerns are left behind: unemployment, North-South relations, East-West conflicts, the polluting of the oceans and the atmosphere, the possibility of human error creating a man-made hell—all become the preoccupations of the unwashed, those poor wretches who see such mundane items as the real problems.

The human potential movement, which is the liberal counterpart to born againism, is equally elitist. Though it at times develops a great sense of camaraderie, it finally demands an elitism of the individual alone. As Martin Buber has pointed out in his argument with Jung, "the others" are included "only as contents of the individual soul that shall, just as an individual soul, attain its perfection through individuation." Against Jung's claim that *gnosis* does not exclude the world of others, Buber goes on to say that the gnostic *self,* "even if it has integrated all of its unconscious elements, remains this single self, confined within itself. All beings existing over against me who become 'included' in myself are possessed by it in this inclusion as an *It.*"[36]

In this most exclusive of all religions, which requires only myself and others insofar as others contribute to or complement my spirituality, a formal, institutional Church becomes a dinosaur. Just as the early gnostics evaluated the orthodox Church as "unknowingly empty" where people are unaware of "who they are, like dumb animals,"[37] so also modern Protestant individualism would look upon the institutional churches as mere relics of former unenlightened ages. Robert Bellah, for example, in his review of Norman O. Brown's *Love's Body,* praises Brown for having understood Christianity apart from its historic roots: "Christianity is seen finally not as 'a religious tradition' or even as 'a great religion' but as a *way of thinking* about what it means to be human." Bellah goes on to applaud Brown's perceptive understanding of this nonhistorical faith: "Christian terminology, then, liberated from its ghetto location in a special group, is released to play its role in the general psychic life of man. What Brown is saying is that Christianity no longer belongs to the self-styled Christians."[38]

Bellah and Brown, like many modern Americans, regard a Christianity that is inextricably bound to a physical community as a lower stage of faith, compared to Christianity "as a way of thinking." It is not by accident that a collection of such essays would be entitled, *Beyond Belief.* (Beyond belief to *gnosis?*) A Christianity, disentangled from such primitive roots, as they see it, could offer positive support to secular psychological and social thought. This way of regarding Christianity would seem to be the awful realization of Walter Rauschenbusch's worst fear, that disillusioned social Christians would one day lose their confidence in Christian community and drift away from the churches into "a disembodied spirit of Christianity" without power or purpose.[39]

What the gnostic spirit cannot tolerate is the notion that a historically bound, tangible *organization* like *church* could in any sense be entrusted with ultimate *truth.* In her discussion of the early gnostics, Pagels explains that the Valentinians did not oppose the existence of a church with traditions and sacraments, under the leadership of priests and bishops; it was just that, for themselves, all this institutionalism was irrelevant. "All who had received *gnosis* . . . had gone beyond the church's teaching and had transcended the authority of its hierarchy."[40] Gnostics of all periods take one look at the Church and say to themselves, "You mean this is it? You mean this is all there is? Only what that simple-minded woman or that acned kid can understand; only what that half-educated preacher is saying?" The ancient gnostic concluded that either Christianity must be disconnected from this embarrassing base or else abandoned altogether.

In modern America, Protestant gnostics have reacted in both ways. Some have tried to appropriate Christian truth to philosophical questions quite apart from any involvement with the Christian Church. Others have identified themselves with voluntaristic sectarian groups in which they can receive the comfort and support of other like-minded spiritual Christians. Many other Protestants who have remained in the various churches, often have been made to feel guilty about being mere institutional Christians.

Meanwhile, institutional Protestantism has experienced a great decline, not only in membership but in influence. Along with the decline in the number of congregations, church members and baptisms, there has been simply a lack of interest in what traditional Protestantism is all about. The born again, charismatic spiritualists dominate television and radio media. Headlines are captured by the Moral Majority, advocating in the name of Christ more "defense" spending, less welfare support, capital punishment and other programs designed to show that life can be acceptable only on an individual level and only for the elite who have been born again.

Since the Vietnam War especially, the voice of traditional Protestantism has been heard in diminuendo. During that crisis, some mainline churches finally did advocate the cause of ordinary humanity, both in terms of the blacks, Appalachians and other disadvantaged Americans who had been conscripted to fight the war as well as for the Vietnamese peasantry who suffered the invasion of their homeland. Despite their belated and cautious opposition to the war, the mainline churches are still being blamed along with others for the defeat in Vietnam. As the Jews were unjustly held responsible for the defeat of Germany following World War I, institutional Christianity is yet bearing the scorn of the political establishment, certainly of the Moral Majority, perhaps even of the Silent Majority, for its small part in opposing the war.

Even a president of the United States did not hesitate to attack the institutional churches for their position on nuclear disarmament as "a dangerous fraud" and as "ungodly." Speaking before a gathering of the National Association of Evangelicals in Orlando, Florida, President Reagan chastised certain Christians for removing themselves "from the struggle between right and wrong, good and evil." The address, which was followed by the singing of "Onward, Christian Soldiers," went on to remind the sympathetic audience that "there is sin and evil in the world, and we are enjoined by Scripture and the Lord Jesus Christ to oppose it with all our might." Then Mr. Reagan identified Soviet communism as "the focus of evil in the modern world" and, again, accused the proponents of disarmament of having ignored "the aggressive instincts of an evil empire."[41]

The judgment that all uprisings and revolutions of the poor have been fomented by "an evil empire" stems from an elitist view of the world. It is a view that fails to take seriously the plight of powerless people who, completely apart from the East-West conflict, desire a decent life for themselves. It is a view that only certain human beings matter—Americans, the privileged, the contributers, the believers, *ourselves*. It is a view that the others do not matter—the Vietnamese, the Salvadorean peasants, the Sandinistas, the welfare recipients. It is a view that if people are poor and wretched they must have brought that condition on themselves. Apart from this elitist theology, how could the atrocities in Vietnam and Central America be explained? Americans are not a cruel folk. In fact, their concern and generosity even for former enemies is legendary. Villages can be burned, cultures can be destroyed, children can be mutilated only where the villages, the cultures and the children do not matter!

Furthermore, a spiritualized Christianity, sympathetic to these American elitist purposes, has become generally accepted as the normal "orthodox" form of the faith.

Everything So Long As It Is Not Anything

That which separates the gnostic from the ordinary person is the conviction that the eternal is in his or her own hands. Life, as the gnostic understands it, even this deficient life, has become manageable through comprehending the universal meaning in all things. Because the search for the ultimate is virtually ended for the gnostic, particular objects, particular events, even particular persons are important only insofar as they help to illustrate the already familiar ultimate. The claim of Kierkegaard that faith is a paradox in which "the particular is higher than the universal"[42] would have no meaning for the gnostic.

Though American theology in its early Puritan expression insisted on particularity in terms of doctrine, sacraments, and church discipline, the gradual acceptance of gnostic ideas culminated in a syncretistic religion that was willing to accept almost anything so long as it did not challenge the conviction that no thing in particular *revealed* the ultimate. Emily Dickinson, noticing the vagueness of New England religion, wrote that she

> Could dimly recollect a Grace—
> I think, they called it "God"—
> Renowned to ease Extremity—
> When Formula, had failed.[43]

Liberal Protestantism, for the most part, has also tried to rid itself of all entanglements with the particular. Doctrine, sacraments and ordinances have all been, at best, aids to understanding and worship. As a result, Alfred North Whitehead observed: "The defect of the liberal theology of the last two hundred years is that it has confined itself to the suggestion of minor, vapid reasons why people should continue to go to Church in the traditional fashion."[44] Without specific means of grace—the reading and preaching of the Word, baptism by water and Spirit, the breaking of bread at Christ's table—the churches have been hard pressed to argue for consistent church attendance. In fact, many essentially faithful Protestants feel little constraint to attend worship services on a regular basis. Professional inconveniences, company from out of town, the need for family recreation, for example, would be acceptable excuses for not being present at Sunday worship. Church attendance, or the lack of it, in the American Protestant scheme, does not signify very much, for what can be found in church that could not be found elsewhere?

What Reinhold Niebuhr wrote in 1955 is probably even more true today than then, "Our religiosity seems to have as little to do with the Christian faith as the religiosity of the Athenians. The 'unknown god' . . . in America seems to be faith itself."[45] In fact, in the last three decades the god "faith" has been elevated within the American pantheon. According to this wisdom, no religion is heretical so long as it serves as "a vehicle for 'inspiration,' for instilling a state of mind that leads to a healthy, positive approach to life." Peter Williams points out that the religious pattern preferred by the *Reader's Digest* and Norman Vincent Peale is non-sectarian and non-theological. Specific concerns based on intensely held convictions from the past could imply criticism of present social arrangements and even show the need for social change. This development would be contrary to the intentions of the *Digest* and Dr. Peale, whose aim is solely to enable individuals to adjust themselves "smoothly and uncritically" into the machinery of the present order.[46]

The Peale theology has culminated in the Church Growth movement. The philosophy behind this movement is that if local churches want to grow, they must find out what the people want and then give it to them. No longer constrained by the leadership of one Lord, the congregation can respond to sociological surveys. Surveys have consistently shown, for example, that "a church usually grows among one kind of person."[47] On this issue, Donald A. McGavran explains, "Men like to become Christian without crossing racial, linguistic, or class barriers." He goes on to urge churches to accommodate this instinct.[48] The apostolic teaching that "there is neither Jew nor Greek, . . . slave nor free . . . male nor female; for you are all one in Christ Jesus"[49] need no longer impede our growth. The important factor is faith. "I remain convinced," writes C. Peter Wagner, a Church Growth advocate, "that without faith, it is impossible for churches to grow. Empirical evidence also validates the absolute necessity of faith *or whatever else you want to call it*—possibility thinking or goal setting—as a prerequisite for church growth."[50]

Within this religious climate, which prefers the blurred to the sharp images, a phenomenon has occurred which could easily be mistaken for Christian tolerance or even for ecumenism. Namely, on the face of things, there would seem to be little of the denominational distinctiveness, certainly not the creedal animosity that separated our Protestant forebears from one another. In actual fact, however, what is happening is neither toleration nor ecumenical harmony. The present condition is better described by Hannah Arendt's insight that within the modern world everything seems to be able to transform itself, "with ever increasing rapidity from one shape into another, as though we were living and struggling with a Protean universe where everything at any moment can become almost anything else."[51] Thus, for example, evangelicalism, which in the past attempted to distinguish itself from the moderates and later the modernists by its insistence on doctrinal purity, seems largely to have abandoned that effort. Now evangelicals call on individuals to make an undefined "decision for Christ" and assure their audiences that "the Lord will bless you real good" or that "God cares about you." Even the sharp distinction between those living under grace and those still under judgment has become blurred, so that regardless of who you are, "something good will happen to you today." With these general platitudes, evangelicals seem to have metamorphosed themselves into the most harmless of liberal Protestants.

On the other hand, Arendt's formula applies to liberals as well. Suddenly, many liberals have concluded that mainline Protestantism has not been urgent enough in appealing to the human instinct for self-understanding and rebirth. Consequently, they have promoted group therapy sessions, a "growth theology" and a noticeable move away from socio-political concerns. Liberalism is still differentiated from evangelicalism, however, in being unmarketable. While the new Fundamentalism enriches itself through the mass media and in the local churches, liberalism is generally finding it difficult to keep its head above the financial waters.

James Wolfe, in his study of three churches in the San Francisco area, states that the Glide Memorial Methodist Church "tolerates any and every religious persuasion, which is to say that no religious position is central to its life. Explicit Christian symbols are absent inside its building, no sacraments are administered, and no profession of faith is required for membership." Of Grace Church (a pseudonym for a nearby non-Methodist congregation), Wolfe informs us that "the high point now of the church year is the annual Yule feast, an extravagant celebration of the twelfth night of Christmas spiced with the wearing of Renaissance clothes, the burning of a yule log, the display and eating of a boar's head spiked with the drinking of wassail before, and wine during, a sumptuous meal." Despite all that can be said of the pagan roots of the Christmas feast, nevertheless, the celebration in Grace Church would seem to have moved a great distance from the medieval Mass of Christ. What is absent from the twelfth night celebration is the central offensive event of the Incarnation, the assertion that the Christ event makes the Christmas feast different from all others. The one biblical truth picked up by the pagan Christmas celebration has been discarded by a new syncretism, open to anything so long as it signifies nothing. Though Wolfe does record that at Grace Church, "Jesus and the humanizing forces he represents . . . are often on the pastor's lips," such language is accompanied by an acknowledged search for "a more adequate conception of the divine which will suit the modern mind."[52] For the time being, at least, Jesus is valuable, along with Chairman Mao, Gandhi and others as a "stimulator of the religious consciousness."[53]

Perhaps the present tendency toward a syncretistic Christianity is related to the issue H. Richard Niebuhr raised over two decades ago in his book, *Radical Monotheism and Western Culture*. In this work Niebuhr defined monotheism not so much as an intellectual concept of divine unity but rather as a unified moral and societal world-view.

Belief in one God holds the faithful together in one value system, one culture. Polytheism, on the other hand, is a sign of a culture in process of disintegration. Formerly accepted values, historical loyalties, basic interpretations of life, everything is up for grabs; as a result one God will no longer suffice. The contemporary theologian, David Miller, in his work *The New Polytheism* seems to confirm Niebuhr's judgment. By 1974 Miller had found that because of the "radical experience of the plurality of both social and psychological life . . . a single story, a monovalent logic, a rigid theology, and a confining morality are not adequate to help in understanding the nature of real meaning." Instead, Miller opts for "the multiple patterns of polytheism [that] allow room to move meaningfully through a pluralistic universe. They free one to affirm the radical plurality of the self, an affirmation that one has seldom been able to manage because of the guilt surrounding monotheism's insidious implication that we have to 'get it all together.' "[54] Such an incredible contradiction of biblical religion in the name of freedom and self-affirmation can only be explained as an example of gnostic syncretism. As the ancient gnostic celebrated "every form of creative invention as evidence that a person has become spiritually alive,"[55] in certain circles of American Protestantism anything goes so long as it is creative, liberating, and expressive of individual freedom.

This uncircumscribed type of religion is characterized by a dislike of any traditional or even natural boundaries and an urge whenever possible to overcome them. Peter Williams has demonstrated how this mentality asserts itself in his discussion of two popular quasi-religious works: *Jonathan Livingston Seagull* and *Love Story*. Both of these narratives have to do with the overcoming of limitations, by means of a sentimental focusing on the individual or the "loving couple." In Richard Bach's *Seagull,* the success of the feathery hero is based entirely on his feelings about himself. Reality is interior; nature, the others, all other factors are beside the point. *Love Story* by Erich Segal involves a similar blurring of all real boundaries in favor of an idealized concept of romantic love. As Williams explains it, "The immortal message of the book—'love is never having to say you're sorry'—is exactly the sort of unfocused, ill-conceived 'beautiful thought' " so characteristic of this contemporary American type. The real distinctions separating male from female, person from person, are avoided by a dishonest depiction of life as inwardly controlled, a fuzzy imprecise space where lovers have become so emotionally unseparate that they no longer need to ask for pardon.[56] Whereas it is possible to say that contemporary

Protestantism has been influenced by such secular blurring of distinctions, given the history of Protestantism in America, the opposite seems more likely. *Seagull* and *Love Story* are among the insipid fruits bred by generations of self-awakenings and feeling-based expressions of Christianity.

No boundary has been more persistently violated in recent times than that between male and female. The Women's Liberation movement has received immense support from liberal Protestantism. When all has been said, which indeed must be said, about the legitimate aims of the movement, one of the alarming themes of some feminists is that any distinctions between sexes in terms of emotional outlook, responsibility, even natural necessity are reactionary and enslaving. This form of world denying, which fails to appreciate the particular contributions of femaleness and maleness to human society and the mystery of *la différence,* is in striking parallel to some of the ancient gnostic writers. In the *Gospel of Thomas* for instance, in answer to the disciples' question as to when they could enter the kingdom, Jesus answered: "When you make the two one, and when you make the inside like the outside and the outside like the inside, and the above like the below, and when you make the male and the female one and the same . . . then you will enter [the Kingdom]."[57]

Gnostic Christians, ancient and modern, agree that only when all distinctions have been overcome, when the individual has crossed all boundaries and the complete person has been recognized as the true and only unit of life, can human existence be tolerable. So long as there are differences—whether male-female, old-young, sick-well, black-white—the gnostic mentality judges the creation as deficient and unacceptable.

Some forces of feminism seem to yoke sexual liberation with deliverance from all authority. Patricia Gundry, for example, the keynote speaker at the Evangelical Women's Caucus held in Seattle, 21–24 July 1982, declared that "Mother God has no illegitimate children," therefore, "*we are* the church—we don't have to fit into the existing institutions, we don't have to change them, we can even ignore them if we want."[58] Once again, real differences of opinion, even antagonisms are not to be overcome by discussion, confrontation and conflict; instead, by pretending that all natural and social divisions do not matter, the individual inherits the kingdom. As always with gnostic thought, however, the inheritance occurs only in the imagination. The liberation of women from male domination in the Church, in this case, occurs only in the mind.

The same sort of blurring that takes place in the sphere of sexuality also occurs in regard to geographic locale. In *The Homeless Mind,* a major study on the American rejection of particularity regarding *place,* the authors attempt to show the consequences of a lack of *place* consciousness.[59] The mind-set is yoked to the lifestyle; it has been estimated that in North America the *average* person moves fourteen times in his or her lifetime and fifty-five percent of adults live over five hundred miles from their childhood home.[60] This uprootedness is, of course, largely a result of the economic demands of a highly mobile society, the need for technicians to be where their techniques are required. The rationale for this lifestyle, however, is supplied by the gnostic philosophy that *place* does not matter. Whether one is in Dallas or Boston is a detail which could not concern a truly liberal-minded person. That a person would refuse to move because he or she *needed* a particular locale would be a definite sign of weakness.

In the same regard, any attempt on the part of a locality to assert its individual distinctiveness is considered a nuisance and the result of perverse narrow-mindedness. Appalachian folk, blacks, Southerners and even New Yorkers have been criticized for the desire to maintain their own recognizably different cultures. Canadians, especially, in daring to claim a national destiny distinct from that of the United States are continually under cultural and economic attack. Some Canadian scholars, such as George Grant, even feel that the struggle for an independent Canadian identity is being lost to the forces of continentalism.[61] If Canadian peculiarities are a challenge to the melting-pot mentality, is there any wonder about the anger engendered by the Nicaraguan revolution? That an impoverished banana republic would dare to opt out of North American culture and maintain its independent culture is an affront to the general gnostic sensibility.

These various secular attempts at line-blurring, which have largely been prompted by a gnosticized Protestant thought, ironically are now indirectly exerting an effect on church life itself. Much earlier, an American Episcopal bishop, Charles Fiske (1868–1941), had discovered "evidence of a sad disintegration of American Protestantism," in which the churches were unable to distinguish between the popular notion of the present and the authentic truth of the eternal.[62] This evidence has grown stronger. The strong barriers our ancestors erected separating Christianity from superstition, true religion from sentimentality, seem to be falling. A typical Protestant sermon is a verbal essay on a contemporary theme, sometimes employing biblical illustrations in support of the essayist's point of view. The preacher who is bound to the text, confined to what he or she perceives as the biblical point of view, is a curiosity. Most often, the congregation is constrained to hear the Gospel according to the *Reader's Digest,* the *National Review* or the *New Republic,* depending on the preacher's orientation.

The increasing liturgical interest within Protestantism is generally a healthy sign. It means that the Gospel is understood as pertaining to nature as well as to grace, that Christians seek to worship God not only with the mind, but with body, music, color, movement—all the gifts of human life—as well. It is especially important for American Protestants that liturgical renewal signifies that faithful people are determined to worship God not only as isolated individuals, but together as Christ's people.

Even in this hopeful area, however, there are discouraging factors. For one thing, many Protestants feel that "new" liturgical practices are artificial, that they have been borrowed from elsewhere, especially from the Roman Catholics, and superimposed on the familiar Protestant worship. Winthrop Hudson noted that in the 1920s, the period of the Gothic revival in architecture and of some liturgical innovation in Protestantism, "Unlike earlier forms of Church architecture and liturgical practice which expressed in one way or another the common faith of the congregation, the new eclecticism betrayed little discernable relationship to any fundamental theological convictions."[63] That judgment still holds true in regard to many liturgically minded Protestant churches. Even though the order is ancient, the music is creative, and the congregation is participating in an act of corporate worship, something is missing. Perhaps Max Thurian, the Reformed liturgist from Taizé, explains it best:

> The liturgial revival . . . has led the Reformed churches to rediscover the ancient structures and sometimes too the texts of the Western Eucharistic celebration. But . . . the problem of celebration itself remains. As a result of a certain fear of forms and gestures, a liturgy which should be experienced is often only *said* or *sung.*[64]

What Thurian indicates is that Protestants do not feel *at ease* with the liturgy; it is still perceived as a practice that is not *their own.* As a result, liturgical renewal, even the attempt to restore the sacraments to their legitimate place in the Christian life, is often misinterpreted as just another example of syncretism, of how anything, even what the Roman Catholics do, can be used within Protestantism. When that misunderstanding occurs, an otherwise valid liturgy can become incorporated into the individualistic Protestant pattern. Worshipers can affirm that this new liturgical style is acceptable insofar as—like charismatic preaching, television evangelism, and religious sentimentality—it is able to turn them on. It is, in other words, seen as merely another aid to personal piety, another gimmick to reach the individual.

Unfortunately, some liturgists and local pastors propagate this misconception themselves by treating the liturgy as if it were but another creative innovation granted to Christianity in these latter days. So the faithful are subjected to choirs dancing down the aisles, celebrants decked out like oriental potentates with no apparent purpose other than to draw attention to themselves, and boars' heads replacing bread as the communal element. In less offensive ways, many celebrants confuse the issue by their apologetic attitude toward liturgical reform, as if the liturgy of the catholic Church were on trial, as if this were another new experiment being tested for practical results, as if like the dialogue sermon and chancel ballet, it is another novelty of these revolutionary times. Little wonder that even the liturgy can be misconstrued as another syncretistic development or that so many faithful Protestants do not feel at home within the corporate worship of the Church.

It is said of atheism that "those who believe in nothing always end up believing in anything." Perhaps it can be said of gnosticism that those who believe in everything always end up believing in nothing.

CHAPTER ELEVEN

The Degnosticizing of Protestantism: The Renewal of Hope

As THE familiar hymn expresses it, the Church is always "by heresies distressed." This work has attempted to state what it is that is particularly distressing about a revitalized gnostic heresy in our own day. It would be a serious mistake, however, to conclude that the problems confronting contemporary Protestantism are overwhelming or insoluble. Every generation of the Church has been threatened in one way or another by a teaching counter to biblical truth. Often the counter-teaching has been so attractive that it has almost captured the Church itself. Gnosticism in its various guises has on several occasions been especially powerful and apparently close to victory. "Mani," as Runciman reminds us, "began his preaching at Ctesiphon in Mesopotamia in A.D. 242 . . . [and] within a century of his death . . . it seemed not unlikely that Mani's faith would dominate the world."[1] Valentinus, often considered the ablest theologian among the ancient heresiarchs, was in the running for and perhaps almost achieved the bishopric of Rome.[2] The extent of gnostic appeal in the fourth century is evident in the fact that the young Ambrose had been a Marcionite and Augustine a Manichee.[3] If those spiritual sojourners could find their way out of the alluring mists of gnostic thought into the clear atmosphere of orthodox faith, indeed to become teaching doctors of that faith, surely there is hope for us.

The unsettling truth is that no generation can simply inherit orthodoxy from the previous one. Orthodoxy must be consciously sought and achieved by a determined Church engaged in an active struggle with itself. This, of course, implies a wrestling with the past in the context of the present under the pressure of the future. In this sense, Christians of all people should be most open to Karl Marx's dicta that "the criticism of religion is the beginning of all criticism" and that "the task is not to interpret the world in various ways but to change it." In the case of Protestantism, its present entanglements with gnosticism cannot be escaped until Protestant church people are prepared to be honestly critical of their own religion, and then determine to do something about it. In what follows, we shall discuss particular areas in which Protestant life can be and must be changed if this expression of faith is to remain a true branch of Christ's Church.

Restoration of a Sure Confidence in a Good God: The Preaching of Grace

The appointed place for the beginning of any reform or purification of the Church must be the pulpit, the platform from which that Word contrary to all our mistaken words is proclaimed. Any successful foray against heresy must be launched from that spot. In fact, insofar as the historical Church has been serious about combating false faith, Gospel preaching has been her primary weapon. Runciman, in his brilliant study of medieval gnosticism, locates much of the Church's decline in the Languedoc area of France with the poor quality of preaching among the parish priests. And to a great extent the response of Dominic to the Albigensian threat was to win the people back by the revitalization of orthodox preaching.[4] What is required at present is nothing at all like a crusade or a witch hunt, for like the author of *Ephesians* "we are not contending against flesh and blood, but against the principalities, against the powers, against the world rulers of this present darkness" and, indeed, "against the spiritual hosts of wickedness" in very "heavenly places."[5]

What could be more Protestant than to begin a new reformation with the preaching of the Word? Calvin wrote that preaching is "the mother who conceives and brings forth, and faith is the daughter who ought to be mindful of her origin."[6] Behind this claim is the conviction that the only preaching that deserves the name is that proclamation which is based on a faithful adherence to the written Word of God as revealed by the Holy Spirit, the conviction that "Behold, *I* have put my words in your mouth."[7] Karl Barth quoted these words of Luther with approval:

> Without God's sending cometh no Word into the world. Hath it grown out of my heart, cling I to Chrysostom, Augustine, and Ambrose, still 'tis not God's Word. For 'tis a vast difference 'twixt the Word that is sent from heaven and that which of my own choice and device I invent.[8]

Among Protestants a confidence in the proclaimed Word of God has certainly been eroded. For one thing, modern psychology has led us to suspect that no one, no matter how well-intentioned or authentically ordained to preach, *could* preach an objective Word as opposed to a word of his own choice, as opposed to a device he invents. At the same time, the idea of a given Word from God in Scripture has been largely undermined by modern critical studies of the biblical texts. After all, is the Bible not just a human book like all the other inspirational books at our disposal?

Such a loss of confidence in the Word of God is, in the context of biblical faith, entirely unwarranted. The prophets and apostles in orthodox teaching have not been regarded as divine persons, free of psychological problems and private opinions. Nor has the written text been received as a dictaphone recording of the Almighty's voice. The Apostle Paul was writing in the best scriptural tradition when he stated, "We have this treasure in earthen vessels [precisely] to show that the transcendent power belongs to God and not to us."[9] That God can communicate through the confusion of human poetry and prose an eternal Word to humanity is a sign of His power. It is also a sign that God is not nearly so embarrassed by the humanity and human imperfections evidenced in preachers and in the Bible as we are ourselves. At the outset, the claim must be restated in something like the fine definition of Karl Barth, that "the Word of God preached now means . . . man's language about God, in which and through which God Himself speaks about Himself."[10]

Meanwhile, the assurance of grace that is part and parcel of the proclamation has often not been heard, and there exists among Protestant people a longing for the certitude that there is some purpose to life, that God is good, that we are not destined to "die here in a rage, like a poisoned rat in a hole."[11] Lacking this assurance of grace through proclamation, why should we not believe that humanity is the result of an evolutionary maze "in which almost all turnings are wrong turnings."[12] When the morning newspaper is read totally apart from the gracious Word of God, why not accept Arthur Koestler's opinion that "*homo sapiens* is a biological freak, the result of some remarkable mistake in the evolutionary process"?[13] The sense of primal alienation experienced by every human generation has been unrelieved in our day by the contrary voice, by the quiet *nevertheless* of the Gospel, assuring the faithful:

> Nevertheless I am continually with
> thee;
> thou dost hold my right hand.[14]

Without that *nevertheless,* the eloquent and unrelieved cry of a North Carolina Presbyterian has a definite Valentinian ring to it: "Naked and alone we came into exile. . . . Which of us has known his brother? . . . Which of us is not forever a stranger and alone?"[15] The Church's response to the legitimate cry of the novelist, the cry of all humanity, must be a Word of assurance to the faithful. But in place of a loaf, the contemporary sermon usually offers a stone; in place of a fish, a serpent.[16]

What has been lost for Protestants is the very gift of certitude that Calvin was so anxious to restore to Christian people. Against the Roman position at that time—which Calvin saw as leaving the sinner *dangling,* wondering about the state of his justification before God and his eternal salvation—the Reformer offered the penitent sinner a *certitude* that "in the end we shall achieve victory in the fight."[17]

Through the preaching of a fallible but ordained Word whose content is defined by and shaped in terms of a flawed but holy text, the Spirit of God speaks to Christ's Church. Such preaching provides the certitude that begins to free its members from despair and desperation and to imbue them personally with a quiet confidence, enabling them to participate in the eternal work being effected in the world.

The confidence, of course, has nothing to do with the false hope that everything will be all right if we do our best, that the world is really not in such desperate shape because we have managed to muddle through in the past or that even though there are greater perils today than ever, there are also greater possibilities because of our advanced technological achievements. In short, the confidence provided by Gospel preaching is not related to an optimistic view of humanity as such. The confidence provided by Gospel preaching has to do with the Bible's consistent witness to the gracious God of humanity and of the Creation as a whole. The dreadful realities of the present are not obscured, but "let those who suffer according to

God's will do right and entrust their souls to a faithful Creator."[18] As opposed to all the stop-gap encouragements that fail to hearten honest spirits very deeply or for very long, the preaching of the Word is a true word of hope because the source of its hope is none other than the Creator and Sustainer Himself.

As each generation is in need of certain emphases in the proclaimed Word to deal with the particular evidence of despair peculiar to that age, so our own generation requires the accenting of specific biblical themes.

First of all, a pervasive spirit of metaphysical alienation must be confronted by a bold proclamation of the goodness and sovereignty of God the Creator. Despite the intricacies of the evolutionary process, these were not merely a series of wrong turns or mistaken moldings; rather the same God who began the process with the words, "Let there be light," kept His eye on the project all along. Of utmost importance is the assurance that at no point in the creative process did the Almighty become preoccupied with other concerns or capricious in His care for any of His creatures; always He was the loving Creator revealed to us in the living Word, Christ himself. "All things were made through him, and without him was not anything made that was made."[19] The fact that we might view the stripes on the zebra and the hump on the camel as strange or the human bone joints as defective products only demonstrates that our human perspective is different from that of the Creator and that our sense of order and excellence is not in accord with His. From the Creator's perspective, even at the end of day six, His work was and remains "very good."[20] The biblical authors were aware of such realities as destructive insects, earthquakes, floods, not to mention the more perplexing problems of deformed children and the long-suffering aged. All of these baffling mysteries of the created world do not obviate faith in a God who knows what He is doing. Nor should the more recently discovered evidence that we humans are biologically descended from sea squirts[21] diminish our gratitude for the good world or our place in it. Accompanied by the preaching which points to the God and Father of Jesus Christ as the goodly Creator, perhaps such scientific theories might lead us to a greater appreciation of sea squirts and a closer feeling of kinship with all our fellow creatures. Proper preaching of the good Creator God leads to human confidence in its own humanity and thereby to the realization that most of our human ills are brought about not by some supposed flaw in the nature of things, but rather by our lack of gratitude for what we have received.

> What causes wars, and what causes fightings among you? Is it not your passions that are at war in your members? You desire and do not have; so you kill. And you covet and cannot obtain; so you fight and wage war.[22]

Modern men and women also need to be assured through biblical preaching that the sovereignty and goodness of God did not stop with creation, but also evidence themselves in human history. Without that Word from the pulpit it would be far too easy to imagine that all the really important decisions are being made in the corridors of earthly power. Why else would such awful atrocities as the Jewish Holocaust or the Hiroshima and Nagasaki bombings have occurred? The preacher, of course, has no answer to the questions posed by recent history. What he does have, however, through the faithful preaching of the Word, is a challenge to those who think they know the answer. To those who have too quickly concluded that God is on the side of the army with the most divisions or the most warheads, biblical preaching continues to assert that "the nations are like a drop from a bucket."[23] And to those, whether in the Kremlin or the Pentagon, who feel that they can make realistic decisions without reference to justice or the Author of justice, preaching issues the warning that

> *He* makes nations great, and he
> destroys them:
> he enlarges nations, and leads
> them away.[24]

The preaching that is a warning to the arrogant is, of course, a promise to the longing—that what appears to be impregnable power is quite vulnerable and that an apparently desperate present is filled with hope.

In biblical preaching, the focus of power is not extra-terrestrial as the gnostics would have it. Neither is it located in high places as worldly wisdom understands it—the exalted precincts of presidential palaces or the mansions of immense wealth. The Word from the Bible persists in seeing power among slave peoples, in shepherds' fields, lying in a manger, resting in fishing boats, hanging on a cross. History, of course, cannot be overcome by wishful thinking. The slaughter of the innocent occurs; Dachau and Buchenwald were all too real; Nagasaki was not a bad dream; the bombing of Cambodia happened. And the awful consequences of these events are still unfolding in terms of divine justice. From the biblical perspective, however, the present reality, far from being *fixed,* is already undergoing transformation and even reversal. For in God's election of Israel, His incarnational act in Jesus the Christ and His forming through Christ of a new humanity, already

> [H]e has put down the mighty from
> their thrones,
> and exalted those of low degree;
> [already] he has filled the hungry with good
> things,
> and the rich he has sent empty away.[25]

This radical reversal is already in the works, but in the works in consequence of and as a participation in the Resurrection victory of the Crucified One. The preaching of grace, then, will necessarily be a preaching of the Crucified Lord both in terms of his crucified lordship and in terms of his lordly crucifixion.

Hope concerning nature and history is therefore engendered by the preaching of grace, namely, that God's gracious purposes introduced from the beginning of all things are being fulfilled in the present to be fully realized in the future. The Creator is also the Sustainer who in Jesus Christ through the Holy Spirit is exercising His power toward the end of achieving His own purpose for the world.

Preaching also must assure Christ's people that they personally matter to the Creator-Redeemer God. In an age of high technology and computerization, it is too easy for personalities to become lost, for people not to matter. There is, in the present cultural setting, the uneasy feeling that persons as persons are not addressed by the spoken word but only manipulated by the communicators for their own purposes of profit or power. Preaching, then, cannot be in the nature of group dynamics: to herd an audience into a predetermined response. Preaching cannot be a dialogue sermon, a dramatic monologue or some other theatrical performance which is intended to entertain and which thereby regards Christ's people as a mere audience. In a Christian sermon, persons are addressed with respect—as persons. Of course, a sermon is not directed to an individual or to a collection of individuals as if each person were standing alone before God. That is not the sense in which the Christian person matters or in which the Christian is personally addressed. On the contrary, the person matters precisely because he or she is not isolated, attempting to stand alone and apart, but rather is found standing alongside the other members of Christ's body, the Church. The Word of grace is spoken to Israel and, therefore, as a member of the New Israel the *per-*

son has access to the Word. The person, then, is given confidence and hope not apart from the others but in terms of the others. One aspect of the Word of grace then becomes that the person as one of the members of the body has a part to play on the most important stage. He is not center-stage; he is not a star; but the important fact is he has been called to act, and the Director has in no sense forgotten his role. It is in this corporate sense that the personal word is spoken which leads the hearer away from despair into a new sense of gratitude.

The preaching within a Christian congregation, if it is to be the preaching of grace, will be liturgical preaching. That is, it will not be a lecture, an educational experience, a talking about the Gospel but rather a sermon (a word), a worshipful experience, a talking *from* the Gospel. In an essay on the Easter service in Faulkner's *The Sound and the Fury,* Thomas Merton contrasts the poetic liturgical preaching of the Reverend Shegog, an uneducated black preacher, with the "truly gruesome Sunday service" that takes place at the white Presbyterian church in *Light in August*. In the black church attended by Dilsey, her daughter and the idiot white boy, Benjy Compson, the congregation is gathered expectantly on Easter morning for the *unburdening,* a real unburdening from the real burdens being carried by Mississippi blacks early in this century. When the congregation spots the visiting clergyman, "undersized, in a shabby alpaca coat [with a] wizened black face like a small, aged monkey," there is a sigh of disappointment. Dilsey's daughter even whispers, "En dey brung dat all de way fum Saint Looey?" To which Dilsey answers, "I've knowed de Lawd to use cuiser tools dan dat." Dilsey's instincts are correct. The sermon is a liturgical recounting of the Gospel story in the sense that it is, in Merton's words, a telling "not only what they know, but *what is present among them*."

> "I sees hit, breddren! I sees hit! Sees de blastin, blindin sight! I sees Calvary, wid de sacred trees, sees de thief en de murderer en de least of dese; I hears de boasting en de braggin: Ef you be Jesus, lif up yo tree en walk! I hears de wailin of women en de evenin lamentations; I hears de weepin en de cryin en de turnt-away face of God: dey done kilt Jesus; dey done kilt my Son!"
>
> [The congregation cries] "Jesus! I sees, O Jesus!"
>
> "O blind sinner! Breddren, I tells you; sistuhn, I says to you, when de Lawd did turn His mighty face, say, Aint gwine overload heaven! I can see de widowed God shet His do'; I sees the whelmin flood roll between; I sees de darkness en de death everlastin upon de generations. Den, lo! Breddren! Yes, breddren! Whut I see? Whut I

> see, O sinner? I sees de resurrection en de light; sees de meek Jesus sayin Dey kilt Me dat ye shall live again; I died dat dem whut sees en believes shall never die. Breddren, O breddren! I sees de doom crack en hears de golden horns shoutin down de glory, en de arisen dead whut got de blood en de ricklickshun of de Lamb!"[26]

This sermon is a profound example of liturgical preaching in the sense that it is a proclamation of grace spoken in the context of a community of faith. And as a result of the proclamation of this strange little man, unburdening occurs which allows the community to endure and overcome.

When the preaching of grace takes place, barriers of alienation between humanity and God are broken down, so that resentments against the God of nature and the God of history are overcome and the faithful are enabled "with confidence [to] draw near to the throne of grace . . . receive mercy and find grace to help in time of need."[27]

The Freedom of Authority: Teaching, Creed and Ministry

Closely connected with the Church's commission to preach the Gospel of grace is the Church's obligation to teach and to teach with authority, for the Church must be a community of people who, as Karl Barth said, know how to speak and comprehend "the language of Canaan." It must be understood that this teaching program is not a rap group, a sharing session or anything that should be construed as a self-educational process; its content is not a secret *gnosis*. On the contrary, the Church's teaching office is under the auspices of the Holy Spirit, pertains to a specific content, to be presented within a certain framework, according to a given order.

The Church, in other words, is not self-authenticating; its teaching is authenticated only by the Lord of the Church. Insofar as the Holy Spirit is its Counselor, teaching it all things and bringing to its remembrance all that Jesus has said and done, the Church's message *is* the very Gospel itself.[28] From a Protestant point of view, the validity of the Church's message cannot be based on an infallible pope or an infallible Bible, but rather on the presence of the living Christ in the midst of his people. A strong statement of this grounding of ecclesiastical authority is given in the ordination vows of a Canadian Church where it is affirmed that, "The Presbyterian Church in Canada is bound only to Jesus Christ her King and Head."[29] Such a clear statement of authority is helpful in overcoming the popular notion that in Protestantism, the power of the pope has been replaced by the power of the people, and that as opposed to monarchial rule, non-Roman Catholics enjoy a pure democracy or even a thoroughgoing anarchy. On the contrary, as the Reformers and even as modern reforming creeds trenchantly state, "The Holy Christian Church whose sole head is Christ, is born of the Word of God, abides in the same and hears not the voice of a stranger" and "The Church lives solely because day by day, it is newly called and upheld, confronted and governed by its Lord."[30]

It is within the context of Christ's Church that the authoritative teaching of Christ is to be received. It has been pointed out that Karl Barth's reforming view of biblical study was at least partly based on his understanding that

> the historical reality of Jesus and the historical reality of his community are inseparable. There can be no historical relation to Jesus Christ which is not at the same time a relation to the men Jesus has made his fellowmen, beginning with his first disciples, but embracing also Israel and the whole church, and including in principle all men.[31]

To claim the Church's teaching office as an authoritative one is certainly not to move beyond Calvin. In one of his polemics against Rome, he explained that "they place the authority of the Church without the Word of God; we annex it to the Word, and allow it not to be separated from it."[32]

Church teaching has nothing to do with arcane knowledge. To say that the Church possesses "revealed" knowledge does not in any way claim that the Church has the knowledge under lock and key. The revelation has, in fact, become public, in that it has become incumbent upon Christ's people "to make all men see what is the plan of the mystery hidden for ages in God who created all things; that through the church the manifold wisdom of God might now be known."[33]

What the Church has to teach, therefore, and this it must be quick to confess, is nothing more than those objective events in which God openly has involved Himself in the world. As distinct from all the religious virtuosi who would claim to have secret, mystical, healing, saving knowledge, the Church must admit that it *knows* nothing except the accounts of the mighty acts of God, which it is more than willing to make available to all who will listen. And the Church need not be ashamed of this admission, as though the mighty acts of God were not enough. "At bottom," Karl Barth assures us,

> knowledge of God in faith is always this *indirect* knowledge of God, knowledge of God *in His works*. . . . What distinguishes faith from unbelief, erroneous faith and superstition is that it is content with this *indirect* knowledge of God. It does not think that the knowledge of God in His works is insufficient. On the contrary, it is grateful really to know the real God in His works . . . it also holds fast to the particularity of these works.[34]

Here, as in other areas, Christ's Church is insisting on standing alongside fellow humans and not over them in confessing: "what you do not know, we also do not know. All that we know are certain events that you can know as well as we; they are . . ."

Having accepted these boundaries of its knowledge, the Church can proceed to teach. What it teaches will be, of course, the long complicated story of the Old Israel, Israel's Messiah and the New Israel, the Church. The story with all its colorful diversions and subplots, accompanied by some apparently extraneous data is the sum of what Christians have to learn and to teach. All of it—and none of it can be written off because the whole of it is the given—represents the sum of our knowledge.

If there is to be a renunciation of the gnostic spirit in our time, there will have to be a renewal of biblical teaching in our churches, a re-grounding in the biblical point of view, so that when the Easter liturgy recalls the Exodus, Protestants will recall more than the novel by Leon Uris. And when the *Magnificat* is sung during Advent season, the faithful will immediately recall the revolutionary history of Israel and the radical demands of Christian discipleship. An effective renewal of biblical teaching will quite naturally require also a repudiation of much of the psychologizing, sociologizing, and peddling of middle-class values that have so often been the core of our Christian education curricula. Perhaps if the Protestant Churches could stick to their real task of teaching the Bible in a creative way—employing drama and music, puppets and art, memorization and debates, anything to make its history, legend and poetry live—young persons would again hear the biblical images with understanding and no longer regard "the God of Abraham, Isaac and Jacob" as a string of nonsense syllables.

Of course, the Bible must be understood and taught as it relates to the present. Of course, the prophets and apostles will speak to our human condition, to the problems of a depressed Third World and to the sense of futility produced by the nuclear arms race. However, if the Church is serious about teaching what it has to teach, it will carefully refrain from any longer *using* the Bible to illustrate our secular wisdom and will instead allow the Scriptures to speak for themselves, unrestrained by our cautious political and social ideas, uncensored by our sense of moral propriety. Instead of the Bible providing illustrations for "real life," "real life" as we perceive it will provide illustrations for biblical truth.

The primary and essential locale for biblical teaching is, of course, not the church school, but the weekly worship service of the people of God. The sermon, again, is not a lecture or a teaching experience; on the other hand, one of the fringe benefits of the sermon, the prayers, the hymns and the sacraments is that through them learning occurs. It is difficult to imagine why parents should feel required to choose between church school and church worship for their children; two hours a week does not seem an inordinate amount of time to spend with the congregation, given the time demanded by secular schooling. However, if it comes to a choice between church school and church, parents should opt for church. The liturgy of the Church, after all, served as the training ground for Christians for centuries before the Protestant Sunday school was invented.

For the church service to offer the fringe benefit of an educated laity will for many congregations require a radical reform of the order of service. Particularly in regard to the service of the Word, it will require the regular use of a lectionary so that the entire Bible will be read in a given time rather than, as is sometimes the case, only the pet texts of the incumbent minister. It will require that the Old Testament be read as well as the New. The gnostic practice of overlooking the Old Covenant as only a marginally Christian document has become common in some Protestant churches. Often the only Scripture heard is when the preacher "reads his own text," which means the text he or she has chosen as a point of departure for the weekly essay. How much better to have an Old Testament lesson and at least one New Testament lesson read by members of the congregation! For the texts do not belong to the preacher; they are the gracious gift of God to Christ's people. Text and sermon together witness to Christ himself to whom the preacher and the people belong.

The teaching of the Bible alone does not ensure orthodox teaching. Gnostics of all times and places have claimed allegiance to the Bible and have argued that only they correctly understood its message. Irenaeus found it discouraging that just as the average person could not tell the difference between cut glass and diamonds or could be induced to drink poison if it were disguised as milk, so most Christians could not distinguish between true teaching and false teaching.[35]

To meet the challenge of a false teaching of the Bible, the Church has often relied upon the formulation of creeds, which provide a framework within which the words of Holy Scripture can be appropriately placed and understood. Creedal statements by their very nature are corporate achievements, and the very writing of them has often represented an effective blow against heresy. The Shepherd of Hermas described the contrast between orthodoxy and heresy as "Men seated on a couch, and another man seated on a chair."[36] At least, in the Shepherd's opinion, the true teachers held the truth in common, whereas the false teacher had isolated himself.

The most familiar creed in Protestant Churches is the Apostles' Creed, which was developed in the early catholic period primarily as a refutation of gnosticism. Candidates for baptism were required to recite it in order to separate themselves from those Christians who did not believe in "God the Father, maker of heaven and earth" or that Jesus had been actually "born of the Virgin Mary, suffered under Pontius Pilate, was crucified, dead and buried."[37]

A creed, of course, is no guarantee against false teaching. Like the Bible itself, creedal formulas are subject to interpretation. As Hans Conzelmann has cautioned, "Orthodoxy is not a possession which can be passed on by inheritance. What can be handed down are doctrinal phrases, explanations of the content of faith, not the content itself."[38] Nevertheless, the "doctrinal phrases," "explanations of content" can help. John Calvin regularly used the Apostles' Creed in his order of service, and he preferred that it be sung.[39] The musical form indicated that the Creed was not an intellectual recitation but a liturgical affirmation of the true and ancient faith.

The Church's use of creeds represents a healthy conservatism in Christianity. It is an acknowledgement that this present generation does not possess the whole truth of the faith but is determined to pass on the apostolic truth it has received. Calvin's conservatism led him to consider his own work as that of restoration rather than of innovation. From his deathbed, he charged the clergy of Geneva to resist change, "since all changes are dangerous and sometimes harmful."[40]

A similar conservatism was expressed by the Barmen Declaration of 1934 against the recent accommodations of the German Churches to the Nazi philosophy:

> We reject the false doctrine that the Church is permitted to form its own message or its order according to its own desire, or according to prevailing philosophical or political convictions.

and

> We reject the false doctrine that the Church can, in human glorification of itself, use the word and work of the Lord to serve any self-chosen desires, purposes and plans.[41]

This essentially conservative view of the Church's message could be a healthy corrective to the Church Management and Church Growth mentality within the North American churches. These recently developed pragmatic notions of the Church's role, urge congregations to determine in a democratic fashion their own goals and then to take the neccessary steps to accomplish those goals. The Church Growth movement seems to have been heavily influenced by the thinking of a consumer society, with its marketing techniques, but little affected by biblical concerns. A conservatism that requires the Church to examine itself in the light of biblical witness and ancient and more recent creeds could help the Church avoid being "tossed to and fro and carried about with every wind of doctrine, by the cunning of men, by their craftiness in deceitful wiles."[42] From a positive point of view, a genuine conservatism could help to ensure that the Church concentrate her energies and resources on the teaching of the one *knowledge* it has to teach, namely, the knowledge of the mighty acts of God as He reveals them through the prophets and apostles.

A conservative use of the historic creeds calls into question even our contemporary inability to believe certain portions of them. Eduard Schweizer, in discussing the hellenistic Church, points out that during that era, Christianity retained certain items of the creed, even though these items were no longer *meaningful* for it. He cites "the expectation of a definite goal to which God leads the world" and "the understanding of the incarnation" as examples of what had become, at that time, outmoded teaching. Schweizer then goes on to say that we are also wise to hold fast to certain creedal items that we cannot preach or even understand today but that "may become of first importance in a new situation."[43]

From the Nicene Creed to the Barmen Declaration, including those creeds that the Church—speaking as Christ's people together—might confess today, the use of creeds can help guide Christians toward an orthodox understanding of the faith. Corporate confession of the catholic faith binds us not only to one another but to our ancient past. Creeds also help us to beware of false religion which denies God as the good Creator, denies the reality of Christ as the crucified, dead and buried one, denies catholicity, communality and everlasting life as essentials of Christianity.

Along with Word and Creed and closely bound to both in the maintaining of authority in the Church is the apostolic ministry. Throughout its history, the Christian Church has been defended against heresies of all sorts by the ordination of men and women trained and dedicated

> to build up the house of Christ and overthrow the house of Satan; to feed the sheep and chase away the wolves; to instruct and exhort the docile, to accuse, rebuke and subdue the rebellious and petulant, to bind and loose; in fine, if need be, to fire and fulminate, but all in the word of God.[44]

The *ministry* of Christ, in the sense of those persons who serve Christ and his Gospel, is not confined to ordained men and women, but it begins there. It begins, in fact, with those first chosen, the Apostles themselves. In his careful statement on "the mission of the Church," T. F. Torrance explained that

> the ministry of the apostolic Church is Christ's own personal ministry . . . the apostolic Church does not act instead of Christ, but He is present in the Church, and though distinct from its ministry acts in and through it, making it His own.[45]

Such a claim has always been an embarrassment to the gnostic mentality, which cannot abide the *mixing* of Holy Spirit with mere human authority. The Church's claim is a further threat to gnosticism in that it endangers the free expression of the individual spark. Holy Spirit and the individual's inner spark are, in gnosticism, of course, identical. When the Church begins to exert its authority, to *test* the spirits and sparks; then, of course, all individual, private, secret *knowledge* is in peril.

Among many North American Protestants today, any assertion of ecclesiastical authority is taken to be an outrage against the Protestant spirit. Regardless of the polity of a given denomination, whether episcopal, presbyterian or congregational, when the Church speaks there are immediate complaints that "all the individual members were not consulted," and even objections that "no church has the right to speak for individual Christians." The ordained clergy themselves in this anti-authoritarian climate have become extremely nervous about exerting the slightest discipline over those committed to their care. What could be worse in our society than being accused of being undemocratic, authoritarian, or above all *rigid*? So, whereas in the more protected environment of general synods, presbyteries and conventions, church leaders have been less reserved in presenting the Christian position in regard to ecological matters, world peace and economic disparity, for example, in the local churches, where North American Christians live and make their primary witness, real authority is for the most part rarely evident. There, economic exploitation, racist bigotry and familial tyranny are allowed to go unchallenged. Outrageous opinions expressing the most hateful political and social outlooks are voiced even in vestry, session and diaconate meetings and are usually unopposed by a docile clergy. The rationale behind this timid exercise of ministry comes from the anarchistic, essentially gnostic, argument that *authority* itself is at best old-fashioned, at worst wicked. The positive counterpart to the argument is that each Christian when left to his or her own conscience will finally think and act in a Christlike way. Such a polity, or rather lack of one, is a denial of Christ's gift of the divine ministry.

This gnostic fear of religious authorities plays into the hands of political tyrants. The Nazi government, for example, was delighted when a weak German Protestantism acquiesced to its demands. In the face of this political terror, however, the small confessing Church, in the Düsseldorf Theses of 1933, reasserted the authority of the Christian ministry. "The Church," it confessed, "lives in all its members by the exercise of the ministry of preachers, teachers, elders and deacons, which was instituted and ordained by Jesus Christ."[46] In contemporary North America, this same ecclesiastical authority must be reasserted against political and social manipulators who indoctrinate individuals through the oft-repeated lie. Whereas individuals standing alone can be easily programmed through the mass media, members of a disciplined Church with a strong Word-bound ministry could resist.

How ecclesiastical authority is to be exercised has been a painful question among Protestants. The New Testament itself does not provide a clear answer, and the early Church's answer of episcopal authority is not acceptable to most non-Anglican Protestants. However, if the Church is to convey Christ's truth to Christ's people, then the various Churches, for the present, must employ their own system of discipline in their traditional manner. There is within episcopal, presbyterian and congregational polity ample means and experience for the restoration of discipline. All that is needed is the confidence and will to exercise it. Confidence and will are present when we understand with Irenaeus that the Church is a divine creation not of human beings but wherein human beings have been appointed to serve as apostles, prophets and teachers. These appointees "preserve this faith of ours in one God who created all things; and they increase that love [which we have] for the Son of God . . . and they expound the Scriptures to us without danger, neither blaspheming God, nor dishonouring the patriarchs, nor despising the prophets."[47]

There is nothing hierarchical or dictatorial about this claim. The recognition of a ministry and its obligation to discipline is simply to state that certain men and women have been set apart by the Holy Spirit in order that under his guidance, always subject to the Word, they might guide the people of God in the way of truth.[48]

If the Church is to restate and restore its traditional gift of ministerial discipline, there will be required, of course, a reform of the ministerial offices. That need is always present in every generation of the Church. Modern Protestantism is no more immune from an unworthy ministry than was medieval Catholicism. The problem is solved not by removing the responsibility of the shepherds but rather by insisting that the shepherds be equipped for and dedicated to their tasks.

Much can be learned from medieval experience. As Roland H. Bainton observed:

> One of the indictments to be brought against the clergy in the Middle Ages is not that they were all ignorant. Some were amazingly versed in Scripture, not to mention theology, but they had developed a technical jargon which the masses did not and were not expected to understand. Theology was almost the pastime of an esoteric clique. As for the ordinary clergy, their learning was manifestly minimal.[49]

As we see the vast gulf that presently lies between academic theology and the pulpit, it is apparent that our situation is not all that different from the medieval one. Certainly, in biblical studies, academic jargon has become too technical and esoteric to help the average preacher achieve a better understanding of the Word. And in other areas from systematics to church history, there often seems to be little concern for the particular problems facing the parish ministers and the congregations. Karl Barth's agenda of writing a theology that would help the preacher with his or her weekly task of preaching the Gospel seems to have been rejected in North America in favor of theology for a professional clique. This is not to suggest that teaching doctors should simplify or modify their labors in order to accommodate an uneducated clergy and laity. Barth's *Church Dogmatics* is not, after all, easy devotional literature for the busy pastor. Rather the problem is one of direction and intention. Theologians, in the various disciplines, are called to be servants of the Church, and therefore to direct their research toward the Church with the intention of edifying it, supporting it, reforming it; they are, above all, to stand within the Church benefiting it with their training and talents.

It would be unfair to single out the academics as the culprits, as if the unfortunate distance between lecture hall and chancel were entirely of their making. There is also, as in the medieval Church, the problem of an uneducated clergy. Most Protestant clergy are not uneducated in the formal sense of the word; they have attended university and seminary and have received the proper academic degrees. The typical clergyperson is uneducated, rather, in the sense that most genuine theological concentration ends with ordination into the parish ministry. All too often both the clergy and the congregation understand the pastor's primary role to be that of managing the organization. What had been the pastor's "study" has become the "office"; the learned journals that may, even yet, decorate the shelves along the wall, are not nearly so important as the telephone or the photocopier. When a parish minister does attempt to devote a great deal of time to study and prayer, he or she is considered an anachronism, something out of a Trollope novel. Very few congregations, in looking for a new minister, would place continuing scholarship and meditation as priorities on their job description.

The clergy are, no doubt, becoming more effective as managers of the organization. Not only are seminary graduates better trained in this area, but also continuing education courses keep ministers abreast of the latest administrative techniques, conflict management and advertising and marketing schemes—all necessary for the managerial tasks. What often goes unquestioned, however, is the concept of the calling itself. Is this managerial model the apostolic ministry for which the ordained person has been set apart? The appointment of the first deacons as recorded in the Acts would seem to be for the express purpose of protecting the Gospel ministry from undue administrative concerns. The Apostles declared, "We will devote ourselves to prayer and to the ministry of the word."[50]

What is required is a thoroughgoing revolt against this comparatively recent revision of the ministerial office. To be successful the revolt would have to be contrived both within the seminary and within the local parish. The seminary would be required to resist the intense pressures to produce managerial types and to insist rather on maintaining high standards in the traditional areas which prepare men and women for the ministry of Word and Sacrament. Also, the seminary would be required to withstand the present drive for further specialization, the training of some students for academic teaching and others for the pastorate by means of a wholly different course of study. The Church does not need specialists in the sense of persons isolated within their field; rather it does need academic theologians who are also trained in pastoral matters and pastors who are well trained in the essentials of academic theology. Above all, Protestant Churches, facing all sorts of challenges within and without, require a genuine intellectual track between seminary and congregation. This track can only be reopened when teaching doctors and pastors prepare for and maintain a common ministry.

In recent years, efforts have been made along this line: continuing education courses and doctor-of-ministry programs, for example, have been promoted by various seminaries. Although these developments are certainly steps in the right direction, for the most part they have been too modest to bring about a genuine reform of the ministry. The continuing education courses for pastors and chaplains usually consist of only two weeks a year and often place unacceptable financial burdens on the individual clergyperson and family. This is certainly the case among those serving in rural areas or small churches who receive basic stipends. Regarding the doctor-of-ministry programs, all too many are designed to enhance the managerial function of the ministry and only succeed in widening the gap between real theological concerns and the pastorate. In all continuing education courses, including the doctor-of-ministry programs, better funding should be provided. In both short- and long-term studies, the emphasis should be shifted from the well-intentioned devices of men to the mighty acts of God.

As the pastor spends more time at the seminary, is it not also possible that the seminary professor could devote more time to the parish? Perhaps every five years or so, a month during the summer could be given to supplying the pulpit and pastoral services within a local congregation. There is a certain Maoist practicality in the idea which might benefit both the seminary and the parish.

Meanwhile, on the parish level it becomes primarily the burden of the pastor to redesign his or her own ministry along New Testament and traditional lines. Certainly, one advantage of the profession is that most pastors and chaplains are still allowed to make up their own time schedule. It is too much to expect that vestries, sessions and deacon boards will suggest that the minister spend more time in prayer and study (including study leaves and sabbaticals) and less in administration. Only the clergy can successfully convert the "office" back into a "study." It is not beyond all imagination, however, to hope that a devotion to "prayer and to the ministry of the Word" would eventually result in a renewal of preaching and pastoral work that would be appreciated by at least some members of the congregation.

Such a concentration on the study of the Word—in terms of the ministerial office and by means of strengthening the ties between academy and parish—would certainly result in a renewal of theological education among the laity. As in other areas of life, actions often speak louder than words. If members of the congregation see their spiritual leader not as one who automatically knows all the answers, but as one who continually needs study and guidance in order to understand, then they also could unashamedly admit their own requirements for direction in understanding the truth of the Gospel.

The renewal of the ministerial office along these lines, of course, implies that the truth is not something we automatically have within, some secret knowledge that is a spinoff of a conversion experience. The knowledge we have in Christ is to be understood and appropriated like any other knowledge. The aid of the Holy Spirit in achieving understanding is an assurance for the diligent, not an excuse for the slothful. The promise of Christ to his disciples was not that the Holy Spirit would unveil secret knowledge so that theological learning no longer need be pursued. Rather the Spirit "will take what is mine and declare it to you."[51]

The fact that the ministry of Word and Sacrament begins with certain persons set aside as teachers, pastors and celebrants does not in any sense imply that ministry ends there. What is important is that the ministry of Christ has direction and purpose, that what is taught within the Church is not the wisdom of individuals, but the truth proceeding from Christ himself. In a practical sense, this means that ministry takes place under the auspices of and guidance of the ministerial offices. Once that is understood, then ministry quite naturally becomes the function of the Christian community as a whole. Within such a discipline, it is not only proper but necessary that theological education should occur within the local parish. In such a congregation wherein ministry is being renewed, lay leaders with the appropriate gifts will be encouraged to read and even preach the Word. Within this context, fathers and mothers can be seen as the priests of the family, and the priesthood of all believers can be realized in terms of each member serving those given to his care.

Willingness to Sacrifice: Acceptance of the Lifelong Pilgrimage

When *knowledge* is understood as having to do with public acts preached and taught openly in a community of faith, such an understanding will undoubtedly affect ethical response. Christians who really believe that God has acted and continues to act in the world will certainly carry out their Christianity in a different way from those who see God only as a revealer, only as the One who provides meaning to a life determined by wholly other, even quite ungodly forces.

The biblical view, as we have seen, is that of a God who acts, who is always free to determine. When, following Jesus' baptism, a heavenly voice said, "Thou art my beloved Son; with thee I am well pleased,"[52] all nature and history had to conform to that judgment. When St. Paul applied Isaiah's prophecy to Christ, he was making the claim that all persons would either stumble or stand according to their relationship to this One in whom the Almighty God is "well pleased."[53]

Once the Church takes the bold step of confessing a God who not only enlightens but intervenes, an appropriate Christian ethic begins to emerge. When, for example, Christians can understand God the Creator of heaven and earth as the same God who addresses us through the Holy Catholic Church, suddenly there is the recognition that there is a plan, a divine scheme for the world. No longer is everything dependent on my insights, my discerning reading of the Revelation or of the *New York Times*. No longer is everything baffling, nor are apparently meaningless events signs that life is chaotic. There is a strategy over and above me which does not require my thorough understanding, but which demands my complete obedience. There is a living body of Christ's people which comes forward from the Apostles, includes all brothers and sisters of the present struggle and moves out into a measureless future.

In a similar way, a belief in the *communion of saints* lifts the burden of omnipotence from the individual Christian. At last, I am able to see myself as a small part of the whole, in time as well as in space.

"Since we are surrounded by so great a cloud of witnesses" we are able to lay aside the close-clinging weights and sins and "run with perseverance the race that is set before us."[54] There will not be the anxious urge to finish everything before the end of my particular race; obviously, the contest will be carried on by my comrades who follow. The only pressure will be to do the task I am given to do, to perform it cheerfully as long as I am given to perform it.

When the *forgiveness of sins* is confessed as a reality going beyond a psychological sense of forgiveness, then the Christian is able to respond in thanksgiving to the God of forgiveness. If, in Christ, my sins have really been overcome and if, in fact, he is really the "Lamb of God, who takes away the sins of the world,"[55] then my compulsion to prove myself wiser, stronger, holier than my fellow worldlings becomes quite unnecessary, and I am free to divert those self-protective energies into grateful service.

The Church, in affirming belief in the *resurrection of the body,* not as a parable for Easter Sunday, but as a sure promise for God's longing people, frees the Christian from an inappropriate pampering of the body and from an obsessive fear of death. When individuals see the end of their individual lives as the permanent end of existence, it is very difficult to muster the sort of courage martyrdom is made of. The boldness of Christians, epitomized in the celebration of the holy martyrs, is not based on James Bond-like nerves of steel, but rather on the assurance that "if the earthly tent we live in is destroyed, we have a building from God, a house not made with hands."[56] This is the true spirituality of the New Testament, a spirituality allowing us to appreciate the present simply for what it is, because we believe in a future that will be what God makes it.

Finally, when the Church confesses a belief in *the life everlasting,* it overcomes the dread of futurelessness which has left so many twentieth-century Christians and non-Christians ethically paralyzed. Given the present disregard for earthly life—human, plant and animal—within the contemporary corridors of power, little wonder that so many thoughtful people have despaired of the survival of this planet. Beyond this "realistic" appraisal of the present threat, however, the Church reaffirms its realistic faith in the sovereign Lord of life, its gratitude for "receiving a kingdom that cannot be shaken."[57]

Confidence in a God who acts, who is still leading His people through deserts and still raising the dead, enables those Christians who are willing to submit to the discipline of the Church to make sacrifices and endure suffering in the name of the Crucified One. Gnostic escape is replaced by faithful pilgrimage.

Since the time of the first Great Awakening, there has been within North American Protestantism a tendency to seek a quick religious *fix,* so that in one brilliant moment a single solution may be found to all the problems of life. Over against this essentially escapist mentality, there has persisted within Protestantism a minority calling for patient Christian maturity, that we might "grow up in every way into him who is the head, into Christ."[58] In his farsighted work, *Christian Nurture,* Horace Bushnell was bold enough to deny the need for a dramatic conversion experience, insisting rather that the normal form of Christian development occurred step by step from infancy. "Let every Christian father and mother understand," wrote Bushnell, "[that] when their child is three years old, . . . they have done more than half of all they will ever do for his character." He even declared that "the child is to grow up a Christian, and never know himself as being otherwise . . . not remembering the time when he went through a *technical experience,* but seeming rather to have loved what is good from his earliest years."[59] It is this essentially orthodox perception that must be recovered by the Protestant Churches.

It could be argued that Bushnell's philosophy of Christian education has been predominant for generations, especially within liberal congregations. And it is quite true that various enlightened church-school curricula have attempted to establish *nurture* as the norm. In practice, however, Christian education at church and in the home is an extremely low-priority item. Were mathematics, science or computer technology to be taught in such a slipshod fashion as are the data of Christian faith, Protestant parents would be rightfully indignant. Most parents openly admit their own inadequacy to teach their young about Israel, the life of Jesus, the Cross, Resurrection and Ascension, and that admission is at least as socially acceptable as not being able to help one's child with calculus. So, they entrust the teaching of religion to their church. Many Protestant congregations undertake this task in inferior academic facilities (unattractive church basements, parlors designed for something else) that are staffed by untrained volunteer (but often unenthusiastic) teachers, within a time frame of about forty-five minutes a week. Even this bleak picture of Christian education does not describe the present state of learning in Protestantism because attendance at church school varies between sporadic and poor. Parents are not concerned because church education is of poor quality; church education is of poor quality because parents are not concerned. Which comes first? I suspect that basic religious education remains impoverished because Protestants have not understood clearly enough that Christian nurture is the normal way to develop Christians. If our children are not taught about the Passover and the Exodus, the Parables and Pentecost, they will *normally* not be Christians. If our children are not in church school and church every Sunday, except for illness or emergency, then the Protestant faith will be for them an optional matter, a strange intrusion into the important routines of existence and a foreign understanding of what life is really about—rather like Hinduism, Buddhism or, more accurately, like Druidism, because it pertains to our ancestral past.

For thousands of Protestant Christians, this description is not in the least overdrawn. On weekend sports outings, coaches often inform their teams that if there are any Roman Catholics present, arrangements will be made to transport them to Mass. The assumption is, of course, that for Protestants, church is not a problem. Protestants can always attend next week—unless something important is going on. Religious holidays such as Ash Wednesday, Maundy Thursday, even Good Friday, are widely thought of as Roman Catholic observances. Again, the predominant Protestant understanding of Christian faith is of something which one either *has* or has not, which one has *within* or not at all.

To counteract this still pervasive view of faith, Protestants must be willing first of all to face up to their own misconceptions about Christianity. Any number of thoughtful, well-planned educational curricula will fail to make a difference as long as Protestants continue to view biblical knowledge as an unnecessary, even irrelevant appendage to true religion. In the same sense, a renewal of the liturgy will have little influence within the churches so long as the liturgy is understood as a mere public expression of a more significant inner reality.

Once Protestantism is able to examine itself and admit the need for biblical truth and liturgical renewal, several practical steps could lead toward effective reform. Christian education would, for one thing, be designed more for the home and less for the church basement. A regular program of family prayer and Bible study would be a practical congregational goal. Simple and usable material would be provided for every home unit: single person, traditional family or single parent. Such material would take into account that at present the Protestant constituency is not strongly motivated toward any religious education and that most persons would be extremely ignorant regarding the Bible. What is needed at this juncture is not regrets or embarrassment but rather confession and a first step. Why not, for instance, begin by building a home curriculum around the three readings of the weekly liturgy as a preparation for the following Sunday worship? Would it not be possible for Christian educators to supply helpful commentary for these readings and at the same time indicate the connection between the particular texts and the broader themes of Holy Scripture?

The church basement or its more adequate equivalent, could then be the place where the church coordinates and reinforces its home educational efforts. Home, church school and the worship service would then all be concentrated on the same theme provided by the three-year ecumenical lectionary. Needless to say, such a concentration would also bring about much closer understanding and trust between the various Protestant denominations as well as between Protestants and Roman Catholics. Such a focusing would be an endorsement of Karl Barth's solid judgment:

> The work of construction in which the community is the true Church is at its centre. . . . This work is its common worship. It is not only in worship that the community is edified and edifies itself. But it is here first that this continually takes place. And if it does not take place here, it does not take place anywhere. . . . Assembling for divine worship is self-evidently the centre and presupposition of the whole Christian life, the atmosphere in which it is lived.[60]

Improving the level of Christian education within the parish will in many cases involve the expenditure of more money. What is involved is remedial education in biblical religion. That implies professional time and training beyond the capacity of most pastors and their volunteer staffs. When motivation increases along with a growing confidence in the possibility of acquiring biblical knowledge, financial support usually is forthcoming.

Even small changes in Christian education and regular church attendance require a greater sense of discipline. In *Love in the Ruins,* Walker Percy's Roman Catholic protagonist compares himself to his Protestant girlfriend:

> Ellen, though she is a strict churchgoer [Presbyterian] and a moral girl, does not believe in God. Rather does she believe in the Golden Rule and in doing right. She doesn't need God. What does God have to do with being honest, hard-working, chaste, upright, unselfish,

> etcetera. I, on the other hand, believe in God, the Jews, Christ, the whole business. Yet I don't do right. I am a Renaissance pope, an immoral believer. Between the two of us we might have saved Christianity. Instead we lost it.[61]

Percy's implication that the Protestant personality still retains a large degree of Puritan discipline, even though the Puritan faith has disappeared, is probably accurate (though I doubt the "strict" churchgoing component). If Protestant faith is able even yet to call forth an ethical response of "doing right," and if that "doing right" can be reconnected to the God of Israel who has so consistently been doing right by us, perhaps Protestant Christians may yet be recalled to a life of discipline: one of prayer, study, stewardship, social and personal morality. What is needed is not a return to the family altar, to the "old time religion," to any of the sentimentalized fantasies of the past, but rather a realistic move toward an attainable lifestyle for the present.

Discipline, of course, is only training for what is to come. Discipline prepares the Christian for the inevitable suffering that lies ahead. Because Christians as ordinary members of humanity are subject to the universal afflictions of the race—loss, disappointment, aging, dying and death—and, in fact, are especially called to witness through their suffering to the dying, death and resurrection of Christ, of all people they are to be prepared. Some religionists, through the assurance of faith healing or some other *exemption* from human life, are pointing away from the Jesus of history; others, through claims of psychological self-perfection are pointing away from Christ the Lord of life. Resisting these gnostic temptations to effect an escape, the Christian will accept the fact that "the same experience of suffering is required of your brotherhood throughout the world" and the assurance that "after you have suffered a little while, the God of all grace, who has called you to his eternal glory in Christ, will himself restore, establish, and strengthen you."[62] If Protestants, through the discipline of the Church, can learn to live as those "afflicted in every way, but not crushed; perplexed, but not driven to despair; persecuted, but not forsaken; struck down, but not destroyed;"[63] surely, no matter how ordinary and unpublicized their lives, they cannot help but be effective witnesses to Christ.

How could brothers and sisters, regardless of their faith or lack of it, help but be impressed by a Protestantism radically willing to admit its humanity? How could North America not feel the impact of a people trained from earliest days not to be seduced by any offer of spiritual escape, a people knowing rather that affliction "is to be our lot"?[64] The commonly accepted idea that Protestant Christianity is a middle-class pastime or a respectable joke would certainly have to be questioned.

A disciplined revolt against the arrogant claims of a gnosticized Protestantism will undoubtedly land the revolutionaries in a great deal of hot water. The gnostic expression of Christianity has in many influential quarters, including at times the White House itself, been accepted as the true representation of historic Christianity. That gnostic expression in cooperation with the existing North American establishment is intent on maintaining the present socio-political arrangement. Those Protestants who beckon to one another to "go forth to him outside the camp, bearing abuse for him," who insist that "here we have *no lasting city,* but we seek the city which is to come"[65] are certainly making themselves vulnerable to political persecution, North American style.

The present crises in North American and global politics cannot be understood in exclusively economic, socio-political or secular historical terms. The present crises—the bomb, unemployment, Third World poverty, ecological peril, sexual unrest—are all in large part theological problems. Ernst Troeltsch, in the early part of our century, pointed out the theological aspect of the impending crises when he observed:

> It [ascetic Protestantism] has founded and evolved the main body of Protestant civilization. But its power is weakening, and Protestantism is thus faced by new tasks, both in its sociological developments and in its corporate connection with civilization.[66]

It would now appear that those "new tasks" foreseen by Troeltsch have reached an acute stage. American Protestantism is now being tempted in even more compelling terms to pretend that Christianity offers an escape from life. From both the theological right and the left, religion is being relegated to the psycho-personal and banned from the socio-political areas of life. Thus immediate problems of environment, economics and nuclear armament are held to be beyond the purview of religious thinking. Given the enormous stakes involved in the present crises, the great amount of money involved in every environmental decision, for example, it is easy to understand the Churches' search for some sort of neutral ground. Also there is constant pressure on the Churches to endorse a position that seeks to refine, but not threaten the present arrangement. Antonio Gramsci, the father of Italian Marxism, has seen the "function of eminent middle-class intellectuals" as that of elaborating "a view of the world that would enable the ruling class to win the allegiance and assent of the lower orders to the institutions under which they live."[67] It would not be surprising if middle-class Protestantism shares the same function because, like the academic institutions, its financial support comes largely from establishment sources.

Biblical Christianity, furthermore, is easily recognized as a threat. When the God of Israel promises Jeremiah:

> See, I have set you this day over
> nations and over kingdoms,
> to pluck up and to break down,
> To destroy and to overthrow,
> To build and to plant.[68]

are the multinational corporations, who have no intention of being "plucked up," expected to hear this prophecy with gladness? And when St. Paul declares:

> God chose what is foolish in the world to shame the wise, God chose what is weak in the world to shame the strong, God chose what is low and despised in the world, even things that are not, to bring to nothing things that are.[69]

are the top echelons of the Pentagon comforted?

Accompanying whatever good motives may be behind the uncompromising separation of church and state in the United States is the lurking fear that an authentically powerful Church might challenge the autonomous claims of the state. The potential is always there. As Karl Barth expressed it:

> The Church—if it be aware of itself and is serious—sets fire to a charge which blows up every sacred edifice which men have ever erected or can ever erect in its vicinity.[70]

The new task of North American Protestantism indeed calls for the blowing up of several sacred edifices. An escape into gnostic fantasy would certainly offer a less painful alternative. For the first edifice to be destroyed, and only dedicated Protestants can properly do it, is the shrine of American nationalism. Despite all that has occurred of late to cast doubt on it, the apocalyptic dream—that America is the hope of the world, a beacon to the nations without which all other nations are destined to live in despair and error—lives on. Even the most liberal-minded Americans, and even some Canadians cling to the idea that the United States has been in some sense uniquely selected to save the world. Protestantism, which has been so influential in building the shrine and providing for its upkeep, is now in a position to call for its demolition. This will involve on the part of Protestants a confession of past error, of having misread the Bible as a prophecy regarding America when the Bible's real story concerns humanity. It will require an assertion that the true community of hope and beacon to the nations is none other than the Church of Jesus Christ in both its ecumenical (spatial) and catholic (temporal) dimensions. It will necessitate the bold and embarrassing admission that the "chosen race, . . . royal priesthood, . . . holy nation, God's own people . . ."[71] is not the United States of America but rather a loosely knit disorganized Church composed of El Salvadorean peasants, Africans, millions of Russians, and even Americans.

This (for America) radical reinterpretation of the biblical message will undoubtedly be understood as unpatriotic and even seditious, not only by the Moral Majority, but by some of the apologists of an American civil religion; yet nothing short of this revision can save the American people and their homeland from an unimaginable self-destruction. Nothing short of a final denial of the false apocalyptic dream can free the great Republic from the impossible occupation of carrying out a divine mission which has never been committed to it. Neither the humiliation of Vietnam nor the continuing military involvements in Central America can be understood and constructively altered until first there is the recognition that America, like every nation on earth, is a land of promise but is not and never will be the Promised Land. What is needed is a Protestant voice calling Americans away from fanciful escape into responsible citizenship.

An even more daunting task faces the Protestant Churches in regard to the present enshrinement of *capitalism*. If faith in the American apocalyptic dream has faded in certain quarters, it would seem that North American belief in the capitalistic way of life is as strong as ever. So entrenched is this gnostic spiritualization of economics in our society that to question its validity is generally considered unsettling if not heretical. For what is accepted as axiomatic is that when unbridled competition is allowed to take place, some "invisible hand" will deal out benefits to a very wide representation of the population. Human nature, according to this wisdom, dictates that some people will benefit from the system a great deal and others not at all; the more compassionate advocates of capitalism support the idea of a social welfare program that aids those necessary victims of the system. The great majority of the Protestant constituency, however, would support "the 'tradition' of political freedom [that] involves the defense of predatory capitalism and the irresponsible acquisition of wealth."[72] This tradition, often called *conservatism,* is in reality a continuation of a liberal faith in unfettered individualism. Most political arguments in North America are, in reality, between those who want capitalism to have a kindlier face and those who do not.

Insofar as Protestants are willing to assert themselves as a People of the Book, their word to the society will be disturbing and even seditious, for within biblical religion the idea of unrestrained greed is quite unacceptable. Even in the agricultural economy of Old Testament times a certain lack of efficiency was enjoined on the landowners on behalf of the less fortunate:

> When you reap your harvest in your field, and have forgotten a sheaf in the field, you shall not go back to get it; it shall be for the sojourner, the fatherless, and the widow . . . . When you beat your olive trees, you shall not go over the boughs again; it shall be for the sojourner, the fatherless, and the widow. When you gather the grapes of your vineyard, you shall not glean it afterward; it shall be for the sojourner, the fatherless, and the widow.

This unbusinesslike ethic is to serve as a reminder to prosperous Israelites "that you were a slave in the land of Egypt."[73] Nor is economic justice to be a matter of largess on the part of the affluent. The affluent are warned that if "your eye be hostile to your poor brother, and you give him nothing, and he cry to the Lord against you" it will be counted as "sin in you." Whereas Yahweh will not tolerate such arrogant behavior, if the well-off "shall give to him freely, and your heart shall not be grudging when you give to him; . . . the Lord your God will bless you in all your work and in all that you undertake."[74] Faithfulness to God is intrinsically connected to the practice of economic justice. Those who are avaricious and uncharitable do not even *know* God:

> The Lord has a controversy
> with the inhabitants of the land.
> There is no faithfulness or kindness,
> and no knowledge of God in the
> land.[75]

The controversy between Yahweh and Israel has to do precisely with Israel's refusal to show the compassion to one another that Yahweh has shown to them. Yahweh's judgment, then, will be severe:

> Therefore I am like a moth to
> Ephraim,
> and like dry rot to the house of
> Judah.[76]

Far from being able to lay claim on divine power, Israel finds Yahweh to be the enemy within its gates.

This same judgment against human greed is pronounced over and over again in the New Testament. The Synoptic Gospels especially present a frightening catalogue of blessing and woes based entirely on the criterion of economic justice. In his Sermon on the Plains, Jesus pronounces a blessing on the poor, "for yours is the kingdom of God," and a woe on the rich, "for you have [already] received your consolation."[77] He prophesies woe for the Pharisees, "for you tithe mint and rue and every herb, and neglect justice and the love of God."[78] Clearly, in this case, the test is not ritualistic purity, which Jesus states they ought to have accomplished "without neglecting the others";[79] the real test is attitude toward the needy. There is the parable of the rich landlord, the poor fool who "lays up treasure for himself, but is not rich toward God."[80] There is the story of the otherwise quite righteous ruler who still lacked one thing. When advised by Jesus to "sell all that [he had] and distribute to the poor . . . he became sad because he was very rich."[81] The disciples as a whole are given this same outrageous command: "Sell your possessions, and give alms; provide yourselves with purses that do not grow old." Provision for the future is, according to Jesus, an unnecessary and unfaithful activity; the crows and the lilies do quite nicely without ever lifting a finger. Therefore, you also are not to "seek what you are to eat and what you are to drink, nor [to] be of anxious mind."[82] There is the terrifying parable about Lazarus and the rich man and the eternal chasm fixed between them,[83] and the equally alarming warning that at the final judgment when all nations are gathered together for the dividing of sheep and goats, the division will be made entirely on the basis of attitude toward the hungry, the naked, the sick and the imprisoned.[84] Again, economic attitude is the primary determining factor because "no one can serve two masters; . . . you cannot serve God and mammon."[85] Obviously, the problem is that mammon, like all idols, has spiritual dimensions. It is not a question of Jesus or the biblical tradition being against materialism. On the contrary, the thrust of the biblical attack is against the spiritualization of economic affluence, the attributing of some absolute value or sense of security to that which, like all earthly gifts, is merely temporal. W. H. Auden joins the attack against a spiritualized economics in his essay, "Postcript: The Almighty Dollar," with this insight: "The great vice of Americans is not materialism but a lack of respect for matter."[86]

It is this attack on capitalism and all its false claims of security and lasting prosperity that the Church of Christ carries within itself. Gutiérrez is certainly correct in seeing the essential connection between politics and religion, Biblical history and secular history, love for God and love for humanity. He is especially astute in understanding that "political theology restores the public meaning of Christian faith over against the privitization of the faith by the Church in its defense against the Enlightenment."[87] Those North Americans who refuse to take Latin American liberation theology seriously, who are unmoved by the persecutions these Churches have endured, are no better than the gnostics of whom Irenaeus wrote: "[They] have reached such a pitch of audacity that they even pour contempt upon the martyrs, and vituperate those who are killed on account of confessing the Lord." Irenaeus goes on to admonish, "If any one supposes there were two natures in Christ, the one who suffered was certainly superior to the one who escaped suffering, sustaining neither injury nor insult." And finally he warns that on the Day of Judgment, when the martyrs "attain to glory, then all who have cast a slur upon their martyrdom shall be confounded by Christ."[88]

North American Protestantism has reached a critical stage. Adherence to biblical truth can no longer be urged upon us as a matter of good conscience or of theological consistency. Rather the crisis has been thrust upon us by historical development and public events. Paul Lehmann has summarized it well:

> According to the coinherence of biblical and revolutionary politics, there is a providential pressure of reality upon human affairs, making time and space make room for the freedom and fulfillment that being human takes. It is this reality that radically alters the Church's time-honored addiction and allegiance to the existing authority of established collectivities, and requires an identification of the people of God with the suppliants of history.[89]

Protestant churches that for a long time have found it too easy to squeeze the camel through the eye of a needle and to ally themselves with capitalism, accepting it as the Protestant solution to man's economic dilemma, are now confronted by a spiritual claim of capitalism so far-reaching that it threatens to destroy Western culture if not the whole of human life on the planet. The claim is that the capitalistic system is so important in terms of function and philosophy that were its existence threatened by Communist aggression, the Northern hemisphere might have to be sacrificed. Such a course of action has been advocated not only by military persons, but also by leading politicians and, of course, is implied by the "defense" budget of the U.S. government. Were the nuclear arms race a contest over land, natural resources, wealth, something tangible, we could only assume that the competitors were mad, that their greed had led them toward the destruction of everything. What we are faced with, however, is not material competition, but spiritual conflict. Whatever the spiritual claims of Russian Marxism might be, the spiritual claim of Western capitalism is that its system is an essential of human life and that everything, literally everything, is to be sacrificed for its preservation. George Kennan has understood the theological nature of the claim and has written these prophetic words in response:

> I hope I am not being unjust or uncharitable. But to me . . . the readiness to use nuclear weapons against other human beings—against people whom we do not know, whom we have never seen, and whose guilt or innocence it is not for us to establish—and, in doing so, to place in jeopardy the natural structure upon which all civilization rests, as though the safety and the perceived interests of our own generation were more important than everything that has ever taken place or could take place in civilization: this is nothing less than a presumption, a blasphemy, an indignity—an indignity of monstrous dimensions—offered to God![90]

The *blasphemy* has been and is being perpetrated by a gnostic view of life, a view that holds the created world and all its creatures in very low esteem, but that, on the other hand, has identified its own *gnosis* with the divine and is willing to risk everything to safeguard that identification.

This, then, is the crisis. Protestantism is being forced by events either to sever the alliance with spiritualized economics or else to endorse its suicidal course. There are certainly hopeful signs that Protestants are beginning to recognize the horrendous consequences of the misalliance between spiritualized religion and spiritualized economics. Most Protestant denominations have spoken out on socioeconomic matters as well as in favor of nuclear disarmament. The critical situation, however, demands more than high-level pronouncements. The real battle must be joined on the local level within ordinary churches. It is there that an escapist Christianity falsely separating the spiritual from the material, faith from responsibility, the compassionate from the practical must be challenged. On that level, the conflict will not be easily or quickly decided. Those who have a great deal at stake both financially and emotionally in Protestantism's support of the system will not simply acquiesce. Undoubtedly, sincere persons will be alienated from one another; courageous ministers of the Gospel will lose their positions. And no amount of conflict-management skills will alleviate the pain.

Rather than technique, what is required is a willingness to bear suffering in the name of Christ for the purifying of his Church. The clergy of all people should be made aware that suffering is the normal state of those who take up the Cross. "Indeed all who desire to live a godly life in Christ Jesus will be persecuted."[91] And especially those who teach should be prepared to "share in suffering as a good soldier of Christ Jesus."[92]

The promise for faithful service is always sure:

> If we have died with him, we shall
> also live with him;
> if we endure, we shall also reign
> with him;
> if we deny him, he also will deny us;
> If we are faithless, he remains
> faithful.[93]

Not escape but pilgrimage. The Roman Catholics in the Second Vatican Council have renewed the Old Testament image in a dynamic and reforming way. Vatican II picks up the theme of Israel moving across the wilderness toward the land of promise. It recalls St. Augustine's words that the Church, "has gone forward on pilgrimage amid the persecutions of the world and the consolations of God."[94] Until North American Protestants are able to reject the compulsion to escape the world, and to adopt the image of pilgrimage, the children of the Reformation are destined to remain unreformed.

Perhaps those Protestants, both clergy and laity, who are discouraged by the present condition of their churches and who are tempted by unbiblical alternatives that offer more immediate rewards, will be strengthened by the far-sighted promise of Karl Barth. In commenting on St. Paul's dilemma, Barth writes:

> All posts which men occupy as men are lost posts. It is this that must be made evident. And, indeed, it is made evident whenever the gospel is proclaimed *in* the Church, whenever in the solidarity of prophet and priest the impossible becomes possible and the possible becomes impossible.[95]

Born Again into the Church

It is indeed in the *Church* where the Gospel is proclaimed and within the context of the Church where the Gospel is received. Nothing is more important for North American Protestantism than the reassertion of that axiom of orthodoxy. Niesel, in discussing the importance of congregations in the history of Protestantism, their strength and endurance even under persecution, points out that their central role was not by accident,

> since the Lord promised His presence, not to individuals but to the congregation gathered in His name. To this He gave the assurance that even the gates of Hell would not prevail against it.[96]

The Church is the source of the Word and of our calling to Christian discipleship. "The Spirit and the *Bride* say, 'Come.' "[97] Unless the invitation to the banquet of life comes from the bride (the Church) as well as the groom (the Spirit of Christ), the invitation may well be a forgery. For the life-giving, saving Word has been entrusted to the community of Christ as surely as the eternal saving Word was entrusted to and incorporated within the Christ of history. A. D. Nock, in dealing with St. Paul's claim, "I have received of the Lord what I also delivered to you," asks the critical question: whether the Apostle gained his knowledge of the eucharistic meal as a direct, personal revelation from Christ or whether he learned of the Supper through the testimony of the Apostles. Nock sensibly concludes that for St. Paul, the apostolic witness has the full authority of the Lord.[98]

The New Testament and the early Church do not, in terms of authority, draw a sharp line of distinction between the Jesus Christ of history and the Jesus Christ, Lord of the Church. Through his many Resurrection appearances, Christ, from time to time, here and there, showed his followers that they would not for very long be bereft of him. As John records it, "a little while, and you will see me no more; again a little while and you will see me."[99]

Protestant Churches, along with their sister Churches, Roman Catholic, Eastern Orthodox and others who are not ashamed of their catholicity, should not hesitate to claim the Bible as the *Church's* Holy Scripture. Against all those who would give the impression that both Testaments dropped out of the sky for the purpose of saving individual souls, the Churches must insist that the Bible is from and for Israel and the Church. When it is read in any other context, as a book of private devotion, or as a collection of salvation techniques or as a guide to self-discovery, it has the same limited value as, say, the *Book of Mormon* and can be equally misleading. Read outside its communal context it is certain to be interpreted in one heretical form or another. Irenaeus, in refuting the false teachings of the gnostics in particular, always relies on the Church itself to be the preserver of the true biblical faith. "By knowledge of the truth," he wrote,

> we mean: the teaching of the Apostles; the order of the Church as established from the earliest times throughout the world: the distinctive stamp of the Body of Christ, preserved through the episcopal succession: for to the bishops the Apostles commited the care of the Church *which is in each place,* safeguarded without any written conditions: . . . the reading of the Scriptures without falsification, and consistent and careful exposition of them, avoiding temerity and blasphemy: and the special gift of love.[100]

Despite all the negative qualities he undoubtedly knew about the Church, Irenaeus was willing to trust her as the bearer of apostolic truth. The Church is the locale where Christ has promised to be present in the world.

What is crucial for American Protestantism is a clear understanding and a stubborn assertion of the truth that when Christians are born again, they do *not* enter again into their mother's womb, nestling back into the fetal position, free of this world's concerns, isolated from pain and trauma by a spiritual water bag. The present state of public religion, from "Christian" television networks to White House prayer breakfasts requires Protestant Churches to declare such born again experiences to be foreign to the nature of Christian faith. For the only escape from the temptations and dangers of the world permitted in biblical tradition is escape into the this-worldly and yet trans-worldly community of faith, Israel or the Church.

During the Babylonian exile when the Israelite was asking, "How shall we sing the Lord's song in a strange land?"—the only acceptable answer was to remember the holy community, its heritage in Jerusalem:

> If I forget you, O Jerusalem,
> let my right hand wither!
> Let my tongue cleave to the roof of
> my mouth,
> if I do not remember you,
> if I do not set Jerusalem
> above my highest joy![101]

Life in the present, with its defects, imprisonments and humiliations can be borne only by a concentration on the past memories and the future hopes of the people of God.

It has been argued that this communal concentration is what separates the Old from the New Covenant. Frans Rosenweig understands the contrast in those terms when he states that "whether Christ is more than an idea—no Christian can know. But that Israel is more than an idea—that he knows, that he sees. For we live."[102] Such a distinction, however, cannot be accepted by orthodox Christians. Is not the very *concreteness* of the blessed community with Christ as its head the explicit theme of the Acts of the Apostles? And the implicit theme of the Gospels? And what else is the author of Ephesians saying in the passage on reconciliation between Jews and Gentile Christians but that the concreteness of ancient Israel has now become the concreteness of the New Israel? "For he is our peace, who has made us both one, and has broken down the dividing wall of hostility."[103]

It is into this concrete community of Jesus Christ, the continuation of the Old Israel, yet still existing alongside of and in the providence of God complementary to the Old Israel, that the Christian person is baptized and in that act born again. The person is born again not in the sense of a psycho-emotional experience, but in the sense that from the moment of baptism his or her entire orientation and destiny has to do with the holy community led by Christ. In his study of infant baptism in the early Church, Jeremias concludes:

> In the New Testament period baptismal grace, as salvation out of this world which is lying under the judgement of God, and incorporation into God's new world which is already coming into being, is experienced as a totality. Any consideration which isolates individual aspects, such as the forgiveness of sins, or the bestowal of the

> Spirit, and enquires about the application of these to infants, overlooks the wholeness of the New Testament theology about baptism, as well as its basic eschatological character.[104]

Without going into the question of infant baptism itself, it must be affirmed that Jeremias is certainly correct in referring to baptism as "a totality." Whether the act occurs in infancy or in adulthood, it is to be understood as a *total* reorientation and redirection of the individual away from the essentially noncommunal, alienating and dying world (establishment) toward the communal, bonding, resurrecting Church of Christ.

Being born again in the Spirit of Christ cannot occur apart from the Body of Christ of which the born again person becomes a member. In the case of infant baptism, this membership is, of course, as yet psychologically unrealized. The French Reformed liturgy is quite consistent with the Gospel when it has the minister, prior to the baptism, take the child in his arms and say:

> Little child, for you Jesus Christ has come, He has fought, He has suffered. For you He entered into the shadows of Gethsemane and the terror of Calvary; for you He uttered the cry "it is finished." For you He rose from the dead and ascended into heaven, and there for you He intercedes. For you, even though you do not know it, little child, but in this way the Word of the Gospel is made true, "We love Him because He first loved us."[105]

No matter when in life the rebirth occurs, it is intrinsically connected to baptism. Like our first birth, it is not self-contrived or self-conscious. It is not a personal trip resulting from spiritual technique, but a corporate "regeneration into God" (*regeneratio in deum)*—to use the terminology of the Fathers. Irenaeus, in speaking of baptism as the objective moment of rebirth, properly credits the One who is responsible for it:

> For he [Jesus] has come to save all of them by himself; all those, I say, who through him are reborn unto God, infants, young children, boys, the mature and older people.[106]

In the face of the extravagant and altogether self-centered claims of born again Christians, Protestant Churches must do all that they can liturgically and educationally to restore the importance of baptism within the community of faith. Infant baptism although quite properly understood as an important occasion for the individual family, and properly understood as a rite hallowing life itself, will be primarily celebrated as the time of rebirth for the infant and also for the entire congregation. Every baptism will represent a renewal of baptismal vows and a reminder of rebirth in Christ. Perhaps, at least for the present, Protestant Churches will have to make this renewal explicit in the liturgy itself.

Rebirth in God is the exact opposite of rebirth into a new and more acceptable self, as the self-acclaimed born again Christians would see the event. In answer to the first question of The Heidelberg Catechism, "What is your only comfort in life and in death?" the answer is given:

> That I belong—body and soul, in life and in death—not to *myself* but to my faithful Saviour, Jesus Christ, who at the cost of his own blood has fully paid for all my sins and has completely freed me from the dominion of the devil.[107]

Rebirth, that is, is the event by which one is freed from the self-concentration required to live in a world dominated by hatred and strife and returned to the free atmosphere where the agenda is not concentrated on the self, but on quite another concern.

The primary concern of the regenerated community is that of obedience to Christ. The mission of the individual becomes identical to the mission of the Church, and the Church's mission is to do whatever she is commanded to do by Christ, her head. Father Kilian McDonnell, in his study of Calvin's ecclesiology, describes how the Reformer sees the Church's relation to Jesus Christ:

> She is strong because she has no strength and no power proper to herself. Her strength is that of her Lord. She consoles the comfortless and gives certitude to the unsure because she herself is nothing and has nothing . . . the Lordship of Christ is effective in her only on condition of her unconditional poverty.[108]

It would be difficult to state a more protestant and at the same time catholic understanding of the Church's role in carrying out Christ's mission.

Participation in the mission of Christ as a member of the Church is the opposite of that condition so attractive to contemporary society and so repugnant to the Old Testament of "every man doing whatever is right in his own eyes."[109] Within the Church of Christ there is rather the opposite scheme, the realization of God's covenant by which "it is a terrible thing that I will do with you."[110] The *terrible* future God has in store for His people reaches its frightening conclusion not only on

Golgotha, but also in Jesus' warning to the disciples: "If any man would come after me, let him *deny himself* and take up his cross and follow me. For whoever would save his life will lose it, and whoever loses his life for my sake will find it."[111] Surely, we discover here a radical contradiction of all our venerable and more recent schemes for self-fulfillment. In these words, we hear a surprising *no* even concerning that axiom of modern faith—the necessity of *self-acceptance*.

Within the context of Christ's community, acceptance of *myself* has been replaced by acceptance of my *humanity:* acceptance of my creatureliness, my bondage to time and space, my unique strengths and weaknesses, my impending death. Because I am no longer standing alone, having to be the complete self-contained unit, I can be, instead, actually myself. Having been accepted by Christ and his people, self-acceptance becomes irrelevant. The important question rather becomes: How can I offer myself, such as I am, with my special talents and my personal limitations, to the Person and people who have already accepted me?

What kind of organization would have the nerve to call modern men and women into a life of *self-denial* rather than a life of self-acceptance? What could possibly be so out of vogue, in an age seeking instant gratification, as the opinion that "love is patient and kind"? Or in this age of self-assertion, that "love does not insist on its own way"? Or in an age in which one is only supposed to have *realistic goals,* that "love bears all things, believes all things, hopes all things, endures all things"?[112] The Pauline definition, which applies to life within the community of Jesus Christ, calls for the same self-denial spoken of by Jesus in the Gospels. It is a self-denial not for the covert purpose of achieving some higher spiritual plane; it is a self-denial made necessary by the infinitely more important mission of Christ's Church.

The mission is summed up in the conclusion to the Pauline statement on self-denial: "So faith, hope, love abide, these three; but the greatest of these is love."[113] The purpose of Christ's people, to witness in faith and hope to the life and death of its risen Lord is realized in love. All other purposes—prophesy (the effort to tell the sinful world the truth about itself) and *gnosis* (the attempt to regulate life through self-knowledge)—are destined to pass away.[114] For those who are anxious for some more dramatic and personal "manifestations of the Spirit," the Apostle admonishes them to "strive to excel in building up the church."[115]

Because this Body of Christ demands self-denial, all attempts at competition, all comparisons between Christians are vigorously suppressed.

> For if any one thinks he is something, when he is nothing, he deceives himself. But let each one test his own work, and then his reason to boast will be in himself alone and not in his neighbour. For each man will have to bear his own load.[116]

The only self-concentration allowed is that which demands an honest appraisal of one's own work as opposed to the too natural tendency to build the self up by putting the neighbor down. This honest appraisal is recommended solely in order that there be "no self-conceit, no provoking of one another, no envy of one another."[117]

Within Christ's Church, the need for self-acceptance becomes irrelevant, for "through him you have confidence in *God,* who raised him from the dead and gave him glory, so that your faith and hope are in God."[118] Whereas *gnosis* most definitely has to do with self-confidence, which is at best problematical and at worst impossible to achieve, the faithful in Christ are to follow a wholly other path of confidence:

> Having purified your souls by your *obedience* to the truth for a sincere love of the brethren, love one another earnestly from the heart. You have been *born anew,* not of perishable seed but of imperishable, through the living and abiding word of God.[119]

The acknowledgement here is that there are different kinds of rebirth. The rebirth that has to do with the *self* rather than with the community is perishable. It leads to "malice and all guile and insincerity and envy and all slander."[120] On the other hand, those who are reborn for the fulfillment of His glory, living in obedience to His truth have been gathered into "a chosen race, a royal priesthood, a holy nation, God's own people, that you may declare the wonderful deeds of him who called you out of darkness into his marvelous light."[121]

Apart from this mission of Christ's Church realized in love, even religion, spirituality, worship of God is rejected by the New Testament. It is significant that John in the well-known *love* epistle does not at any point speak approvingly of loving God. Instead, there are only the warnings against a false love of God: "Little children, let us not love in word [*logo*] or speech [*tē glossē*] but in deed and in truth."[122] The Christian's attitude toward brothers and sisters and particularly those in need reveals the extent to which he or she has been freed from the unreal world of sin to live in the real world of Christ's Church.

It is, indeed, the unreal *world* that is being opposed by the Church. It is not that the Church has a quarrel with the Creation, the earth and sky, the creatures; certainly not with fellow human creatures. The Church has a quarrel with the established unreal view of created life: with the unreal view that *self* is the center of life; with the unreal view that personal happiness is the purpose of life; with the unreal view that putting down others leads to fulfillment; with the unreal view that spiritual prowess reaps salvation. And orthodoxy's dispute with gnosticism is that the gnostics fail to challenge this unreal world at the very point where it counts. For the unreal world and the gnostics stand together in defining human life in terms of the *self*. In the critical matter of human relationships, gnosticism capitulates to the established order. For that reason, even if for no other, the Church today has the obligation to expose gnostic Christianity as a false expression of the faith.

Too often theologians, pastors, church leaders seem to have been reluctant to oppose false alliances between Christianity and secular thought. The framers of the Hartford Appeal of January 1975 were an exception to the general American caution regarding the criticism of religion, any religion. When the Hartford Appeal stated that widely accepted themes such as "to realize one's potential and to be true to oneself is the whole meaning of salvation" were "false and debilitating to the Church's life and work,"[123] it was not only correct but courageous. Perhaps it would be helpful if the Churches themselves were willing as national bodies to denounce a false individualistic piety and to make real efforts to bring church-promoted literature into conformity with biblical teaching.

A head-on confrontation with American individualism is, of course, a dangerous undertaking. Both in religious and in secular life, individualism is usually considered sacrosanct. As Paul Lehmann has described the prevailing conviction, "it has become axiomatic, and on the alleged authority of Jesus himself, to link Christianity with the exaltation of the individual. Jesus' major concern, so the claim runs, was with the individual." No one has so clearly corrected this presumption as has Lehmann, who argues that

> Jesus' alleged individualism must be understood with reference to his own conception of himself. It is not accidental that Mark declares, "Jesus came . . . preaching the gospel of God and saying,

> 'The time is fulfilled, and the kingdom of God is at hand; repent and believe in the gospel.' " Jesus did not come saying, "Are you saved?—You! and You! and You!" He did not come with an invitation to come forward, give yourself to Christ, fill out a card, and join the church! Individuals are 'saved' into the *koinonia,* not one by one! . . . Even the prodigal son, when he comes to himself, returns to the Father's house and is received again into a *family.*[124]

It is therefore through the Church as *family* that true selfhood is revealed and realized. This family into which the Christian has been born again, in which she or he is being raised, provides the only safety and comfort the individual can know in this present life. In this context, the Christian person is assured that, "you are no longer strangers and sojourners, but you are fellow citizens with the saints and *members of the household of God* [*oikeioi tou theou*]."[125] No longer isolated in his own sinfulness, the individual finds himself in a milieu of reconciliation where the problems of immaturity and aggression are looked upon not as an outrage, but as common to all.

Thomas Merton explained:

> God reveals himself to the world in the mystical Christ, the Church, which is the community of those who are reconciled to the Father, in Christ, because they are united with one another in the Holy Spirit. . . . [I]f men tend unfortunately to conflict and division by reason of their weakness, selfishness and sin, then the will to reconciliation and pardon is necessary if the Church is to make God visible in the world. Nor can this pardon, this communion in forgiveness, remain interior and invisible. It must be clearly manifest. So the mystery of the Church demands that Christians love one another in a visible and concrete way—and that they love all men.[126]

The fulfillment of such an understanding of the Church requires much of the local congregation and, in fact, demands much more discipline than has been exercised in recent North American Protestantism. The live and let live attitude of most congregations, which will tolerate almost any sort of scandalous or hateful behavior in its members and any degree of laxity in church attendance even among its officers, amounts, in the final analysis, to neglect. Just as parents who fail to confront their teenage children concerning harmful and wrongheaded practices are in reality showing a lack of love, so the Church in its failure to discipline is giving the message that its individual members do not matter.

Without applying some rigid backward-looking regulations to the contemporary scene, how can a Protestant church arrive at an effective discipline? These questions are not easily answered and undoubtedly would have to be dealt with by church bodies in a careful and compassionate manner. Nevertheless, something must be done if the Church is to be at all faithful to its calling. The present neglect is contributing not only to the decline of Protestantism in terms of its population and effectiveness, but also to a latent hostility felt against the Church for its uncaring silence. As opposed to the patristic and Calvinistic picture of the Church as a mother who nurses, comforts, scolds, punishes, in short, loves her children into a healthy maturity, the present image of Church is that of an organization that cashes our checks, mails us notices and newsletters, but otherwise leaves us to our own devices.

In one way or the other, what needs to be affirmed is the reality of each member of the congregation's belonging no longer to himself or herself alone but to Christ. "I am the vine, you are the branches . . . apart from me you can do nothing."[127] That statement is not a pious sentiment but an indispensable basis for Christian practice. The statement also requires interpretation in terms of the interconnection between all members of Christ's Church. It is impossible to be related to the One without being related to the others. The Pauline advice that "as therefore you received Christ Jesus the Lord, so *live in him,* rooted and built up in him and established in the faith"[128] must be understood in the corporate sense of life within Christ's community or it cannot be understood at all. That Paul's words are strictly related to discipline is made clear by the further admonition: "See to it that no one makes a prey of you by philosophy and empty deceit, according to human tradition, according to the elemental spirits of the universe, and not according to Christ. For in him the whole fullness of deity dwells *bodily*." Here Paul has taken a gnostic term *pleroma* (fullness) and linked it, alarmingly no doubt for the gnostics, with the word *somatikos* (bodily), the point being that if this fullness of the godhead is to be grasped, it will be in and through the concrete community in which the Christ is incarnate. It is in him "who is the head of all rule and authority" by whom "you have come to fullness of life."[129] The Word that "became flesh and dwelt among us" has not therefore reverted to disembodied Word, but continues to dwell among us in our corporate life "full of grace and truth" and "we have beheld his glory."[130]

The image of vine and branches requires an understanding of discipline which, rather than coming from the top down as a bolt of lightning, seeps up by osmosis through an organism well planted in the good earth. So it is certain that discipline should not become primarily a function of a hierarchy as in the episcopal system or of church courts as in the Calvinist tradition, but rather of a priesthood of all believers under the guidance and oversight of the pastoral ministry. As Paul Lehmann has reminded us, the Reformation doctrine, priesthood of all believers, refers not at all to the unbiblical idea of every person being his own priest, but precisely to the opposite:

> Every man his neighbor's priest, "one the Christ of the other"—this is the Christian life, life in and of the *koinonia!* The incarnate, resurrected, and ascended Christ has no real presence in the world apart from the fellowship-creating relationship in which the "one" confronts the "other" in the maturing humanity of man. This is what the "head and the body" in the New Testament, and in the Reformation doctrine of the *communio sanctorum,* are all about. We have to do with a society in which all the parts properly function in so far as all the parts, in one way or another, minister Christ to all the other parts.[131]

When the need for discipline is linked to the common priesthood of believers, it becomes clear that corrective discipline will be not so much a matter of punishment, of public rebuke or excommunication, as of private admonition. Under the pastoral leadership of clergy or lay leaders who are not afraid to describe the requirements of the Christian life, members of the congregation can be encouraged to help one another. They will be present in times of illness and death; they will be encouraging in times of trial, and also they will care enough to speak "the truth in love" and even to "be angry but not sin."[132] A renewed sense of discipline, far from cutting people off from one another, can assure Christian individuals that the community cares, that what they do or fail to do matters a great deal, that they are not lonely victims of societal conditioning, but belong to and are thereby being liberated by the Christ himself.

Apart from the loving and forgiving discipline of Christ's people, we are certainly all destined to be victims of contemporary society. Who alone could withstand the constant brainwashing through television and the other mass media, not to mention the propagandizing by governments and multinational corporations? Without the counter message of the Gospel applied to our own life together, how could anyone not succumb to the

> waterless springs and mists driven by a storm; . . . For uttering loud boasts of folly, they entice with licentious passions of the flesh men who have barely escaped from those who live in error. They promise them freedom, but they themselves are slaves of corruption . . . For if, after they have escaped the defilements of the world through the *knowledge* of our Lord and Savior Jesus Christ, they are again entangled in them and overpowered, the last state has become worse for them than the first. For it would have been better for them never to have known the way of righteousness than after knowing it to turn back from the holy commandment delivered to them.[133]

Knowledge alone is not only insufficient; apart from the care and love of the community, it is extremely dangerous. To be an isolated Christian convert in the hands of a hateful, even suicidal, society is worse than never having been acquainted with the Gospel.

It will not be easy for North American Protestantism to move away from its individualistic moorings. To renounce a born-againism that centers the faith in the individual's emotional achievements will bring down the wrath of the religious right and the charge that the Churches are abandoning "historic Christianity." To question the claims of liberalism that personal fulfillment is the primary duty and goal of humanity will no doubt evoke the hostility of the religious left. For example, it would be dangerous to renounce the popular middle-class wisdom that "no unwanted child should be born" and the cry that "abortion is a matter between the woman and her doctor." On the other hand, because Christ was most certainly at one point an unwanted child, how can his disciples and members of his *community* allow such monstrous and anti-communal assertions to go unchallenged? How can Protestants leave to their Roman Catholic brothers and sisters the burden of defending humanity in its most helpless and voiceless form? Although abortion is in some cases therapeutically necessary or otherwise advisable, nevertheless, it remains a communal matter. If it is considered an individual matter, then the sense of our corporate humanity in Christ has been finally swallowed up by the philosophy of personal fulfillment. The Human Potential movement will have arrived at the ultimate conclusion that the individual's maximum potential can be reached only through the death of others. The human race returns to a frightening primal theme, that through child sacrifice, the adult generation can find health, economic security and peace of mind. As the early Church stood against the gnostic disdain for child-bearing, Protestant Christianity must have the will to oppose this contemporary anti-life religion in the name of Christ for the sake of the world he died to save.

So long as Christianity is understood as an individual matter, it becomes impossible for evangelical or liberal Protestants to react, ethically, to the questions of the day in a manner different from that of any other person in the secular society. Neither manifestation of Protestantism is able to assert itself independently, free of right-wing or left-wing stereotypes, because neither has a sense of commitment to Christ in terms of a commitment to his people. The question then, for North American Protestants, is not whether they have been born again, but rather whether they have been born again into Christ's Church.

An Affirmation of Ordinary Christianity

The Protestant Church in North America must furthermore reject the elitism that leads to snobbishness and exclusiveness, both on a local and a global level. A positive understanding of its election in biblical terms rather than in a gnostic sense will help the Church overcome its class distinctions and its contempt for ordinary humanity.

Gnostic Christianity always distorts the doctrine of divine election in such a way as to distinguish between the worthy and the unworthy. No wonder gnostics are so consistently repelled by the election of Israel and so anxious to spiritualize and thereby neutralize Old Testament history. For Israel, of course, was not elected because of her worthiness, not even because of her distinctiveness. On the contrary, because Israel is indistinguishable from the others ("a wandering Aramean was my father"), Israel must be distinguished by the commandments of God. "You shall not do as they do in the land of Egypt, where you dwelt, and you shall not do as they do in the land of Canaan, to which I am bringing you."[134] Only by conformity to the words of Yahweh can the Israelites *look* any different from their neighbors. However, whether they look different or not, nevertheless, they are the elected people. Isaiah refers to the special people as the *Gomorrah* people, in that they are wholly given over to pagan ways and refuse to listen to the warnings of God's prophets. The *Gomorrah* people, however, are still "*my* people." It has thus become Isaiah's task to help the people fulfill the purpose of their election.[135] The point here is that even when the elected people, Israel, are disobedient and indistinguishable from humanity as a whole, they nevertheless remain elected. T. F. Torrance explains that

> the election of Israel as the servant of the Lord meant that it was elected to be used even in its refusal of grace that through it the ultimate self-giving of God to man in spite of his sin and because of his sin might take place—elected, that is, to act in a representative capacity for all peoples in their rejection of God's will.[136]

Is it not possible that what was true for sinful Israel is also true of the Christian Church? Could it not be that the calling of Christ's people is also a *representative* calling and that we must begin to read our history in non-idealistic terms, no longer searching for the true Church in the sense of a faithful church, but accepting the Holy (set apart, elected) Catholic Church as simply the historic earthly body identified as and identifying itself as the communion of Christ?

Certainly, the Gospels concentrate on the power of God to work miracles within the people of God's choice. If in the Old Covenant God has the power to find His elect "in a desert land, and in the howling waste of the wilderness,"[137] now He is able "from these stones to raise up children to Abraham."[138] God has the right to call out His servants and separate them from the others, but the servants are not allowed to concern themselves with the task of separating themselves. The elitist attitude is, in other words, forbidden by the Holy Gospel.

Within North American society iself, the distortion of the biblical image of election takes the form of what can only be called snobbishness. The class distinctions so marked in Protestant churches, and in striking contrast to most Roman Catholic congregations, are generally thought to be an irreversible feature of Protestant Christianity. The rationale is that mainline Protestantism simply appeals to persons of a certain level of education and economic stability and the others will be spiritually nourished by Pentecostalists and Roman Catholics.

The New Testament, on the other hand, does not view class distinctions as a trivial matter at all. Not only does Jesus consider it as the fundamental question in the separation of the sheep from the goats,[139] but also James regards "respect for persons" in the congregation as a transgression of the whole law:

> For if a man with gold rings and in fine clothing comes into your assembly, and a poor man in shabby clothing also comes in, and you pay attention to the one who wears the fine clothing and say, "Have a seat here, please," while you say to the poor man, "Stand there," or, "Sit at my feet," have you not made distinctions among yourselves, and become judges with evil thoughts?[140]

Most Protestant congregations are not confronted with such radical choices between rich and poor, for the shabbily clothed poor simply do not enter their sanctuaries. It is tacitly understood that poverty and Protestantism are incompatible. Protestants can be most generous in supporting programs to help *them:* Christmas boxes, day care centers, nutrition classes, and other charitable efforts will be made so long as *they* are kept distinctly separate from *us*. Generally, however, the last thing Protestants would do for the poor is to invite them to church as potential brothers or sisters in Christ. As a result, economically and educationally deprived people quickly recognize Protestant charity for what it is—a fraud, a further evidence of snobbishness. Despite the well-meaning intentions of liberal Protestantism to effect positive changes in the social scene, churches and church people can accomplish nothing really helpful until the present "respect for persons" has been faced, confessed and dealt with as a fundamental flaw within Protestant practice.

No self-justifying declarations about the need for homogeneity will work: doctors, lawyers, professional people are simply more at home in their own sort of church, whereas working people are more at home in their sort. Whether the appeal for homogeneity comes from the market-oriented Growth movement or from more sophisticated circles, it is always an excuse, an excuse for an inexcusable affront to Jesus Christ!

Once Protestant churches have become properly embarrassed and are no longer smug about this middle-class constituency, perhaps genuine efforts will be made to reach out and embrace those people especially blessed by Christ in the Beatitudes. If working-class and poor people are welcomed to the liturgy of the Word and the simple Sacrament of the Table, they will gradually come to feel that they are respected members of the family. Class fears will be overcome; class blindness will be healed; a large emptiness in Protestantism will have been filled.

Irenaeus, in his polemic against the gnostics, insisted that the Church recognize that the real heroes of the faith were those who simply followed Christ in fulfilling their common tasks, and attending the weekly Eucharist. Such a view of the faith has always seemed scandalous to those who understand Christianity in terms of separating themselves from ordinary people. In recent times, it has become almost axiomatic for church officers and Christian educators to heap ridicule on those *mere* Christians who only attend weekly services. Apparently, there is no one more worthless than the weekly churchgoer who simply sits in the pew and drops something in the offering plate when it comes around. The authentic Christians are those who become involved in mission studies, take part in organizational activities, and in one way or another show an understanding of the profound implications of Christian faith.

There is little doubt that such a differentiation between the *involved* Christians and the ordinary *nominal* Christians serves the purpose of the ecclesiastical bureaucrats. But at the same time, it is a classic example of elitism, an insult to thousands of simple, nonorganizational Protestants who desire the Word and Sacraments and other means of grace and who on a day-to-day basis witness to the faith in their homes and on the job. Against both the extravagant elitism of born again evangelicalism and the unfair demands of bureaucratic liberalism, there must emerge within Protestantism an appreciation of *ordinary* Christians. The emphasis should be precisely on participation in the liturgy. All other ecclesiastical functions are secondary and responsive to the Church's essential gathering about Christ's Table. Those who are inclined to serve on church boards and committees should, of course, be encouraged in their labors. Ordinary Christians, however, have been maligned long enough.

In a similar way, *ordinary* congregations have been made to feel inferior to innovative ministries, mission fields and other more avant-garde endeavors. Again, ecclesiastical bureaucrats often appeal for financial support by urging local (*ordinary*) congregations to spend as much on the greater ministry as they spend on *themselves*. As if support of local work—the comforting of the sick, burial of the dead, preaching of the Gospel, ministration of Holy Baptism, serving of Holy Communion—were spending money on *themselves,* as if money paying the bureaucrat's salary is holier than money supporting the local pastor. Ordinary congregations also need to be affirmed and encouraged in performing the necessary tasks they have been ordained to do. The Protestant clergy should stand with their congregations in denouncing an elitism that fails to honor the essential work of the ordinary congregation in its own locale.

The class stratification within Protestantism underscores the need for a genuine ecumenism that understands the need for every congregation to be holy, catholic and apostolic not only in concept, but in practice. Denominationalism, especially the acceptance of the denominational system as a Christian norm, is in itself elitist and a sign of unfaithfulness. T. F. Torrance describes the Church as

> the restoring into one of broken and scattered humanity to form the one people of God; it is the community of the reconciled brought into organic unity with Jesus Christ; and gathered together in His name, partaking of His fulness as the one Body of which He is the head.[141]

Such an orthodox vision of the Church as the body in which humanity is organically united rather than systematically divided must be recaptured if Protestantism is to move away from its present elitist position.

Perhaps the ardor of the ecumenical spirit of the 1960s has been partially cooled by the Roman Church's diminished interest in visible unity. Also, there has been a certain well-grounded suspicion on the part of Protestants that a union of the churches might lead merely to heavier bureaucracy than now exists in the separate denominations. Despite these discouraging factors, Protestants could initiate new contacts with Rome in theological dialogue and cooperative liturgical and social programs. In the full tide of Vatican II, most of the overtures were made by Roman Catholics. Perhaps now it is Protestantism's turn to offer the kiss of peace. Meanwhile, innovative efforts must be made among Protestants to arrive at a catholicity which can include within one body "all sorts and conditions of men" and women. Without sacrificing the essentials of the faith and the integrity of liturgical practice, some scheme must be arrived at which will allow non-Roman Christians to be visibly united in one communion which is, at the same time, catholic and reformed. Perhaps such a body could avoid bureaucratic dehumanization by allowing for immense local autonomy. Bishops or presbyteries, or both could be responsible for a very small area of particular churches. A compromise plan such as that of the Church of South India might be possible. A genuine North American ecumenism would also recognize what, in fact, already exists, namely, a high degree of congregational autonomy. Such ecumenism could not help but make Christians aware of the vital connection between themselves and all brothers and sisters in Christ. The common lectionary and the renewed interest in the liturgy of the Church must be taken as positive signs of a genuine desire for the realization of one Holy Church.

Snobbishness within the Church also has global ramifications. An elitist misunderstanding of election has caused some persons to be regarded as blessed with divine favor, whereas others are obviously born to lose. This gnostic misunderstanding of divine election as an immutable separation between real men and animal-like people[142] and the further corruption of that elitism in terms of class and schooling have opened the door for every sort of atrocity by the chosen few against the unchosen many. It is doubtful that America can be led out of the psychological malaise of Vietnam or enabled to avoid future Vietnams until Protestant elitism has been overcome.

If, for example, it became clear that American Protestant Christians (not merely national church officials) would not accept their government's waging a military campaign against a weak, impoverished nation, the military campaign would not occur. If it became known that American Protestants regard Latin Americans in the same way that they regard Scandinavians or regard themselves, would not foreign policy in the Western Hemisphere be radically altered? Is it possible that trust and cooperation might begin to take the place of resentment and armed hostility?

As the Church needs to respect ordinary Christians who seek the means of grace and attempt to live in response to grace, so also the Church is called to recognize its solidarity with all humanity. As opposed to the exclusive claims of born-againism, with its fanciful and even magical ideas of separateness from the *others,* Christians are asked to accept with gratitude their unity with the human race. Irenaeus, in his defence of the ordinary, continually reminded his readers that whereas we humans can fail to comprehend our proper relation to God, God, on the other hand, in His eternal and ingenerate simplicity *is related* to every creature.[143] Nothing essential then separates any of us from any other. Our connectedness is not through common understanding, but through a common subjection to the sovereign grace of God. Hopefully, the Christian would have a better grasp of the real situation than, say, an atheist, but in no way are the two fundamentally divided. Both are, in one way or another, bound by their relatedness to God.

Christians, of course, are chosen to carry out an exclusive task in the world. Their exclusive task, however, is to proclaim and enact the inclusive purpose of God. In *Crime and Punishment,* the drunken father of the prostitute Sonia is the spokesman for Dostoevsky's orthodox understanding of Christian faith:

> And He will judge and will forgive all, the good and the evil, the wise and the meek . . . And when He has done with all of them, then He will summon us. "You too come forth," He will say, "Come forth ye drunkards, come forth, ye weak ones, come forth, ye children of shame!" And we shall all come forth, without shame

> and shall stand before him. And He will say unto us, "Ye are swine, made in the Image of the Beast and with his mark; but come ye also!"[144]

It is this universality of divine love that "makes his sun rise on the evil and the good,"[145] which defines the particular area of the Church's concerns. In this sense, it is quite proper to speak of the Church as existing *in* mission for humanity, for the world! That is quite different from the statement that the Church exists only *for* mission. The former claim expresses the biblical truth that humanity, sinful yet in the process of redemption, is our natural milieu. The latter assertion is merely another way of expressing the bourgeois idea of the *cause*. A church existing only *for* mission sets itself apart for the *cause* of saving the *others*. Whether evangelical or liberal, such a church is basically elitist, embarrassed to identify itself with humanity until humanity has been given a spiritual bath.

Karl Barth in describing the Church's role *in* mission explains:

> Solidarity with the world means that those who are genuinely pious approach the children of the world as such, that those who are genuinely righteous are not ashamed to sit down with the unrighteous as friends, that those who are genuinely wise do not hesitate to seem to be fools among fools, and that those who are genuinely holy are not too good or irreproachable to go down "into hell" in a very secular fashion.[146]

Restoration of Ritual: Affirmation of the Concrete in Terms of Sacrament, Sexuality, and Family Life

Christian gnostics of every age have been repelled by *ritual* because ritual by its very nature is dependent on material *things*, on times and seasons and on routine, all those elements of religious practice that are such rude reminders of human limitation, of the paucity of all religion. Furthermore, ritual is the living vestige of the primitive origins of all religion, a vestige the gnostic feels must be left behind.

Karen Horney, from her psychological perspective, observes:

> Man under the pressure of inner distress reaches out for the ultimate and the infinite which—though his limits are not fixed—it is not given for him to reach; and in this very process he destroys himself, shifting his very best drive for self-realization to the actualization of

> his idealized image and thereby wasting the potentialities he actually possesses.[147]

Orthodox Christianity clings to ritual because it is aware of humanity's destructive reaching out for the ultimate and humanity's necessary dependence on that "which we have seen with our eyes, which we have looked upon and touched with our hands." It is through this fellowship with those who originally "have heard . . . seen . . . and touched" that each generation of the Church hears and sees and touches those things "concerning the word of life."[148] Orthodoxy understands that biblical religion, like all religion, can be but a dim vision of the truth and beauty of its object. "For now we see through a glass darkly"[149] is not only a repudiation of gnosticism, but a confession of orthodoxy.

On the North American scene, Protestantism has been especially wary of any commitment to ritual. Ritualistic practices were perceived to be a sellout to Romanism or, what was almost as bad, to Anglo-Catholicism. When an individual congregation became concerned with such matters as the liturgy, sacramental life or the Christian year, it was generally accepted that the congregation had given up on the attempt to be really religious. Despite recent interest in the liturgical movement in some mainline Protestant churches, ritual seems to be approached with an uneasy conscience, with the feeling that the Church really should be doing something better if it could only be inspired to know what that something is. Meanwhile, there are voices from the theological right calling for yet another American revival and from the left urging middle-class communicants to concentrate on contemporary issues—let the world set the agenda for the Church.

Is the time not long overdue for an unashamed restoration of ritual within the sanctuaries and homes of Protestant Christians? The biblical witness as well as the long experience of the Church insists on the necessity for the means of grace. Ordinary Christians should have the right of access to those tangible means through which the Church and Israel before her have received the Word of life for thousands of years.

The first step of restoration is the recognition that the enemy of true religion today is a different enemy than that facing the Protestant reformers. Calvin's principal foe might well have been, as he apprehended it, Roman idolatry (the false materializing of the spiritual). The arch foe today, however, is Protestant gnosticism (the false spiritualizing of the material). Restoration of an authentic ritual will require a repudiation of all spirituality that separates Christianity from the material world. Martin Buber's argument must be heard and accepted:

> God is not an object beside objects, and hence cannot be reached by renunciation of objects. God is indeed not the cosmos, but even less is he being *minus* cosmos. He is not to be found by subtraction, and not be loved by reduction.[150]

Against the claims of a "religionless Christianity," faith severed from all cultic and ritualistic ties, a reforming Protestantism will agree with Troeltsch's prophetic understanding that the heart of the Christian faith is not to be discovered in "dogma and idea" but in "cult and community."[151] Apart from the concretely received revelation of Christ within the cultus of the community, the concrete revelation of God's Messiah is not to be comprehended at all. When *knowledge* of Christ is apprehended and applied apart from this concrete communal experience, it is reduced to a mere historical illustration, at best a clarifying example of truth already discernible through other means.

Protestantism must admit, with Karl Barth, the profound limitation of all religion in expressing the truth about God and the sense in which Christian ritual, like all ritual, is unable in itself to *accomplish* anything. Yet Protestants must also heed Barth's warning that the present threat is not the arrogance of religious practice but the arrogance of non-practice:

> The religious interest and desire which was once in play expressing and manifesting itself, now prefers to live itself out without expression or manifestation. The same non-needy, religious need now seeks its satisfaction in solemn non-satisfaction, in a pathetic renunciation of self-expression, in a pathetic silence, in a pathetic cessation of soul, in the solemn emptiness which it thinks it would now prefer to its former equally solemn fulness.[152]

Liberal Protestantism in North America may have heeded Barth's warning about the arrogance of religion; it may have recognized the similarity between Christian external forms and that of other religions. What has not been admitted, however, is that the revelation of God, that which is unique to our faith, must be externalized. Either it is carried in an earthen vessel or it is not carried at all. The normal vessel in which revelation has been at the same time carried and received is the simple liturgy of Word and Sacrament. Protestants have retained the Word portion of the liturgy, though we have noted some serious misuses of the Word service. The eucharistic meal, however, is not a regular part of Protestant liturgy, and it is difficult to see how any genuine renewal of Protestantism can take place until this neglect has been faced and dealt with.

The eucharistic feast must be restored to its rightful place if the churches of the Reformation are to be reformed. The account given in the Acts of the Apostles makes it clear that teaching, preaching, prayer and the breaking of bread were from the beginning the essential elements of Christian worship.[153] Indeed, the Church's teaching, preaching and praying culminate in the breaking of bread with Christ and all his people. "This is the joyful feast of the people of God" where and when the eyes of the faithful are opened and they recognize the Lord.[154] Historically, the simple reenactment of the Last Supper and of the post-Easter meals of Christ and his disciples has been the central act of the Christian community.

The irony of Protestant history is that although the sixteenth-century Reformers fought like tigers to restore the wine to the people, their descendents have now deprived the people of both bread and wine. The Protestant celebration, when it is on rare occasions held, has been spiritualized to the extent that it could scarcely be recognized as a meal at all. The purely symbolic wafer of the Roman celebration, which John Knox thundered against as a distortion of Christ's "common bread," has in most Protestant churches been replaced by minute, carefully diced pieces of bread unlike any other bread ever eaten by any culture. The common cup which the medieval Church withheld from the faithful is, except among Anglicans, still the sole possession of the clergy. The unordained are now given thimble-like glasses filled with Welch's grape juice. The symbolism is quite clear. We all come before God individually; with our individual bits of bread and our individual cups of juice, we are not of one loaf and one chalice. Our relationship to Christ is private and personal. What may be even more significant is that by partaking of this unearthly meal with our unbreadly bread and our unwinely wine we are making a clear statement that the bread and wine of spiritual communion has no connection with earthly communion. It is an unmistakable gnostic witness against the significance of ordinary meals: common bread, wine, the table fellowship of laughter and tears.

A renewal of Protestant liturgy will require a restoration of the sacramental life that has slowly but surely been lost since the Reformation. Certainly, there must again be frequent celebration of the Eucharist with the goal being a weekly celebration in every congregation. Although many Protestant liturgical studies have called the service of Word and Sacrament the norm for which the churches should be striving, so far frequent communion has not been considered important enough for a major conflict within the Church.

Frequent communion, of course, would call for a simple, less elaborate service than the unmeal-like rite now practiced. The funereal procession of clergy and lay leaders passing the diminuitive dishes to the solemnly sitting or kneeling communicants would probably have to be replaced by the crowded gathering of the faithful about the Holy Table for a breaking of the common loaf and the passing of a common cup. Those who argue that the intimacy and the everyday quality of such a celebration would take away the sense of mystery simply do not understand the nature of drama and mystery. It was Jean Cocteau who said "vagueness is unsuitable to the fairy world . . . mystery exists only in precise things."[155] Concreteness, the preciseness of home-baked bread and earthy red wine, in pottery plates and chalices, received with much chewing and swallowing, witnesses to the mystery of the Word made flesh. The present practice unwittingly undercuts the mystery and leaves us with the vague and unhelpful feeling that some undefined perfunctory act must be taking place.

Along with the restoration of frequent communion within the sanctuaries, a reforming Protestantism will also take seriously the ministering of the Sacrament to ill and confined persons. John Calvin was at his most eloquent in referring to the eucharistic meal as "medicine to the sick" and in attacking the Roman Church for denying communion to the needy.[156] And he lamented the fact that Protestants had adhered to this abuse: "It displeases me that we do not have the custom of administering the Supper to the sick; but it is not I who have deprived those departing this life from enjoying this consolation."[157] Now the situation has become reversed. Roman Catholics are extremely punctilious about ministering the Mass to the sick and dying whereas to our great shame, in many Protestant parishes, the ill rarely if ever receive Holy Communion. Among many Protestants, this central, normal means of grace would be viewed as an extraordinary *last rite,* too frightening an offer to be made to the sick and the aged.

This strange unsacramental attitude spills over into an even more incredible neglect of the Church's pastoral functions. A significant number of clergy do not normally pray during hospital or nursing home visitation. Only when the patient requests a prayer does the visitor offer one. Is it any wonder that so many Protestant clergy have been suffering from identity crises? After all, if the minister or priest is not at the bedside of the sick and dying to comfort with Word, prayer and Sacrament, why is he there? Who is he?

Baptism, which is ministered in the midst of the eucharistic community, has remained a more human, less gnostic ritual within Protestantism largely because of the presence of one or more babies in the service. It is difficult to maintain too much formality with these natural little creatures in the sanctuary. Even here, however, Protestants seem to be embarrassed by *things,* in this case, *water*. The ritualistic cleansing bath is often given with only the slightest use of water, the damp hand of the clergyperson sufficing because, of course, baptism is "only" symbolic. On the other hand, when there is an uninhibited splashing of water, wetting of the baby's head, and carrying of the infant about the sanctuary to introduce her to her new family in Christ, then the meaning of the Sacrament becomes clearer. The child has been received from her parents, covered with the water of Holy Baptism, born again of water and the Spirit, received into the family of faith and then returned to her parents as a person set apart, a member of the household of God. The precise enactment of what the Church has been commissioned to do distinguishes Holy Baptism from a mere rite of passage. It reminds the congregation dramatically of the graciousness of the Lord in loving our children before they can recognize their love for him. It leads the faithful of all ages to a "remembrance" of their own baptism; it is a reminder to all that they also have been born again.

Public celebrations of the wedding and funeral ordinances within the Protestant churches require a thorough revamping. Because both services have become completely gnosticized, there must be a return to basic orthodox practice. Most important of all, these critical moments require the celebration of Holy Communion. If the wedding rite follows a traditional order of readings, vows, prayers and Eucharist accompanied by the songs of Zion rather than of Hollywood, already a giant step will have been taken. The funeral service, held in the church rather than the funeral "home," also following the ancient order of Word and Sacrament, would reclaim the celebration of the Resurrection as the Church's celebration. During the committal at graveside, "earth shall be cast upon the body by some standing by." At that point, the final act will have been snatched from all gnostic despisers of dirt, from all who refuse to recognize that "we are dust and to dust we shall return."[158]

The observance of the Christian year, which in some form or other has been practiced since ancient times, has always been an irritant to the gnostic spirit. It recognizes gnosticism's ancient foe, *time,* as having an important role within the Christian faith. Thomas Merton expressed the orthodox view well when he wrote that "the Liturgy accepts our common, everyday experiences of time: sunrise, noonday, sunset . . . the church has no quarrel with time."[159]

The Christian year from Advent through Pentecost is a reminder that God has not approached His creatures in a general unidentifiable way, but in the particularity of space and time. As Martin Buber argues in his polemic against neo-gnosticism: biblical religion represents a "hallowing of the everyday."[160] Through the reinactment of the past event, Holy Baptism and the Eucharist, in the context of the lectionary reading for the day and the traditional concern of the day, the eternal becomes real in the particular, and past and future are brought to bear on the reality of the present.[161] There is, indeed, in the Church a transcendence of time. At the *sursum corda,* there is a lifting up of hearts to the place of Christ at the right hand of the Father. Time is transcended, however, not by escaping it in gnostic fashion, but by recognizing our given place within it and the eternal God's gracious gift in entering time and redeeming it for our sakes.

Because acceptance of times and seasons involves a recognition of God's acceptance of ourselves as we are in the particular present, Protestants must be willing to restore the rhythm of celebrating the Christian year. Perhaps the Protestant Reformers were forced to abandon the ancient and medieval Church seasons for the sake of disentangling the faith from its complex pagan and secular interconnections. That decision, though, is now almost half a millennium behind us, and the problems facing the Church have changed drastically since that time. Now the problem is a gnostic fear of particularity. The particularity of the Christmas message, for example, is a scandal to the North American mind. That the real meaning of such a celebration could be bound to the one Messiah of God coming into one point of history in one place is an affront to the contemporary understanding of truth. As a result, Christmas has been, in the secular culture, departicularized. Thus it is acceptable to play Mozart's "Exultate Jubilate" on the department store holiday tape so long as it is sandwiched between "White Christmas" and "Winter Wonderland." Mozart's anthem, filled with devotion for the Incarnate Christ, is robbed of its meaning by the other two, which carefully signify nothing. With countless such devices, the society robs the season of its mood of celebration, its hope for light in the midst of winter darkness. In place of the particular message, there emerges a general, sad, and confusing longing for what has never been. "I'm dreaming of a white Christmas"; Christmases are not what they used to be, because they never were.[162]

Meanwhile, many churches cave in to the secular pressure to generalize and remove the scandal of particularity. Too often, the Protestant message is that Christmas is a time for warm good feelings toward others or for family closeness. Sermon diatribes, reflecting a strange misunderstanding of the problem are directed against the *materialism* of the season. There are pious calls to "put the Christ back in Xmas"—even though the crying need is to put the *mass* back in Christmas. The obligation of the Church is to gather the faithful once again for a particular celebration (the Eucharist) of the particular event (the Incarnation).

Because the secular community has little to say about the Easter celebration, Protestantism finds the Lenten-Easter season more and more baffling. Easter morning might still be illustrative of immortality, of eternal springtime, of hoping against impossible odds; however, the serious celebration of Christ's rising from the dead does not generally occur in liberal Protestant churches. Among evangelicals, because the Resurrection is understood as unrelated to the particularity of the present, the Easter event remains an event which has occurred in the past, morbidly remote from the contemporary world. The Protestant failure in celebrating Easter is closely connected to the Protestant failure to observe the Lenten season. Again, there is an embarrassment about setting aside a season different from other seasons to remember Christ's life, sacrifice and death. Lent would be an admission that Christians, like all their fellow creatures, are not only captives of time, but in need of times and seasons. Even Good Friday has become, like Ash Wednesday, a Roman Catholic holy day, as removed from many Protestants as is Yom Kippur. Without a particular remembrance of Golgotha in terms of the present, is there any wonder that Easter Sunday is unfulfilling for so many Protestants?

It would seem almost impossible to bring about any significant change in what amounts to the Protestant non-practice of the Christian religion. There are signs, however, that the paucity of Protestant life is beginning to be recognized by many believers. There is an emerging hunger for ritual, which will be filled in one way or the other. To take advantage of this mood, Protestant Churches will need to establish definite disciplinary norms. Parents will be informed as to what the Church expects of them in terms of nurture. Members of congregations will be instructed as to their obligations to attend services and to participate in the various seasons of the Christian year. Discipline cannot be forced on the faithful, but it can be urged on them. Threats will not accomplish this reformation, but perhaps promises can, the assurance that through availing themselves of the *means* of grace, Christian people will be rewarded with the definite blessing of a life in which union with Christ has become normative.

> If you turn back your foot from the
> sabbath,
> from doing your pleasure on my
> holy day,
> and call the sabbath a delight
> and the holy day of the Lord
> honourable;
> . . . then you shall take delight in the
> Lord,
> and I will make you ride upon the
> heights of the earth;
> I will feed you with the heritage of
> Jacob your father,
> for the mouth of the Lord has
> spoken.[163]

The anti-particularity and line-blurring of gnostic Protestantism are nowhere more clearly seen than in the expression of the sexual revolution sponsored by some branches of the feminist and gay rights movements. Among the former, sexual identification is not accepted as a defining factor; among the latter, sexual identification is a matter of individual preference. In both cases, we encounter a spiritualization of sexuality.

Walker Percy, in his *Love in the Ruins,* gives the Church the role of restoring humanity to a proper earthiness. Doris, Dr. Tom More's wife, asks her Roman Catholic husband: "My God, what is it you do in Church?" More explains,

> What she didn't understand, she being spiritual and seeing religion as spirit, was that it took religion to save me from the spirit world, from orbiting the earth like Lucifer and the Angels, that it took nothing less than . . . eating Christ himself to make me mortal

man again and let me inhabit my own flesh and love her in the morning.[164]

Against the growing conviction that sexual distinction is at best an accident and at worst a curse, the Church is called upon to affirm human maleness and femaleness as a providential and gracious fact. Our sexuality defines us, sets our limitation as human beings; it is a constant reminder that individually, alone, we are incomplete and unfulfilled. Certainly, the Church will not inveigh against women who cannot or do not wish to fulfill the maternal role, any more than against men who do not fulfill the paternal role. Nor will the Church disparage homosexual Christians who are unable to function within the confines of a male-female sexuality. The Church, however, will insist that the male-female sexual partnership is God-given, that family life is the norm of which we all partake as children and then as parents, either natural or surrogate. To confess anything less would be a sellout to gnostic spiritualism and a denial of Christian commitment to the human race. Our sexual distinctions along with all other distinctions are miraculously transcended in the celebration of the Eucharist, in the miracle whereby, "through love [we are] being changed into each other."[165] This miracle, however, occurs only when we are gathered together as distinctive persons who, regardless of our ability or inability to cope with it in a positive way, can accept sexuality as a gracious blessing of the Lord.

Such an admittedly *conservative* view of sexuality must not become for the Church an endorsement of marriage and family life as popularly conceived in North American culture. Marriage as the fulfillment of all romantic dreams and the nuclear family as the complete unit of humanity are both bourgeois notions that are not only fanciful but, from a Christian perspective, positively evil.

A successful marriage is, at best, a blessed union between two persons who are psychologically, sexually, intellectually and spiritually imperfect. The two persons can and should be helpmates to one another. It is impossible, however, that they could so perfectly complement one another, fill the other's gaps, that anything like "earthly bliss" or "living happily ever after" could occur. The present epidemic of divorces, often after twenty-five years of marriage or more, is not a result of marriage being taken too lightly. The problem may be quite the opposite. Marriage has been idealized in our society to the point that any imperfections in marriage are taken as a sign that the union is not blessed by the gods. A couple's failure to be perfectly happy is evidence that the marriage is not working.

It becomes the Church's task to demythologize such a view of marriage, to remind all who call themselves Christians that marriage, like all human institutions, is flawed and imperfect and that those who undertake it will be faced with continual difficulties, economic and physical. They will be asked to think seriously about those old-fashioned vows: "for better for worse, for richer for poorer, in sickness and in health, to love and to cherish, till death us do part,"[166] as descriptions of what could and no doubt will happen in the course of their life together.

The Church will also remind the faithful that marriage is not a decision to exclude the human race in favor of a model man or model woman. On the contrary, in marriage, humanity is made present to the one in the particularity of the other. A sexual knowing of one person is able to relate the individual to the opposite sex, to open the individual to the counter theme of maleness or femaleness. When, in Christian marriage, there is a commitment to fidelity, to the particular *other,* outsiders will not be turned away from the home as a threat to marital harmony, but confidently welcomed as brothers and sisters. When Christians are true to their marital vows and aware of the limitations of sexual fulfillment, they will be able to have close friends of the opposite sex not outside of marriage but within it. They will be able to experience marriage not only as an enclosure, which to some extent marriage must always be, but as an enclosure with an open door to humanity.

Marriage normally implies family life. There are instances, of course, where a man and wife cannot have children because of a physical or emotional disability or because of advanced age. The Church, however, ordinarily should not be a party to performing marriages in which a young, physically able man and woman have determined, with malice aforethought, not to have children. Certainly, there would have to be some extraordinary circumstance to justify a husband and wife making such a decision. Personal ambition, career fulfillment and other selfish concerns could not be an adequate excuse for excluding children at the outset of a marriage. Procreation is not the sole purpose of sexuality, but the necessary connection between sexuality and procreation cannot be ignored. "We do not have children. We do not want children. . . . I want the Riviera in January"[167] is not an acceptable declaration for Christian people.

The Church insists upon the particularity, the restriction in time and space implied by family life. Husbands and wives, of course, require times of being alone together, but normal sexuality from a Christian perspective is achieved in the context of family work and play. Children growing up in such a context will not be made to feel excluded but included, not unwanted impediments to their parents' fulfillment, but the blessed fruits of their parents' sexuality. In achieving a healthier view of sex and marriage, the Church needs to recall the earthiness of its Old Testament roots.

> How graceful are your feet in
> sandals,
> O queenly maiden!
> Your rounded thighs are like jewels,
> the work of a master hand.
> Your navel is a rounded bowl
> that never lacks mixed wine.
> Your belly is a heap of wheat,
> encircled with lilies.
> Your two breasts are like two fawns,
> twins of a gazelle.[168]

The Song of Solomon plus the Jewish concept of family are always healthy antidotes to Christian gnosticism.

Again, the Christian family itself will not be exclusive, but inclusive. Father, mother and children cannot constitute a self-contained unit. They are in constant need of an older generation, of single aunts and uncles, of friends who can view problems from a different, sometimes clearer perspective. In light of the mobility, the uprooted nature of many North American families, it becomes more and more necessary for members of the Christian congregation to serve as grandparents, uncles, aunts, and close friends. The larger family of those particular persons providentially drawn together will offer support and fulfillment to one another beyond the possibility of the nuclear family. In such a community of varied ages and approaches, love will be understood not as a vague spiritual ideal, but as a concrete reality. The solitary will be gathered into a family of God; the communal meal of the congregation will on occasions be shared similarly in homes.[169]

When the family is defined in broader, less romanticized terms, everyone benefits. Fathers and mothers are relieved of the total burden of child-rearing; children are provided with adult support and understanding beyond the capacity of their parents; the elderly are given lively purpose through their contacts with the young; and single persons are protected from utter loneliness and assured that their living and dying matters. The greater family supports the parent-child relationship as normative, but it makes *room* for many varied life situations.

A Protestant Christianity freed from its misalliances with gnostic syncretism, insisting on the importance of a genuine sexuality and the earthly family, can be a blessing to the entire North American community. Once again, this branch of the faith can fulfill the ancient prophecy concerning God's people:

> I will give you as a light to the nations,
> that my salvation may reach to
> the end of the earth.[170]

Epilogue

In his introductory note to *Against Heresies,* A. Cleaveland Coxe states that the principal task of Irenaeus was twofold: "(1) To render it impossible for anyone to confound Gnosticism with Christianity, and (2) to make it impossible for such a monstrous system to survive, or ever to rise again."[1] The second task, we have argued, was an impossible undertaking because there would seem to be an eternal temptation within the religious drive itself to go beyond belief as trust to belief as knowledge. Furthermore, there is the persistent longing to *know* God as He allegedly exists within the self rather than as He has revealed Himself through the history and life of His community. Assuredly, the Church will be cursed by elements of gnosticism as long as the Church exists in its militant form.

The first task, however, was and is a realistic one. Given the strong resurgence of the gnostic movement in our own day, it becomes the burden of all who cherish the positive tradition of Protestant Christianity and long for a renewal of its witness, to clarify the distinctions between gnosticism and the faith of the Church. For every teacher, preacher, and lay leader within the Church, the need is to make plain the differences between infinite claims and earthly gratitude, between *gnosis* and faith, between escape and pilgrimage, between self and community, between the exclusive and the inclusive and between the nebulous and the concrete.

The task will not be an easy one, for as Irenaeus observed in his preface to Book I, "Error indeed is never set forth in its naked deformity, lest being thus exposed, it should at once be detected. But it is craftily decked out in an attractive dress, so as, by its outward form, to make it appear to the inexperienced . . . more true than the truth itself."

There will be no short cuts. If these distinctions are to be explained, in Irenaeus's words, "to all those with whom thou art connected" that they might "avoid such an abyss of madness and of blasphemy against Christ,"[2] then study, debate, discipline, devotion, prayer and fasting will be required.

In denying the false claims of gnostic faith, it will be necessary to confess with Irenaeus that "perfect knowledge cannot be attained in the present life: many questions must be submissively left in the hands of God."[3] That statement itself could serve as a concise warning to North American Protestants. For our religious expectations have been too high; our claims of religious prowess have been too great. We have failed to regard the distance between the temporal and the eternal, between what we know and what there is to know.

By opposing a gnostic Protestantism in our generation, already a positive step will have been taken and a way will have been opened for a wholly different claim and a wholly other Voice. For when the false has been exposed, Irenaeus promises, then we have become enabled to follow "the only true and steadfast Teacher, the Word of God, our Lord Jesus Christ, who did, through His transcendent love, become what we are, that He might bring us to be even what He is Himself."[4]

Notes

CHAPTER ONE

1. See Steven Runciman, *The Medieval Manichee* (Cambridge: Cambridge University Press, 1960), pp. 7ff. According to Runciman, what the gnostic seeks is knowledge of the origin of evil.

2. In I Tim. 6:20, Paul was not ironic when he warned against *pseudo-gnosis*. Note also that the full title of Irenaeus's great work, *Against Heresies*, was *A Refutation and Subversion of Knowledge Falsely So Called*.

3. Arthur Darby Nock, "Gnosticism," *Harvard Theological Review*, 57 (1964), p. 261.

4. *The Apocryphon of James*, I, 2, trans. Francis E. Williams, ed. Dieter Mueller in *The Nag Hammadi Library: In English*, gen. ed. James M. Robinson (San Francisco: Harper & Row, 1977), pp. 30ff. (Hereafter cited as *NHL.)*

5. *The Apocryphon of James*, I, 2, in Robinson, *NHL*, p. 30.

6. *Excerpta ex Theodota* 78:2, in Hans Jonas, *The Gnostic Religion* (Boston: Beacon Press, 1963), p. 45.

7. Luke 1:4 (my literal translation; italics added).

8. Nock, "Gnosticism," p. 277.

9. Frederik Wisse, "Stalking Those Elusive Sethians," in *The Rediscovery of Gnosticism*, II, ed. Bentley Layton, proceedings of the Yale Conference on Gnosticism, March 1978 (Leiden: E. J. Brill, 1981), p. 576.

10. Walter Bauer, *Orthodoxy and Heresy in Earliest Christianity*, trans. by a team

from the Philadelphia Seminary on Christian Origins (Philadelphia: Fortress Press, 1971), pp. xxii ff.

11. Hans Conzelmann, *History of Primitive Christianity,* trans. John E. Steely (Nashville: Abingdon Press, 1973), pp. 123–124.

12. A. S. Atiya, *A History of Eastern Christianity* (London: Methuen, 1968), pp. 41–42.

13. Irenaeus, *Against Heresies,* I:29:1.

14. Acts 8:9–24.

15. Adolf von Harnack, *History of Dogma,* I, trans. Neil Buchanan (New York: Dover, 1961), p. 224.

16. Ibid., pp. 227–228, 244.

17. Nock, "Gnosticism," p. 266.

18. Jean Daniélou, *The Theology of Jewish Christianity,* Vol. I of *A History of Early Christian Doctrine,* trans. John A. Baker (London: Darton, Longman and Todd, 1964), p. 34n., p. 69n., pp. 69–70. See also R. M. Grant, *Gnosticism and Early Christianity* (New York: Harper & Row, 1966), pp. 13–26.

19. Jonas, *Gnostic Religion,* p. 34.

20. Discussion of Weber's method may be found in H. H. Gerth and C. Wright Mills, eds. and trans., *From Max Weber: Essays in Sociology* (New York: Oxford University Press, 1946), pp. 55–61.

21. Ernst Troeltsch, *The Social Teaching of the Christian Churches,* I, trans. Olive Wyon (London: Allen & Unwin, 1931), pp. 331–343.

22. Grant, *Gnosticism and Early Christianity,* p. 34.

23. Troeltsch, *Social Teaching,* I, p. 105.

24. See Carl A. Raschke, *The Bursting of New Wineskins: Reflections on Religion and Culture at the End of Affluence* (Pittsburgh: Pickwick Press, 1978),p. 7.

25. A. E. Housman, *A Shropshire Lad* (Mount Vernon, N. Y.: Peter Pauper Press, 1961), XLVIII, p. 50.

26. *Pleroma*—the fullness of the godhead, the divine world. See R. McL. Wilson, *The Gnostic Problem* (London: A. R. Mowbray, 1958), pp. 129–132; and R. A. Norris, *God and World in Early Christian Theology* (New York: Seabury Press, 1965), p. 79.

27. *Excerpta ex Theodota* 78:2, in Jonas, *Gnostic Religion,* p. 45.

28. Clement of Alexandria, *Stromata* IV:12. Quoted in Gilles Quispel, *Gnostic Studies* (Istanbul: Nederlands Historisch-Archaeologisch Instituut in het Nabije Oosten, 1974), I, p. 126.

29. Runciman, *Medieval Manichee,* p. 6.

30. Quispel, *Gnostic Studies,* I, p. 57 (translation mine, italics mine).

31. Harold Bloom, "Lying Against Time: Gnosis, Poetry, Criticism," in Layton, *Rediscovery of Gnosticism,* I, pp. 57ff.

32. *Gospel of Truth,* I, 3, trans. George W. MacRae, in Robinson, *NHL,* p. 38.

33. Ibid., p. 39. See also Richard H. Drummond, "Studies in Christian Gnosticism," *Religion in Life,* 45 (Spring 1976), p. 16.

34. Arthur Darby Nock, *Early Gentile Christianity and Its Hellenistic Background* (New York: Harper & Row, 1964), pp. xiv, xv.

35. *Gospel of Truth,* I, 3, in Robinson, *NHL,* p. 37.

36. Ibid., p. 48.

37. Quispel, *Gnostic Studies,* I, p. 165 (italics mine).

38. Nock, *Early Gentile Christianity,* p. 90.

39. Nock, "Gnosticism," p. 278.

40. See Gilles Quispel's fascinating reinterpretation of the Narcissus legend from a gnostic perspective ("Gnosis and Psychology," in Layton, *Rediscovery of Gnosticism,* I, p. 30). See also the gnostic (though not Christian gnostic) recycling of the story in terms of Nature and Man finding their complementary forms in the water and thus falling in love and bringing about man's double nature, mortal and immortal, the *Poimandres,* 14, 15, in *Corpus Hermetica,* I, ed. Walter Scott (Oxford: Clarendon Press, 1924), pp. 120–123.

41. I Cor. 1:26.

42. Harnack, *History of Dogma,* I, pp. 227, 234.

43. Quoted in Nock, "Gnosticism," p. 260.

44. John Herman Randall, *Hellenistic Ways of Deliverance and the Making of the Christian Synthesis* (New York: Columbia University Press, 1970), p. 160.

45. Examples of works that tend to favor gnosticism over orthodoxy are: Drummond, "Christian Gnosticism," see especially pp. 12, 13; Jacques Lacarrière, *The Gnostics,* trans. Nina Rootes (London: Peter Owen, 1977); Geddes MacGregor, *Gnosis* (Wheaton, Ill.: Theosophical Publishing House, 1979); G. R. S. Mead, *Fragments of a Faith Forgotten* (New Hyde Park, N.Y.: University Books, 1962).

46. Jonas, *Gnostic Religion,* p. 25.

47. Henry Chadwick, "The Domestication of Gnosis," in Layton, *Rediscovery of Gnosticism,* I, p. 3.

48. David Miller, *The New Polytheism* (New York: Harper & Row, 1974). Quoted in Raschke, *New Wineskins,* p. 79.

CHAPTER TWO

1. Mark 9:38–41 and Luke 9:49–50. However, see also Matt. 12:30, Luke 11:23 and even Mark 9:42.

2. Augustine, *De baptismo contra Donatistas,* II:17, in *Nicene and Post-Nicene Fathers of the Christian Church,* IV, ed. Philip Schaff, trans. J. R. King (Grand Rapids: Eerdmans, 1983).

3. Jude 3.

4. Ibid.

5. Luke 12:1.

6. Luke 11:44.

7. Matt. 23:15.

8. Matt. 23:13–36.

9. Hans von Campenhausen, *The Fathers of the Greek Church,* trans. Stanley Godman (New York: Pantheon, 1959), p. 23.

10. A. S. Atiya, *A History of Eastern Christianity* (London: Methuen, 1968), pp. 41–42.

11. See Steven Runciman, *The Medieval Manichee* (Cambridge: Cambridge University Press, 1960).

12. Martin Buber, *The Eclipse of God,* trans. Stanley Godman (New York: Harper & Bros., 1952), p. 175.

13. Will Herberg, ed., *The Writings of Martin Buber* (Cleveland: World, 1968), pp. 260–261.

14. Gen. 1:1, 31.

15. John 1:2–3.

16. Hans Jonas, *The Gnostic Religion* (Boston: Beacon Press, 1963), p. 42.

17. Ibid., p. 43.

18. Ibid., p. 137. Adolf von Harnack refused to classify Marcion as a gnostic and accepted some of his critique of orthodoxy.

19. Ibid., p. 138.

20. Gilles Quispel, *Gnostic Studies* (Istanbul: Nederlands Historisch-Archaeologisch Instituut in het Nabije Oosten, 1974), I, pp. 29, 33, 35.

21. Runciman, *Medieval Manichee,* p. 7.

22. Quoted in G. R. S. Mead, *Fragments of a Faith Forgotten* (New Hyde Park, N.Y.: University Books, 1962), p. 302.

23. The parable is found in Luke 3:17. Irenaeus, *Against Heresies,* I:3:4–5, in Pagels, *The Johannine Gospel in Gnostic Exegesis* (Nashville: Abingdon Press, 1973), p. 74.

24. Eph. 6:12. For a contemporary use of this contrary view of the human problem, see Harold Bloom, *The Flight to Lucifer: A Gnostic Fantasy* (New York: Farrar, Straus & Giroux, 1979), p. 23.

25. Henry Chadwick, "The Domestication of Gnosis," in *The Rediscovery of Gnosticism,* I, ed. Bentley Layton, Proceedings of the Yale Conference on Gnosticism, March 1978 (Leiden: E. J. Brill, 1980), p. 10.

26. Clement of Alexandria, *Stromata* III:63:2. Quoted in R. M. Grant, *Gnosticism and Early Christianity* (New York: Harper & Row, 1966), pp. 105, 106. See also Jean Daniélou, *The Theology of Jewish Christianity,* Vol. I of *A History of Early Christian Doctrine,* trans. John A. Baker (London: Darton, Longman and Todd, 1964), p. 74.

27. Ps. 24:1.

28. Ps. 139:13.

29. Job 38:3, 41.

30. R. McL. Wilson, *The Gnostic Problem* (London: A. R. Mowbray, 1958), p. 82.

31. Eph. 3:9.

32. Col. 1:16.

33. Rev. 4:11.

34. I Tim. 4:2–3.

35. R. A. Norris, *God and World in Early Christian Theology* (New York: Seabury Press, 1965), p. 89. von Campenhausen, *Fathers of the Greek Church,* p. 25.

36. Heb. 1:1–2.

37. Quispel, *Gnostic Studies,* I, pp. 124, 125 n. 27 (italics mine).

38. Ibid., p. 30 (italics mine). Quispel here is referring not to the *Gospel of Truth* but to Irenaeus's account of Valentinus's poem.

39. Pagels, *Johannine Gospel,* pp. 11–14.

40. von Campenhausen, *Fathers of the Greek Church,* p. 24.

41. Pagels, *Johannine Gospel,* p. 76.

42. *Gospel of Truth,* I, 3, in Robinson, *NHL,* p. 38.

43. John 1:18, I John 5:20. See John Painter, *John: Witness and Theologian* (London: S.P.C.K., 1975), p. 108.

44. Adolf von Harnack, *History of Dogma,* I, trans. Neil Buchanan (New York: Dover, 1961), pp. 227–228.

45. As in Gen. 4:1, 17, 25; Num. 31:18, 35; Judg. 21:12.

46. Rudolf Bultmann, "Yada," in *The Theological Dictionary of the New Testament,* I, ed. Gerhard Kittel (Grand Rapids: Eerdmans, 1964), p. 698. Examples of various uses of *yada:* Deut. 11:2, Isa. 41:20, Hos. 11:3, Mic. 6:5.

47. Bultmann, op. cit., pp. 689–692.

48. I Tim. 6:20–21.

49. Irenaeus, *Against Heresies,* III:6:4 (italics mine). See also bk. IV for Irenaeus's argument that the true God is author of both the Old and New Testaments.

50. Phil. 3:12–14.

51. Bultmann, "Yada," p. 695.

52. Johann Wolfgang von Goethe, *Faust,* trans. George Madison Priest (New York: Knopf, 1963), I:1112–17.

53. Quispel, *Gnostic Studies,* I, p. 120.

54. See Carl A. Raschke, *The Bursting of New Wineskins: Reflections on Religion and Culture at the End of Affluence* (Pittsburgh: Pickwick Press, 1978), p. 223, for a discussion of the connection between the quest for God *alone* and idolatry.

55. e. e. cummings, "pity this busy monster, manunkind, not," in *Poems 1923–1954* (New York: Harcourt, Brace, 1954), p. 397.

56. Harold Bloom, "Lying Against Time: Gnosis, Poetry, Criticism," in *Rediscovery of Gnosticism,* I, p. 69.

57. I Cor. 13:2, 8–9.

58. Painter, *John,* pp. 136, 137.

59. I John 1:8; 2:3–4.

60. I John 4:20.

61. I John 3:14.

62. Arthur Darby Nock, *Conversion* (London: Oxford University Press, 1963), p. 14.

63. James Loder, "Transformation in Christian Education," *Princeton Seminary Bulletin,* NS 3, No. 1 (1980), 20.

64. Rom. 7:24.

65. II Cor. 5:8.

66. Hans Jonas, "Delimitation of the Gnostic Phenomenon—Typological and Historical," in *Le origini dello gnosticismo,* ed. Ugo Bianchi. Proceedings of the Colloquio di Messina, April 1966 (Leiden: E. J. Brill, 1967), p. 97.

67. Richard H. Drummond, "Studies in Christian Gnosticism," *Religion in Life,* 45 (Spring 1976), p. 7. Also Gilles Quispel, "Gnosis and Psychology," in Layton, *Rediscovery of Gnosticism,* I, p. 21.

68. Raschke, *New Wineskins,* pp. 219–220.

69. Karen Horney, M.D., *Neurosis and Human Growth: The Struggle Toward Self-Realization* (New York: W. W. Norton, 1950), pp. 375–377.

70. Quispel, "Gnosis and Psychology," p. 23.

71. Bloom, "Lying Against Time," p. 59.

72. Bultmann, "Yada," pp. 695–96.

73. Arthur Darby Nock, "Gnosticism," *Harvard Theological Review,* 57 (1964), p. 275.

74. From the *Agrapha,* quoted in G. R. S. Mead, *A Faith Forgotten,* p. 596.

75. The *Gospel of Thomas,* II, 2, trans. Thomas O. Lambdin, in Robinson, *NHL,* p. 118. (See chap. 1, n. 4.)

76. Ibid., p. 122.

77. Ibid, p. 129. See also Drummond, "Studies."

78. Matt. 18:20.

79. From the *Oxyrhynchus Papyrus,* quoted in G. R. S. Mead, *A Faith Forgotten,* p. 601.

80. Ibid., p. 602.

81. Matt. 4:12–17, Mark 1:15, Luke 4:14–15.

82. Quispel, *Gnostic Studies,* I, p. 133.

83. Leslie Newbigin, *The Open Secret* (Grand Rapids: Eerdmans, 1978), p. 201.

84. Gen. 1:3 (italics mine).

85. Ps. 1:2.

86. Ps. 63:6.

87. Ps. 77:12.

88. Deut. 26:5–7.

89. Hos. 2:23.

90. Ps. 139:1, 6.

91. Gen. 35:10–11.

92. Deut. 11:19–20.

93. Deut. 30:20.

94. Isa. 62:4–5.

95. Matt. 4:1–11.

96. Matt. 10:39.

97. Matt. 16:24–25; see also Mark 8:34–35, Luke 17:33.

98. Luke 18:18–22.

99. Luke 18:15–17.

100. I Pet. 2:9–10.

101. I Cor. 1:9.

102. Gerhard Kittel, ed., *The Theological Dictionary of the New Testament,* vol. 3 (Grand Rapids: Eerdmans, 1964), pp. 804ff.

103. Phil. 1:5.

104. I Cor. 10:16.

105. II Cor. 13:11–14.

106. From Ignatius, *Ep. ad Smyrnaeos* 8, 2, quoted in Johannes Quasten, *Patrology,* I (Utrecht-Antwerp: Spectrum, 1966), p. 66.

107. Robert R. Williams, *A Guide to the Teachings of the Early Church Fathers* (Grand Rapids: Eerdmans, 1960), p. 17.

108. Drummond, "Studies," pp. 12–13.

109. Pagels, *Johannine Gospel,* pp. 121–122.

110. *Gospel of Thomas,* II, 2, in Robinson, *NHL,* p. 125.

111. From Epiphanius, *Panarion* 24:5, 2, quoted in Quispel, *Gnostic Studies,* I, p. 119.

112. *Gospel of Thomas,* II, 2, in Robinson, *NHL,* p. 129.

113. Matt. 18:10–14.

114. Luke 15:3–7.

115. See also Bertil Gärtner, *The Theology of the Gospel According to Thomas,* trans. Eric J. Sharpe (New York: Harper & Bros., 1961), pp. 235–236.

116. Quispel, *Gnostic Studies,* I, p. 122.

117. *Gospel of Truth,* I, 3, in Robinson, *NHL,* p. 40.

118. Ibid., p. 40.

119. Ibid., p. 40.

120. Max Weber, *The Sociology of Religion* (London: Methuen, 1965), p. 131.

121. See J. B. Bauer, ed., *Encyclopedia of Biblical Theology,* II (London: Sheed & Ward, 1970), pp. 472–474.

122. Jer. 22:15–16 (italics mine).

123. Despite Amos 3:7.

124. Exod. 29:45–46. See also Exod. 6:7, 16:12; Deut. 4:35, 7:9–11 (italics mine).

125. Isa. 11:9; also Hab. 2:14.

126. Deut. 29:29.

127. Job 15:7–9.

128. Isa. 45:15, 19; also Isa. 48:16.

129. Acts 20:29–30.

130. II Cor. 11:13.

131. Rudolf Bultmann, *Theology of the New Testament,* I, trans. Kendrick Groebel (New York: Scribner's, 1954), pp. 170–171.

132. Walter Schmithals, *Gnosticism in Corinth* (Nashville: Abingdon Press, 1971); and *Paul and the Gnostics* (Nashville: Abingdon Press, 1972).

133. Günther Bornkamm, *Paul* (New York: Harper & Row, 1971), p. 71; I Cor. 2:6; 3:1ff.; 8:1.

134. I Cor. 8:1–2 (italics mine).

135. II Cor. 11:5–6.

136. I Cor. 2:1–2.

137. I John 2:19.

138. I John 2:20 (trans. *RSV* footnote).

139. I John 3:14.

140. I John 4:2.

141. Quoted in von Campenhausen, *Fathers of the Greek Church*, p. 27.

142. Irenaeus, *Against Heresies*, III:3; I:10:2.

143. Joachim Jeremias, *The Origins of Infant Baptism*, trans. D. M. Barton (London: SCM Press, 1963), p. 85.

144. Athenagoras, *Apology*, 11, in Quasten, *Patrology*, I, p. 230.

145. I Cor. 2:2.

146. Frederick C. Grant, ed., *Hellenistic Religions: The Age of Syncretism* (New York: Liberal Arts Press, 1953), p. xiii.

147. Jonas, *Gnostic Religion*, p. 26.

148. Hans Jonas, Response to Gilles Quispel, "Gnosticism and the New Testament," in *The Bible in Modern Scholarship*, ed. J. Philip Hyatt. Papers read at the 100th Meeting of the Society of Biblical Literature, 28–30 December 1964 (Nashville: Abingdon Press, 1965), p. 293.

149. *The Apocryphon of John*, II, 1, trans. Frederick Wisse, in Robinson, *NHL*, p. 99.

150. I Cor. 2:2.

151. Augustine, *Contra Faustem* XX, 2, vol. XLII, col. 369, quoted in Runciman, *Medieval Manichee*, p. 14.

152. Ignatius, *To the Smyrnaeans*, 7, in *Early Christian Fathers, I*, ed. Cyril C. Richardson (Philadelphia: Westminster, 1953), pp. 65–66.

153. Irenaeus, *Against Heresies*, I: 21:4, quoted in J. G. Davies, *The Early Christian Church* (Garden City, N.Y.: Doubleday, 1967), p. 103.

154. Quoted in Pagels, *Johannine Gospel*, p. 59.

155. Frederik Wisse, "Stalking Those Elusive Sethians," in *Rediscovery of Gnosticism*, II, p. 584.

156. Bultmann, *New Testament Theology*, I, p. 107.

157. See Runciman, *Medieval Manichee*, p. 172.

158. II Cor. 4:2.

159. Bultmann, *New Testament Theology*, I, p. 295.

160. Gal. 4:4.

161. II Cor. 13:4.

162. I Cor. 1:23.

163. "Nihil vacuum neque sine signo apud Deum," quoted in J. Huizinga, *The Waning of the Middle Ages* (London: Edward Arnold, 1924), p. 183.

164. Irenaeus, *Against Heresies* IV: 17:5, quoted in J. A. Jungmann, *The Mass of the Roman Rite,* I (New York: Benziger Brothers, 1951), p. 27.

165. Jungmann, *Mass,* p. 27.

166. Ignatius, *Ep. ad Ephesios* XX:I:V, quoted in Joseph Cullen Ayer, Jr., *Sourcebook for Ancient Church History* (New York: AMS Press, 1913/1970), p. 31.

167. Quoted in R. R. Williams, *Guide to Early Church Fathers,* p. 137.

168. Nock, "Gnosticism," p. 279.

CHAPTER THREE

1. Eric Voegelin, *Order and History* (Baton Rouge: Louisiana State University Press, 1974), IV, pp. 20–27; see also 13ff. See in addition Thomas J. J. Altizer, "A New History and a New but Ancient God? A Review Essay," *American Academy of Religion Journal,* 43, (1975), p. 758.

2. Hans Conzelmann, *An Outline of the Theology of the New Testament,* trans. John Bowden (New York: Harper & Row, 1969), p. 15.

3. II Cor. 4:6; Col. 1:12f; Rom. 13:12; I Thess. 5:4f.

4. I Cor. 7:31.

5. Col. 2:20

6. I John 5:19. For an excellent discussion of the New Testament use of *cosmos,* see C. E. B. Cranfield, "The Message of James," *Scottish Journal of Theology,* 18, No. 2 (1965), p. 189.

7. II Cor. 4:18.

8. Rom. 5:10.

9. Rom. 4:15; 5:9; 9:22.

10. See Rudolf Bultmann, *Essays,* trans. James C. Q. Greig (New York: Macmillan, 1955), pp. 148–49.

11. Rom. 1:20, 21.

12. Rom. 5:12.

13. Rom. 8:22.

14. John 1:2–5.

15. John 1:5.

16. John 3:19.

17. John 8:12; 12:35; 12:46.

18. John Painter, *John: Witness and Theologian* (London: S.P.C.K., 1975), p. 31.

19. Rudolf Bultmann, *Theology of the New Testament,* I, trans. Kendrick Groebel (New York: Scribner's, 1954), pp. 164–165.

20. John 1:29; also John 8:21, 24; I John 1:10.

21. John 3:16–17 (*cosmos* my substitution).

22. II Cor. 5:17.

23. II Cor. 1:20.

24. I John 1:5.

25. I John 2:8.

26. I John 2:9.

27. Gilles Quispel, *Gnostic Studies* (Istanbul: Nederlands Historisch-Archaeologisch Instituut in het Nabije Oosten, 1974), I, p. 26.

28. R. M. Grant, *Gnosticism and Early Christianity* (New York: Harper & Row, 1966), p. 198.

29. Robinson, *NHL*, p. 1 (italics mine). (See chap. 1, n. 4.)

30. Augustine, *The Confessions* I, 1. *Basic Writings of Saint Augustine*, vol. 1, ed. Whitney J. Oates (New York: Random House, 1948).

31. Luke 10:3, 17.

32. Ernst Troeltsch, *The Social Teaching of the Christian Churches*, I, trans. Olive Wyon (London: Allen & Unwin, 1931), pp. 106–107.

33. Jean Daniélou, *Gospel Message and Hellenistic Culture*, vol. II of *A History of Early Christian Doctrine*, trans. John A. Baker (London: Darton, Longman and Todd, 1973), p. 446.

34. Ibid., p. 465.

35. I Cor. 15:50.

36. Werner Jaeger, *Early Christianity and Greek Paideia* (Cambridge: Harvard University Press, Belknap, 1965), pp. 54–56, 64, 65.

37. Paul Ricoeur, *The Conflict of Interpretation* (Evanston: Northwestern University Press, 1974), p. 272.

38. Ibid., p. 273.

39. Rom. 5:12.

40. Ricoeur, *Conflict*, pp. 276–281.

41. J. G. Davies, *The Early Christian Church* (Garden City, N.Y.: Doubleday, 1967), p. 258.

42. J. F. Bethune-Baker, *An Introduction to the Early History of Christian Doctrine* (London: Methuen, 1958), p. 368.

43. Ibid., p. 369.

44. Henry S. Bettenson, *Documents of the Christian Church* (London: Oxford University Press, 1953), p. 103.

45. Henry S. Bettenson, ed. and trans., *The Early Christian Fathers* (London: Oxford University Press, 1956), p. 103.

46. Roland H. Bainton, *The Medieval Church* (Princeton: D. Van Nostrand, 1962), pp. 52–53.

47. Phyllis McGinley, *Saint-Watching* (New York: Viking, 1969), p. 142.

48. Bainton, *Medieval Church*, p. 40.

49. J. A. Jungmann, *The Mass of the Roman Rite* (New York: Benziger Brothers, 1955), II, pp. 262–263.

50. J. Huizinga, *The Waning of the Middle Ages* (London: Edward Arnold, 1924), pp. 54, 140.

51. John 17:15, 16 (*cosmos* my substitution).

52. Hans Jonas, "Delimitation of the Gnostic Phenomenon—Typological and Historical," in *Le origini dello gnosticismo,* ed. Ugo Bianchi. Proceedings of the Colloquio di Messina, April 1966 (Leiden: E. J. Brill, 1967), p. 91.

53. Ibid., p. 95.

54. The Westminster Confession of Faith, II:1, in *The Book of Confessions* (Philadelphia: General Assembly of the United Presbyterian Church in the U.S.A., 1967).

55. Voegelin, *Order and History,* I, p. 454.

56. Quoted in Voegelin, *Order and History,* III, p. 193.

57. Jonathan Sumption, *The Albigensian Crusade* (London: Faber and Faber, 1978), p. 252.

58. See Rom. 5:1; 3:28; Eph. 2:8, 9; Gal. 2:16; among others.

59. Martin Luther, "Preface to New Testament," in *Martin Luther: Selections from His Writings,* ed. John Dillenberger (Garden City, N.Y.: Doubleday, Anchor, 1961), pp. 18–19.

60. Luther, *The Bondage of the Will,* in *Martin Luther,* ed. Dillenberger, p. 170.

61. Luther, "Preface to New Testament," in *Martin Luther,* ed. Dillenberger, p. 19.

62. Luther, "Address to the Imperial Diet at Worms, 1521," in *Martin Luther,* ed. Dillenberger, p. xxiii (italics mine).

63. Wilhelm Niesel, *Reformed Symbolics: A Comparison of Catholicism, Orthodoxy and Protestantism,* trans. David Lewis (Edinburgh: Oliver and Boyd, 1962), pp. 253–254.

64. Luther, "Sermon in Castle Pleissenburg, Leipzig, 1539," in *Martin Luther,* ed. Dillenberger, pp. 247–248.

65. Niesel, *Reformed Symbolics,* p. 12.

66. Quoted in R. L. Greaves, "Luther's Doctrine of Grace," *Scottish Journal of Theology,* 18, No. 4 (1965), p. 394.

67. Quoted in Niesel, *Reformed Symbolics,* p. 234.

68. Quoted in Greaves, "Luther's Doctrine," p. 392.

69. Luther, *The Pagan Servitude of the Church,* in *Martin Luther,* ed. Dillenberger, p. 279.

70. Quoted in Greaves, pp. 385–386.

71. Dillenberger, *Martin Luther,* pp. xxviii, xxix.

72. Luther, "Sermon Delivered at Marburg, October 5, 1529," in *What Luther Says,* vol. 3, ed. Ewald M. Plass (Saint Louis: Concordia, 1972), p. 1466.

73. Quoted in Greaves, p. 389.

74. Luther, "Treatise on Christian Liberty," in *Martin Luther,* ed. Dillenberger, p. 53.

75. Quoted in Greaves, p. 393.

76. Ibid.

77. Quoted in Paul Lehmann, *Ethics in a Christian Context* (New York: Harper & Row, 1975), pp. 63–64 (italics mine).

78. Luther, "Table Talk, December 12, 1538," in *What Luther Says,* vol. 1, ed. Plass, p. 272.

79. Luther, "Sermons on the Catechism, 1528," in *Martin Luther,* ed. Dillenberger, p. 233.

80. Ibid., p. 237.

81. See François Wendel, *Calvin,* trans. Philip Mairet (London: William Collins, 1976), pp. 346–351, for a discussion of Luther's concept of *ubiquity,* the idea that Christ himself becomes bodily present at every celebration of the Eucharist. As we shall see, this attempt to concretize the sacrament might have had an unfortunate opposite effect.

82. John Calvin, *Institutes of the Christian Religion,* trans. Henry Beveridge (Grand Rapids: Eerdmans, 1953), I, 1, 1.

83. Wendel, *Calvin,* p. 216; see also Calvin, *Institutes,* II, 12, 1.

84. Wendel, *Calvin,* pp. 185, 216; see also Calvin, *Institutes,* I, 15, 4; II, 6, 4.

85. Wendel, *Calvin,* p. 252; see also Calvin, *Institutes,* III, 9, 1 and 2.

86. Calvin, *Commentary on Philippians, Colossians and Thessalonians,* trans. John Pringle (Grand Rapids: Eerdmans, 1957), p. 135 [Col. 3:5].

87. Wendel, *Calvin,* p. 151.

88. Calvin, *Institutes,* I, 15, 1.

89. Ibid., I, 15, 2.

90. Ibid.

91. Ibid., II, 1, 1.

92. See chap. 1, p. 2, in this work.

93. John Calvin, *Commentary on the Catholic Epistles* (Grand Rapids: Eerdmans, 1959), p. 159.

94. Wendel, *Calvin,* p. 225.

95. See Bainton, *Medieval Church,* p. 85. Note that both Calvin and Loyola were taught at the Sorbonne by one of the Brethren of the Common Life, a movement depreciating the externals of religion.

96. Calvin, *Institutes,* I, 11 (title of his chapter).

97. Calvin, *Institutes,* I, 11, 1.

98. Calvin, *Institutes,* I, 11, 9. See also Kilian McDonnell, *John Calvin, the Church and the eucharist* (Princeton: Princeton University Press, 1967), p. 162.

99. Calvin, *Institutes,* I, 11, 7.

100. Wendel, *Calvin,* p. 314; *Institutes,* IV, 14, 3.

101. See Calvin, *Institutes,* IV, 17, 12–15.

102. Calvin, *Institutes,* IV, 17, 19.

103. Wendel, *Calvin,* p. 353. Fr. McDonnell in *John Calvin* (p. 381) takes a different view: "Though rough of edge and left hanging in perpetual dialectical motion [Calvin's eucharistic doctrine] is admirably worked out in the framework of his Christology, pneumatology, ecclesiology, and of his doctrine of predestination and grace."

104. Calvin, *Institutes,* I, 5, 9 (italics mine).

105. Calvin, *Institutes,* I, 5, 1.

106. Calvin, *Institutes,* I, 13, 21; quoted in Wendel, *Calvin,* p. 152.

107. Calvin, *Institutes,* I, 6, 2; quoted in Wendel, *Calvin,* p. 153.

108. Wendel, *Calvin,* p. 158.

109. Ibid., p. 154.

110. Calvin, *Institutes,* I, 5, 15.

111. Calvin, *Institutes,* II, 6, 4.

112. Calvin, *Institutes,* I, 10, 2.

113. J. K. S. Reid, ed. and trans., *Calvin: Theological Treatises,* XX, Library of Christian Classics (Philadelphia: Westminster Press, 1954), p. 228.

114. Calvin, *Institutes,* III, 12, 7–8; see also III, 13, 2.

115. Calvin, *Institutes,* III, 7, 1.

116. Calvin, *Institutes,* IV, 9, 1.

117. Calvin, *Institutes,* IV, 9, 8.

118. Reid, *Calvin: Theological Treatises,* p. 252.

119. G. S. M. Walker, "Calvin and the Church," *Scottish Journal of Theology,* 16, No. 4 (1963), p. 377.

120. Calvin, *Institutes,* IV, 19, 35.

121. Calvin, *Institutes,* IV, 17, 22, trans. Walker, in "Calvin," p. 382, n. 4.

122. John Calvin, *Sermons on Ephesians* (Carlisle, Penn.: Banner of Truth Trust, 1973), pp. 122–123.

123. Calvin, *Institutes* IV, 1, 4, trans. Walker, in "Calvin," p. 376.

124. Calvin, *Commentary on Isaiah* 54:13, trans. Walker, in "Calvin," p. 376.

125. Wendel, *Calvin,* p. 297.

126. Quoted in Walker, "Calvin," p. 377.

127. See Calvin, *Institutes,* IV, 5–11. Entire section deals with the Roman Church as a sect.

128. Reid, *Calvin: Theological Treatises,* p. 230 (italics mine).

129. Calvin, *Institutes,* IV, 1, 9.

130. Calvin, *Institutes,* IV, 1, 4. Note that the starting point of Calvin's ecclesiology is the necessity of the Church and the absolute condemnation of schism.

131. Reid, *Calvin: Theological Treatises,* pp. 231–232. See also Walker, "Calvin," p. 373.

132. McDonnell, *John Calvin,* p. 184 (italics mine).

133. Calvin, *Institutes,* IV, 1, 1; IV, 14, 1.

134. Ibid., IV, 14, 6 (italics mine).

135. Ibid., IV, 14, 19.

136. Walker, "Calvin," p. 375.

137. Calvin, *Institutes,* IV, 15, 3.

138. Ibid., IV, 16, 32.

139. Ibid., IV, 16, 31.

140. Ibid., IV, 15, 19, trans. McDonnell in *John Calvin,* p. 185.

141. Calvin, *Corpus Reformatorum* 47:153, trans. McDonnell in *John Calvin,* pp. 283–284. See also p. 176.

142. McDonnell, *John Calvin,* p. 178. See Calvin, *Institutes,* IV, 17, 5.

143. Calvin, *Institutes,* IV, 17, 7.

144. Ibid., IV, 17, 16–17.

145. Ibid., IV, 17, 19 (italics mine).

146. Ibid., IV, 17, 24–26. See also Wendel, *Calvin,* p. 349; McDonnell, *John Calvin,* p. 211 (italics mine).

147. Calvin, *Institutes,* IV, 17, 19.

148. Wendel, *Calvin,* p. 343.

149. Ibid., p. 340.

150. Ibid., p. 351 (italics mine).

151. McDonnell, *John Calvin,* p. 186.

152. Ibid., p. 380. See also G. C. Coulton, *Ten Medieval Studies:* "Those [during the Middle Ages] who wished to communicate too frequently were constantly discouraged by the clergy. Anything like weekly communion was very rare indeed among the laity; the few who desired it could very rarely obtain it," p. 198.

153. Calvin, *Institutes,* IV, 17, 43–44 (italics mine). See also *Institutes,* IV, 17, 5; 42; 46; IV, 18, 19; 20; and Wendel, *Calvin,* p. 71; Walker, "Calvin," p. 388 (italics mine).

154. John T. McNeill, *The History and Character of Calvinism* (New York: Oxford University Press, 1962), p. 191. See also Calvin, *Institutes,* IV, 20, 32.

155. Wendel, *Calvin,* pp. 61, 78, 79, 105, 148, 293.

156. Ibid., p. 243.

157. Calvin, *Institutes,* IV, 1, 5; 3, 2; 9, 5; 11, 1–6; 12, 1–2; 12, 7. See also Walker, p. 385; McDonnell, p. 187.

158. Walker, "Calvin," pp. 381, 386.

159. Walker, "Calvin," p. 387.

160. Calvin, *Institutes,* IV, 20, 4.

161. See Lehmann, *Ethics,* p. 71.

162. Wendel, *Calvin,* p. 49.

163. The following statement by Walker gives some idea of the universal significance of Calvinism: "Catholicism and Calvinism, . . . are the only two absolute types of Christianity. It would be more accurate to say that there are two types of Catholicity, one Roman, one Reformed. They stand in fundamental opposition because of a fundamental likeness, for Geneva offered to Rome an alternative which was ultimate and in itself complete. A partial synthesis was indeed achieved by Canterbury, but at the price of creating parties which finally sundered the religious unity of England. . . . Calvin stood closer to the Latin tradition of churchmanship, and on the formal basis of *sola scriptura,* he sought to realize at least some ideals of the great medieval popes," p. 389. See also Troeltsch, *Social Teaching,* II, pp. 677, 681, 687, 690, 691, 808, 815, 819.

164. Perry Miller, ed., *The American Puritans: Their Prose and Poetry* (Garden City, N.Y.: Doubleday, 1956), p. ix.

165. Walker, "Calvin," p. 379.

166. Perry Miller, *The New England Mind: The Seventeenth Century,* (Cambridge: Harvard University Press, 1954), pp. 407–31.

167. Robert Middlekauf, *The Mathers: Three Generations of Puritan Intellectuals, 1596–1728* (New York: Oxford University Press, 1971), p. 99.

168. Miller, *New England Mind: Seventeenth Century*, p. 147.

169. Philip Greven, *The Protestant Temperament: Patterns of Child-Rearing, Religious Experience and the Self in Early America* (New York: Knopf, 1977), p. 259.

170. Quoted in Greven, ibid., pp. 259, 260 (italics mine).

171. Ibid., pp. 194, 196. Greven also points out that the Anglicans shared this *organic* view of nature and society: "Like the moderates, they also believed in the necessity for the fulfillment of duties and obligations—within the family, the community and in the world at large generally," p. 297.

172. Troeltsch, *Social Teaching*, II, p. 690.

173. Walker, "Calvin," p. 379. See also Charles S. McCoy, "Johannes Cocceius: Federal Theologian," *Scottish Journal of Theology*, 16, No. 4 (1963), pp. 360ff. For a complete critique of the federal theology as opposed to pure Calvinism, see Karl Barth, *Church Dogmatics*, IV/1, ed. G. W. Bromiley and T. F. Torrance, pp. 54–66.

174. Greven, *Protestant Temperament*, p. 236.

175. Wendel, *Calvin*, p. 360.

176. Ibid., p. 241.

177. Walker, "Calvin," p. 381. See also Calvin, *Institutes*, IV, 1, 8; Wendel, *Calvin*, pp. 140, 141, 297, 298.

178. Westminster Confession, III, 3.

179. Ibid., III, 8.

180. Greven, *Protestant Temperament*, pp. 257, 258, 193.

181. James W. Jones, *The Shattered Synthesis: New England Puritanism Before the Great Awakening* (New Haven: Yale University Press, 1973), p. 91.

182. Greven, *Protestant Temperament*, pp. 257, 258.

183. Martin E. Marty, *Righteous Empire: The Protestant Experience in America* (New York: Dial Press, 1970), pp. 80, 81.

184. Jones, *Shattered Synthesis*, p. 16.

185. Ibid., pp. 16, 17, 31.

186. Ibid., pp. 143–197. See also Vernon L. Parrington, *The Romantic Revolution in America, 1800–1860*, Vol. II of *Main Currents in American Thought* (New York: Harcourt, Brace, 1959), pp. 317ff.

187. Henry Steele Commager, *The American Mind* (New Haven: Yale University Press, 1964), pp. 366, 367.

188. Quoted in Parrington, *Main Currents*, II, p. 380.

189. I Cor. 1:23.

190. Parrington, *Main Currents*, II, p. 319.

CHAPTER FOUR

1. See Rodger Van Allen, ed., *American Religious Values and the Future of America* (Philadelphia: Fortress Press, 1978), pp. 13, 14. See also Martin E. Marty, *Righteous Empire: The Protestant Experience in America* (New York: Dial Press, 1970), p. 210.

2. Vernon L. Parrington, *The Romantic Revolution in America, 1800–1860*, Vol. II of *Main Currents in American Thought* (New York: Harcourt, Brace, 1959), p. 313.

3. See William R. Hutchison, *The Modernist Impulse in American Protestantism* (Cambridge: Harvard University Press, 1976), p. 203; see also Marty, *Righteous Empire,* p. 82.

4. Marty, *Righteous Empire,* p. 144.

5. Sidney E. Mead, *The Lively Experiment: The Shaping of Christianity in America* (New York: Harper & Row, 1963), p.x.

6. From the "General Thanksgiving," *Book of Common Prayer* (New York: Oxford, 1944).

7. From the "Great Prayer of Thanksgiving," *Book of Common Prayer.*

8. John 1:3.

9. Col. 2:14, 15; II Cor. 5:21; Heb. 10:12, 13.

10. François Wendel, *Calvin,* trans. Philip Mairet (London: William Collins, 1976), p. 177.

11. Ibid., p. 178.

12. Ibid., p. 247.

13. From an unpublished article by Eda W. Martin, "Jonathan Edwards's Early Works," Williamsburg, Virginia, October 6, 1982.

14. William A. Clebsch, *American Religious Thought* (Chicago: University of Chicago Press, 1973), p. 53.

15. Ibid., p. 172.

16. See chap. 3, pp. 12ff. in this work.

17. John T. McNeill, *The History and Character of Calvinism* (New York: Oxford University Press, 1962), p. 265.

18. Paul Ricoeur, *The Conflict of Interpretation* (Evanston: Northwestern University Press, 1974), p. 269. Some verses by Anne Bradstreet summarized the New England acceptance of the ultra-Calvinist position:

> Stained from birth with Adam's sinfull fact,
> Thence I began to sin as soon as act:
> A perverse will, a love to what's forbid,
> A serpents sting in pleasing face lay hid.

So much for the innocence of infancy. (Quoted in *The Protestant Temperament: Patterns of Child-Rearing, Religious Experience and Self in Early America* by Philip Greven, [New York: Knopf, 1977] p. 29.)

19. Ricoeur, *Conflict,* p. 283.

20. Ibid., p. 273.

21. See Gilles Quispel, *Gnostic Studies* (Istanbul: Nederlands Historisch-Archaeologisch Instituut in het Nabije Oosten, 1974), I, p. 127.

22. Gen. 1:26.

23. Hans Jonas, "Delimitation of the Gnostic Phenomenon—Typological and Historical," in *Le origini dello gnosticismo,* ed. Ugo Bianchi, Proceedings of the Colloquio di Messina, April 1966 (Leiden: E. J. Brill, 1967), p. 97.

24. Greven, *The Protestant Temperament,* pp. 67–68.

25. Ibid., p. 199.

26. Sidney E. Ahlstrom, *A Religious History of the American People* (New Haven: Yale University Press, 1972), p. 301.

27. Jonas, "Delimitation," p. 100.

28. Greven, *Protestant Temperament*, p. 338.

29. Jonas, "Delimitation," p. 100 (italics mine).

30. Ahlstrom, *Religious History*, p. 145.

31. See Will Herberg, ed., *The Writings of Martin Buber* (Cleveland: World, 1968), p. 263.

32. Martin E. Marty, *Righteous Empire: The Protestant Experience in America* (New York: Dial Press, 1970), p. 117.

33. Ibid.

34. Vernon L. Parrington, *The Romantic Revolution in America, 1800–1860,* Vol. II of *Main Currents in American Thought* (New York: Harcourt, Brace, 1959), pp. 441–442 (italics mine).

35. T. Walter Herbert, Jr., *Moby Dick and Calvinism* (New Brunswick, N.J.: Rutgers University Press, 1977), pp. 171ff.

36. Lawrance Thompson, *Melville's Quarrel with God* (Princeton: Princeton University Press, 1952), pp. 242–243.

37. Herman Melville, *The Confidence Man* (New York: Airmont, 1966), p. 21.

38. Parrington, *Main Currents,* II, p. 250.

39. Emily Dickinson, *The Complete Poems of Emily Dickinson,* ed. Thomas H. Johnson (Boston: Little, Brown, 1960), No. 1270, p. 555.

40. William R. Hutchison, *The Modernist Impulse in American Protestantism* (Cambridge: Harvard University Press, 1976), p. 16.

41. Parrington, *Main Currents,* II, p. 411.

42. Henry David Thoreau, *A Week on the Concord and Merrimack Rivers,* in *The Works of Thoreau,* ed. Henry Seidel Canby (Boston: Houghton Mifflin, 1937), p. 90.

43. Parrington, *Main Currents,* II, p. 364.

44. Ibid., p. 319.

45. See Herberg, *Martin Buber,* p. 263. Buber reminds us that Protestant liberalism has also at times followed Marcion in its rejection of the Old Testament. He cites a statement of Adolf von Harnack that the preservation of the Old Testament as a canonical text is "the consequence of religious and ecclesiastical paralysis."

46. Marty, *Righteous Empire,* pp. 116–117.

47. Ralph Waldo Emerson, *Journals of Ralph Waldo Emerson,* ed. Edward Waldo Emerson and Waldo Emerson Forbes, 10 vols. (Boston: Houghton Mifflin, 1909–14), vol. 8, p. 259. Quoted in Parrington, *Main Currents,* II, p. 383.

48. Parrington, *Main Currents,* II, p. 392.

49. Hutchison, *Modernist Impulse,* p. 192, n. 14.

50. Quoted in Marty, *Righteous Empire,* p. 207.

51. Hutchison, *Modernist Impulse,* pp. 192, 227.

52. Ibid., p. 219.

53. Charles Y. Glock and Robert N. Bellah, *The New Religious Consciousness* (Berkeley: University of California Press, 1976), pp. 361–362.

54. Quoted in Arthur Koestler, *The Ghost in the Machine* (New York: Macmillan, 1967), pp. 127, 200.

55. Owen Chadwick, *The Secularization of the European Mind in the 19th Century* (Cambridge: Cambridge University Press, 1975), pp. 169, 178.

56. H. Shelton Smith, Robert T. Handy and Lefferts A. Loetscher, *American Christianity: An Historical Interpretation with Representative Documents* (New York: Scribner's, 1963), II, pp. 250–253.

57. Koestler, *Ghost,* pp. 267, 296, 331, 339.

58. Herberg, *Martin Buber,* pp. 263–264.

59. Marty, *Righteous Empire,* p. 139.

60. This occurred with the distribution of pamphlets entitled *The Fundamentals* by evangelists A. C. Dixon and R. A. Torrey. See Marty, *Righteous Empire,* p. 216.

61. Ibid., pp. 216–217.

62. Ibid., pp. 256–257.

63. Winthrop S. Hudson, *Religion in America* (New York: Scribner's, 1965), pp. 385–386.

64. Ahlstrom, *Religious History,* p. 962.

65. Walter Lippmann, *New York Herald Tribune,* 4 August 1964. Quoted in Roger L. Shinn, *Tangled World* (New York: Scribner's, 1965), p. 151.

66. Marty, *Righteous Empire,* p. 237.

67. Hudson, *Religion in America,* p. 381.

68. Ahlstrom, *Religious History,* p. 946.

69. John C. Bennett, "A Changed Liberal—But Still a Liberal," *Christian Century,* 56 (8 February 1939), p. 180.

70. See Robert C. Neville, *Creativity and God: A Challenge to Process Theology* (New York: Seabury Press, 1980).

71. Harvey Cox, *The Secular City: Secularization and Urbanization in Theological Perspective* (New York: Macmillan, 1965), pp. 76, 83, 84, 264.

72. Ahlstrom, *Religious History,* p. 1094.

73. Ibid.

CHAPTER FIVE

1. Isa. 45:18, 19; see also Isa. 48:16.

2. Acts 2:23.

3. Acts 26:25, 26 (italics mine).

4. Irenaeus, *Against Heresies,* I:10:2. Quoted in Robert R. Williams, *A Guide to the Teachings of the Early Church Fathers* (Grand Rapids: Eerdmans, 1960), p. 331.

5. Will Herberg, ed., *The Writings of Martin Buber* (Cleveland: World, 1968), p. 75.

6. G. S. M. Walker, "Calvin and the Church," *Scottish Journal of Theology,* 16, No. 4 (1963), p. 381.

7. James W. Jones, *The Shattered Synthesis: New England Puritanism Before the Great Awakening* (New Haven: Yale University Press, 1973), p. 7.

8. William A. Clebsch, *American Religious Thought* (Chicago: University of Chicago Press, 1973), p. 28. See also Jerald C. Brauer, ed., *Reinterpretation in American Church History* (Chicago: University of Chicago Press, 1968), p. 42.

9. Rodger Van Allen, ed., *American Religious Values and the Future of America* (Philadelphia: Fortress Press, 1978), p. 16 (italics mine).

10. Quoted in Philip Greven, *The Protestant Temperament: Patterns of Child-Rearing, Religious Experience and the Self in Early America* (New York: Knopf, 1977), p. 232.

11. Martin E. Marty, *Righteous Empire: The Protestant Experience in America* (New York: Dial Press, 1970), p. 116.

12. H. Richard Niebuhr, *The Social Sources of Denominationalism* (Hamden: Shoe String Press, 1954), pp. 103–104.

13. Paul Ricoeur, *The Conflict of Interpretation* (Evanston: Northwestern University Press, 1974), p. 293.

14. Hans Jonas, "Delimitation of the Gnostic Phenomenon—Typological and Historical," in *Le origini dello gnosticismo,* ed. Ugo Bianchi. Proceedings of the Colloquio di Messina, April 1966 (Leiden: E. J. Brill, 1967), pp. 98–99.

15. Arthur Koestler, *The Ghost in the Machine* (New York: Macmillan, 1967), pp. 302, 327.

16. Harvey Cox, *The Secular City: Secularization and Urbanization in Theological Perspective* (New York: Macmillan, 1965), p. 119.

17. Karl Menninger, *Whatever Became of Sin?* (New York: Hawthorne Books, 1973).

18. Jonas, "Delimitation," p. 98 (italics mine).

19. Arthur Darby Nock, "Gnosticism," *Harvard Theological Review,* 57 (1964), p. 269.

20. Gilles Quispel, *Gnostic Studies* (Istanbul: Nederlands Historisch-Archaeologisch Instituut in het Nabije Oosten, 1974), I, p. 117.

21. Sidney E. Mead, *The Lively Experiment: The Shaping of Christianity in America* (New York: Harper & Row, 1963), p. 96.

22. John Painter, *John: Witness and Theologian* (London: S.P.C.K., 1975), pp. 5–6.

23. Rudolf Bultmann, *Theology of the New Testament,* I, trans. Kendrick Groebel (New York: Scribner's, 1954), p. 302. See also J. G. Gibbs, "Rudolf Bultmann and His Successors," *Scottish Journal of Theology,* 18, No. 4 (1965), p. 403.

24. Peter W. Williams, *Popular Religion in America* (Englewood Cliffs, N.J.: Prentice-Hall, 1980), p. 12.

25. Henry Nelson Wieman, "A Religious Naturalist Looks at Reinhold Niebuhr," in Charles W. Kegley and Robert W. Bretall, eds., *Reinhold Niebuhr: His Religious, Social and Political Thought* (New York: Macmillan, 1961), p. 348.

26. Paul L. Lehmann, "The Christianity of Reinhold Niebuhr," in Kegley and Bretall, eds., *Reinhold Niebuhr,* p. 279.

27. See Paul L. Lehmann, *Ethics in a Christian Context* (New York: Harper &

Row, 1963); and *The Transfiguration of Politics* (New York: Harper & Row, 1975), especially p. 289.

28. Cox, *Secular City*, p. 119.

29. Rodney M. Booth, *The Winds of God: The Canadian Church Faces the 1980s* (Winfield, B.C., Canada: World Council of Churches in cooperation with Wood Lake Books, 1982), p. 119.

30. I Thess. 1:5.

31. Mead, *The Lively Experiment*, p. 122 (italics mine).

32. Ibid., p. 123.

33. See Donald E. Miller, "Sectarianism and Secularization: The Work of Bryan Wilson," *Religious Studies Review*, 5, No. 3 (1979), 161–174.

34. Frederick Kirschenmann, "Horace Bushnell: Cells or Crustacea?" in Brauer, *Reinterpretation*, pp. 67–89.

35. Ibid.

36. William R. Hutchison, *The Modernist Impulse in American Protestantism*, (Cambridge: Harvard University Press, 1976), pp. 273f.

37. Luke 16:8, King James Version.

38. II Cor. 4:7.

39. Sidney E. Ahlstrom, *A Religious History of the American People* (New Haven: Yale University Press, 1972), p. 1090.

40. Mead, *The Lively Experiment*, p. 124.

41. Marty, *Righteous Empire*, p. 224.

42. Emily Dickinson, *The Complete Poems of Emily Dickinson*, ed. Thomas H. Johnson (Boston: Little, Brown, 1960), No. 185, p. 87.

43. See Ahlstrom, *Religious History*, pp. 1037–1054.

44. Charles Y. Glock and Robert N. Bellah, *The New Religious Consciousness* (Berkeley: University of California Press, 1976), p. 346 (italics mine).

45. Heb. 12:1.

46. Samuel L. Terrien, *The Elusive Presence* (San Francisco: Harper & Row, 1978), p. 458. Terrien goes on to admit to Paul's experience of mystical ecstasy (II Cor. 12:1ff.), but points out that Paul takes no stock in it. In fact, Paul uses his own experience to discount gnostic pretensions.

CHAPTER SIX

1. Calvin, *Institutes*, I, 13, 1.

2. H. Richard Niebuhr, *The Social Sources of Denominationalism* (Hamden: Shoe String Press, 1954), p. 97.

3. Calvin, *Institutes*, Prefatory Address, 5.

4. Perry Miller, *The New England Mind: From Colony to Province* (Cambridge: Harvard Univ. Press, 1953), pp. 484–485.

5. Jonathan Edwards, "Memoirs," *The Works of President Edwards* (New York,

1881), 1:16. Quoted in Herbert W. Richardson, *Toward an American Theology* (New York: Harper & Row, 1967), p. 60.

6. Philip Greven, *The Protestant Temperament: Patterns of Child-Rearing, Religious Experience and the Self in Early America* (New York: Knopf, 1977), p. 85 (italics mine).

7. Emily Dickinson, *The Complete Poems of Emily Dickinson,* ed. Thomas H. Johnson (Boston: Little, Brown, 1960), No. 77, p. 40.

8. Walter Scott, ed., *Corpus Hermetica,* I (London: Oxford University Press, 1924), pp. 239–255.

9. John 3:3, 3:7, King James Version.

10. Jerald C. Brauer, ed., *Reinterpretation in American Church History* (Chicago: University of Chicago Press, 1968), p. 27.

11. Martin E. Marty, *Righteous Empire: The Protestant Experience in America* (New York: Dial Press, 1970), p. 147.

12. Quoted in Elaine Pagels, *The Gnostic Gospels* (New York: Random House, 1979), p. 135.

13. Arthur Darby Nock, *Early Gentile Christianity and Its Hellenistic Background* (New York: Harper & Row, 1964), p. 16.

14. Gilles Quispel, *Gnostic Studies* (Istanbul: Nederlands Historisch-Archaeologisch Instituut in het Nabije Oosten, 1974), I, p. 118.

15. Henry Chadwick, "The Domestication of Gnosis," in *The Rediscovery of Gnosticism,* I, ed. Bentley Layton, Proceedings of the Yale Conference on Gnosticism, March 1978 (Leiden: E. J. Brill, 1980), p. 14. See also Gal. 6:14 (*cosmos* my substitution).

16. See Will Herberg, ed., *The Writings of Martin Buber* (Cleveland: World, 1968), pp. 270–271.

17. Gen. 3:19; Psalm 103:13, 14.

18. Greven, *Protesant Temperament,* pp. 35, 44.

19. Ibid., p. 31.

20. Marty, *Righteous Empire,* p. 12.

21. See Margaret Atwood, *Survival: A Thematic Guide to Canadian Literature* (Toronto: House of Anansi Press, 1972), pp. 87–106, for a brilliant comment on the American and Canadian literary treatment of the "first people."

22. Marty, *Righteous Empire,* pp. 24–33.

23. Greven, *Protestant Temperament,* p. 110.

24. Steven Runciman, *The Medieval Manichee* (Cambridge: Cambridge University Press, 1960), p. 133.

25. Peter W. Williams, *Popular Religion in America* (Englewood Cliffs, N.J.: Prentice-Hall, 1980), pp. 145f.

26. Mark 16:18.

27. Mark 16:17; Acts 2:4.

28. Ralph Waldo Emerson, *Nature* VIII, in *Selected Prose and Poetry,* ed. Reginald L. Cook (New York: Rinehart, 1950), p. 43.

29. Henry David Thoreau, *Walden,* in *The Works of Thoreau,* ed. Henry Seidel Canby (Cambridge: Riverside Press, 1937), p. 305.

30. Vernon L. Parrington, *The Romantic Revolution in America 1800–1860,* Vol. II of *Main Currents in American Thought* (New York: Harcourt, Brace, 1959), p. 395.

31. A. R. Ammons, "Corson's Inlet," in *Collected Poems: 1951–1971* (New York: Norton, 1972), p. 148.

32. Harold Bloom, *The Ringers in the Tower* (Chicago: University of Chicago Press, 1975), pp. 274–275.

33. A. R. Ammons, "For Harold Bloom," dedicatory lines in *Sphere: The Form of a Motion* (New York: Norton, 1974), p. 5. Quoted in Harold Bloom, *A Map of Misreading* (New York: Oxford University Press, 1975), pp. 200–201.

34. See Donald Stone, "The Human Potential Movement," in *The New Religious Consciousness,* Charles Y. Glock and Robert N. Bellah, eds. (Berkeley: University of California Press, 1976), pp. 93–115.

35. Elisabeth Kübler-Ross, *On Death and Dying* (London: Macmillan, 1969).

36. Harold Bloom, "Lying Against Time: Gnosis, Poetry, Criticism," in Layton, *Rediscovery of Gnosticism,* I, pp. 69–70.

37. Ralph Waldo Emerson, *Journals of Ralph Waldo Emerson,* ed. Edward Waldo Emerson and Waldo Emerson Forbes, vol. 5, p. 288. Quoted in Parrington, *Main Currents,* II, p. 378.

38. Quoted in Pagels, *Gnostic Gospels,* p. 132.

39. Thomas Jefferson, *The Complete Jefferson, Containing his Major Writings, Published and Unpublished, Except his Letters,* ed. Saul K. Padover (New York: Duell, Sloan & Pearce, 1943), p. 940. Quoted in Sidney E. Mead, *The Lively Experiment: The Shaping of Christianity in America* (New York: Harper & Row, 1963), p. 106.

40. Mead, *The Lively Experiment,* pp. 108–111.

41. Emerson, *Journals,* vol. 4, p. 242. Quoted in Parrington, *Main Currents,* II, p. 391.

42. See Hans Jonas, "Delimitation of the Gnostic Phenomenon—Typological and Historical," in *Le origini dello gnosticismo,* ed. Ugo Bianchi. Proceedings of the Colloquio di Messina, April 1966 (Leiden: E. J. Brill, 1967), p. 102. See also Pagels, *Gnostic Gospels,* p. 36.

43. Marty, *Righteous Empire,* pp. 184, 187.

44. Emerson, *Journals,* vol. 8, p. 316. Quoted in Parrington, *Main Currents,* II, pp. 385, 391, 392.

45. Quoted in Parrington, *Main Currents,* II, pp. 397–399.

46. Marty, *Righteous Empire,* p. 180.

47. Parrington, *Main Currents,* II, p. 320.

48. H. H. Gerth and C. Wright Mills, eds. and trans., *From Max Weber: Essays in Sociology* (New York: Oxford University Press, 1946), pp. 18, 19, 331.

49. Fernand Braudel, *Afterthoughts on Material Civilization and Capitalism* (Baltimore: Johns Hopkins University Press, 1977), pp. 40–44.

50. Marc. H. Tanenbaum, "Response [to Michael Novak]," in Rodger Van Al-

len, ed., *American Religious Values and the Future of America* (Philadelphia: Fortress Press, 1978), p. 195.

51. Quoted in Mead, *The Lively Experiment,* p. 158.

52. Marty, *Righteous Empire,* pp. 144–145.

53. Ibid., pp. 207–208.

54. Henry Steele Commager, *The American Mind* (New Haven: Yale University Press, 1964), p. 179.

55. Quoted in Marty, *Righteous Empire,* p. 256.

56. Ibid., pp. 184, 227. See also Commager, *American Mind,* p. 180.

57. Reinhold Niebuhr, *The Nature and Destiny of Man: A Christian Interpretation,* (New York: Scribner's, 1955 [Gifford Lectures; one-volume edition]), II, p. 22.

58. Reinhold Niebuhr, *Moral Man and Immoral Society: A Study in Ethics and Politics* (New York: Scribner's, 1960), pp. 256, 277.

59. Glock and Bellah, *New Religious Consciousness,* p. 150.

60. Quoted in Pagels, *Gnostic Gospels,* p. 146. Pagels goes on to recall that to maintain the consistency of his sanctifying theory Irenaeus held Jesus to have been more than fifty years old when he died.

61. Ibid., p. 101.

62. I Cor. 6:20.

63. Pagels, *Gnostic Gospels,* pp. 101, 145, 146.

64. Quoted in Pagels, ibid., p. 73.

65. Greven, *Protestant Temperament,* p. 65.

66. Runciman, *Medieval Manichee,* p. 173.

67. Jonathan Edwards, *The Works of President Edwards: With a Memoir of His Life,* ed. Sereno E. Dwight (New York, 1881), 1:16. Quoted in Greven, *Protestant Temperament,* p. 70.

68. Greven, *Protestant Temperament,* p. 73.

69. Ibid., p. 23. Note that the parallel with the famous Valentinian formula is striking.

70. Ibid., pp. 66, 67.

71. Ibid.

72. William R. Hutchison, *The Modernist Impulse in American Protestantism* (Cambridge: Harvard University Press, 1976), p. 190.

73. Quoted in Pagels, *Gnostic Gospels,* pp. 26, 27.

74. Walker Percy, *Love in the Ruins* (New York: Farrar, Straus & Giroux, 1971), pp. 191, 282–283, 383. See also Cleanth Brooks, "Walker Percy and Modern Gnosticism," *Southern Review,* 13, No. 4 (1977), 677–687.

75. Ernst Troeltsch, *The Social Teaching of the Christian Churches,* II, trans. Olive Wyon (London: Allen & Unwin, 1931), p. 809.

76. Greven, *Protestant Temperament,* p. 313.

77. Ibid., p. 130.

78. Runciman, *Medieval Manichee,* p. 76.

79. Greven, *Protestant Temperament,* p. 131.

80. Herman Melville, *Billy Budd, Foretopman,* in *Selected Tales and Poems,* ed. Richard Chase (New York: Rinehart, 1956), p. 326. See also Lawrance Thompson, *Melville's Quarrel with God* (Princeton: Princeton University Press, 1952), p. 354.

81. Max Weber, *The Sociology of Religion* (London: Methuen, 1965), pp. 123–124 (italics mine).

82. Anthony J. DeLuca, *Freud and Future Religious Experience* (New York: Philosophical Library, 1976), p. 357.

83. Percy, *Love in the Ruins,* p. 403.

84. From the *Agrapha;* quoted in G. R. S. Mead, *Fragments of a Faith Forgotten* (New Hyde Park, N.Y.: University Books, 1962), p. 598.

85. Runciman, *Medieval Manichee,* p. 96; see also pp. 120, 150–152, 175, 176.

86. Winthrop S. Hudson, *Religion in America* (New York: Scribner's, 1965), p. 66.

87. Greven, *Protestant Temperament,* p. 30.

88. Ibid., p. 34.

89. Ibid., p. 138.

90. See Marty, *Righteous Empire,* p. 173.

91. Carl A. Raschke, *The Bursting of New Wineskins: Reflections on Religion and Culture at the End of Affluence* (Pittsburgh: Pickwick Press, 1978), p. 119.

92. Marty, *Righteous Empire,* p. 173.

93. Ellen Peck, *The Baby Trap,* (New York: Bernard Geis Associates, 1971).

94. See Pagels, *Gnostic Gospels,* pp. 49, 67.

95. Ibid., p. 67.

CHAPTER SEVEN

1. J. R. R. Tolkien, "On Fairy Stories," in *Tree and Leaf* (London: Unwin Books, 1964), p. 54.

2. Gilles Quispel, *Gnostic Studies* (Istanbul: Nederlands Historisch-Archaeologisch Instituut in het Nabije Oosten, 1974), I, p. 10 (italics mine).

3. Quoted in Elaine Pagels, *The Gnostic Gospels* (New York: Random House, 1979), pp. xix–xx.

4. Philip Greven, *The Protestant Temperament: Patterns of Child-Rearing, Religious Experience and the Self in Early America* (New York: Knopf, 1977), p. 259.

5. Calvin, *Institutes,* II, 2, 27. (Quoted from Augustine's *Sermones de verbis apostole* 10, shortly before the statement, "Of our own we have nothing but sin.")

6. Greven, *Protestant Temperament,* pp. 12, 13, 70 (italics mine).

7. See ibid., pp. 124, 299.

8. Karen Horney, M.D., *Our Inner Conflicts* (New York: W. W. Norton, 1966), pp. 98–99, 112.

9. See Vernon L Parrington, *The Romantic Revolution in America, 1800–1860,* Vol. II of *Main Currents in American Thought* (New York: Harcourt, Brace, 1959), p. 331.

10. Greven, *Protestant Temperament,* p. 79.

11. See Jerald C. Brauer, ed., *Reinterpretation in American Church History* (Chicago: University of Chicago Press, 1968), p. 61.

12. See Parrington, *Main Currents,* II, p. 318. See also pp. 319–330.

13. Ibid., p. 374.

14. William R. Hutchison, *The Modernist Impulse in American Protestantism* (Cambridge: Harvard University Press, 1976), p. 127.

15. Mark Twain, *Huckleberry Finn* (Bungay, Suffolk: Penguin Books, 1966), p. 302.

16. Greven, *Protestant Temperament,* pp. 259, 260, 300–303.

17. Matt., 13:24–30.

18. See Sidney E. Ahlstrom's article of the same title in Rodger Van Allen, ed., *American Religious Values and the Future of America* (Philadelphia: Fortress Press, 1978), p. 14. Ahlstrom holds that subjective experience was an essential of Puritanism from its beginning.

19. Joseph Haroutunian, ed. and trans., *Calvin: Commentaries,* Commentary on Jeremiah 24:7 (Philadelphia: Westminster Press, 1958), p. 229.

20. Sidney E. Mead, *The Lively Experiment: The Shaping of Christianity in America* (New York: Harper & Row, 1963), pp. 123–124 (italics mine).

21. Greven, *Protestant Temperament,* pp. 75–76.

22. Rev. 21:2, 9; 18:23; 22:17. See also John 3:29; Eph. 5:21–32.

23. Greven, *Protestant Temperament,* pp. 126, 137.

24. Ibid., pp. 147–148.

25. Harold Bloom, *A Map of Misreading* (New York: Oxford University Press, 1975), p. 24 (italics mine).

26. Harold Bloom, *The Ringers in the Tower* (Chicago: University of Chicago Press, 1971), p. 334.

27. Jean-Paul Sartre, *Being and Nothingness: Existentialism and Human Emotion* (New York: Philosophical Library, 1957), pp. 63, 90.

28. Arthur Koestler, *The Ghost in the Machine* (New York: Macmillan, 1967), p. 220.

29. Quoted in J. G. Gibbs, "Rudolf Bultmann and His Successors," *Scottish Journal of Theology,* 18, No. 4 (1965), pp. 403–404.

30. Pagels, *Gnostic Gospels,* p. 124.

31. Gilles Quispel, "Gnosis and Psychology," in *The Rediscovery of Gnosticism,* I, ed. Bentley Layton, Proceedings of the Yale Conference on Gnosticism, March 1978 (Leiden: E. J. Brill, 1980), pp. 21–23.

32. William A. Clebsch, *American Religious Thought* (Chicago: University of Chicago Press, 1973), pp. 175–176. Also Winthrop S. Hudson, *Religion in America* (New York: Scribner's, 1965), p. 361.

33. Greven, *Protestant Temperament,* p. 204.

34. Hutchison, *Modernist Impulse,* p. 21.

35. Parrington, *Main Currents,* II, p. 382.

36. Quoted in J. R. S. Mead, *Fragments of a Faith Forgotten* (New Hyde Park, N.Y.: University Books, 1962), p. 602.

37. See Quispel, *Gnostic Studies,* I, p. 228.

38. Parrington, *Main Currents,* II, p. 374.

39. Ibid., p. 376.

40. Henry David Thoreau, *Walden and Other Writings,* ed. Joseph Wood Krutch (New York: Bantam Books, 1977), p. 173 (italics mine).

41. Martin E. Marty, *Righteous Empire: The Protestant Experience in America* (New York: Dial Press, 1970), p. 118.

42. Mead, *The Lively Experiment,* p. 172.

43. Ibid., p. 136.

44. Hutchison, *Modernist Impulse,* p. 35 (italics mine).

45. Ibid., p. 97.

46. Marty, *Righteous Empire,* p. 177 (italics mine).

47. Hutchison, *Modernist Impulse,* p. 165.

48. Walter Rauschenbusch, *Christianity and the Social Crisis* (New York: Macmillan, 1912), p. 29.

49. Peter W. Williams, *Popular Religion in America* (Englewood Cliffs, N.J.: Prentice-Hall, 1980), pp. 138–139.

50. D. D. Williams, "Niebuhr and Liberalism," in *Reinhold Niebuhr: His Religious, Social and Political Thought,* ed. Charles W. Kegley and Robert W. Bretall (New York: Macmillan, 1961), p. 203.

51. Reinhold Niebuhr, *The Nature and Destiny of Man: A Christian Interpretation* (New York: Scribner's, 1955 [Gifford Lectures; one-volume edition]), I, pp. 59, 66, 74–92.

52. Hudson, *Religion in America,* p. 387. See also Charles Y. Glock and Robert N. Bellah, *The New Religious Consciousness* (Berkeley: University of California Press, 1976), p. 336.

53. John E. Biersdorf, "The Human Potential Movement and the Church," *Christianity and Crisis,* 35 (1975–1976), p. 56, quoted in Carl A. Raschke, *The Bursting of New Wineskins: Reflections on Religion and Culture at the End of Affluence* (Pittsburgh: Pickwick Press, 1978), p. 72 (italics mine). I am indebted to Dr. Raschke for his penetrating study of the movement. Also see Glock and Bellah, *New Religious Consciousness,* pp. 93–115.

54. Harvey Seifert, *Reality and Ecstasy* (Philadelphia: Westminster Press, 1974), p. 90.

55. Donald Berry, "Seeking a Theology of the Finite," *Christian Century,* 29 September 1982, pp. 953, 956.

56. Tom F. Driver, *Patterns of Grace: Human Experience as Word of God* (New York: Harper & Row, 1977), pp. 5, 14.

57. Irenaeus, *Against Heresies,* I:11:4.

58. Marty, *Righteous Empire,* p. 86.

59. Glock and Bellah, *New Religious Consciousness,* p. 214.

60. Ibid., pp. 214–215.

61. Ibid., pp. 151–153.

62. Herbert W. Richardson, *Toward an American Theology* (New York: Harper & Row, 1967), pp. 55–56.

63. Harvey Cox, *The Seduction of the Spirit* (New York: Simon & Schuster, 1973), pp. 222–223.

64. Will Herberg, ed., *The Writings of Martin Buber* (Cleveland: World, 1968), pp. 109, 235.

65. Helmut Koester, "The Structure of Early Christian Beliefs" in *Trajectories Through Early Christianity* (Philadelphia: Fortress, 1971), p. 231.

66. Pagels, *Gnostic Gospels*, p. 145.

67. Haroutunian, *Calvin: Commentaries*, Commentary on Isa. 2:1, p. 90.

68. John Calvin, *Commentary on the Letter of Saint Paul to the Ephesians*, CR, LXXIX, 203. Quoted by Paul L. Lehmann, *Ethics in a Christian Context* (New York: Harper & Row, 1963), p. 66.

69. Abraham Kuyper, *Lectures on Calvinism* (Grand Rapids: Eerdmans, 1964), pp. 102, 109 (italics mine).

70. John Lawson, *A Theological and Historical Introduction to the Apostolic Fathers* (New York: Macmillan, 1961), p. 10.

71. Marty, *Righteous Empire*, p. 153.

72. Mead, *The Lively Experiment*, p. 137.

73. Ernst Troeltsch, *The Social Teaching of The Christian Churches*, I, trans. Olive Wyon (London: Allen & Unwin, 1931), pp. 331ff., 341 (italics mine).

74. H. Richard Niebuhr, *The Social Sources of Denominationalism* (Hamden: Shoe String Press), p. 65. See Mead, *The Lively Experiment*, p. 55.

75. Brauer, *Reinterpretation*, p. 12.

76. John 15:16.

77. Brauer, *Reinterpretation*, p. 3.

78. Troeltsch, *Social Teaching*, II, p. 796 (italics mine).

79. Harvey Cox, *The Secular City: Socialization and Urbanization in Theological Perspective* (New York: Macmillan, 1965), pp. 156–157.

80. G. R. S. Mead, *Fragments of a Faith Forgotten* (New Hyde Park, N. Y.: University Books, 1962), p. xix.

81. Richardson, *Toward an American Theology*, pp. 120, 122. For an incisive discussion of Tillich on holiness and church, see A. J. McKelway, *The Systematic Theology of Paul Tillich* (Richmond, Va.: John Knox Press, 1964), pp. 202–209.

82. I Pet. 2:9. See also Ex. 19:6; Deut. 7:6, 14:2, 21; Luke 1:75; Heb. 12:10; I Pet. 1:15, 16, among many others.

83. Thomas J. J. Altizer, "Overt Language About the Death of God," *Christian Century*, 7–14 June 1978, p. 626.

84. Williams, *Popular Religion*, p. 199.

85. Carl A. Raschke, *The Interruption of Eternity: Modern Gnosticism and the Origins of the New Religious Consciousness* (Chicago: Nelson Hall, 1980), p. 243.

86. Mead, The *Lively Experiment,* pp. 112, 123. For a complete study of the Mercersburg school, see James Hastings Nichols, *Romanticism in American Theology* (Chicago: University of Chicago Press, 1961). See also Sidney E. Ahlstrom, *A Religious History of the American People* (New Haven: Yale University Press, 1972), pp. 616–621, note especially p. 620.

87. Robert T. Handy, *A History of the Churches in the United States and Canada* (New York: Oxford University Press, 1979), p. 259.

88. Benson Y. Landis, ed., *A Rauschenbusch Reader* (New York: Harper & Bros., 1957), pp. 43, 67.

89. Lehmann, *Ethics,* pp. 25, 47 (italics mine).

90. Matt. 13:33, King James Version.

CHAPTER EIGHT

1. I Cor. 8:1.

2. Elaine Pagels, *The Gnostic Gospels* (New York: Random House, 1979), p. 104.

3. Hans von Campenhausen, *The Fathers of the Greek Church,* trans. Stanley Godman (New York: Pantheon, 1959), p. 27.

4. John Herman Randall, *Hellenistic Ways of Deliverance and the Making of the Christian Synthesis* (New York: Columbia University Press, 1970), p. 200.

5. Calvin, *Institutes,* III, 21, 1.

6. The Westminster Confession of Faith, V:6, in *The Book of Confessions* (Philadelphia: General Assembly of the United Presbyterian Church in the U.S.A., 1967).

7. Ernst Troeltsch, *The Social Teaching of the Christian Churches,* II, trans. Olive Wyon (London: Allen & Unwin, 1931), p. 590.

8. Quoted in James W. Jones, *The Shattered Synthesis: New England Puritanism Before the Great Awakening* (New Haven: Yale University Press, 1973), p. 79.

9. Ibid., pp. 83–85.

10. Quoted in Clyde A. Holbrook, ed. *The Ethics of Jonathan Edwards* (Ann Arbor: University of Michigan Press, 1973), p. 185 (italics mine).

11. Jonathan Edwards, *The Works of President Edwards,* ed. Sereno Edwards Dwight (New York: 1829–30), 4:334. Quoted in William A. Clebsch, *American Religious Thought* (Chicago: University of Chicago Press, 1973), p. 29.

12. James Carse, *Jonathan Edwards and the Visibility of God* (New York: Scribner's, 1967), p. 184.

13. Quoted in Philip Greven, *The Protestant Temperament: Patterns of Child-Rearing, Religious Experience and the Self in Early America* (New York: Knopf, 1977), p. 117.

14. Quotation conflated from Irenaeus III:15:2 and II:16:4 by Pagels, *Gnostic Gospels,* p. 43.

15. Donald G. Bloesch, *The Invaded Church* (Waco, Tex.: Word Books, 1975).

16. From the *Agrapha;* quoted in G. R. S. Mead, *Fragments of a Faith Forgotten* (New Hyde Park, N.Y.: University Books, 1962), p. 597.

17. Martin E. Marty, *Righteous Empire: The Protestant Experience in America* (New York: Dial Press, 1970), p. 112.

18. Quoted in Vernon L. Parrington, *The Romantic Revolution in America, 1800–1860,* Vol. II of *Main Currents in American Thought* (New York: Harcourt, Brace, 1959), pp. 377–378 (italics mine).

19. Ralph Waldo Emerson, *Journals of Ralph Waldo Emerson,* ed. Edward Waldo Emerson and Waldo Emerson Forbes, vol. 8, p. 363; vol. 9, p. 215. Quoted in Parrington, *Main Currents,* pp. 390–391.

20. Troeltsch, *Social Teaching,* II, p. 795.

21. Quoted from Lyman Abbott in Mead, *The Lively Experiment,* p. 209, n. 56; see also p. 173 (italics mine).

22. Ibid., pp. 97, 104.

23. Eric Voegelin, *Order and History* (Baton Rouge: Louisiana State University Press, 1964), III, p. 278.

24. H. H. Gerth and C. Wright Mills, eds. and trans., *From Max Weber: Essays in Sociology* (New York: Oxford University Press, 1946), p. 305.

25. Max Weber, *The Sociology of Religion* (London: Methuen, 1965), pp. 148, 204–205, 220–221.

26. H. Richard Niebuhr, *The Social Sources of Denominationalism* (Hamden: Shoe String Press, 1954), p. 87.

27. Sidney E. Mead, *The Lively Experiment,* pp. 159–162; see also Marty, *Righteous Empire,* pp. 144ff., 169.

28. Marty, *Righteous Empire,* p. 228; see also Niebuhr, *Social Sources,* p. 76.

29. Margaret Laurence, *The Diviners* (Toronto: McClelland and Stewart, 1974), pp. 63, 89. See Kenneth C. Russell, "God and Church in the Fiction of Margaret Laurence," *Studies in Religion,* 7, No. 4 (1978), pp. 444–445.

30. Niebuhr, *Social Sources,* pp. 31–32.

31. Hans Jonas, "Delimitation of the Gnostic Phenomenon—Typological and Historical," in *Le origini dello gnosticismo,* ed. Ugo Bianchi. Proceedings of the Colloquio di Messina, April 1966 (Leiden: E. J. Brill, 1967), p. 98.

32. Weber, *Sociology,* p. 227.

33. Quoted in Marty, *Righteous Empire,* front matter.

34. Quoted in Marty, ibid., p. 88.

35. Jerald C. Brauer, ed., *Reinterpretation in American Church History* (Chicago: University of Chicago Press, 1968), p. 136.

36. Marty, *Righteous Empire,* front matter.

37. A familiar quotation from G. K. Chesterton, used by Sidney E. Mead as title to his article in *Church History,* 36, No. 3 (September 1967) and as title to his later book (New York: Harper & Row, 1975).

38. Marty, *Righteous Empire,* p. 238 (italics mine).

39. See Dennis P. McCann, *Christian Realism and Liberation Theology* (Maryknoll, N.Y.: Orbis Books, 1981), especially pp. 106–110.

40. Robert N. Bellah, "Civil Religion in America," in *American Civil Religion* ed. Russell E. Richey and Donald G. Jones (New York: Harper & Row, 1974), p. 40.

41. Greven, *Protestant Temperament*, p. 355.

42. Ibid., p. 347.

43. Jonas, "Delimitation," p. 98.

44. Greven, *Protestant Temperament*, p. 193.

45. Marty, *Righteous Empire*, p. 118.

46. William R. Hutchison, *The Modernist Impulse in American Protestantism* (Cambridge: Harvard University Press, 1976), pp. 86, 87, 95.

47. Walter Rauschenbusch, *Christianity and the Social Crisis* (New York: Macmillan, 1912), p. 127.

48. Sidney E. Mead, "Reinterpretation in American Church History," in Brauer, *Reinterpretation*, p. 176.

49. Weber, *Sociology*, p. 121.

50. Richard Shaull, "The Death and Resurrection of the American Dream," in Gustavo Gutiérrez and Richard Shaull, *Liberation and Change*, ed. Ronald H. Stone (Atlanta: John Knox Press, 1977), p. 157.

51. Harvey Cox, *The Secular City: Secularization and Urbanization in Theological Perspective* (New York: Macmillan, 1965), pp. 44, 156, 157, 125–148, 158.

52. Harvey Cox, *Religion in the Secular City: Toward a Postmodern Theology* (New York: Simon & Schuster, 1984), pp. 173, 196.

53. von Campenhausen, *Fathers*, p. 24.

54. Schubert M. Ogden, *Christ Without Myth: A Study Based upon the Theology of Rudolf Bultmann* (London: William Collins, 1962), pp. 31ff.

55. Colin Gunton, "The Knowledge of God According to Two Process Theologians: A Twentieth-Century Gnosticism," *Religious Studies*, 2 (1975), p. 95.

56. A. J. McKelway, *The Systematic Theology of Paul Tillich* (Richmond, Va.: John Knox Press, 1964), p. 25. See also pp. 101–102.

57. Pagels, *Gnostic Gospels*, p. 33.

58. Weber, *Sociology*, p. 124.

59. See Paul L. Lehmann, *The Transfiguration of Politics* (New York: Harper & Row, 1975), p. 289. Lehmann's work represents a serious attempt to understand, revise and appropriate Liberation theology in light of the biblical witness and, in particular, in light of the Transfiguration of Jesus Christ.

60. Irenaeus, *Against Heresies*, I:13:6, in Pagels, *Gnostic Gospels*, p. 21.

CHAPTER NINE

1. Hans Jonas, *The Gnostic Religion* (Boston: Beacon Press, 1963), pp. 25–26.

2. Kilian McDonnell, *John Calvin, the Church and the Eucharist* (Princeton: Princeton University Press, 1967), p. 182. See Calvin, *Institutes of the Christian Religion*, II, trans. Henry Beveridge (Grand Rapids; Eerdmans, 1953), II, 15, 2.

3. François Wendel, *Calvin*, trans. Philip Mairet (London: William Collins, 1963), p. 353.

4. Jer. 6:16.

5. See McDonnell, *John Calvin,* p. 169.

6. Max Weber, *The Protestant Ethic and the Spirit of Capitalism,* trans. Talcott Parsons (New York: Scribner's, 1958), pp. 104–105.

7. Quoted in Lawrance Thompson, *Melville's Quarrel with God* (Princeton: Princeton University Press, 1952), p. 2.

8. Emily Dickinson, *The Complete Poems of Emily Dickinson,* ed. Thomas H. Johnson (Boston: Little, Brown, 1960), No. 502, pp. 243–244.

9. Quoted from John Weiss in Vernon L. Parrington, *The Romantic Revolution in America, 1800–1860,* Vol. II of *Main Currents in American Thought* (New York: Harcourt, Brace, 1959), p. 407; see also pp. 410, 413.

10. William R. Hutchison, *The Modernist Impulse in American Protestantism* (Cambridge: Harvard University Press, 1976), p. 22.

11. Parrington, *Main Currents,* II, p. 383; see also pp. 380–381 as well as Hutchison, *Modernist Impulse,* p. 30.

12. Perry Miller, ed., *The American Transcendentalists: Their Prose and Poetry* (New York: Doubleday, 1957), p. ix.

13. Karl Löwith, *From Hegel to Nietzsche: The Revolution in Nineteenth-Century Thought,* trans. David E. Green (London: Constable, 1965), p. 20.

14. II Cor. 5:19. See Hutchison, *Modernist Impulse,* p. 113.

15. Hutchison, *Modernist Impulse,* pp. 223–224 (italics mine).

16. Quoted in Hutchison, ibid., p. 201; see also p. 201, n. 28.

17. Ibid., pp. 205–206.

18. Sidney E. Ahlstrom, *A Religious History of the American People* (New Haven: Yale University Press, 1972), p. 946 (italics mine).

19. Hutchison, *Modernist Impulse,* p. 308.

20. Harvey Cox, *The Secular City: Secularization and Urbanization in Theological Perspective* (New York: Macmillan, 1965), pp. 185, 186, 222, 225.

21. Frederick Herzog, "Reformation Today," *Christian Century,* 27 October 1982, p. 1079.

22. Colin Gunton, "The Knowledge of God According to Two Process Theologians: A Twentieth Century Gnosticism," *Religious Studies,* 2 (1975), p. 95.

23. Hutchison, *Modernist Impulse,* pp. 121, 221, 229.

24. For the medieval background leading to the practice of an infrequent Eucharist, see J. A. Jungmann, *The Mass of the Roman Rite* (New York: Benziger Brothers, 1955), II, pp. 359–367.

25. Walker Percy, *Love in the Ruins* (New York: Farrar, Straus & Giroux, 1971), p. 400.

26. Marty, *Righteous Empire,* p. 216.

27. Calvin, *Institutes,* IV, 18, 18.

28. Jungmann, *Mass of the Roman Rite,* II, p. 38.

29. See A. K. Robertson, "The Individual Cup: Its Use at Holy Communion," *Liturgical Review,* 8, no. 2 (November 1978), pp. 2–12.

30. Paul Lehmann, *Ethics in a Christian Context* (New York: Harper & Row, 1963), p. 65.

31. A. J. McKelway, *The Systematic Theology of Paul Tillich* (Richmond, Va.: John Knox Press, 1964), pp. 239–240 (italics mine).

32. Herbert W. Richardson, *Toward an American Theology* (New York: Harper & Row, 1967), pp. 116–118.

33. Ibid., p. 108.

34. Ahlstrom, *Religious History,* p. 954.

35. Quoted by Marty in *Reinterpretation in American Church History* (Chicago, University of Chicago Press, 1968), p. 201.

CHAPTER TEN

1. See Martin Buber, *The Eclipse of God,* trans. Stanley Godman (New York: Harper & Bros., 1952), pp. 113–114.

2. Philip Greven, *The Protestant Temperament: Patterns of Child-Rearing, Religious Experience and the Self in Early America* (New York: Knopf, 1977), pp. 132–133.

3. Margaret Atwood, *Survival: A Thematic Guide to Canadian Literature* (Toronto: House of Anansi Press, 1972), pp. 32–33.

4. For Sidney Ahlstrom's views on the subject, see his article of the same title in *American Religious Values and the Future of America,* ed., Rodger Van Allen (Philadelphia: Fortress Press, 1978), p. 3.

5. *Wall Street Journal,* 5 May 1981, p. 1; see also *US News & World Report,* 30 March 1981, p. 8.

6. Margaret Laurence, "The Merchant of Heaven," *The Tomorrow-Tamer and Other Stories* (Toronto: McClelland & Stewart, 1984), pp. 67, 74. See also Kenneth C. Russell, "God and Church in the Fiction of Margaret Laurence," *Studies in Religion,* 7, No. 4 (1978), 435–446.

7. George F. Kennan, *The Nuclear Delusion: Soviet-American Relations in the Atomic Age* (New York: Pantheon Books, 1982), p. 206.

8. Ernst Troeltsch, *The Social Teaching of the Christian Churches,* II, trans. Olive Wyon (London: Allen & Unwin, 1931), p. 796.

9. William R. Hutchison, *The Modernist Impulse in American Protestantism* (Cambridge: Harvard University Press, 1976), p. 37.

10. e. e. cummings, "no time ago," *Xaipe,* in *Poems 1923–1954* (New York: Harcourt Brace, 1954), p. 455.

11. Gal. 6:7.

12. Rev. 19:15; Rom. 1:18.

13. See Winthrop S. Hudson, *Religion in America* (New York: Scribner's, 1965), pp. 371–372.

14. Steven Runciman, *The Medieval Manichee* (Cambridge: Cambridge University Press, 1960), p. 132.

15. Quoted from sermon in Washington, D.C., 1952. Martin E. Marty, *Righ-*

teous Empire: The Protestant Experience in America (New York: Dial Press, 1970), p. 258.

16. *Montreal Gazette,* 14 March 1983.

17. "An Approach for Theological Affirmation" in Peter L. Berger and Richard John Neuhaus, eds., *Against the World for the World* (New York: Seabury Press, 1976), theme 10, p. 4.

18. Sidney E. Mead, *The Lively Experiment: The Shaping of Christianity in America* (New York: Harper & Row, 1963), pp. 141, 142. See also Marty, *Righteous Empire,* p. 265.

19. See Herbert W. Richardson's excellent article, "Civil Religion in Theological Perspective," in *American Civil Religion,* ed. Russell E. Richey and Donald G. Jones (New York: Harper & Row, 1974), pp. 161–184.

20. Louisa May Alcott, lines from journal, in Martha Saxton, *Louisa May: A Modern Biography of Louisa May Alcott* (Boston: Houghton Mifflin, 1977), p. 141.

21. Tom Wolfe, "The Me Decade and the Third Great Awakening," *Mauve Gloves & Madmen, Clutter & Vine* (New York: Bantam Books, 1977), pp. 111–147, esp. pp. 129, 145–147.

22. J. G. Gibbs, "Rudolf Bultmann and His Successors," *Scottish Journal of Theology,* 18, No. 4 (1965), p. 403.

23. Herbert W. Richardson, *Toward an American Theology* (New York: Scribner's, 1965), pp. 109–111; see also pp. 158–159.

24. Jer. 18:12–16.

25. See H. Richard Niebuhr, *The Social Sources of Denominationalism* (Hamden: Shoe String Press, 1954), pp. 86–87.

26. Rosemary R. Reuther, "Women's Liberation and Reconciliation with the Earth," in *Conversations* (Graymoor Garrison, N.Y.: Graymoor Institute), December 1971, p. 10.

27. Wolfe, "The Me Decade," p. 141.

28. Erica Jong, *How to Save Your Own Life* (Winnipeg: New American Library of Canada, 1978).

29. Jim Gardner, "Narcissism in Contemporary Literature," *Katallagete,* 8, no. 2 (Spring 1983), p. 17. See William Faulkner, *The Wild Palms* (New York: Vintage Books, 1939).

30. Max Weber, *The Protestant Ethic and the Spirit of Capitalism,* trans. Talcott Parsons (New York: Scribner's, 1958). See especially pp. 105–107.

31. Marty, *Righteous Empire,* p. 152. See also pp. 149–150.

32. Ahlstrom, "American Religious Values," p. 21 (italics mine).

33. See Carl A. Raschke, *The Bursting of New Wineskins: Reflections on Religion and Culture at the End of Affluence* (Pittsburgh: Pickwick Press, 1978), pp. 92f.

34. Quoted in Marty, *Righteous Empire,* pp. 207–208.

35. Karen Horney, M.D., *Our Inner Conflicts* (New York: W. W. Norton, 1966), pp. 99–112.

36. Buber, *Eclipse of God,* pp. 117–118 (italics mine).

37. Elaine Pagels, *The Gnostic Gospels* (New York: Random House, 1979), p. 102.

38. Robert N. Bellah, *Beyond Belief: Essays on Religion in a Post-Traditional World* (New York: Harper & Row, 1976), pp. 233–234 (italics mine).

39. See Marty, *Righteous Empire,* p. 208.

40. Pagels, *Gnostic Gospels,* p. 25.

41. *Montreal Gazette,* 9 March 1983, p. H–8; *Montreal Gazette,* 11 March 1983, p. B-3.

42. Søren Kierkegaard, *Fear and Trembling,* in *Fear and Trembling* and *The Sickness unto Death,* trans. Walter Lowrie (New York: Anchor Books, 1955), p. 65.

43. Emily Dickinson, *The Complete Poems of Emily Dickinson,* ed. Thomas H. Johnson (Boston: Little, Brown, 1960), No. 293, p. 137.

44. Alfred North Whitehead, *Adventures of Ideas* (New York: Macmillan, 1933), p. 218.

45. Quoted in Marty, *Righteous Empire,* p. 259.

46. Peter W. Williams, *Popular Religion in America* (Englewood Cliffs, N.J.: Prentice-Hall, 1980), pp. 206–208.

47. C. Peter Wagner, "Confused About Church Growth?" *Church Growth Canada,* 2, No. 3 (Winter 1975), (Regina, Saskatchewan), p. 3.

48. Donald A. MacGavran, *Understanding Church Growth* (Grand Rapids: Eerdmans, 1970), p. 62.

49. Gal. 3:28.

50. C. Peter Wagner, *Your Church Can Grow* (Glendale, Calif.: Regal Books, 1976), p. 55.

51. Quoted in Marty, *Righteous Empire,* p. 255.

52. James Wolfe, "Three Congregations," in *The New Religious Consciousness,* ed. Charles Y. Glock and Robert N. Bellah (Berkeley: University of California Press, 1976), pp. 231–233.

53. See Ernst Troeltsch, *Social Teaching,* p. 796.

54. H. Richard Niebuhr, *Radical Monotheism and Western Culture* (New York: Harper & Row, 1960), p. 32. David Miller, *The New Polytheism* (New York: Harper & Row, 1974), pp. ix, 2, 11. For this contrast between Niebuhr and Miller, I am entirely indebted to Raschke, *New Wineskins,* pp. 77–79.

55. See Pagels, *Gnostic Gospels,* p. 25.

56. Williams, *Popular Religion,* pp. 210–211.

57. Quoted in Pagels, *Gnostic Gospels,* p. 129.

58. "Report on the Evangelical Women's Caucus," *Christian Century,* 29 (September 1982), p. 959.

59. Peter L. Berger, Brigitte Berger, and Hansfried Kellner, *The Homeless Mind* (New York: Random House, 1973).

60. Harold Warlick, "Loneliness: Peril and Promise of the Communities of Faith," *Harvard Divinity Bulletin,* 9, No. 1 (October–November 1978), p. 12.

61. George Grant, *Lament for a Nation* (Toronto: McClelland & Stewart, 1965).

62. Winthrop S. Hudson, *Religion in America* (New York: Scribner's, 1965), p. 379.

63. Ibid., p. 376.

64. *The Eucharistic Liturgy of Taizé,* intro. Max Thurian (London: Faith Press, 1962), p. 1.

CHAPTER ELEVEN

1. Steven Runciman, *The Medieval Manichee* (Cambridge: Cambridge University Press, 1960), p. 16.

2. Gilles Quispel, *Gnostic Studies* (Istanbul: Nederlands Historisch-Archaeologisch Instituut in het Nabije Oosten, 1974), I, p. 12.

3. Walter Bauer, *Orthodoxy and Heresy in Earliest Christianity,* trans. by a team from the Philadelphia Seminary on Christian Origins (Philadelphia: Fortress Press, 1971), p. 59, n. 57.

4. Runciman, *Medieval Manichee,* pp. 136–137.

5. Eph. 6:12.

6. John Calvin, *Calvin's Commentaries: The Second Epistle of Paul to the Corinthians,* trans. T. A. Smail (Grand Rapids: Eerdmans, 1964), 2 Corinthians 13:5, p. 173.

7. Jer. 1:9 (italics mine).

8. Karl Barth, *Church Dogmatics,* I/1, ed. G. W. Bromiley and T. F. Torrance, (Edinburgh: T. & T. Clark, 1936), p. 101.

9. II Cor. 4:7.

10. Barth, *Church Dogmatics,* I/1, p. 106.

11. Jonathan Swift, quoted in Arthur Koestler, *The Ghost in the Machine* (New York: Macmillan, 1967), p. 339.

12. Julian Huxley, *Man in the Modern World* (New York: Harper, 1964), p. 13.

13. Ibid., p. 267.

14. Ps. 73:23. See Barth's sermon, "Nevertheless I Am Continually with Thee," *Deliverance to the Captives* (New York: Harper & Bros., 1961), pp. 13–19.

15. Thomas Wolfe, *Look Homeward, Angel* (New York: Scribner's, 1952), p. 1.

16. Matt. 7:9–10.

17. John Calvin, *Commentary on Romans,* 6:6. Quoted in François Wendel, *Calvin,* trans. Philip Mairet (London: William Collins, 1963), p. 244.

18. I Pet. 4:19.

19. John 1:3.

20. Gen. 1:31.

21. Koestler, *Ghost in the Machine,* p. 163.

22. James 4:1–2.

23. Isa. 40:15.

24. Job 12:23 (italics mine).

25. Luke 1:52–53.

26. William Faulkner, *The Sound and the Fury,* in *The Sound and the Fury* and *As*

I Lay Dying (New York: Random House, 1946), pp. 312–313. See also Thomas Merton, "Time and the Unburdening and the Recollection of the Lamb: The Easter Service in Faulkner's *The Sound and the Fury*," *Katallagete,* 4, no. 4 (Summer 1973), pp. 7–15.

27. Heb. 4:16.

28. John 14:26.

29. *The Book of Forms* (Don Mills, Ontario: Presbyterian Publications, 1981), p. 125.

30. The Düsseldorf Theses (Theses 1, 5 [1933]) in Wilhelm Niesel, *Reformed Symbolics* (Edinburgh: Oliver and Boyd, 1962), pp. 355–356.

31. David L. Migliore, "Christology and New Testament Studies," *Princeton Seminary Bulletin,* 59, No. 2 (1966), p. 23.

32. John Calvin, *Institutes of the Christian Religion,* IV, 8, 13.

33. Eph. 3:9, 10.

34. Barth, *Church Dogmatics,* II/1, p. 17 (italics mine).

35. Cited in Elaine Pagels, *The Gnostic Gospels* (New York: Random House, 1979), p. 32.

36. Quoted in John Lawson, *A Theological and Historical Introduction to the Apostolic Fathers* (New York: Macmillan, 1961), precept 11, p. 242.

37. For a discussion of the Apostles' Creed's development and use, see John Herman Randall, *Hellenistic Ways of Deliverance and the Making of the Christian Synthesis* (New York: Columbia University Press, 1970), p. 161.

38. Hans Conzelmann, *History of Primitive Christianity,* trans. John E. Steely (Nashville: Abingdon Press, 1973), p. 125.

39. G. S. M. Walker, "Calvin and the Church," *Scottish Journal of Theology,* 16, No. 4 (1963), p. 388. See also Calvin, *Institutes,* IV, 10, 27.

40. Walker, "Calvin and the Church," p. 372.

41. Quoted in Niesel, *Reformed Symbolics,* Articles 3 and 6, pp. 357–360.

42. Eph.4:14.

43. Eduard Schweizer, "Two New Testament Creeds Compared," in *Curent Issues in New Testament Interpretation,* ed. William Klassen and Grayden F. Snyder (London: SCM Press, 1962).

44. Calvin, *Institutes,* IV, 8, 9.

45. T. F. Torrance, "The Mission of the Church," *Scottish Journal of Theology,* 19, No. 2 (1966), pp. 131–132.

46. Thesis 6, quoted in Niesel, *Reformed Symbolics,* p. 355.

47. Irenaeus, *Against Heresies* III: 26: 5.

48. See Robert R. Williams's discussion of Church discipline in *A Guide to the Teachings of the Early Church Fathers* (Grand Rapids: Eerdmans, 1960), p. 21. Also Johannes Quasten, *Patrology,* I (Utrecht-Antwerp: Spectrum, 1966), pp. 66, 68, 283.

49. Roland H. Bainton, *The Medieval Church* (Princeton: D. Van Nostrand, 1962), p. 83.

50. Acts 6:2–4.

51. John 16:14.

52. Luke 3:22.

53. Rom. 9:33; see also I Pet. 2:8.

54. Heb. 12:1.

55. John 1:29.

56. II Cor. 5:1.

57. Heb. 12:28.

58. Eph.4:15.

59. Quoted in Philip Greven, *The Protestant Temperament: Patterns of Child-Rearing, Religious Experiences and the Self in Early America* (New York: Knopf, 1977), pp. 172, 230 (italics mine).

60. Barth, *Church Dogmatics,* IV/2, pp. 638, 640. Quoted in Horace T. Allen, Jr., *A Handbook for the Lectionary* (Philadelphia: Geneva Press, 1980), p. 21.

61. Walker Percy, *Love in the Ruins* (New York: Farrar, Straus & Giroux, 1971), p. 157.

62. I Pet. 5:9–10.

63. II Cor. 4:8–9.

64. I Thess. 3:3.

65. Heb. 13:13–14 (italics mine).

66. Ernst Troeltsch, *The Social Teaching of the Christian Churches,* II, trans. Olive Wyon (London: Allen & Unwin, 1931), p. 820.

67. Quoted from Gramsci's *Notebooks* in George Novack, *Pragmatism vs. Marxism* (New York: Pathfinder Press, 1975), p. 9.

68. Jer. 1:10.

69. I Cor. 1:27, 28.

70. Karl Barth, *The Epistle to the Romans,* trans. Edwyn C. Hoskyns (London: Oxford University Press, 1953), p. 375.

71. I Pet. 2:9–10.

72. Carl A. Raschke, *The Bursting of New Wineskins: Reflections on Religion and Culture at the End of Affluence* (Pittsburgh: Pickwick Press, 1978), p. 90.

73. Deut. 24:19–22.

74. Deut. 15:9–10.

75. Hos. 4:1. See a discussion of this connection in J. B. Bauer, ed., *Encyclopedia of Biblical Theology,* I (London: Sheed & Ward, 1970), p. 473.

76. Hos. 5:12.

77. Luke 6:20, 24.

78. Luke 11:42.

79. Ibid.

80. Luke 12:15–21.

81. Luke 18:22, 23.

82. Luke 12:24–33.

83. Luke 16:19–31.

84. Matt. 25:31–46.

85. Matt. 6:24.

86. W. H. Auden, "Postcript: The Almighty Dollar," in *The Dyer's Hand and Other Essays* (New York: Random House, 1962), p. 336.

87. Gustavo Gutiérrez, "Freedom and Salvation: A Political Problem," in Gustavo Gutiérrez and Richard Shaull, *Liberation and Change,* ed. Ronald H. Stone (Atlanta: John Knox Press, 1977), p. 57. See also Ismael Garcia, Review Article, *The Journal of Religion,* 59, no. 1 (January 1979), p. 108.

88. Quoted in Pagels, *The Gnostic Gospels,* p. 87.

89. Paul L. Lehmann, *The Transfiguration of Politics* (New York: Harper & Row, 1975), p. 289.

90. George F. Kennan, *The Nuclear Delusion: Soviet-American Relations in the Atomic Age* (New York: Pantheon Books, 1982), p. 207.

91. II Tim. 3:12.

92. II Tim. 2:3.

93. II Tim. 2:11–13.

94. Augustine, *City of God* XVIII, 51.2, in *Basic Writings of Saint Augustine,* ed. Whitney J. Oates (New York: Random House, 1948). See also J. K. S. Reid's article "Vatican Council II and the People of God," *Reformed and Presbyterian World,* 29, No. 1 (1966–1967), pp. 13–14.

95. Barth, *Romans,* pp. 335–336.

96. Niesel, *Reformed Symbolics,* p. 255.

97. Rev. 22:17 (italics mine).

98. Arthur Darby Nock, *Early Gentile Christianity and Its Hellenistic Background* (New York: Harper & Row, 1964), pp. 69–70.

99. John 16:16.

100. Henry S. Bettenson, ed. and trans., *The Early Christian Fathers* (London: Oxford University Press, 1956), pp. 121–122 (italics mine).

101. Ps. 137:4–6.

102. Quoted in Frederick Herzog, *Theology of the Liberating Word* (Nashville: Abingdon Press, 1971), p. 107.

103. Eph. 2:14.

104. Joachim Jeremias, *Infant Baptism in the First Four Centuries,* trans. David Cairns (London: SCM Press, 1960), p. 84.

105. George S. Yule, "The Incarnation and the Unity of the Church," *Reformed World,* 37, No. 5 (1983), p. 152.

106. Irenaeus, *Against Heresies,* II:33:2, quoted in Jeremias, *Infant Baptism in the First Four Centuries,* p. 73.

107. The Heidelberg Catechism, Answer to Q. 1, *Book of Confessions* (Philadelphia: General Assembly of the United Presbyterian Church in the U.S.A., 1967).

108. Kilian McDonnell, *John Calvin, the Church, and the Eucharist* (Princeton: Princeton University Press, 1967), pp. 171–172.

109. Deut, 12:8.

110. Exod. 34:10.

111. Matt. 16:24–25 (italics mine).

112. I Cor. 13:4–7.

113. I Cor. 13:13.

114. I Cor. 13;8–9. See Nock, *Early Gentile Christianity*, pp. 88–89.

115. I Cor. 14:12.

116. Gal. 6:3–5.

117. Gal. 5:26.

118. I Pet. 1:21 (italics mine).

119. I Pet. 1:22–23 (italics mine).

120. I Pet. 2:1.

121. I Pet. 2:9.

122. I John 3:18.

123. Peter L. Berger and Richard J. Neuhaus, eds., *Against the World for the World* (New York: Seabury Press, 1976), pp. 1, 3.

124. Paul L. Lehmann, *Ethics in a Christian Context* (New York: Harper & Row, 1963), p. 57.

125. Eph. 2:19 (italics mine); see also Gal. 6:10.

126. Thomas Merton, *Seasons of Celebration* (New York: Farrar, Straus & Giroux, 1965), p. 216.

127. John 15:5.

128. Col. 2:6–7 (italics mine).

129. Col. 2:8–10.

130. John 1:14.

131. Lehmann, *Ethics in a Christian Context,* pp. 67–68.

132. Eph. 4:15, 26 (altered wording).

133. II Pet. 2:17–21 (italics mine).

134. Dt. 26:5; Lev. 18:3.

135. Is. 1:1–10 (italics mine). See also Douglas Jones, "Exposition of Isaiah Chapter One Verses Ten to Seventeen," *Scottish Journal of Theology,* 18, No. 4 (1965), p. 470.

136. Torrance, "Mission," p. 119.

137. Deut. 32:10.

138. Matt. 3:9.

139. Matt. 25:31–46.

140. James 2:1–13. See also James 5:1–6; I Tim. 6:6–10, 17–19. An excellent article on the subject can be found in the *Scottish Journal of Theology,* 18, No. 2 (1965) by C. E. B. Cranfield, "The Message of James." See especially pp. 190–191.

141. Torrance, "Mission," p. 133. For John Calvin's strong ecumenical position, see *Institutes,* IV, 1, 3, and 12; also Wendel, *Calvin,* pp. 101, 310–311.

142. See chapter 2, p. 57, n. 110 (quote from Basilides), this work.

143. See R. A. Norris, *God and World in Early Christian Theology* (New York: Seabury Press, 1965), p. 86.

144. Feodor Dostoevsky, *Crime and Punishment,* trans. Constance Garnett (Cleveland: Fine Editions Press, 1947), p. 32. See also Eduard Thurneysen, *Dostoevsky,* trans. Keith R. Crim (Richmond, Va.: John Knox Press, 1964), p. 47.

145. Matt. 4:45.

146. Barth, *Church Dogmatics,* IV/3, Second Half, p. 774.

147. Karen Horney, M.D., *Neurosis and Human Growth: The Struggle Toward Self-Realization* (New York: W. W. Norton, 1950), p. 377.

148. I John 1:1–3.

149. I Cor. 13:12.

150. Will Herberg, ed., *The Writings of Martin Buber* (Cleveland: World, 1968), p. 80.

151. Ernst Troeltsch, *Die Bedeutung der Geschichtlichkeit Jesu fur den Glauben* (Tübingen: J. C. B. Mohr, 1911), p. 25. Quoted in D. L. Deegan, "The Ritschlian School: The Essence of Christianity and Karl Barth," *Scottish Journal of Theology,* 16, No. 4 (1963), pp. 409–410.

152. Barth, *Church Dogmatics,* I/2, 17, p. 318.

153. Acts 2:42, 46; 20:7. See Oscar Cullmann, *Early Christian Worship,* trans. A. Stewart Todd and James B. Torrance (London: SCM Press, 1969), p. 12.

154. Luke 24:30–35.

155. René Filson, *Jean Cocteau, an Investigation into His Films and Philosophy* (New York: Crown, 1969).

156. Calvin, *Institutes,* IV, 17, 42.

157. Calvin, *Corpus Reformatorum* 17:311, 312, trans. by McDonnell, in *John Calvin,* p. 188.

158. "The Order for the Burial of the Dead," *The Book of Common Prayer* (New York: Oxford, 1944).

159. Merton, *Seasons of Celebration,* p. 45.

160. Herberg, *Martin Buber,* pp. 270–271; see also pp. 109, 264.

161. See J. G. Davies, *The Early Christian Church* (Garden City, N.Y.: Doubleday, 1967), pp. 57–63.

162. See Peter W. Williams, *Popular Religion in America* (Englewood Cliffs, N.J.: Prentice-Hall, 1980), pp. 212–214.

163. Isa. 58:13, 14. See also Jer. 6:16.

164. Walker Percy, *Love in the Ruins* (New York: Farrar, Straus & Giroux, 1971), p. 254. See also Percy's development of a similar theme in *The Moviegoers* (New York: Knopf, 1962). In that novel, the character Kate Cutrer, "longs to be an anyone who is anywhere," p. 190.

165. Martin Luther, *W.A.,* 2, 750, quoted in Lehmann, *Ethics,* p. 65.

166. "The Form of Solemnization of Matrimony," *The Book of Common Prayer.*

167. Ellen Peck, *The Baby Trap,* (New York: Bernard Geis, 1971), pp. 8–9. See also Raschke, *New Wineskins,* p. 129.

168. Song of Sol. 7:1–3.

169. Acts 2:46.

170. Isa. 49:6.

EPILOGUE

1. A. Cleaveland Coxe, "Introductory Note to Irenaeus *Against Heresies*," in *The Ante-Nicene Fathers: Translations of the Writings of the Fathers Down to A.D. 325*, Vol. 1, ed. Alexander Roberts and James Donaldson (Grand Rapids: Eerdmans, 1977), p. 310.

2. Irenaeus, *Against Heresies*, I: Preface.

3. Irenaeus, *Against Heresies*, II:28:title.

4. Irenaeus, *Against Heresies*, V: Preface.

Bibliography

Alhstrom, Sidney E. "American Religious Values and the Future of America." In *American Religious Values and the Future of America*. Ed. Rodger Van Allen. Philadelphia: Fortress Press, 1978.

———. *A Religious History of the American People*. New Haven: Yale University Press, 1972.

Allen, Horace T., Jr. *A Handbook for the Lectionary*. Philadelphia: Geneva Press, 1980.

Altizer, Thomas J. J. "A New History and a New but Ancient God? A Review Essay." *American Academy of Religion Journal*, 43, No. 4 (1975), pp. 757–764.

———. "Overt Language About the Death of God." *Christian Century*, 14 June 1978, pp. 624–627.

Ammons, A. R. *Collected Poems: 1951–1971*. New York: Norton, 1972.

———. *Sphere: The Form of a Motion*. New York: Norton, 1974.

Atiya, A. S. *A History of Eastern Christianity*. London: Methuen, 1968.

Atwood, Margaret. *Survival: A Thematic Guide to Canadian Literature*. Toronto: House of Anansi Press, 1972.

Auden, W. H., "Postcript: The Almighty Dollar." In *The Dyer's Hand and Other Essays*. New York: Random House, 1962.

Augustine. *City of God*, XVIII. In *Basic Writings of Saint Augustine*. Vol. II. Ed. Whitney J. Oates. New York: Random House, 1948.

———. *The Confessions*, I. In *Basic Writings of Saint Augustine*. Vol. 1. Ed. Whitney J. Oates. New York: Random House, 1948.

———. *De baptismo contra Donatistas.* In *Nicene and Post-Nicene Fathers of the Christian Church,* IV. Trans. J. R. King. Ed. Philip Schaff. Grand Rapids, Mich.: Eerdmans, 1983.

Ayer, Joseph Cullen, Jr. *Sourcebook for Ancient Church History.* New York: AMS Press, 1913/1970.

Bainton, Roland H. *The Medieval Church.* Princeton, N.J.: D. Van Nostrand, 1962.

Barth, Karl. *Church Dogmatics,* I/1. *The Doctrine of the Word of God.* Ed. G. W. Bromiley and T. F. Torrance. Edinburgh: T. & T. Clark, 1936.

———. *Church Dogmatics,* II/1. *The Doctrine of God.* Ed. G. W. Bromiley and T. F. Torrance. Edinburgh: T. & T. Clark, 1957.

———. *Church Dogmatics,* IV/1. *The Doctrine of Reconciliation.* Ed. G. W. Bromiley and T. F. Torrance. Edinburgh: T. & T. Clark, 1958.

———. *Church Dogmatics,* IV/2. *The Doctrine of Reconciliation.* Ed. G. W. Bromiley and T. F. Torrance. Edinburgh: T. & T. Clark, 1958.

———. *Church Dogmatics,* IV/3, 2. *The Doctrine of Reconciliation.* Ed. G. W. Bromiley and T. F. Torrance. Edinburgh: T. & T. Clark, 1965.

———. *Deliverance to the Captives.* New York: Harper & Bros., 1961.

———. *The Epistle to the Romans.* Trans. Edwyn C. Hoskyns. London: Oxford University Press, 1953.

Bauer, J. B., ed. *Encyclopedia of Biblical Theology.* Vol. II. London: Sheed & Ward, 1970.

Bauer, Walter. *Orthodoxy and Heresy in Earliest Christianity.* Trans. by a team from the Philadelphia Seminary on Christian Origins. Philadelphia: Fortress Press, 1971.

Bellah, Robert N. "Civil Religion in America. In *American Civil Religion.* Ed. Russell E. Richey and Donald G. Jones. New York: Harper & Row, 1974.

———. *Beyond Belief: Essays on Religion in a Post-Traditional World.* New York: Harper & Row, 1976.

Bennett, John C. "A Changed Liberal—But Still a Liberal." *Christian Century,* 56, 8 February, 1939, pp. 179–181.

Berger, Peter L., Brigitte Berger, and Hansfried Kellner. *The Homeless Mind.* New York: Random House, 1973.

Berger, Peter L., and Richard J. Neuhaus, eds. *Against the World for the World.* New York: Seabury Press, 1976.

Berry, Donald. "Seeking a Theology of the Finite." *Christian Century,* 99, 29 September 1982, pp. 953–956.

Bethune-Baker, J. F. *An Introduction to the Early History of Christian Doctrine.* London: Methuen, 1958.

Bettenson, Henry S., ed. *Documents of the Christian Church.* London: Oxford University Press, 1953.

———, ed. and trans. *The Early Christian Fathers.* London: Oxford University Press, 1956.

Bibliography

Biersdorf, John E. "The Human Potential Movement and the Church." *Christianity and Crisis,* 35, 1975–1976.

Bloesch, Donald G. *The Invaded Church*. Waco, Tex.: Word Books, 1975.

Bloom, Harold. *The Flight to Lucifer: A Gnostic Fantasy*. New York: Farrar, Straus & Giroux, 1979.

———. "Lying Against Time: Gnosis, Poetry, Criticism." In *The Rediscovery of Gnosticism,* I. Ed. Bentley Layton. Proceedings of the Yale Conference on Gnosticism, March 1978. Leiden: E. J. Brill, 1980.

———. *A Map of Misreading*. New York: Oxford University Press, 1975.

———. *The Ringers in the Tower*. Chicago: University of Chicago Press, 1971.

The Book of Common Prayer. New York: Oxford University Press, 1944.

The Book of Forms. Don Mills, Ont.: Presbyterian Publications, 1981.

Booth, Rodney M. *The Winds of God: The Canadian Church Faces the 1980s*. Winfield, B.C.: World Council of Churches (Geneva) in cooperation with Wood Lake Books, 1982.

Bornkamm, Günther. *Paul*. New York: Harper & Row, 1971.

Brauer, Jerald C., ed. *Reinterpretation in American Church History*. Chicago: University of Chicago Press, 1968.

Braudel, Fernand. *Afterthoughts on Material Civilization and Capitalism*. Baltimore: Johns Hopkins University Press, 1977.

Brooks, Cleanth. "Walker Percy and Modern Gnosticism." *Southern Review,* 13, No. 4 (1977), pp. 677–687.

Buber, Martin. *The Eclipse of God*. Trans. Stanley Godman. New York: Harper & Bros., 1952.

Bultmann, Rudolf. *Essays*. Trans. James C. Q. Greig. New York: Macmillan, 1955.

———. *Theology of the New Testament*. Vol. I. Trans. Kendrick Groebel. New York: Scribner's, 1954.

———. *Theology of the New Testament*. Vol. II. Trans. Kendrick Groebel. New York: Scribner's, 1955.

———. "Yada." In *The Theological Dictionary of the New Testament*. Ed. Gerhard Kittel. Grand Rapids, Mich.: Eerdmans, 1964.

Calvin, John. *Calvin's Commentaries: The Second Epistle of Paul to the Corinthians*. Trans. T. A. Smail. Grand Rapids, Mich.: Eerdmans, 1964.

———. *Commentary on the Catholic Epistles*. Grand Rapids, Mich.: Eerdmans, 1959.

———. *Commentary on Philippians, Colossians and Thessalonians*. Trans. John Pringle. Grand Rapids, Mich.: Eerdmans, 1957.

———. *Institutes of the Christian Religion*. 2 vols. Trans. Henry Beveridge. Grand Rapids, Mich.: Eerdmans, 1953.

———. *Sermons on Ephesians*. Carlisle, Penn.: Banner of Truth Trust, 1973.

Campenhausen, Hans von, *The Fathers of the Greek Church*. Trans. Stanley Godman. New York: Pantheon, 1959.

Carse, James. *Jonathan Edwards and the Visibility of God*. New York: Scribner's, 1967.

Chadwick, Henry. "The Domestication of Gnosis." In *The Rediscovery of Gnosticism,* I.

Ed. Bentley Layton. Proceedings of the Yale Conference on Gnosticism, March 1978. Leiden: E. J. Brill, 1980.

———. *The Early Church*. Harmondsworth, Middlesex, Eng.: Penguin Books, 1977.

Chadwick, Owen. *The Secularization of the European Mind in the 19th Century*. Cambridge: Cambridge University Press, 1975.

Clebsch, William A. *American Religious Thought: A History*. Chicago: University of Chicago Press, 1973.

———. *From Sacred to Profane America*. New York: Harper & Row, 1968.

Commager, Henry Steele. *The American Mind*. New Haven: Yale University Press, 1964.

Conzelmann, Hans. *History of Primitive Christianity*. Trans. John E. Steely. Nashville, Tenn.: Abingdon Press, 1973.

———. *An Outline of the Theology of the New Testament*. Trans. John Bowden. New York: Harper & Row, 1969.

Coulton, G. C. *Ten Medieval Studies*. Gloucester, Mass.: Peter Smith, 1967.

Cox, Harvey. *Religion in the Secular City: Toward a Postmodern Theology*. New York: Simon & Schuster, 1984.

———. *The Secular City: Secularization and Urbanization in Theological Perspective*. New York: Macmillan, 1965.

———. *The Seduction of the Spirit*. New York: Simon & Schuster, 1973.

Coxe, A. Cleaveland. "Introductory Note to Irenaeus *Against Heresies*." In *The Ante-Nicene Fathers: Translations of the Writings of the Fathers Down to A.D. 325*. Vol. 1. Ed. Alexander Roberts and James Donaldson. Grand Rapids, Mich.: Eerdmans, 1977.

Cranfield, C. E. B. "The Message of James." *Scottish Journal of Theology*, 18, No. 2 (1965), pp. 182–193.

Cullmann, Oscar. *Early Christian Worship*. Trans. A. Stewart Todd and James B. Torrance. London: SCM Press, 1969.

cummings, e. e. *Poems: 1923–1954*. New York: Harcourt, Brace, 1954.

Daniélou, Jean. *A History of Early Christian Doctrine*. Vol. I: *The Theology of Jewish Christianity*. Trans. John A. Baker. London: Darton, Longman and Todd, 1964.

———. *A History of Early Christian Doctrine*. Vol. II: *Gospel Message and Hellenistic Culture*. Trans. John A. Baker. London: Darton, Longman and Todd, 1973.

Davies, J. G. *The Early Christian Church*. Garden City, N.Y.: Doubleday, 1967.

Deegan, D. L. "The Ritschlian School: The Essence of Christianity and Karl Barth." *Scottish Journal of Theology*, 16, No. 4 (1963), pp. 390–414.

DeLuca, Anthony J. *Freud and Future Religious Experience*. New York: Philosophical Library, 1976.

Dickinson, Emily. *The Complete Poems of Emily Dickenson*. Ed. Thomas H. Johnson. Boston: Little, Brown, 1960.

Dillenberger, John, ed. *Martin Luther: Selections from His Writings*. Garden City, N.Y.; Doubleday (Anchor), 1961.

Dostoevsky, Feodor. *Crime and Punishment*. Trans. Constance Garnett. Cleveland, Ohio: Fine Editions Press, 1947.

Driver, Tom F. *Patterns of Grace: Human Experience as Word of God*. New York: Harper & Row, 1977.

Drummond, Richard H. "Studies in Christian Gnosticism." *Religion in Life*, 45 (1976), pp. 7–21.

Edwards, Jonathan. *The Works of President Edwards: With a Memoir of His Life*. Ed. Sereno E. Dwight. New York, 1829.

Emerson, Ralph Waldo. *Journals of Ralph Waldo Emerson*. Ed. Edward Waldo Emerson and Waldo Emerson Forbes. 10 vols. Boston: Houghton Mifflin, 1912.

———. *Selected Prose and Poetry*. Ed. Reginald L. Cook. New York: Rinehart, 1950.

The Eucharistic Liturgy of Taizé. Intro. Max Thurian. London: Faith Press, 1962.

Faulkner, William. *The Sound and the Fury* and *As I Lay Dying*. New York: Random House, 1946.

———. *The Wild Palms*. New York: Vintage Books, 1939.

Filson, René. *Jean Cocteau: An Investigation into His Films and Philosophy*. New York: Crown, 1969.

Garcia, Ismael. Review Article. *The Journal of Religion*, 59, No. 1 (January 1979), pp. 108–110.

Gardner, Jim. "Narcissism in Contemporary Literature." *Katallagete* 8, No. 2 (Spring 1983), pp. 11–22.

Gärtner, Bertil. *The Theology of the Gospel According to Thomas*. Trans. Eric J. Sharpe. New York: Harper & Bros., 1961.

Gerth, H. H., and C. Wright Mills, eds. and trans. *From Max Weber: Essays in Sociology*. New York: Oxford University Press, 1946.

Gibbs, J. G. "Rudolf Bultmann and His Successors." *Scottish Journal of Theology*, 18, No. 4 (1965), pp. 396–410.

Glock, Charles Y., and Robert N. Bellah, eds. *The New Religious Consciousness*. Berkeley: University of California Press, 1976.

Goethe, Johann Wolfgang von. *Faust*. Trans. George Madison Priest. New York: Knopf, 1963.

Grant, Frederick C., ed. *Hellenistic Religions: The Age of Syncretism*. New York: Liberal Arts Press, 1953.

Grant, George. *Lament for a Nation*. Toronto: McClelland & Stewart, 1965.

Grant, R. M. *Gnosticism and Early Christianity*. New York: Harper & Row, 1966.

Greaves, R. L. "Luther's Doctrine of Grace." *Scottish Journal of Theology*, 18, No. 4 (1965), pp. 385–395.

Greven, Philip. *The Protestant Temperament: Patterns of Child-Rearing, Religious Experience and the Self in Early America*. New York: Knopf, 1977.

Gunton, Colin. "The Knowledge of God According to Two Process Theologians: A Twentieth-Century Gnosticism." *Religious Studies*, 2 (1975), pp. 87–96.

Gutiérrez, Gustavo, and Richard Shaull. *Liberation and Change*. Ed. Ronald H. Stone. Atlanta, Ga.: John Knox Press, 1977.

Handy, Robert T. *A History of the Churches in the United States and Canada.* New York: Oxford University Press, 1979.

Harnack, Adolf von. *History of Dogma.* Vol. I. Trans. Neil Buchanan. New York: Dover, 1961.

Haroutunian, Joseph, ed. and trans. *Calvin: Commentaries.* Philadelphia: Westminster Press, 1958.

The Heidelberg Catechism. *The Constitution of the United Presbyterian Church in the United States of America. Part I: Book of Confessions.* Philadelphia: General Assembly of the United Presbyterian Church in the U.S.A., 1967.

Herberg, Will, ed. *The Writings of Martin Buber.* Cleveland, Ohio: World, 1968.

Herbert, T. Walter, Jr. *Moby Dick and Calvinism.* New Brunswick, N.J.: Rutgers University Press, 1977.

Herzog, Frederick. "Reformation Today." *Christian Century,* 27 October 1982, pp. 1078–1081.

———. *Theology of the Liberating Word.* Nashville, Tenn.: Abingdon Press, 1971.

Holbrook, Clyde A. *The Ethics of Jonathan Edwards.* Ann Arbor: University of Michigan Press, 1973.

———, ed. *Works of Jonathan Edwards.* Vol. II: *Original Sin.* New Haven: Yale University Press, 1970.

Holder, Alan. *A. R. Ammons.* Boston: Twayne, 1978.

Horney, Karen, M.D. *Neurosis and Human Growth: The Struggle Toward Self-Realization.* New York: W. W. Norton, 1950.

———. *Our Inner Conflicts.* New York: W.W. Norton, 1966.

Housman, A. E. *A Shropshire Lad.* Mount Vernon, N.Y.: Peter Pauper Press, 1961.

Hudson, Winthrop S. *Religion in America.* New York: Scribner's, 1965.

Huizinga, J. *The Waning of the Middle Ages.* London: Edward Arnold, 1924.

Hutchison, William R. *The Modernist Impulse in American Protestantism.* Cambridge: Harvard University Press, 1976.

Huxley, Julian. *Man in the Modern World.* New York: Harper, 1964.

Irenaeus. *Against Heresies.* In *The Ante-Nicene Fathers: Translations of the Writings of the Fathers down to A.D. 325.* Vol. 1. Ed. Alexander Roberts and James Donaldson. Grand Rapids, Mich.: Eerdmans, 1977.

Jaeger, Werner. *Early Christianity and Greek Paideia.* Cambridge: Harvard University Press (Belknap), 1965.

Jefferson, Thomas. *The Complete Jefferson, Containing his Major Writings, Published and Unpublished, Except his Letters.* Ed. Saul K. Padover. New York: Duell, Sloan and Pearce, 1943.

Jeremias, Joachim. *Infant Baptism in the First Four Centuries.* Trans. David Cairns. London: SCM Press, 1960.

———. *The Origins of Infant Baptism.* Trans. D. M. Barton. London: SCM Press, 1963.

Jonas, Hans. "Delimitation of the Gnostic Phenomenon—Typological and Historical." In *Le origini dello gnosticismo.* Ed. Ugo Bianchi. Proceedings of the Colloquio di Messina, April 1966. Leiden: E. J. Brill, 1967.

———. *The Gnostic Religion*. Boston: Beacon Press, 1963.

———. Response to Gilles Quispel, "Gnosticism and the New Testament." In *The Bible in Modern Scholarship*. Ed. J. Philip Hyatt. Papers read at the 100th Meeting of the Society of Biblical Literature, 28–30 December 1964. Nashville: Abingdon Press, 1965.

Jones, Douglas. "Exposition of Isaiah Chapter One Verses Ten to Seventeen." *Scottish Journal of Theology*, 18, No. 4 (1965), pp. 457–471.

Jones, James W. *The Shattered Synthesis: New England Puritanism Before the Great Awakening*. New Haven: Yale University Press, 1973.

Jong, Erica. *How to Save Your Own Life*. Winnipeg, Manitoba: New American Library of Canada, 1978.

Jungmann, J. A. *The Early Liturgy*. Trans. F. A. Brunner. Notre Dame, Ind.: University of Notre Dame Press, 1959.

———. *The Mass of the Roman Rite*. Vol. I. New York: Benziger Brothers, 1951.

———. *The Mass of the Roman Rite*. Vol. II. New York: Benziger Brothers, 1955.

Kegley, Charles W., and Robert W. Bretall, eds. *Reinhold Niebuhr: His Religious, Social and Political Thought*. New York: Macmillan, 1961.

Kennan, George F. *The Nuclear Delusion: Soviet-American Relations in the Atomic Age*. New York: Pantheon Books, 1982.

Kierkegaard, Søren. *Fear and Trembling* and *The Sickness Unto Death*. Trans. Walter Lowrie. New York: Anchor Books, 1955.

Kirschenmann, Frederick. "Horace Bushell: Cells or Crustacea?" In *Reinterpretation in American Church History*. Ed. Jerald C. Brauer. Chicago: University of Chicago Press, 1968.

Kittel, Gerhard, ed. *The Theological Dictionary of the New Testament*. Vols. 1 and 3. Grand Rapids, Mich.: Eerdmans, 1964.

Koester, Helmut. "The Structure of Early Christian Beliefs." *Trajectories Through Early Christianity*. Philadelphia: Fortress Press, 1971.

Koestler, Arthur. *The Ghost in the Machine*. New York: Macmillan, 1967.

Kübler-Ross, Elisabeth. *On Death and Dying*. London: Macmillan, 1969.

Kuyper, Abraham. *Lectures on Calvinism*. Grand Rapids, Mich.: Eerdmans, 1964.

Lacarrière, Jacques. *The Gnostics*. Trans. Nina Rootes. London: Peter Owen, 1977.

Landis, Benson Y., ed. *A Rauschenbusch Reader*. New York: Harper & Bros., 1957.

Laurence, Margaret. *The Diviners*. Toronto: McClelland & Stewart, 1974.

———. *The Tomorrow-Tamer and Other Stories*. Toronto: McClelland & Stewart, 1984.

Lawson, John. *A Theological and Historical Introduction to the Apostolic Fathers*. New York: Macmillan, 1961.

Layton, Bentley, ed. *The Rediscovery of Gnosticism*. Vol. I of Proceedings of the Yale Conference on Gnosticism, March 1978. Leiden: E. J. Brill, 1980.

———, ed. *The Rediscovery of Gnosticism*. Vol. II of Proceedings of the Yale Conference on Gnosticism, March 1978. Leiden: E. J. Brill, 1981.

Lehmann, Paul L. "The Christianity of Reinhold Niebuhr." In *Reinhold Niebuhr: His*

Religious, Social and Political Thought. Ed. Charles W. Kegley and Robert W. Bretall. New York: Macmillan, 1961.

———. *Ethics in a Christian Context.* New York: Harper & Row, 1963.

———. *The Tranfiguration of Politics.* New York: Harper & Row, 1975.

Loder, James. "Transformation in Christian Education." *Princeton Seminary Bullletin,* NS 3, No. 1 (1980), pp. 11–25.

Löwith, Karl. *From Hegel to Nietzsche: The Revolution in Nineteenth-Century Thought.* Trans. David E. Green. London: Constable, 1965.

Marty, Martin E. *Righteous Empire: The Protestant Experience in America.* New York: Dial Press, 1970.

McCann, Dennis P. *Christian Realism and Liberation Theology.* Maryknoll, N.Y.: Orbis Books, 1981.

McCoy, Charles S. "Johannes Cocceius: Federal Theologian." *Scottish Journal of Theology,* 16, No. 4 (1963), pp. 352–370.

McDonnell, Kilian. *John Calvin, the Church and the Eucharist.* Princeton, N.J.: Princeton University Press, 1967.

MacGavran, Donald. *Understanding Church Growth.* Grand Rapids, Mich: Eerdmans, 1970.

McGinley, Phyllis. *Saint-Watching.* New York: Viking Press, 1969.

MacGregor, Geddes. *Gnosis.* Wheaton, Ill.: The Theosophical Publishing House, 1979.

McKelway, A. J. *The Systematic Theology of Paul Tillich.* Richmond, Va.: John Knox Press, 1964.

McNeill, John T. *The History and Character of Calvinism.* New York: Oxford University Press, 1962.

Mead, G. R. S. *Fragments of a Faith Forgotten.* New Hyde Park, N.Y.: University Books, 1962.

Mead, Sidney E. *The Lively Experiment: The Shaping of Christianity in America.* New York: Harper & Row, 1963.

———. *The Nation with the Soul of a Church.* New York: Harper & Row, 1975.

Melville, Herman. *Billy Budd, Foretopman.* In *Selected Tales and Poems.* Ed. Richard Chase. New York: Rinehart, 1956.

———. *The Confidence Man.* New York: Airmont, 1966.

Menninger, Karl. *Whatever Became of Sin?* New York: Hawthorne Books, 1973.

Merton, Thomas. *Seasons of Celebration.* New York: Farrar, Straus & Giroux, 1965.

———. "Time and the Unburdening and the Recollection of the Lamb: The Easter Service in Faulkner's *The Sound and the Fury.*" *Katallagete,* 4, No. 4 (Summer 1973), pp. 7–15.

Middlekauf, Robert. *The Mathers: Three Generations of Puritan Intellectuals, 1596–1728.* New York: Oxford University Press, 1971.

Migliore, David L. "Christology and New Testament Studies." *Princeton Seminary Bulletin,* 49, No. 2 (1966), pp. 19–28.

Miller, David. *The New Polytheism.* New York: Harper & Row, 1974.

Miller, Donald E. "Sectarianism and Secularization: The Work of Bryan Wilson." *Religious Studies Review,* 5, No. 3 (1979), pp. 161–168.

Miller, Perry. *The New England Mind: From Colony To Province.* Cambridge: Harvard University Press, 1962.

———. *The New England Mind: The Seventeenth Century.* Cambridge: Harvard University Press, 1954.

———, ed. *The American Puritans: Their Prose and Poetry.* Garden City, N.Y.: Doubleday, 1956.

———*The American Transcendentalists: Their Prose and Poetry.* Garden City, N.Y.: Doubleday, 1957.

Neville, Robert C. *Creativity and God: A Challenge to Process Theology.* New York: Seabury Press, 1980.

Newbigin, Leslie. *The Open Secret.* Grand Rapids, Mich.: Eerdmans, 1978.

Nichols, James Hastings. *Romanticism in American Theology.* Chicago: University of Chicago Press, 1961.

Niebuhr, H. Richard. *Radical Monotheism and Western Culture.* New York: Harper & Row, 1960.

———. *The Social Sources of Denominationalism.* Hamden, Conn.: Shoe String Press, 1954.

Niebuhr, Reinhold. *Moral Man and Immoral Society: A Study in Ethics and Politics.* New York: Scribner's, 1960.

———. *The Nature and Destiny of Man: A Christian Interpretation.* New York: Scribner's, 1955. (Gifford Lectures, one-volume edition.)

Niesel, Wilhelm. *Reformed Symbolics: A Comparison of Catholicism, Orthodoxy and Protestantism.* Trans. David Lewis. Edinburgh: Oliver & Boyd, 1962.

Nock, Arthur Darby. *Conversion.* London: Oxford University Press, 1963.

———. *Early Gentile Christianity and Its Hellenistic Background.* New York: Harper & Row, 1964.

———. "Gnosticism." *Harvard Theological Review,* 57 (1964), pp. 254–279.

Norris, R. A. *God and World in Early Christian Theology.* New York: Seabury Press, 1965.

Novack, George. *Pragmatism vs. Marxism.* New York: Pathfinder Press, 1975.

Ogden, Schubert M. *Christ Without Myth: A Study Based upon the Theology of Rudolf Bultmann.* London: William Collins, 1962.

Pagels, Elaine. *The Gnostic Gospels.* New York: Random House, 1979.

———. *The Gnostic Paul.* Philadelphia: Fortress Press, 1975.

———. *The Johannine Gospel in Gnostic Exegesis.* Nashville, Tenn.: Abingdon Press, 1973.

Painter, John. *John: Witness and Theologian.* London: S.P.C.K., 1975.

Parrington, Vernon L. *Main Currents in American Thought.* Vol. II: *The Romantic Revolution in America, 1800–1860.* New York: Harcourt, Brace, 1959.

Peck, Ellen. *The Baby Trap.* New York: Bernard Geis Associates, 1971.

Percy, Walker. *Love in the Ruins.* New York: Farrar, Straus & Giroux, 1971.

———. *The Moviegoer*. New York: Knopf, 1962.

Quasten, Johannes. *Patrology*. Vol. I. Utrecht and Antwerp: Spectrum, 1966.

Quispel, Gilles. "Gnosis and Psychology." In *The Rediscovery of Gnosticism*, I. Ed. Bentley Layton. Proceedings of the Yale Conference on Gnosticism, March 1978. Leiden: E. J. Brill, 1980.

———. *Gnostic Studies*. Vol. I. Istanbul: Nederlands Historisch-Archaeologisch Instituut in het Nabije Oosten, 1974.

———. *Gnostic Studies*. Vol. II. Istanbul: Nederlands Historisch-Archaeologisch Instituut in het Nabije Oosten, 1975.

Randall, John Herman. *Hellenistic Ways of Deliverance and the Making of the Christian Synthesis*. New York: Columbia University Press, 1970.

Raschke, Carl A. *The Bursting of New Wineskins: Reflections on Religion and Culture at the End of Affluence*. Pittsburgh, Pa.: Pickwick Press, 1978.

———. *The Interruption of Eternity: Modern Gnosticism and the Origins of the New Religious Consciousness*. Chicago: Nelson Hall, 1980.

Rauschenbusch, W. *Christianity and the Social Crisis*. New York: Macmillan, 1912.

Reid, J. K. S., ed. and trans. *Calvin: Theological Treatises*. Vol. XX. Library of Christian Classics. Philadelphia: The Westminster Press, 1953.

———. "Vatican Council II and the People of God." *Reformed and Presbyterian World*, 29, No. 1 (1966–67), pp. 12–22.

Reuther, Rosemary R. "Women's Liberation and Reconciliation With the Earth." *Conversations*. Graymoor/Garrison, N.Y.: Graymoor Institute, December 1971.

Richardson, Cyril C., ed. *Early Christian Fathers*. Vol. I. Philadelphia: Westminster Press, 1953.

Richardson, Herbert W. "Civil Religion in Theological Perspective." In *American Civil Religion*. Ed. Russell E. Richey and Donald G. Jones. New York: Harper & Row, 1974.

———. *Toward an American Theology*. New York: Harper & Row, 1967.

Ricoeur, Paul. *The Conflict of Interpretation*. Evanston, Ill.: Northwestern University Press, 1974.

Roberts, Alexander, and James Donaldson, eds. *The Anti-Nicene Fathers: Translations of the Writings of the Fathers Down to A.D. 325*. Vol. I. Grand Rapids: Eerdmans, 1977.

Robertson, A. K. "The Individual Cup: Its Use at Holy Communion." *Liturgical Review*, 8, No. 2 (November 1978), pp. 2–12.

Robinson, James M., gen. ed. *The Nag Hammadi Library: In English*. San Francisco: Harper & Row, 1977.

Runciman, Steven. *The Medieval Manichee*. Cambridge: Cambridge University Press, 1960.

Russell, Kenneth C. "God and Church in the Fiction of Margaret Laurence." *Studies in Religion*, 7, No. 4 (1978), pp. 435–446.

Sartre, Jean-Paul. *Being and Nothingness: Existentialism and Human Emotion*. New York: Philosophical Library, 1957.

Saxton, Martha. *Louisa May: A Modern Biography of Louisa May Alcott*. Boston: Houghton Mifflin, 1977.

Schmithals, Walter. *Gnosticism in Corinth*. Nashville, Tenn.: Abingdon Press, 1971.

———. *Paul and the Gnostics*. Nashville, Tenn.: Abingdon Press, 1972.

Schweizer, Eduard. "Two New Testament Creeds Compared." In *Current Issues in New Testament Interpretation*. Ed. William Klassen and Grayden F. Snyder. London: SCM Press, 1962.

Scott, Walter, ed., *Corpus Hermetica*. Vol. I. Oxford: Clarendon Press, 1924.

Seifert, Harvey. *Reality and Ecstasy*. Philadelphia: Westminster Press, 1974.

Shafer, William J. "SK 124C41+." *Katallagete* 8, No. 2 (Spring 1983), pp. 29–34.

Shinn, Roger L. *Tangled World*. New York: Scribner's, 1965.

Smith, H. Shelton, Robert T. Handy, and Lefferts A. Loetscher. *American Christianity: An Historical Interpretation with Representative Documents*. Vol. II. New York: Scribner's, 1963.

Stone, Donald. "The Human Potential Movement." In *The New Religious Consciousness*. Ed. Charles Y. Glock and Robert N. Bellah. Berkeley: University of California Press, 1976.

Sumption, Jonathan. *The Albigensian Crusade*. London: Faber and Faber, 1978.

Terrien, Samuel L. *The Elusive Presence*. San Francisco: Harper & Row, 1978.

Thompson, Lawrance. *Melville's Quarrel with God*. Princeton, N.J.: Princeton University Press, 1952.

Thoreau, Henry David. *Walden and Other Writings*. Ed. Joseph Wood Krutch. New York: Bantam Books, 1977.

———. *A Week on the Concord and Merrimack Rivers*. In *The Works of Thoreau*. Ed. Henry Seidel Canby. Boston: Houghton Mifflin, 1937.

Thurneysen, Eduard. *Dostoevsky*. Trans. Keith R. Crim. Richmond, Va.: John Knox Press, 1964.

Tolkien, J. R. R. "On Fairy Stories." In *Tree and Leaf*. London: Unwin Books, 1964.

Torrance, T. F. "The Mission of the Church." *Scottish Journal of Theology*, 19, No. 2 (1966), pp. 129–143.

Troeltsch, Ernst. *The Social Teaching of the Christian Churches*. 2 vols. Trans. Olive Wyon. London: Allen & Unwin, 1931.

Twain, Mark. *Huckleberry Finn*. Bungay, Suffolk: Penguin Books, 1966.

Van Allen, Rodger, ed. *American Religious Values and the Future of America*. Philadelphia: Fortress Press, 1978.

Voegelin, Eric. *Order and History*. Vol. I. Baton Rouge: Louisiana State University Press, 1956.

———. *Order and History*. Vol. III. Baton Rouge: Louisiana State University Press, 1964.

———. *Order and History*. Vol. IV. Baton Rouge: Louisiana State University Press, 1974.

Wagner, C. Peter. "Confused About Church Growth?" *Church Growth Canada*, 2, No. 3 (Winter 1975), Regina, Saskatchewan.

———. *Your Church Can Grow*. Glendale, Cal.: Regal Books, 1976.

Walker, G. S. M. "Calvin and the Church." *Scottish Journal of Theology*, 16, No. 4 (1963), pp. 371–389.

Warlick, Harold. "Loneliness: Peril and Promise of the Communities of Faith." *Harvard Divinity Bulletin*, 9, No. 1 (October–November 1978).

Weber, Max. *The Protestant Ethic and the Spirit of Capitalism*. Trans. Talcott Parsons. New York: Scribner's, 1958.

———. *The Sociology of Religion*. London: Methuen, 1965.

Wendel, François. *Calvin: The Origins and Development of His Religious Thought*. Trans. Philip Mairet. London: William Collins, 1976.

The Westminster Confession of Faith. *The Constitution of the United Presbyterian Church in the United States of America. Part I: Book of Confessions*. Philadelphia: General Assembly of the United Presbyterian Church in the U.S.A., 1967.

Whitehead, Alfred North. *Adventures of Ideas*. New York: Macmillan, 1933.

Wieman, Henry Nelson. "A Religious Naturalist Looks at Reinhold Niebuhr." In *Reinhold Niebuhr: His Religious, Social and Political Thought*. Ed. Charles W. Kegley and Robert W. Bretall. New York: Macmillan, 1961.

Williams, D. D. "Niebuhr and Liberalism." In *Reinhold Niebuhr: His Religious, Social and Political Thought*. Ed. Charles W. Kegley and Robert W. Bretall. New York: Macmillan, 1961.

Williams, Peter W. *Popular Religion in America*. Englewood Cliffs, N.J.: Prentice-Hall, 1980.

Williams, Robert R. *A Guide to the Teachings of the Early Church Fathers*. Grand Rapids, Mich.: Eerdmans, 1960.

Wilson, R. McL. *The Gnostic Problem*. London: A. R. Mowbray, 1958.

Wisse, Frederick. "Stalking Those Elusive Sethians." In *The Rediscovery of Gnosticism*, II. Ed. Bentley Layton. Proceedings of the Yale Conference on Gnosticism, March 1978, Leiden: E. J. Brill, 1980.

Wolfe, James. "Three Congregations." In *The New Religious Consciousness*. Ed. Charles Y. Glock and Robert N. Bellah. Berkeley: University of California Press, 1976.

Wolfe, Thomas. *Look Homeward, Angel*. New York: Scribner's, 1952.

Wolfe, Tom. "The Me Decade and the Third Great Awakening." *Mauve Gloves & Madmen, Clutter & Vine*. New York: Bantam Books, 1977.

Yule, George S. "The Incarnation and the Unity of the Church." *Reformed World*, 37, No. 5 (1983), pp. 149–159.

Index